Our Father Planned It All

Our Father Planned It All

by

Esther Peters Balisky

Our Father Planned It All

To the best of our ability, we have recalled events that took place years ago. Some stories have been changed slightly, due to the fact we could not remember every detail exactly. A few names have also been altered to protect certain individuals in Eastern Europe and Russia...but the events are factual.

ISBN: 1-55383-017-2

Published by
Marshall Foundation
PO Box 77808
Seattle, WA 98177

Cover and book design by
Long Drive Design, Abbotsford, BC

Printed in Canada by
Friesens Corporation, Altona, Manitoba

Our Father Planned It All.

Our heavenly Father knew about us
long before our birth,
Though we are weak and finite,
to Him we have much worth!
He knew the path that we would take,
and scheduled all our days,
Through sunshine and dark shadows,
He taught us how to praise.

Sometimes we do not understand
why His children go through pain,
It seems He hides His face awhile
and allows the storms and rain.
But for our good, He gently molds us
into His image fair,
Our Father planned it all for us,
because He loves and cares.

He gently guides our footsteps
along life's weary road,
Tenderly He lifts our burdens
and carries all our load.
He knows all our tomorrows—
so we have no need to fear,
He's gone before—He knows the way,
and He is always near.

He led to faraway countries—
places where no one would go,
Dangers and perils surrounding
His gracious mercies to show.
He knew we would go—
leaving home and loved ones behind,

And in that joyful surrender,
    His peace we would find.
Someday in that celestial city,
    we'll bow down at His feet,
And those we've won to Christ on earth—
    there in that land we'll meet.
What can compare to Heaven's bliss
    where we shall wear a crown,
And all our sorrows, trials and burdens
    are at His feet laid down?

Because we shared His love with others
    and obeyed the Master's call,
From grateful hearts of joy we know—
    our Father planned it all!

Esther M. Balisky

Dedication

With a grateful heart I dedicate this book to:
The glory of God

> "How can I say thanks
> for the things You have done for me?
> Things so undeserved,
> Yet You gave to prove Your love for me;
> The voices of a million angels
> could not express my gratitude,
> All that I am, and ever hope to be;
> I owe it all to Thee."

–Andraé Crouch

My husband, Gordon—without him none of the encounters in Eastern Europe and Russia would have taken place.

Charlene and Corinne—our daughters who have faithfully stood with us through times of victory and difficult situations.

Steve—who is an exemplary husband, father, and son-in-law.

Alexis and Nicholas—our grandchildren, who continue to give us joy every day.

Table of Contents

Acknowledgements

To the following, I gratefully say, Thank you:

J. Murray Marshall, for writing the Foreword.

Marilyn, Cheryl, and Karen who capably, efficiently, and willingly spent dedicated hours typing this manuscript.

Jordan, whose computer skills assisted us in various ways.

Gordon, who remembered facts and details to add to some of the stories which took place so long ago.

To our faithful contributors throughout the years, who, without their prayer and financial support, this work could not have been accomplished.

Beryl Henne, who capably edited my manuscript. Her encouragement caused me to realize that the task of writing and publishing this book would become a reality.

Thank you to Corinne, who years ago drew the black and white drawings featured in this book.

To my journals, without which it would have been impossible to record the various details and encounters experienced over twenty-eight years.

will come on proof stage

Introduction

Esther and I had just been commissioned to work in East Europe and Russia. One of the presiding ministers leaned over and asked, "Gordon, why are you doing this? You will never change anything. You have just completed graduate school, and ought to continue in a practice and prepare for retirement." For a moment, many thoughts and ideas flooded my mind. Maybe he was right.

Leonid Breznev, a stern and crafty communist diplomat had taken control of the communist "Evil Empire" from Nikita Kruschev... who had promised to bury America and the rest of the non-communist world as he pounded the pulpit with his shoe while speaking to the United Nations. President Kennedy had narrowly averted a nuclear war with Kruschev, and communism was viewed as an impossible foe. Christians were being persecuted and martyred for their faith. It was officially impossible to propagate Christianity in the communist world.

After a few short moments I responded. "My friend, God is not calling us to change anything but to obey Him, we are simply going to obey Him." Sounds simple, doesn't it?

Some time later I stood by the statue of Lenin in the gardens of Red Square in Moscow, and my thoughts traced back in time to when I had first learned about him, Stalin, Karl Marx, and Engels, each of whom played a part in what had become this vast political movement. My grandparents, the Machuks, who migrated from the Ukraine, my aunts and uncles and other friends and families would gather at the Highland Park community hall in Alberta, Canada for various funtions. There I first saw the pictures of Lenin, Marx and Stalin and learned to know about them. The pictures hung above the stage platform in this log building constructed by the early settlers who came to this community. I remember in my early childhood how we were encouraged to attend

"Sobraniya" (a term for solemn gathering used in Ukrainian, Russian, Polish and other Slavic languages.) The same is also used by Orthodox, Catholic and Protestant Christians.

A hammer and cycle, very artisticly painted on the large canvas curtain, was lowered by the use of rope and pulley and operated with dignity and respect. It seemed that only the trusted could have the honor of attending to the operation of that curtain.

In my early years in this immigrant Canadian community, I learned the languages and cultures of the Slavaic community where my parents operated their businesses; a general store, blacksmith & welding shop and sawmill.

It had been a great preparation to have those growing up years in that community, and later to stand beside the statue of Lenin, and view his embalmed body so heavily guarded in Red Square. For us to change anything in Russia and the communist world was out of the question. Our responsibility was to obey God. We endeavored to do this and have realized our inadequacies.

My wife Esther whom I met at Peace River Bible College always carried a diary, keeping careful notes in a language that she made up as she went. This included several dialects of her native German, Dutch, English, Polish and some Ukrainian.

God has answered the faithful prayers of His people and we thank you for praying. There are more challenges and He has promised to be faithful.

Gordon W. Balisky

will come on proof stage

Foreword

Eastern Europe and Russia in the mid-twentieth century was an austere place. The totalitarian Soviet regime was rigid and often brutal. Behind the so-called "Iron Curtain" ordinary citizens conformed to the system and struggled to find their way through the tasks of daily living.

For Christians, the scene was particularly grim. Atheistic Soviets had little tolerance for those who acknowledged God, treasured the Holy Scriptures, and sought to gather themselves for worship, nurture, and fellowship. They met under difficult, often dangerous circumstances to worship the Lord and to encourage one another. Despite intolerant oppression and frequent imprisonment, they persevered.

Gordon Balisky, a pastor of Slavic ancestry, and Esther, his wife, were ministering in the Pacific Northwest in the mid-1970s when they sensed the call of God to focus ministry toward believers behind this Iron Curtain. Gifted in Slavic languages and burdened for the people of their forefathers, they were ready to give up the comforts of ministry in America to reach out to a people they dearly loved.

Our Father Planned It All, written by Esther Balisky, is a series of vignettes in which she traces the story of this venture. Gordon, Esther, and their two young daughters, Charlene and Corinne, moved to Europe and traveled frequently behind the Iron Curtain. There they met and ministered to people who were hungry for love, open to the teaching of the Bible, and were prepared to bear witness to Jesus, consequences notwithstanding.

The Balisky family encountered a series of adventures in which threatening, dangerous situations were taken in stride—although often in fear and trembling. These accounts give insights into life and private travel in Eastern Europe and

Russia in those days. Food, accommodations, sanitary conditions, border controls, clandestine worship, and surveillance all provided situations which, while daunting at the moment, became occasions to recall God's goodness, grace, and mercy. Faithful Christian believers welcomed the Balisky ministries of music, proclamation, teaching, and encouragement.

Now, years later, the political horizon is radically altered. In Eastern Europe and the former Soviet Union, Christians no longer face the cruel intensity of political oppression. Gordon and Esther Balisky minister today to Slavic people who have emigrated to Western Canada and the United States. While the political situation is different, the social needs and spiritual hunger of these people, both in Europe and North America, are as intense as ever.

Esther Balisky tells these stories with intimate, often touching, details of the challenges that she, her husband, and family encountered. These are tales of the deep commitment of two of the Lord's servants to faithful, costly pursuit of the call that God placed upon them. Eternity alone will reveal the accomplishments of these endeavors.

J. Murray Marshall
Seattle, Washington
Easter 2002

1 SAYING FAREWELL

The church sanctuary was full the morning Gordon announced his resignation from Fifteenth Avenue Bible Church. The atmosphere was hushed, sacred. No one moved. Were they really losing their pastor and his wife so soon?

Tears were shed freely as, one by one, embracing the departing family, with regret, the people said good-bye.

When most of the people had left, Esther stole into the bathroom and sobbed. Loving every part of the work, she wanted to hold on. But knowing God had called them away, hastily she wiped her tears and went to say good-bye to the few still remaining in the foyer.

Charlene and Corinne, too, bid their friends farewell. But they were not weeping. Knowing God had called their parents to a ministry in Eastern Europe and Russia, they looked with anticipation to broadening their horizons in other countries.

Disturbing News

But Esther had a problem. In the shower one day, she detected a lump on her right breast. Wondering how to handle this new development, she went to tell her husband.

"Esther, I will call the doctor right away," he responded in alarm.

Carefully the doctor examined the affected area.

"I think, Mrs. Balisky, this will have to come out," he cautioned. "But we will take some tests first."

After x-rays and a mammogram, surgery was scheduled.

Gordon was confused. Both he and Esther had given their lives to Christ unreservedly.

Esther was willing to give up her church and beautiful house. She had committed her mother into God's hands during the traumatic time when she broke her hip, counting it more important to obey God than to stay at home.

"God, what more do you want?" asked Gordon, head in his hands. "Will you take my wife, too?"

But God is always gracious and never allows His children to bear more than they are able as they rely on Him.

"Esther, are you awake?" called Gordon a few hours later. "I have good news, Honey! Please wake up!"

It was an effort to open her eyes through the aftereffects of the anesthetic.

Squinting, she saw her husband through a hazy cloud. Why was her head so heavy?

"Honey, you have come through the surgery just fine, and the lump is not malignant!"

Vaguely, she could see her children, smiling through their tears.

"Mom, I love you," said Charlene, moving closer.

Corinne, standing nearby, assured her mother she was there, too.

After her family left the hospital, Esther, now more awake, gratefully thanked God for another miracle. Lying in bed, staring at the ceiling, her thoughts turned toward Katy, her mother.

Reminiscing

How could she forget driving to the Peace River country in Canada to say good-bye to their loved ones? The Peters gang had a farewell party for them there. Most of their dear ones were present.

Realizing her children would be in jeopardy while going into Communist countries, didn't make it any easier for Katy, Esther's mother.

She knew that even now, many who professed the name of Christ were being persecuted for their faith. Lenin's thrust was to have them all annihilated. He worked diligently toward this goal, as he continued to harass believers.

Esther remembered another day so long ago. Saying good-bye to her eldest brother on his way to Trinidad had not been easy for her parents, either.

Turning in her bed to become more comfortable, Esther could remember the details as if it were yesterday. Where had the time gone?

Esther felt a tenderness toward her God. He would give her mother grace to see her go away, too!

She remembered how the family had gathered in the hallway to commission Gordon and Esther, the new missionaries. Prayerfully they commended them and their girls to God's safekeeping.

Later that day, by the time Esther and Gordon left, Katy, holding her cane, was standing beside the big picture window in the living room.

Esther waved as long as she could. Gradually the bent

form of her mother disappeared, but the young woman in the back seat of the big car, cried all the way to Edmonton. Would she see her mother again?

Still Esther reminisced.

The invitation to work in Eastern Europe and Russia had come again and again.

"Gordon," Peter Deyneka, from the Slavic Gospel Association, said in his broken English, "our people need someone like you to teach them. You are familiar with the native language and know the culture and ways of the Slavic people. Please consider what God would have you do, Son. Consider it prayerfully and carefully."

A move to Europe would be inevitable. This was not the first time he'd asked. But now this request from the elderly gentleman was brought up once again. Knowing her mother needed her didn't make it easy for Esther to consider this challenge. Also, how would a move such as this affect her girls?

The rest of the Peters family lived in various parts of the country. How could she leave her mother alone? God had the unexpected answer.

Giving Through Pain

Stirring in her bed again, Esther winced as pain shot through her right arm.

Groggily, she remembered reaching for the telephone one morning. Switching on the light, she saw the hour was only 6:00 A.M. Who could be calling this early?

"Esther?"

Marguarite Johnson, Katy's pastor's wife, was calling from Abbotsford, Canada. "I am phoning to tell you that your mom broke her hip last night," she said.

"How did she do that?" Esther asked, anxiety etched in her voice.

"Your mom fell while going out of the store," continued Marguarite. "She was taken by ambulance to the hospital. Surgery is scheduled for this morning."

Thanking Mrs. Johnson and assuring her that she would be there as soon as possible, Esther hung up the phone. Taking a few deep breaths, she went to tell her girls.

It wasn't long before they were speeding toward Canada in her small Toyota. Many thoughts raced through her mind as she drove.

Her dad had passed away a few months before. Living in their home alone, her mother bravely endeavored to cope. During the adjustment period, friends and family came to her side. And slowly, gradually, the pain in her heart was beginning to mend.

Now tragedy had struck again. How would she cope with it?

Soon the hospital loomed before them, reminding her acutely that her mother was there.

Surgery over, Katy lay on her bed exhausted, looking older than the last time they'd met.

"Esther!" she murmured, her tongue dry and swollen, her usual active mind dulled due to pain medication.

"Mama!" Esther whispered, bending down to plant a kiss on her pale cheek. "When this is all over, I'm taking you home with me to Seattle. Don't worry about anything."

Charlene and Corinne stood close to her bed.

"We are praying for you, Grandma," said Corinne.

"It will be nice to have you living at our house—you can help me learn to sew," said the industrious Charlene.

Katy smiled and closed her eyes for a moment to rest. "Esther?"

"Yes, Mom."

"When will you be moving to Germany and going into

Eastern Europe and Russia?" she asked, her eyes fixed steadily on Esther's.

Esther knew her mom needed her more now than ever before. Pain filled her heart. She had no answers yet.

That night Esther prayed earnestly. Her mother's situation weighed heavily on her heart. How could she leave her?

Katy did come to live with them in Seattle after her hospital stay.

Happily the girls helped her unpack as she settled into the large master bedroom on the main floor. Day after day, Esther tended to her many needs.

It was encouraging to see Katy become stronger again. Pushing a walker, courageously she even helped with the cooking. Everything took a great deal of effort, but she improved every day. Gradually she became adjusted to her new surroundings and fit in well. Esther loved to have her near. Happily the girls shared their days' events with their grandma. She had become an important part of the family. Quietly watching events unfold, Esther prayed for God's blessing on their future trusting Him to care for His own.

Katy knew Esther's heart was aching. Rarely did they talk about the impending move, but she knew it was inevitable.

Katy and Henry had given their children to God even before they were born. Never did her mother want to go back on her word, no matter how impossible the situation. Every day she prayed.

Esther trusted God to look after Katy while they were in Europe—but how? Never did she dream that her mother would have to break her hip so they could make arrangements for her to go to Alberta to live with Esther's oldest sister, Martha. It was a long journey, so Charlene made plans to go along to be of assistance to her aging grandmother. Katy would be leaving the West Coast. Winters were long and cold in Alberta. Her house in British Columbia must be sold. There were numerous details needing immediate attention.

Esther would never forget how, during those days, her mother became her role model. Her faith in a living God was challenged and she responded positively.

One day Esther heard Katy call. "Yes, Mom, I'm coming," she answered, hastily putting aside the task at hand.

"Esther, I never want to stand in your way, my child. God has called you and Gordon to work in Europe. It is important that you obey Him. He has promised to care for me. Now you go with my blessing! Remember, too, dear, you are going to lands where our forefathers bled and died for their faith. Remember as well, that Gordon's ancestors were born in the Ukraine and many suffered. Now God has chosen both of you to minister in these countries."

Holding onto her walker with one hand, tenderly she touched Esther's cheek with the other. Looking into her mom's big brown eyes, now brimming over with unshed tears, Esther knew she meant it.

Without reservation, Esther renewed her own commitment to God, telling Him she would go wherever He led. There was no need to be anxious or troubled. God would care for her mother, and He would look after her family as well.

Interrupting these thoughts, Esther heard a nurse say, "Time to sleep now, Mrs. Balisky!"

Knowing that in order to heal, sleep was essential, she put these nostalgic thoughts aside, turned over on her back and drifted off. Tomorrow, hopefully, she would be released from the hospital and go home. This was something to positively anticipate.

2 HECTIC DAYS OF PACKING AND MOVING

Time passed quickly. The house had been a hive of feverish activity for days. Everywhere, Esther saw signs of chaos.

The family was in the process of packing to leave for Europe. To store some things, sell others, give away many, and pack to take overseas, was a very frustrating experience. In the last throes of decision-making, they still had many hours of work ahead. The house, of course, must be left spotless for renters to move in.

Their plane reservations, booked for some time, had already been canceled once, due to Esther's surgery. Now they really had no choice. Ready or not, they must leave. The Slavic Gospel Association was anxious for them to be in Europe to begin their work there as soon as possible.

Esther, still not strong, had been out of the hospital for only two weeks, but was doing her best to help straighten up the general chaos and confusion around the place.

"Mrs. Balisky, shall I put these books in the storage, or do you want to take them with you?" came a call from the garage.

"Just put them in the basement with the others," she answered, turning to the task at hand.

"Mom, can I take my Barbie dolls and clothes?" pleaded Corinne.

"Yes, Honey, pack them in your suitcase. You will want them when you are there," her mother answered.

Turning back to her work, Esther heard another call from the kitchen. "Esther, we're hungry. Bob hasn't had lunch yet. Could you please make something soon?"

Sighing, she got up from the floor where she was sorting papers, and went into the kitchen to see if there was anything left to eat. There wasn't. Taking her car keys she went out to her Toyota. Her heart was heavy as she started the motor. Purring like a kitten, she remembered that this car had been trouble-free since they purchased it. Now the ad to sell it was in the *Seattle Times* and there had been calls from potential buyers. Esther found it hard to part with many things she held dear—and this car was one of them. But she knew it had to go.

Sincerely she prayed, "Lord make me strong enough to relinquish material things so dear to me. With so much work to do before we leave, give wisdom and courage. Help me to part with this car with dignity. Amen."

The words of a song came to mind:

He giveth more grace as the burdens grow greater
He addeth more strength as the labors increase
To added affliction, He addeth His mercy
To multiplied trials, His multiplied peace!

Esther knew she needed to draw liberally from the strength and grace He was ready to supply on a daily basis.

She stopped at the familiar store where her family had done their shopping for years. In a few minutes, bread, butter, vegetables, and fruit filled her shopping cart.

Driving into her yard, she noticed there were several unfamiliar cars that had not been there when she left. It seemed these days, there were always people coming to assist or visit. Many wanted to say good-bye. It was hard to drop everything to visit, but sometimes it was necessary.

Sure enough, there was company from Canada. They had stopped for a short while, they said. Wearily sitting down on the piano bench, the only place left to sit in the living room, she put on a fixed smile and began to visit.

"Esther, the phone is ringing, will you get it please?" said Gordon, as he went into the other room to answer the doorbell. A man was there who had seen the ad in the *Seattle Times* and was interested in the truck.

Excusing herself, Esther went to answer the phone. A friend wanted to talk and asked how their plans were coming with regards to their departure.

"Is there anything I can do to help?" she offered kindly. Esther told her that when they'd worked through some of the chaos, they would call her. Thanking her cordially, she hung up the phone and went to visit with her company in the living room.

Later she had just settled down between boxes when Florence came into the house through the back door.

"Esther, I hate to bother you," she said, "but I will take those groceries now if that's all right with you."

Many cans of fruits and vegetables that obviously couldn't be taken to Europe stood on the shelf. Excusing herself, Esther went into the kitchen and helped her pile them into boxes.

Meanwhile, Bob came in, looking hungry and tired.

Quickly, Esther made lunch. Taking it out, he sat under the trees in the back yard and began to eat.

"An angel in disguise," is what they called him. And he was! Bob Dolhanyk had been working since very early that morning. A long-time friend, never once did he complain as he worked the long hours. Esther silently thanked God for willing people like himself. He usually went around the house whistling, and always had a smile for each of them.

Gordon was back in the living room with their guests when his wife returned. "Did the man buy the truck?" she asked hopefully.

"No, but he is interested," replied Gordon.

They had several big trucks to sell, which had been used in a boys' work therapy program earlier, and they weren't moving. Having talked to God about this dilemma, they knew He would help them.

A huge motorcycle roared into the yard. Gordon went to the window to see who this was. Gil, another friend, had come to offer his services around the yard.

"Yes," Gordon said, "We certainly could use your help, Gil. Just stay around for a few minutes. I will show you what needs to be done."

Their company finally excused themselves and said they had to go. Thanking them for coming, Esther apologized for the interrupted visit. Of course they understood.

"Mom, we're hungry!" called Corinne from outside. Her little face streaked with dirt, she and Charlene had been helping Gil pick up the branches from trees he and Gordon had cut yesterday.

"I'll run out, Gordon," Esther said, "and buy hamburgers. Bob may be hungry again, too."

"Do you want to eat as well?" Esther questioned, while opening the door to her car.

"No," Gordon answered. "I really don't have time." His face lined with weariness, he had already lost twenty pounds during the pending move. These weeks had not been easy for any of them.

Because of Esther's recent surgery, Gordon had said, "Esther, don't worry about a thing. I will take full responsibility." He was working hard to keep this promise.

The drive-in restaurant was very busy, as she stood in line waiting to buy hamburgers and fries for her "gang."

A short time later, the family, Gil, and Bob, sat down to enjoy their humble dinner. Esther, too, munched on a burger, talking to Bob about work that was still undone. They would be leaving in a few days, and the tasks seemed insurmountable.

"Don't worry about it, Mrs. Balisky," he comforted. "We'll get it done."

Watching him eat, Esther appreciated the enthusiasm and optimism of youth, but couldn't see how they possibly could be ready on time for their departure.

That night, several friends came by to help them pack. Just being there to tell them what had to be done was a big job. With everything in disarray, Esther really wasn't sure herself. A 6,000 square foot house filled with furniture and memorabilia, plus a large yard, complicated the situation.

While they were in the bedroom sorting things, the doorbell rang. She started, not really wanting company at that time.

A Car for Sale

"Esther, Brian is here to buy your car," Gordon smiled. She didn't feel like smiling at that moment. Every bone in her body hurt and resistance was low.

Sucking in her breath, and trying hard to be brave, she

walked outside. The men were talking about the fantastic features on the car and admiring its fine condition.

When Gordon handed Esther's keys to the buyer, her heart felt sad. Trying to look calm, she murmured, "I hope you enjoy the car as much as I have, Brian." Tears began to trickle down her cheeks while she turned away and cried.

Brian Johnson was a pastor's son. Bowing their heads in prayer, they committed the young man and his newly acquired vehicle to the Lord.

Quietly, Esther watched as he slipped inside, started the motor, and drove away. Feeling almost as if they had sold a family member, everyone had mixed emotions. Giving her feelings to God, who always heard and understood, Esther was comforted.

Everyone was strangely quiet when they went back into the house to resume unfinished tasks.

Finally, excusing herself, Esther went to bed. Their friends stayed up until late, diligently sorting and packing.

Newspaper Article

Esther's eyes were heavy as someone called her early the next morning. "Mom, the newspaper man is here, and wants to take some pictures of the house and all of us, too," bubbled Corinne. "Come on down, Mom—quick!"

As she dressed and combed her hair, she noticed dark circles surrounding her eyes from fatigue and lack of sleep. Certain she would not make a good picture in this condition, she decided not to go into the next room, but the girls called again.

The newspaper photographer was already taking pictures of Charlene and Corinne packing in the bedroom, and a reporter was interviewing Gordon in the living room.

Esther smiled woodenly as the camera clicked. Busy in

the kitchen, she continued packing dishes so he could take an action shot.

The next morning, Gordon called, "Hey, everyone, get up! You're picture is on the front page of the newspaper!"

The girls giggled as they saw themselves sitting on the floor, packing Russian dolls. A rather lengthy article followed:

FAMILY TO SEEK ITS ROOTS IN THE OLD WORLD

by Lynn Napier, *Shoreline Journal*, Wed. August 3, 1977

Tense excitement and apprehension filled the Balisky household on Fremont Avenue North last week. The family was moving and the scene was a typical one with stacked boxes, hurried instructions, and organized disarray.

Typical, however, with one exception. The Baliskys are moving to West Germany to work in Eastern Europe and Russia as missionaries.

Gordon Balisky said that he, his wife, and daughters were looking forward to the move, which was scheduled last Friday. "We'll never move there to stay," Balisky qualified, but we expect to stay an undetermined length of time abroad.

"My work has been in the area of Social Psychology," Balisky explained, noting that he will help German-Russian families who have recently immigrated to West Germany, with cultural adjustment.

Balisky said that another reason for the move, is to get in touch with his family's own cultural heritage. His grandfather, an officer in the Czar's army, immigrated

to North America with his family before the 1918 revolution, because he realized that things were falling apart. Balisky said the revolution marked the Soviet take-over of Russia.

"My wife's ancestors from Holland and Germany, migrated to Russia and then on to the United States," said Balisky, who speaks several Slavic languages fluently. His wife speaks German and will act as interpreter for the family.

He and his family will live at first in Kandern, a town in the Black Forest region of West Germany, north of Basel, Switzerland.

Balisky has toured Europe and the Soviet Union twice. On his first trip he spent a week in the South Central Kiev area.

"I found it very shocking. Everything was so structured as if Big Brother was watching everything, and of course, he is," he claimed.

Last year he toured Russia by auto with his wife, from Leningrad to the Black Sea.

Noting that the Soviet government strictly regulates tourist travel, he said, "You're given a route, an itinerary, and a deadline. Officials await your designated arrival at camp grounds along their route. Certain areas are restricted to tourists entirely. If you are on the wrong road, they will soon find you," he said, adding, "most roads are small, two-lane streets ravished by potholes. The Soviet Union has come a long way industrially in the past sixty years, but at a high price in the form of less personal freedom."

The article went on to tell of some of the activities in which the family would be involved in Europe.

The days were rapidly going by.

In addition to the chaos upstairs, hammer and saws were busy in the family room downstairs. A remodeling project taking place near the day of their departure seemed a bit odd. However, the kind man who volunteered his services had some spare time to help. What a transformation took place in a few days! They were truly grateful.

Garage Sale Remnants

The garage sale in their front yard had been going on for over a week. The girls did a fine job of selling many things they didn't need. Their "junk" became someone else's treasure.

"Mom, the Salvation Army truck is here to pick up the rest of the stuff!" shouted Charlene one afternoon.

Esther, running over to see if there was anything of value they would still like to keep, hastily chose a few desirable items to put into a keepsake box. Putting these into the storage area, she noticed that the piles were growing too fast. Even after weeks of sorting and giving away, there still seemed to be too much stuff!

They all heaved a sigh of relief to see the remainder packed into the truck, and taken to the store where it was later sold.

In their wallets, the girls carried a few dollars which they knew would come in handy. Smiling, they closed the garage door and knew this effort had been a job well done. And Mom was pleased, too.

Paul and Florence, dear friends and neighbors, were a wonderful source of comfort and assistance during those last busy days before departure.

"Come on over for breakfast," Florence called. The

Baliskys were only too happy to oblige. Offering one meal after another, it was great to break away from the chaos and walk into a quiet, clean house to enjoy a home-cooked meal. This always refreshed them and gave strength to carry on.

Florence had a cozy "prophet's chamber" in her basement. "Would you like to stay with me?" she offered kindly.

"It's what the doctor ordered," Esther answered gratefully. So at night, when the Balisky house was still lit up like a thousand florescent light bulbs, Esther could sneak into her friend's basement, crawl under soft white covers, and drift off to sleep until too soon, the light of a new day dawned once again.

Last minute instructions came on the day before their flight. "Della," she said to Gordon's sister, "please don't forget to send my books."

"I'll send them as soon as possible," she promised. She, too, had been consistent and helpful during those busy days. Without people who were there as pillars while Esther and Gordon dismantled their home, the task they had undertaken would have been overwhelming. But they made it through.

Going to bed early the night before their flight, Esther knew there were still people working to pack remaining boxes and tie the last knot.

But sleep didn't come easily that night. Too full of nervous energy and exhaustion, Esther stared at the ceiling and wondered what the future held for her family.

3 CHICAGO BOUND

It seemed as if she had just entered the realm of blissful sleep, when someone called, "Time to get up everyone! Hurry up!"

Pulling herself out of bed, Esther dressed. After a hot breakfast with Paul and Florence, Esther, Gordon, and the girls left for the airport. The time had finally arrived!

Mixed emotions filled their hearts as they drove out of the yard on Fremont Avenue North that morning.

Bonnie, a friend from the church, had come for them in her big Cadillac. Russ and Bob had already left for the airport with the boxes and suitcases.

This was it! It seemed so final! They were on their way! Watching as long as possible, Della, Paul, and Florence waved from the front porch step, until the car disappeared.

The lump in Esther's throat grew larger as they left the spacious yard, the enormous fir trees, the lovely flower garden, Gordon's favorite roses.... *How many years will go by before we come home again?* she wondered.

Snuggling back into the seat of the luxurious car, Esther blinked back the tears that wanted to take control. But she had said yes to God and she meant it! There was no turning back now!

Sea-Tac airport was busy, as usual, when they arrived. Bob and Russ, already there, waited with rows of boxes and suitcases.

As they boarded the plane for Chicago, Bob, putting his big arms around Esther, hugged her tightly. “Thank you for your family, and what you mean to me,” he said.

The lump in her throat didn’t go away. Swallowing hard, she returned Bob’s gesture.

Walking into the huge craft, they were soon seated. The girls seemed to enjoy themselves, as they settled down in the crowded seats allotted to them.

“Please fasten your seat belts,” droned the stewardess in a nasal voice.

They were on their way! They watched their beautiful city disappear as the clouds gradually covered buildings and scenery. Seeing snow-capped Mount Rainier in the distance, resplendent in the sunshine, Esther knew this familiar landmark would vanish soon, as well.

Eventually all the familiar and precious things relating to home faded out of sight, and they settled down in their seats to relax. Esther, closing her eyes, was relieved to be on the way at last. Those last few days of packing were over and a new life lay ahead.

The huge aircraft continued to soar upward into the blue, azure skies. The unknown lay ahead, but God had already charted the way, so Esther and Gordon put their trust in Him.

When the stewardess brought lunch, the girls pulled out their trays, and in short order cleared their plates. They had been too excited to eat breakfast, so this meal tasted especially good!

Chicago

The flight was pleasant enough, and it didn't take long before the Baliskys saw the great city of Chicago beneath them. The cars looked like small matchbox toys as they drove along narrow snakelike roads. As the plane descended, the cars appeared larger.

Feeling the huge aircraft go down as it sped toward the runway, with seat belts fastened securely, they waited for the familiar thump as the wheels touched the pavement below.

It took some time to pack all their luggage into the waiting vehicle. A Slavic Gospel Association worker helped Gordon load the heavy luggage and soon they were on their way to SGA mission headquarters. Remembering how humid it had been when they had been in this area before, true to Chicago's weather pattern, they found it to be the same again. Esther's hair limply clinging to her face, was wet with perspiration. Wiping her brow with the back of her hand, she climbed into the van.

The rooms assigned to them were air conditioned. Relieved, the girls sank into a freshly-made bed and rested comfortably. They were all in need of a good sleep before tackling the long flight across the water.

The air conditioner hummed softly as the drape beside the bed gently blew in the night air. Gordon's soft breathing gradually became a grand crescendo as he began to snore. It did not bother his wife, however, because she was just too tired to care. In a few minutes they were all in dreamland.

Across the Water

Coworkers, Larry, Trish, and Dave, accompanied them to the airport the next day. With all the luggage stacked carefully into the van, they drove through the busy streets of the city during heavy traffic. It took some time to check in. Thankfully, they had come early enough to accomplish all this in good time.

Charlene and Corinne hugged their friend, Larry, as they said good-bye. Were those tears in his eyes? They thought so.

Larry Gray had been very dear to the Baliskys throughout the years, and the girls regarded him as an older brother or uncle. He had known them since they were very young, and held a brotherly love toward them, too.

After boarding the huge aircraft, the stewardess informed them they would be making one stop in Iceland, and then flying straight through to Luxembourg. It had been arranged that, upon arrival, Bill Neudorf, a Black Forest Academy school teacher, would be picking them up with his van.

The flight would take nine hours, so they would be flying all night, and changing their clocks. It was confusing to leave in the morning, and arrive in Luxembourg in the morning! Missing a night's sleep takes its toll, and this night was no exception. Oh well, they would have to get used to this, too.

Many around them were fast asleep, but the girls and Esther stayed awake all night. Gordon, beside them, blissfully snored his way into oblivion. Before they knew it, the light of day began to show through the darkness. Brilliant hues of scarlet and tints of gold covered the wide, crimson sky as the sun came up from behind the billowy clouds. Then it was impossible to sleep! Charlene and Corinne sat in crowded seats, while cigarette smoke curled into the blue-gray atmosphere. Both of them were weary and cramped when breakfast came around.

Eating at this unusual hour seemed abnormal. In Seattle it was time for bed! Thinking of their big, comfortable bedrooms at home made them long for "the leaks and garlic" of more comfortable days, but when the pungent aroma of freshly brewed coffee reached them, they felt more awake and ready to participate in new adventures.

The hours droned by while they tried to rest, read magazines, and look out of the little windows beside them.

Arrival—Luxembourg

What a thrill it was to hear the stewardess announce, "We are nearing Luxembourg, ladies and gentlemen. Please fasten your seat belts. The weather is warm and balmy. We hope you had a pleasant flight."

"Hey, we are nearing our new home!" said Esther, as they craned their necks to see out of the little windows.

Luscious green grasses stretched as far as the eye could see. Interchanging hills and valleys dipping and soaring, reminded them of pictures they had seen in magazines. With no words to describe the beauty below, they expressed their thanks to the Creator who fashioned the world so long ago.

Eventually, buildings and cars appeared. At first they seemed small and insignificant, but gradually grew larger as the plane began to descend. Mixed emotions overwhelmed them all when they realized their new home was just a short distance away. They would soon be there! What did the future hold for them in a culture so different from their own?

"Please fasten your seat belts," repeated the captain over the intercom. Once more they felt the steady descent of the airplane as it glided toward the runway beneath them.

As she stood up, Esther's legs felt weak and shaky. Even her purse seemed heavy!

Trying not to burden his wife, Gordon carried the sewing machine, his camera bag, overnight case, and many smaller articles. Even without carry-on luggage to contend with, Esther felt the effects of recent surgery, as she struggled to lift one foot in front of the other. Why did her legs feel like rubber? Would she make it?

Thankfully she did!

Strangers in a foreign land, they watched familiar boxes and cases come down the ramp. Finally, when all were accounted for, they saw Bill Neudorf and his son, Duane, walking toward them. Greeting each other warmly, they proceeded to pack their luggage into the van. It is amazing how much one can pack into one vehicle. Every corner was filled. In fact, there was barely enough room for all the people, but finally, after a little strategic planning, they each found a small section in which to sit.

At close range this time, Esther marveled at the beauty of this country, as they drove by grasslands, great mountains, and peaceful valleys. Cattle, contentedly grazing in luscious meadows, wore cow bells that tinkled with each movement.

A few hours later, they decided to stop for time to unravel their cramped legs. Blessed stillness filled the peaceful countryside. The air, fresh and balmy, was a sharp contrast to the city's pollution and noise.

Bedtime

Traveling made them all weary.

"Shall we stop for the night?" asked Bill. No one objected, so they found a quaint *Gasthaus* in which to retire.

Charlene, Corinne, and Duane were starved. It had been hours since they'd stopped to eat along the roadside.

"Let's buy some *schnitzel*, Dad!" said Duane. The suggestion was appealing.

Checking into the *Gasthaus*, Esther went into the clean, quiet room alone and gratefully crawled into bed, while the men and ravenous young people went to find a restaurant.

When Gordon arrived back at the room with a delightful, hot dinner for Esther, she was already sleeping. Shaking herself, while prying open her eyes, she saw the *schnitzel*! Deep fried to a succulent golden brown, the aroma was one of a kind. Crisp Pommes Frites (French Fries) and a salad completed the typically German entrée.

Forgetting for a moment that she was sleepy, she sat up in bed, and ate every bite!

Like a person drugged, she settled back into the feather bed, and dozed off again. They say the need for sleep is retroactive. Not having slept a great deal during those last hectic days of packing in Seattle, she was now relaxed.

Meanwhile, the others went for a walk in the quiet, refreshing countryside.

The Last Mile

Esther, feeling much more refreshed, awakened at 6:30 A.M. Counting back, she realized that meant it was 10:30 P.M. at home. What a mix-up, but they knew it wouldn't take long to adapt to this new schedule.

Breakfast, too, was delicious. Strong European coffee mixed with rich, fresh cream revived everyone.

The girls and Duane finished first, and asked to be excused in order to continue their conversation.

The car was crowded and the day very warm, however they enjoyed God's great handiwork as they sped along the smooth ribbon of road. While Bill, Gordon, and Esther talked endlessly in the front seat, the girls and Duane had

their own animated conversation in the cramped stuffy rear of the van.

They had a difficult time to even look out, because boxes were piled in front of the windows blocking their view. They ignored this problem and talked about the new school they would soon be attending. Patiently Duane answered one question after another.

Black Forest Academy was founded by the Janz brothers from Canada, when they realized a school was needed to educate missionary children while their parents went to other parts of Europe.

Charlene and Corinne listened as Duane told them about the teachers, fellow students, and curriculum. Soaking up this information like sponges, they learned a lot about the place where they would be spending the majority of their time.

4 KANDERN , SOUTHWEST GERMANY

Bill Neudorf's wife, Erma, had packed a delightful lunch, so in order to eat and exercise a bit, they stopped beside the road. The scenery there, as well, was delightful. Esther drew in long, deep breaths of clean country air.

Almost before they knew it, the town of Kandern appeared. Settled in the midst of hills and greenery, it appeared like a picture out of a storybook.

Esther's heart skipped a beat, realizing this *dorf* would be their home for several years. Passing Bruckers Clothing store, the post office where many letters would soon be mailed to the States, and Gottlieb, the grocery store where they would buy their food, they knew this would all be familiar territory soon.

The girls stretched to see all they could from the crowded back seat. When the car came to a stop in Blumenplatz market place, they jumped out excitedly.

Our home in Kandern, Germany

"This is where my family lives, and here you will be catching the school bus every morning," Duane smiled. Right now, even through the beauty, everything seemed strange and new to them.

Erma came to the door of their apartment extending her hand in greeting.

"Welcome to Kandern," she smiled. "I'm so glad you have arrived. We have been waiting for you."

Giving her Bill a hug, she invited everyone into their home.

Charlene and Corinne shyly came from around the van.

"Erma, I'd like you to meet our daughters," Esther said, naming them. Shaking her hand, they, too, followed her inside as she led them all into the cool, spacious apartment. Josilyn, their youngest, took Corinne's hand as if they were old friends, and invited her to see gifts she had received at a recent birthday party.

Sighing gratefully, Charlene stretched out on the couch, happy to unravel cramped legs and arms.

Erma began setting out the hot meat loaf, potatoes fixed the German way, salad, vegetables, and juices on the ample dining room table.

Calling everyone to "come and dine," it wasn't long before they were seated. Sensing they had found a home away from home, they clasped hands around the dinner table while Bill thanked the Lord for their safe arrival. The food was passed around, and they all fell to.

Home: Steinenstrasse 1B

Charlene and Corinne couldn't wait to drive to their new home on Steinenstrasse 1B, so the men and the girls took the van and left for the house. The Schick's, their new landlords, had been waiting for them all day. A delicious lunch was spread on the spacious table in the living room. Could they eat again?

Meanwhile, Esther stayed at the Neudorf's to assist Erma with the dishes.

"Esther," Erma gently reprimanded, "You look so tired. Go and lie down on our bed until your husband comes back for you. I know about fatigue while making a trip such as you have done." Esther was reluctant.

"Please go now," she said, giving her a gentle shove. Esther complied. As she rested on the big, cozy bed, her busy mind went over the past days' events. She was happy to finally be home!

It wasn't long before the gang came back from the house and said the Schicks were eagerly waiting to meet her. The girls' eyes sparkled as they told her about their new home.

"Mom, the living room is sunken, and has so much room! The yard is like a park, and the bedrooms are all ready for us!" chirped Corinne. "Hurry Mom, come with us! We want to get unpacked and settled. Char and I each have our own bedroom, too," she smiled.

While Esther slipped into her shoes and reached for her sweater, the girls waited impatiently. "Hold on!" she laughed. "I'm coming!" She, too, was excited as they told about the beautiful yard.

Thanking the family for their wonderful hospitality, they climbed into the van and left for their new home just a kilometer away.

"Mom, there is a river that flows past the back yard," said Charlene, her eyes shining. "And Mom, wait until you hear the birds in the yard…and see the flowers Frau Schick planted."

"There it is!" shouted Corinne.

Looking ahead, Esther saw a typical, charming German chalet with a slanted roof, situated in the middle of trees, flowers, and hills.

Frau and Herr Schick came toward them as they climbed out of the car.

"*Guten Tag*," Esther said, extending her hand.

"Hello!" they greeted. "Welcome to Kandern!" Smiling, they led the family into the sunken living room for a cup of hot German coffee and a variety of cakes.

"I think I will burst if I eat one more bite!" whispered Gordon when Frau Schick had gone into the kitchen for more goodies.

Esther had spoken German since she was a child, but due to lack of practice, she felt awkward in the beginning, trying to articulate the big words. But as time went on, she became more fluent.

In a few minutes, everyone was laughing and talking as if they had known each other for years! Yes, they would get along fine with these delightful people. There was a chemistry between them, and they all felt it.

In broken English, Frau Schick said, "You must be very tired after your long journey. Come, I will show you where the bedrooms are located."

She had carefully made their beds with her own sheets, pillow cases, and quilts. They were impressed!

The girls, following Frau Schick upstairs to their bedrooms, were delighted for the privacy.

Later, under their pillows, each found a Toblerone chocolate bar. These bars would become their favorite chocolate treats.

Touched by these gestures of kindness, they looked toward a long-lasting friendship with this German couple.

That night, with renewed energy (or was it adrenaline?), Esther even unpacked some of the boxes to make this place a real home. Planning a trip to Poland soon, there would be numerous tasks that needed immediate attention.

Charlene helped, as together, they put their few dishes into the small kitchen cupboards. Carefully unpacking the linens and towels, Esther placed them in available drawers. Frustrated already due to lack of space, she knew they would have to buy a storage unit (*schrank)* soon.

Momentarily, holding a sweet-smelling towel to her face, nostalgia washed over her as she thought of home. What was happening there? And was Mother making the necessary adjustments?

Turning to her work, she knew God would care for all the details. She would follow one day at a time.

Climbing into bed their first night in Kandern, and snuggling down into the warmness of Frau Schick's colorful

quilt, she could hear the Kander River rushing past, while trees gently rustled in the warm wind.

But before sleep completely enveloped her, she gratefully thanked God for leading their family safely to a new home—away from home.

Asking God to bless her girls, she was grateful they were now sleeping in their own bedrooms. God had promised to look after them and she knew He would.

"Lord," Esther continued, "help them to become adjusted quickly. Bring new friends along their path soon, and cause them to grow in grace during this period of upheaval and adjustment. Thank You, Father. Amen."

The stream rushed on peacefully and Esther went to sleep, secure in the knowledge that her God had opened up the way. There was no need to fear. Closing her eyes, she was soon dreaming of the blessed future God had planned for them.

Kandern

The school bus arrived in Kandern at 8:00 A.M., so the girls were expected to be up early.

"Charlene and Cori, time to get up!"

"Coming Mom."

Sleepily they crawled out of bed. It didn't take long to find that schoolwork in Germany was more difficult, and the standard of education higher, than in the U.S.A., but enthusiastically they tackled the challenge. Making new friends quickly, the adjustment period was not as hard as Esther thought it might be.

Coming downstairs, they quickly had breakfast and hurried to catch a bus at Blumenplatz in Kandern.

"Come on!" challenged their new classmates. "Hurry or you'll be late!"

Corinne and Miriam quickly became close friends. Everywhere they went, they were linked together. After school, it was interesting to explore the ancient *dorf* together as graveyards, old houses, river beds, and shops became alive to the eager youths. Sampling cookies and other sweets in local shops after school became a daily ritual. Shopkeepers smiled and waited on the hungry pair.

Charlene too had a special friend. Tim, a senior, older in years than she, found himself attracted to the flaxen-haired junior who had so recently joined their ranks at Black Forest Academy. Often coming to the Balisky home to visit, he became a familiar and good friend to the family—especially Charlene.

Years ago, Tim's father and Esther's sister had become so attached that, though it never happened, the family wondered if a wedding would be coming. Now Esther's daughter was enjoying the company of Neil's handsome son!

Another Ministry

Many of the young people attending BFA were lonely. Parents, going to various mission fields, left their children at the BFA dorms in the care of dorm parents, but no one would ever be able to fill the void of absent loved ones. Though friends were plentiful and dorm parents kind, the young people longed for a more homelike atmosphere to fill the void in their hearts.

Esther decided to befriend them. Volunteering to teach Sunday School to the high school girls, she found this to be a needy field of service. Gradually the young women warmed up. Eventually they began coming to the house and Charlene and Corinne had new friends. Slumber parties, with lots of love and a warm home atmosphere, brought a new dimension into the lives of the lonely students. Esther had become a substitute mom, as she tried to help those who came to her with problems.

Being active in the local BFA assembly also brought joy to the woman who'd had concerns that she and her family would be lonely in Germany.

A Day in a German Village

A new day dawned without a cloud, as sunshine burst through between the great Black Forest trees. It glistened on the grass, still wet with early morning dew.

A myriad of birds had awakened several hours before. In grand crescendo, a great chorus of music swelled from their throats. It reached to the ears of the waking village people.

Pulling up the shades on her windows that morning, Esther sucked in her breath as she looked at the beautiful countryside. Hills, arrayed in festive shades of green, rose majestically before her eyes. In the far distance, snow-capped mountains towered high into the blueness of the clear sky. The manicured countryside was covered with a variety of colorful flowers. The stream quietly, gently, flowed over the slippery rocks, while little fish darted here and there in daily pursuit of food.

Then Esther heard the church bell in the village toll the hour of six o'clock. The sound echoed loud and clear over the waking town.

It wasn't long before the village women came out of their houses. Emerging one by one, each carried a shopping bag or basket. Carried on for generations before them, it has always been a ritual to go to the store every morning to purchase fresh food for the day.

Breathing the crisp clean air, Esther, too, hurried toward her destination. Seeing one of her friends ahead and quickening her pace, she called, "Good morning, Frau Schmidt!"

"Hello, Frau Balisky. How are you today?"

"I am happy to be alive on such a lovely day," she smiled. Together they walked toward the bustling shopping center.

Frau Schmidt was short of stature and pleasantly plump. Her laughter was infectious, and Esther liked her from the beginning of their friendship.

As they entered the crowded store, the aroma of freshly baked bread greeted them. The shelves were lined with fragrant brown cracked wheat, pumpernickel, sour dough, and white bread. Brown crusty rolls, just out of the oven, were steaming and hot. Both women put several into their baskets.

Tantalizing aromas of freshly brewed coffee awakened them completely. They inhaled long and deep.

Large eggs, white and clean, were neatly stacked in their crates. Bacon, sausages, and steaks had just been brought in from a nearby farm.

As Frau Schmidt and Esther walked toward home, baskets full, they saw the restaurants were already open. They heard the clanking of forks and knives against ceramic dishes as people ate breakfast. There, too, the aroma of coffee and fragrant food filled the morning air.

"I'm getting hungry," Esther laughed.

"So am I," she answered.

They hurried to their respective homes to make breakfast for waiting families.

"Mom, I'm starved!" said eleven-year-old Corinne as she opened the door for Esther. She looked hungrily into the bulging bag to see what it contained.

After breakfast, Esther walked with the girls to the gate.

Swinging lunch pails and skipping on the stone path, they waved back to her.

"Bye Mom! See you after school!" Charlene called over

her shoulder. Corinne was in too much of a hurry to look back.

Esther stood and watched until they disappeared around the corner.

The German women appeared to be fastidiously clean. She saw Frau Schmidt and others diligently sweeping their already immaculate sidewalks. Frau Schmidt turned and waved. Her clean windows sparkled in the morning sunlight.

Sighing, Esther went into her own house to make the beds and tidy a messy kitchen.

At noon, the church bells tolled once more. It was time for shops to close. Now the villagers ate their main meal of the day. After satisfying hungry stomachs, the entire town became still as the people rested. At 2:00 P.M., shops became a hive of bustling activity once more. Later, children were welcomed home from a long day at school. Shoppers crowded the streets. Everywhere villagers chatted about events occurring in their town. Cars, bicycles, and pedestrians lined the busy streets. Horns honked and brakes squealed, as vehicles tried to maneuver in this hub of activity.

The day wore on until dusty twilight. Slowly the sun set, casting brilliant colors of various hues against a darkening sky, then withdrew at length behind the silent hills, leaving the village shrouded in darkness.

Birds, safe in their nests, softly chirped an evensong, before putting their heads under downy wings and contentedly going to sleep.

One by one, lights in homes went out. Another day was over and it was time to rest.

"Good night," Esther murmured to her sleepy husband as she settled down under the feather comforter in her cozy bed.

5 Penetrating Iron Barriers

"Where could that church be?" asked Gordon as they circled the city of Budapest, Hungary. Billy Graham was scheduled to speak that evening, and no one seemed to be able to give the necessary instructions. Stopping at the Bahnhof (train station), they had a family conference and decided to go back to their hotel room. Their day had been filled with numerous activities and they were tired.

Gordon had just started the motor when Charlene cried, "Hey, wait a minute! I see Chris and her friend beside that little red car! Quick, Dad! Go over there!"

Could it be? Gordon drove over to where Charlene was sure she had seen one of her parents' coworkers. Chris' eyes grew wide when she saw the Baliskys coming toward her. How incredible! To meet friends in a city the size of Budapest unplanned, could not merely be chance.

"Where are you going?" Gordon asked.

"We are on our way to hear Billy Graham," she smiled. "Are you going there, too?"

"Yes, we want to, but we don't know where to find the church building."

"Oh, we know where it is!" said Chris. "Why don't you just follow us?"

Carefully they drove behind the little red car, careful not to lose each other in the congested traffic.

Delighted to realize that God had arranged for them to meet the girls in a specific spot, though they knew nothing about it previously, each agreed that surely, this was a divine encounter. Who but God cared about these little details?

Finally Chris pulled her little red car toward the curb and stopped. Gordon drove close behind, parked the vehicle, and got out.

Noticing others who were obviously in a hurry, they realized these people, too, were going to the church where the well-known evangelist would be speaking.

After carefully locking the cars, they began to walk toward the church. It was several blocks away, but eventually they saw the large building ahead.

"Mom, I hope we find a place to sit down tonight," said Corinne. "Come, let's hurry!"

The evening was stifling hot and humid, and to stand during the long service would be exhausting. Though they quickened their pace, hundreds of people were already there before them. Crowds of humanity swarmed everywhere! Trying to keep together as a family was not easy. Suddenly they heard music—not the trashy sort often heard in restaurants and camping grounds, but the familiar strains of an old hymn floating clearly across the evening air. Thrilled to hear the message of hope, just as others around them were hearing it, Esther choked back a lump in her throat as tears filled her eyes.

Blessed assurance, Jesus is mine!
Oh, what a foretaste of glory divine!
Heir of salvation, purchase of God,
Born of His Spirit, washed in His blood.
This is my story, this is my song,
Praising my Savior all the day long!

—Fanny J. Crosby

Here in a Communist country, where the precious name of Jesus was dishonored, the words of truth and life were clear for all to hear.

"I can't believe this," Chris said as slowly—ever so slowly—they inched their way through the crowds. Once inside, they were sorry they had not stayed outdoors! The heat closed in oppressively as the people waited. Some had come hours before and were seated, waiting for the service to begin. Others continued walking around looking for a place to sit.

There were no vacant seats inside, so they decided to go out where at least they could breath.

"But how do we get out of here?" Corinne wailed as she looked at the blocked exit doors.

"It's a challenge, but let's try!" said her mother.

Shoving and pushing, others were coming from different directions. Perspiration flowed freely. Odors of garlic and onions were pungent.

"Mom, I'm trapped!" called Corinne, and indeed she was. Being so much smaller than most of the people in the building, she was pressed from all sides. Esther could do nothing to stop the heaving crowd as they pushed against them. Holding tightly to the child's hand, she encouraged her to stay close as Charlene followed.

Finally, to their relief, they were out the door and

under a darkening sky. The air here, too, was humid, but better than it had been inside. Corinne sighed and took a deep breath.

"Thank God, we're out of there!" she said.

Still everywhere, there were people coming to hear the evangelist. Men, women, children, teenagers, uncles, aunts, and grandparents swarmed into the crowded church, or stood restlessly outside.

Meanwhile, Gordon went into the church to take pictures. They didn't see him for the rest of the evening.

The choir continued to sing familiar hymns with a wonderful message for a waiting, expectant people.

Charlene, Corinne, and Esther stood at the side door of the church, realizing they could do nothing else. Chris and her friend were inside. Billy Graham arrived and the preliminaries began.

Suddenly a leader, with a badge on his lapel, opened the side door and gestured for the girls and Esther to come with him. Needing no further prompting, they followed to where miraculously, there were vacant seats near an outside door. Certainly, God had provided!

No longer were the people shoving and pushing. Most sat silent now in their seats. Some expressed a desire to hear from God, while others were just curious. Perhaps some came to jest at this American preacher from the West. But all were hearing the message of hope.

Watching the television crew taking pictures, they knew the program would be aired in America soon afterward.

As the baritone voice of the colored soloist rang through the crowded church, there was an air of expectancy. The people listened in rapt attention. What did this preacher have to offer them?

When Billy Graham rose to speak, the audience was

hushed and waiting. Speaking through an interpreter, he expressed joy to be with them.

"Just before I left America," he went on to say, "I talked with the President of the United States, and he told me to send special greetings to the people of Hungary! We, as Americans, have so much to learn from you," his voice rang out clear and strong.

Pleased, some nodded, flattered to realize the President even thought about them.

Billy Graham spoke at length about Jesus, the Light of the World, and the Good Shepherd of His sheep.

One hour went by and still the service continued. The air was stifling, oppressive, yet the people listened. Finally, at the end of the service, the evangelist asked them to bow their heads. The choir softly sang a song of invitation. Many bowed their heads and prayed. Some asked Jesus to be Lord of their lives.

While making their way down the stairs, the music continued to resound to the four corners of the old building and beyond, into the streets of the great city of Budapest, proclaiming the Gospel of Christ to a needy people.

Everywhere outdoors, police were anxiously watching and directing congested traffic.

What sway did this preacher from the West have over their people? Perhaps they, too, would find out.

God's Word cannot be silenced. As it is proclaimed, even in a Communist country, His power cannot be stopped. It flows on and on like a mighty current.

In deep thought, the family climbed into their waiting vehicle and drove to the hotel. Grateful to have the opportunity of hearing this man of God proclaim the Gospel in a Hungarian city, they knew that time and eternity would reveal the outcome of this wonderful evening. Perhaps there

will be new believers in glory one day because they accepted the challenge given that night. Esther and Gordon would be able to shake their hands in welcome and say, “Yes, we remember. We were in Budapest the night Billy Graham was there. Welcome into the family of God!”

The Haunted House—Szcezecin, Poland

While Esther stayed home with the girls, Gordon and a coworker, Alex, made another trip to Poland.

As Gordon and Alex bumped along the corrugated road toward Szcezecin, in northwest Poland, they shivered as a cold wind blew in from the North.

Red and gold leaves, hanging tenaciously from the now almost-bare trees, finally let go of their strong hold on the solid branches of the maple trees to which they had clung since spring. Gracefully flying through the air, one by one, they fell to mingle with others to become part of mother earth.

Gordon shivered. Pulling his coat around him, he heard Alex say, “This old ’65 Volkswagen bus has seen better days, don’t you think?”

Nodding his head, Gordon agreed.

With no source of heat inside, it seemed to absorb the cold from the outside.

“We’re almost there,” encouraged Alex.

Lost in thought, they resumed their journey toward the new church in Szcezecin, which would be dedicated in the next few days. Both men had been to Poland before, but this trip would be the first time they would visit this particular church.

Pastors from all across the country planned to come to this big event, coupled with a weekend conference.

Everyone was excited! Truly God had opened the door

to purchase the big building. Insurmountable problems had stood in the way, and now it belonged to God's people. They planned to use it wisely.

Gordon silently thought about his family in Kandern. They had settled just recently in the small *dorf.* Would it be a difficult time of adjustment, or would they fit in? Praying for them, he could only trust God to work out the details.

Resuming conversation, Alex and Gordon commented on groups of aggressive men, women, and children as they worked in the fields along the main road. The potato and sugar beet harvest had come. They must gather their vegetables in before the winter snows arrived. They depended on these provisions to sustain them through the long, cold winter ahead. The days were going by rapidly. Would they finish their job before it snowed?

Even children, dressed in warm coats, filled pails of vegetables and carried them to the rubber-tired wagon standing nearby. Horses, waiting patiently, still hitched to the conveyance, would soon drive home, where they would be fed and released from this burden.

Gordon's thoughts turned toward the church building. Looking at his partner, he said, "Surely it is a myth that the building they will dedicate this week is haunted?"

"I have heard it isn't a myth," answered Alex. "People who have lived there in the past always move out soon afterward. So, what do *you* think, Gordon?"

"It has been reported by many Poles to be haunted," answered Gordon. "Strange noises are evident at various times of the month and year. No one, they say, wants to live there!"

"But now it is God's house," answered Alex. "No one expects it to be haunted anymore! Surely, God will look after this if there really is a problem. Pastor Tadeuez and Lydia

seem to be happy there since they moved into the apartment on the second floor."

"And no one has heard of ghosts in a church," laughed Gordon.

Alex pressed his foot on the accelerator. The old van shot forward.

Both Alex and Gordon eagerly anticipated being able to assist Polish pastors financially. With a burden on their hearts for men who worked in the church and couldn't hold jobs as ministers living in the system, SGA had sent gifts of money with Alex and Gordon.

This remuneration would be distributed to various pastors in Poland so they could continue to teach their own people from the precious Word of God. So few others seemed to be well-versed in the Scriptures. Many had a hunger to know more, but if the pastors left, where could they go to learn?

These gifts of money would also be spread around to assist and support the Evangelical Union in Poland, in aiding the Bible School in Warsaw, where young men and women studied to go into the ministry. The finances would also help in youth and children's camp ministries, literature, and radio in that country.

Besides distributing these necessary funds, Gordon would minister in the large conference. The pastors always longed for deep truths from the Word of God, so they, in turn, could teach their people. From past experience, they knew they would be fed.

Gordon knew Szcezecin was not far away now. It was a beautiful city and was a leading port of Poland. Lying on the Baltic Sea on the Oder River, it served as a port for Czechoslovakia, East Germany, and Hungary, as well as for Poland.

This city became part of Poland at the end of World War

II in 1945. Previously it had been part of Germany and was spelled Stettin.

Finally driving through the crowded city, Gordon looked for the church that was reported to be haunted. Surely this was only a myth—or could it be true? They would soon find out!

"There it is!" reported Alex, pointing to a rather weather beaten, but renovated building.

"We're here," sighed Gordon, "finally here!"

Stopping, they stepped out and stretched their cramped muscles.

"Welcome!" greeted Pastor Tadeuez.

"We are so happy you have come to the conference and dedication of our new church! Most of the pastors are already here, but a few are still on their way."

Inviting them in, Tadeuez led his guests from America into the small kitchen, where the teakettle boiled on the stove, and *kinapke* was already prepared.

"Hello," smiled his dark-haired wife, Lydia, extending her hand.

BEDTIME: WAS THE HOUSE HAUNTED?

The hot liquid went down well. Soon, warmed and fed, Alex and Gordon were escorted to their bedroom on the main floor.

"But where are you sleeping?" Gordon asked, concerned. "Is this not your bedroom?"

"Yes, but that is fine. We will retire in the living room," replied their gracious host.

"Often, when we have guests, they sleep in our room. We are happy to share it with you both for the duration of the conference. Just enjoy it."

"*Dobra niez*! And sleep well," he concluded, walking

toward his sleeping quarters in the living room.

Alex, on the floor in a sleeping bag, rolled over and was soon oblivious to everything and everyone around him. Gordon, too, was sleeping almost before his head touched the pillow.

Suddenly Alex froze! What was that terrible noise? Had the reported ghost come to haunt them on their first night in the big house?

Closing his ears with the palms of his hands, he preferred to think that what he had heard was his overactive imagination. After all, his mother told him he was good at fantasizing when he was young. He lay motionless. Perhaps it would go away.

"Oh, no! There it is again!" A strange, rattling noise like he had never heard before drummed in his ears.

This was not imagination. What he heard was real—very real.

"Gordon!" he whispered.

No answer.

"Gordon!" he cried. "Do you hear that unearthly sound?"

Gordon startled. Sitting up, he whispered, "Is this really the reported ghost? It can't be!"

But what, then, was that infernal noise?

Gordon cupped his hand to one ear and propped his other elbow on the floorboard. He shuttered.

There it was again!

Loud, eerie, ominous, it rattled through the room. Where did it come from? What could it be? Alex and Gordon looked at each other—and hoped it would go away. Surely it would!

But Gordon had another problem. Mother nature was urgently calling. "Go now, or you'll wish you had," said an urgent voice within.

"I can't," he reasoned. "With that noise so close—I just can't! How can I leave this room?"

Hugging his legs together, he tried to ignore the appalling situation. But how long can one ignore mother nature's warning?

"I can't wait! I've got to go *now*!" he groaned.

The hands of the clock, pointing to 2 A.M., brought back recollection of the tea he had consumed earlier that night. It had to be released soon—or what?

Gingerly, cautiously, he crawled out of bed and walked toward the closed door.

What, or who lay behind this mystery? And what or who was on the other side of that closed door?

He did not know—nor did he want to know.

Alex squelched a smile in spite of the uneasy feeling gnawing in the pit of his stomach. The tea, consumed earlier, was becoming a bit of a problem for him, as well, but he chose to ignore it—at least for a little longer. How much longer, he didn't know. He didn't care to know. He had to hold on!

Opening the door a crack, Gordon peered into the darkness.

The noise was louder now. Tiptoeing, hurriedly he slunk toward the bathroom. Would he make it? Was the ghost—or whatever it was—behind him?

The ghostly rattle reverberated louder and louder.

Coming close to the study, he stopped a moment. Were the sounds coming from inside?

Cautiously opening the door, the rattling noise sounded loudly in his ears.

What? What was this?

He couldn't believe it!

There, Brother Meranty, the secretary of the Polish

Evangelical Union of Churches, lay fast asleep on the couch. With his mouth wide open, voluptuous rattling sounds emanated from his throat. The man was snoring—simply, blissfully snoring his way into oblivion.

So much for the haunted house!

Laughing—relieved—Gordon closed the door and ran toward the bathroom. Now he knew no ghosts were following him.

Only the sounds of a man deep in sleep reverberated throughout the apartment. In the morning, the big house would be quiet again. Hopefully the reported ghosts would stay away!

The Conference and the church dedication was an occasion everyone would remember for a long time.

Driving toward Legnicia, Alex and Gordon shivered in the unheated van. Cold winds seeped through the doors and windows of the unheated van, causing the two men to cover their legs with sleeping bags while they drove. Knowing the weather would not grow warmer, they braced themselves. In a short time they planned to leave for southwest Germany. Hopefully it would not be so cold there.

The Calisia Piano

Esther, who had played the piano since she was a child, longed for her instruments in Seattle. She wondered how she could cope without a piano in Germany.

Gordon, of course, saw the need. Both musical, they used their talents to minister in many churches. The girls too, were taking music lessons from a teacher at BFA. They asked Gordon if he could purchase a piano in Poland. They were all becoming excited at this prospect. Would it be possible to buy one at the factory price—and with the American dollar, too? Gordon did his homework well.

As he and Alex drove toward the factory, they hoped the big instrument would fit into the old van.

The Calisia was a beauty! Gordon smiled, knowing how much pleasure it would give his family There was a place reserved in the sunken living room at home for this cherished gift. Seeing the light in Esther's eyes would be well worth any inconvenience they may have in taking it home.

When they were told at the factory that a trip to Warsaw would be necessary to facilitate the financial transaction, the men found themselves driving toward that city. Returning later, after the piano was paid for, they planned to load it into the van and leave for home. Meanwhile, in Warsaw, it was difficult to leave as soon as planned.

Invitations to speak in various churches sparked the interest of the people. Becoming involved in the Zigorna Street Evangelical Church and the Bible School, they spent long hours teaching.

The people were always happy when they came. Knowing there would be "meat" from the Word of God, they arranged times of fellowship with believers in the area.

It was well into November now. Ice and snow covered the potholes on the frozen road. Could they transport a piano in weather conditions such as these? Gordon sincerely hoped so. As they drove back to the factory, the men knew winter had arrived. Having been in Poland when ten-foot snow banks surrounded the narrow roadway, they could hardly wait to arrive back in Germany again.

Loading the instrument was not a problem. Taking the back seat out, with three quarters of an inch to spare, the piano slid in easily. Paid for and ready to leave, the men drove toward the border into East Germany.

Border Crossing

"Get out of your vehicle!" ordered the austere border guard. The men knew he meant what he said.

Roughly, a group of officials herded Alex into one room and Gordon into another. If found guilty, these Americans would get the punishment they deserved!

But what were they guilty of? Alex and Gordon didn't know. It was true that Alex had been involved in smuggling Bibles into Russia on a previous occasion. On a cold, foggy night in northeast Poland, his old van, similar to the one they were driving now, was hit by an on-coming train. Fortunate to be alive, he was hospitalized for some time. The Bibles, of course, were all confiscated and destroyed.

No doubt, this situation was recorded in their archives. The Russians always knew their comings and goings even before they entered the country. They knew the officials had their vehicle license registration number, and all other important information, documented. Every thing was on file. They would never forget.

Was Alex on a black list now? Perhaps this was the reason they were being questioned?

Now that they wanted to leave for Germany, what had gone wrong?

Gordon, following the border guard, was led into a steaming, hot room. Roughly, the officer commanded him to take off his clothes—all of them—even his watch and glasses.

Sweating profusely, helpless, he stood before his interrogators. Rapidly throwing questions at him, the officials demanded answers.

Gordon, wet with perspiration, longed for a breath of fresh air. Humid and hot, there was little air in the small room. Gasping, and putting his head in his hands, he sat down on the nearest chair. What could he do but call on his heavenly Father? Clearly he remembered stories of horror told by the Russian believers when they were persecuted. But they always stood true to their faith. Come what may, he resolved to do the same.

Doing a strip search, they probed every part of his body and his clothing, which had been flung on a nearby couch. Using various instruments, deliberately, the officers made their captive squirm! His warm body, drenched with sweat, was probed with icy cold magnets. If this was an effective method of torture, they were doing a good job. Thorough in their search, they didn't seem to want to stop, but this was only phase one of interrogation. What would the next procedure be? Heart pounding, Gordon waited.

Quietly praying for his wife and family, he wondered if he would ever see them again. And what was happening to his friend, Alex, silently he wondered. Crying to God, he sensed his Father's presence in the darkness.

"Now, follow me!" ordered the largest official.

Gordon quietly followed as they led him into another room. This one was as cold as a bitter winter day. Below freezing—the crisp air took Gordon's breath away. The officials, clad in warm winter coats and fur hats, didn't feel the cold as it stung Gordon's bare skin.

"Now," barked an older border guard, "Climb on top of this table!"

It was high and covered with a thick metal sheet, about 3 feet by 8 feet, and freezing cold!

With sweat still pouring from his body, he lay prone on the frozen table. Shivering from head to toe, he felt sick—really sick. His body struggled to cope with the sudden change from hot, humid temperature to frigid weather. It seemed impossible.

While the men roughly spread his arms and legs in a

prone position, Gordon's warm body froze to the cold metal. His body temperature dropped quickly.

Interrogators stood around and shot one question after another at him. They went on and on. It was difficult for Gordon to concentrate. He was so cold! Frost stinging his arms, legs, and torso, dulled his mind, too.

They showed him a photo in a SGA magazine where Gordon was pictured with several young people who had been at a winter youth camp with him. He and his colleagues had prayed that in the future, they would become the spiritual leaders in their country. Even the future son-in-law of one of the pastors, who had once been a communist propaganda organizer, but was now gloriously born-again, smiled at the guards from the page of the magazine.

"Do you know this man?" they queried. "Tell us about his activities. Is he now a church leader? He says he is born again," they jeered. On and on they probed.

Asking about each individual on the photo, relentlessly they probed. Fortunately, Gordon didn't really know enough about any of them to give reliable information. This was his first trip into Poland since moving to Germany and he could not honestly give information about them at that time.

Praying for wisdom, Gordon closed his eyes. The room was hushed now. The only sounds he heard were the voices of the border guards as they spoke in hushed tones about what they should do with Wasyl Was Ylovitch. They were not getting the information they needed, and it seemed this man knew little. Or was he really telling the truth?

Time went by. They resumed their questioning, but eventually they became weary. Maybe he was telling the truth. Finally, they decided to let him go.

With teeth chattering, and his entire body trembling with cold, Gordon propped himself up. But what was this?

Warm, soft skin from his body had frozen onto the slab. Wincing in pain, he tore himself off the cold table. With his skin peeling, chunks of raw flesh remained on the frozen slab. Open sores covered his body, back, legs, and arms.

Painfully putting his clothes back on, he wondered what kind of medical provisions they had in the van. Perhaps there were none. Later he found hand lotion, which he spread liberally on his wounds. Like a burn, they absorbed the soft liquid.

Alex had received the same treatment, but God gave grace to both men.

Before getting into the cold bus, carefully they defrosted the frozen windows with rubbing alcohol. Gradually the frost patterns melted and they could see through the windows again.

Gratefully they drove toward Germany. The word *home* never seemed so sweet! Gordon's family was there, and he would see them again. Praise the Lord!

While snow fell, and cold wind blew into their unheated vehicle, from Dresden to Berlin, they covered themselves with sleeping bags again. They had time to express their feelings along the way.

"They know," said Gordon, his teeth chattering, "that we from the West greatly influence the citizens of Poland. This, of course, is frowned upon by the leadership because they want complete control of their people. They know that often, because of us, their people—after making a decision to follow Christ—in time become the spiritual leaders of the country. Naturally, this is frowned upon. Only the dictates of Communism are accepted by the hierarchy of their country."

"Yes," agreed Alex, "they don't want outside forces to control their people. Today we experienced their way to try to stop us from spreading the Gospel so we won't do it again."

The officers could have retaliated in other ways, as well. Gordon and Alex could have been put in jail, or their van confiscated, or they could have been deported from the country. The officials, this time, had chosen an even more effective way to punish. But would the men ever learn?

Gordon had learned a lesson. Later he told Esther, "I have come to respect these border guards because it is their job to protect their own people. Now, in spite of these cruel tactics, I have a proper attitude toward them."

Purposing not to smuggle literature or Bibles into that country, he was determined not to be involved in any illegal activities. Sometimes, however, he was allowed to bring gifts to the people because he was careful to report what he had brought. There would be no future involvement in smuggling for him!

HOME

West Germany seemed like paradise when they arrived. Green, manicured fields and lawns, paved, wide roads, an orderly populace, and freedom were a normal part of this society. Gordon's heart beat with anticipation, knowing he would see his family soon. Would they like the piano? He knew they would!

Smiling, he drove into the yard on Steinenstrasse Ib. He wanted to pinch himself to see if this was real. His wife and children ran out to meet him, and greeted him royally.

"Is it here?" cried Esther.

"It's here, Mom!" called Charlene, peering into the interior of the crowded van.

"Come and look!" laughed Corinne.

There stood the beautiful Calisia. Shiny and new, it was no worse for the terrible experience at the border, nor for the inclement weather they had encountered. Unloading and placing it in the big, sunken living room, the family took turns playing. Soon they were all singing around the piano.

Once again, God had intervened. As music sounded to the far corners of the big, German house, the family was together again. That was all that really mattered!

Anita's Decision

Anita is banished from her home because of her stand for Christ

As Esther listened to testimonies from young people who were attending youth camp in Poland that year, Anita came to mind.

Noticing she was not present, Gordon and Esther prayed for her and trusted God to give her courage as she lived for Him in difficult circumstances.

Sharing at youth camp the previous August, many were touched by her testimony. "When I came to camp last year," she said, "I accepted Christ as my Savior from sin. I wanted to tell everyone what had happened in my life because now I was a new creature," she beamed.

However, many did not share this enthusiasm and joy. Her parents were livid, when glowing, she told them about her decision to follow Christ.

"You have become a heretic!" screamed her angry father. "There is no God and you know it! We are Communists. We always have been and always will be! Forget about the whole thing," he warned, "or it will be hard for all of us in the future!"

Fear filled his faded blue eyes as he looked accusingly at his only daughter. How could she bring this disgrace on their entire family? What would their friends say, or worst of all, what would happen when the government officials found out?

However, Anita did not forget. The Lord's promises were new and fresh each day. Desperately she clung to them. While her irate parents continued to berate and threaten, Anita remained true. How could she forsake her new Friend?

When former friends at school became distant and began taunting her about the God she served, Anita smiled and told them more. When loneliness overwhelmed her, she knew her heavenly Father was there. He always understood.

THREATS

One day Anita's father snatched the Bible, Anita's treasure, out of her room, and destroyed it before the girl's astonished eyes. This was her joy! How could she live without the Word of God?

"Perhaps now you will see this is a dead book!" he ranted. But by this time Anita had memorized great portions of Scripture. Daily she repeated promises over and over, until they became strength and balm to her thirsty soul. They were her rod and staff. No one, but no one, could take away the treasures hidden safely within her heart.

Anita's parents watched in amazement, as their daughter continued to glow with happiness. How could she have such joy in spite of difficulties? Quietly her mother, yearning for peace, found her eyes brimming with unshed tears. Turning to the wall, roughly she wiped them away on her sleeve before her angry husband saw what was going on.

"How can my parents understand my joy, though all outward circumstances are against me?" Anita reasoned.

As time went on, no one could daunt Anita's spirits, nor snuff out the flame she had within.

The day her father snatched up an old broom, telling his daughter he would beat her, did not frighten the girl. As in a rage he advanced toward her, she silently prayed that God would give her strength and courage to withstand this new test of faith. "And God," she added, "give me the right attitude toward my angry father. Help me to love my persecutor!"

While lifting the broom high to strike his defenseless child, somehow he could not hit her. Though he tried again and again, he was unable to carry out his threat. Throwing the offending broom to the side, he spat on the floor and in utter frustration stomped out of the house.

God had intervened.

"The angel of the Lord encampeth round about them that fear him, and delivereth them," she smiled[1].

The situation at school did not grow any easier but the courageous young teen continued to struggle forward, always putting Christ first. With her testimony ringing clear, everyone in the village knew about her stand for Christ.

"I do not believe there should be any compromise in my life," she smiled. "Following Christ is giving everything, or nothing at all!" And she meant it.

GIVING ALL

Anita's heart beat rapidly under her thin blouse when her father asked again, "Are you willing to give up this heresy?"

"No, Dad. First of all, it is not heresy, and I cannot give up the Lord who is more precious to me than life itself," she whispered.

His face red with rage, he shouted, "Okay then!" Pointing to the outside door, he stormed, "Leave this house at once. I disown you as a daughter until you are ready to believe as I do!"

Her mother, silently watching her daughter go into the bedroom to pack a few belongings, wondered how her husband could be so cruel. Though she did not believe in God, her heart was broken. How could she intervene? Of course, she could not.

Tears filled the young woman's eyes, as she sadly said good-bye and walked out into an unknown future. God would intervene somehow, she knew.

"Psalm 27 became very precious to me during those difficult days," she said. Reaching for the well-worn Bible a friend had recently given her, she began to read the verses that had become her daily strength.

> *The Lord is my light and my salvation; whom shall I fear? the Lord is the strength of my life; of whom shall I be afraid? When the wicked, even mine enemies and my foes, came upon me to eat up my flesh, they stumbled and fell. Though an host should encamp against me, my heart shall not fear: though war should rise against me, in this will I be confident.*
>
> *One thing have I desired of the Lord, that will I seek after; that I may dwell in the house of the Lord all the days of my life, to behold the beauty of the Lord, and to enquire in his temple. For in the time of trouble he shall hide me in his pavilion: in the secret of his tabernacle shall he hide me; he shall set me up upon a rock. And now shall mine head be lifted up above mine enemies round about me: therefore will I offer in his tab-*

ernacle sacrifices of joy; I will sing, yea, I will sing praises unto the Lord.

Hear, O Lord, when I cry with my voice: have mercy also upon me, and answer me.

When my father and my mother forsake me, then the Lord will take me up.

I had fainted, unless I had believed to see the goodness of the Lord in the land of the living.

Wait on the Lord: be of good courage, and he shall strengthen thine heart: wait, I say, on the Lord
(Psalm 27:1-7,10,13-14).

"I have renewed my commitment to God in spite of all the difficulties," she said. "He means more to me than ever before. He has been faithful in supplying a place for me to live, as well. I knew He would help!"

"Please pray for my parents," she concluded with concern in her eyes. "They need Christ in their lives. He is the only source of true joy and love. He is the meaning of life!"

Silently Anita bowed her head. She had made the resolution to serve Christ, though it meant hardship and trials.

Does He mean that much to you and me?

Illness

Another lump! Carefully Esther touched the affected area on her breast.

"You must see a doctor," emphasized Gordon. "Soon!"

The Kantonspital in Basel, Switzerland, specialized in "*Frauen*" problems, so they decided to go there for the necessary treatment.

"How long have you had this problem?" asked Doctor Bundelray, the Gynecology specialist in Kantonspital.

"I just found the lump yesterday," answered Esther in a small voice.

Lying on a high, white table, she felt the doctor probe and press the affected area.

"We do a procedure here in Switzerland where we perform a biopsy with a needle," he said, pulling off his glasses. "After fluid has been drained from the lump, we insert another needle and fill the area with air. That way we can see the walls of the tumor."

Esther squirmed uneasily on the hard table.

Carefully he cleaned and anesthetized the breast. In a moment there was no feeling there. She watched as he inserted the long needle, while pink fluid filled the tube above the needle. All had gone well so far. Esther breathed a sigh of relief. But what would the biopsy show? Somehow, she was not afraid of the outcome and, by faith, believed her heavenly Father would do what was best. He always did.

Doctor Bundelray inserted the second needle.

"Now we will fill the tumor with air to see what we have here," he said.

Suddenly Esther gasped! Something had gone wrong. Sharp pain filled her left lung making it difficult to breathe. What had happened?

The doctor, concerned, took her pulse and blood pressure, and checked her heart beat. Alarmed, he realized this was far from normal. But soothingly he said, "You will be fine, Mrs. Balisky. Just try and relax." But he knew something had gone wrong. Never had he encountered a situation such as this.

After lying still in the hospital for some time, while the doctor sat beside her, he reluctantly released his patient to go home.

Concerned, Gordon took his wife's arm and helped her into the car.

On the way home, pain exploded in her lung. Breathing came in short gasps. Now she was really afraid.

During the night, she struggled. Her heart pounded in her chest, as cold wind howled around the house, banging a loose board against the wall.

Morning finally came. Pink streaks across an awakening sky signaled a new day, but what would this day hold for Esther?

That night the long drive from Kandern to Basel took place again. Concerned, Doctor Bundelray examined his patient's chest. More tests were taken.

Unwilling at first to admit that he had made a mistake, now, reluctantly, he acknowledged that the procedure had gone wrong. The second needle, when inserted to blow air into the tumor, had pierced the left lung, collapsing the vital organ. Later, infection of the lining of the heart caused strong, irregular palpitations and pain.

Coming into Emergency a number of times was a trying experience.

CHRISTMAS DAY

Christmas day dawned cold and clear. The *dorf* was shrouded in a blanket of new, white snow. Carillons rang throughout the vast countryside, announcing the birth of Christ. The Broughtons, missionaries with the Janz team, had invited the Balisky family to their home for Christmas dinner.

Slowly Esther, putting on her clothes, felt sharp pain filling her chest until sometimes she wanted to choke.

Sorrowfully thinking of home, her heart ached for her mother. Yearning for her presence, she visualized Katy putting the last touches on the Christmas dinner table and calling her youngsters in. Tears came to the surface and spilled down Esther's pale cheeks. She roughly wiped them away and tried to think positively. But she couldn't help it. She still yearned for her mother.

"Come on, Mom, let's go!" called Charlene. Taking her

mother's arm, they walked down the slippery stairs toward the car.

Dinner, though elegantly served, had little taste for Esther. Turkey cooked to perfection, along with bread stuffing and cranberries, stuck in her throat.

That long Christmas day was the crisis in her illness. Gordon rubbed her back when she went to bed that night, while the girls stood nearby, ready to help if necessary. They could hear Esther's heart pounding loudly against her ribs. Taking deep breaths did not alleviate the difficulty in breathing. Was she going to die?

Longing for her mother, as her chest rose and fell, she envisioned Katy's cool hand on her brow.

Her family, though nearby, seemed far away—unreal. Clinging to Gordon's hand, her own was damp and clammy.

Sharp winter winds blew around the house, causing snow crystals to beat against the windows. The night was black as she cried to God. But where was He?

The drive to Kantonspital was not pleasant. Courageously she tried to calm herself as they sped toward the city.

In the Emergency room, vaguely she saw a dim light above. A clear voice came peacefully, reassuringly. Straining to hear, and realizing it must be God's voice, she whispered, "Yes, God, I'm listening!"

"Be still and know that I am God! Be still! Be still!"

In the hospital room that night, the voice repeated the message—specifically for her—and quietly listening, she knew that God was there. He stood beside her in the darkness. He would never leave nor forsake her. Desperately she clung to this promise.

Recovery was slow and difficult, but steadily Esther regained her strength. The tumor diagnosis was negative. Together Gordon and Esther praised God for His goodness.

6 FINNJET–JUNE, 1978

Another trip into Russia was planned. Esther, now strong enough to go, looked with anticipation to being in the East again.

"Hey! We made it!" cried Gordon triumphantly, as they entered the city of Hamburg, Germany, just a half-hour before the great Finnjet would sail. Everyone heaved a sigh of relief.

Leaving Wetzler at noon, they had taken time to shop for electrical equipment which they planned to take into Russia.

The faithful yellow van was piled high with relief to leave behind the Iron Curtain, as well as their own personal belongings, food, and water. It was difficult to even sit comfortably. Charlene and Corinne, squeezing into the back seat, had patiently endured the heavy trip. Before leaving Wetzler in the morning, they had a special time of prayer, asking God to guide them and keep them safe as they traveled to

Hamburg, across the channel on the Finnjet, stay overnight in Helsinki, Finland, and then drive into Russia the next day.

"I'm looking forward to sailing instead of sitting in this crowded van," sighed Charlene.

"So am I!" Cori emphatically replied. They all were. This new part of the journey would be novel. They had never taken a cruise before, and looked with anticipation to a time of fun and relaxation. Also, instead of driving for hundreds of kilometers, they would save valuable time and mileage.

Corinne's eyes grew wide as they approached the great Finnjet.

"This is awesome!" she cried.

"Incredible!" smiled her sister.

Before them stood the massive ship. Holding 350 cars, plus caravans, she was over 200 meters long and as wide as two tennis courts. The Finnjet had cabin space for 1,532 passengers, and the gas powered engines produced 75,000 hp to cruise at 30 knots. The Finnjet was unique in its class of ship.

They had imagined the vessel would be more like a ferry, but were delighted to realize it was a floating hotel and restaurant, as well.

Leaving most of their belongings in the locked van, and taking a few small overnight bags, they climbed up into the ship.

Having specific instructions on how to find their cabin, they walked slowly down the massive hallways.

The reception room was spacious and eloquently furnished. The dining room, from which gourmet aromas wafted, made them realize it was almost dinnertime.

"Hey, let's move and get settled!" encouraged Gordon. "I'm hungry!"

Esther realized they had not eaten for many hours. "I'm hungry, too," she added. Looking forward to a buffet dinner, they hurried to their room to freshen up and dress.

Number 110 showed clearly on a door ahead.

"Here it is! Let's go in!" said Charlene. They were all excited when the key turned and they walked into their home on the water.

The room was small. Most of them were, but there was ample space for four if they took turns getting dressed.

Choosing top bunk beds, the girls knew they would have more privacy there.

Gordon and Esther put their bags on the beds below, took a quick shower, and dressed for dinner.

The restaurant seated thirty-two passengers at one time. There they boasted that their passengers had not seen an original smorgasbord, until they had seen the one on board the Finnjet. Delicacies from all over Scandinavia were displayed on the smorgasbord, ranging from caviar, giant crayfish, fresh shrimp, dolphin, and fresh salads, to the best cheeses.

Tasting and enjoying, they were convinced the boasting was true. It was a feast none of them would ever forget! Eating until they could eat no more, they then had a glass of wine to settle their stomachs.

The four of them stood at the big window and watched as the great ship slid through calm and peaceful waters. Leaving a silver trail behind her, effortlessly, gracefully, she transported her passengers to their destination.

Tired by this time, they went back to their cabin, put on their pajamas, climbed under clean, white sheets, pulled the covers over their heads, and listened while the huge ship gently lulled them to sleep.

Helsinki, Finland

Morning arrived.

The ship, continuing to slide gently over calm, untroubled waters, made them want to keep on sleeping. The room,

shrouded in complete darkness, didn't make it any easier for them to pull out of bed.

However, the ambitious Charlene, wanting to use the bathroom first, climbed out of her warm quarters. Yawning, she slipped out of the room to have a shower. They each followed soon afterward.

Refreshed and awake at last, they made their way to the dining room. Again, another gastronomical buffet was served. Knowing they probably would not have need for food all day after this feast, they ate heartily.

Sometimes while traveling, it was difficult to find good restaurants. And stopping always takes valuable time out of busy schedules.

Corinne, especially, looked with anticipation to spending time in Finland. Her friend, Miriam, whose family was born there, had moved to the Black Forest where they were headquartered.

Bonding strongly, the girls became best friends. Miriam had told Cori about her homeland many times. Now she wanted to see it for herself.

Arriving in Helsinki about 6:00, Finish time, they drove into the city. Helsinki is the capital of modern Finland and has been called the White City of the North, and, the Daughter of the Baltic. The people boast of the beautiful landscapes and thousands of lakes with innumerable islands.

The Fins say that it would be hard to find a holiday country which offers the variety they have to offer—hunting, fishing, lumberjacking, skiing, and gold panning in the rivers make this a country to be enjoyed.

Staying with a Christian family, the Baliskys explored a little, eating delicious Finnish ice cream, and walking from place to place. Ornate, old churches were open for them to see. Stores, which had a great deal to offer, and scenery which almost left them speechless, were all there to enjoy and explore.

That night, the evening was warm and balmy as they walked under a great, silver moon toward their friend's house they where they would spend the night.

THE UNEXPECTED

Trying to settle down in their respective rooms and go to sleep, the girls were wound up and didn't feel like resting. Laughing, talking, but trying to whisper so they wouldn't disturb their parents, they shared about the events of the day.

A pillow fight followed. Still excited, playing and jumping around, they began to push each other, giggling all the while.

"Stop it and go to sleep!" called their father from the next room. "You will need your rest tonight. Tomorrow we go over the Russian border. It could be exhausting!"

Finally, everyone settled down. Esther covered her ears, as Gordon presented a familiar concert. In grand crescendo, his breathing rose and fell. Putting the feather pillow over her head to drown out the noise, Esther, too, was soon asleep.

Maternal instinct caused her to wake up early in the morning to hear weeping in the girl's room.

Gordon, already out of bed, was getting ready for the trip. Running into their room, concerned, Esther realized it was Corinne who was crying.

Face ashen, hair disheveled, eyes dilated, painfully she looked at her mother.

"Whatever is the matter, Sweetheart?" she cried, cradling the child in her arms.

"Mom, I'm dizzy. I have a headache, and I have to throw up!"

Pulling herself away from Esther, she ran toward the

bathroom. Following her, Esther held her head while Cori lost last night's dinner.

This did not relieve her symptoms.

Charlene, standing nearby, soberly told her mother that last night, while she and Cori were playing and wrestling, her younger sister had hit her head on the hard, cement wall. Not wanting to wake her parents, she had tried to go to sleep. Knowing that if this was a concussion, she should not have slept, Esther became even more concerned for her youngest.

"Charlene, go get Dad," she ordered.

He immediately called a local hospital. He was told to take her to a children's hospital and given the address and directions on how to find it. They lost no time.

Putting a child's-size gown on the little girl, the doctors checked her and went to take an X-ray immediately.

Their suspicions confirmed, the family was informed that Corinne had suffered a severe concussion. They assumed this had happened when she'd hit her head on the wall last night.

Esther sat with her daughter all day. Nurses came and went. Light food was served, but Corinne was not interested in eating. Quietly, she lay on her bed. Getting up brought dizziness, pain, and nausea.

Charlene, Gordon, and Esther seriously prayed for healing for this youngest member of their family.

"Mom, I feel a lot better!" she said the next morning. "I want something to eat."

"Thank You, God!" said a grateful mother, as she placed the sausages and eggs on the delivered tray next to her daughter.

A little listless, but some excitement showing in her eyes, Cori asked when they would leave for Russia.

"Not until you are completely well,' Esther answered,

grateful that her daughter had an appetite again. "The journey into Russia will be grueling. Strength and health will be necessary for you to travel the vigorous journey ahead."

Esther knew her daughter would be well soon. God would see to that!

God's Way with a Quella Catalog—1975

Esther settled down in her comfortable bed in Finland with a prayer on her heart. Tomorrow they would enter Russia, the foreboding country they had only heard about.

For a year they had planned this trip—praying that the Lord would use them in this Communist country where the name of Jesus was dishonored and believers were persecuted.

In the semi-darkness, from her bed, she could see the dim outline of stacks of Christian literature where they rested on a table beside the window. Earlier in the evening, they had carefully selected material to take into Russia, leaving the rest with their missionaries from Finland to take in at a later date. Careful not to jeopardize their opportunities for future trips into Russia, they decided to take only a minimum amount at a time.

Esther had just closed her eyes, it seemed, when she heard the wake-up call.

"Time to get up, Honey," came the retort from Gordon who had slept in a twin bed next to her. The night had fled so quickly. She rubbed her eyes sleepily, yawned, and slipped out of bed. When her feet hit the cold cement floor, she was awake instantly! It was time to start a new day. What would it hold?

Quickly getting dressed, she hurried into the kitchen where the tantalizing aroma of freshly-ground coffee filled the room, and white, crispy rolls and cheese graced the breakfast table.

After they ate, their Finnish friends helped them load the suitcases and literature into the Volkswagen camper bus. They did not forget to join in prayer before leaving. Standing in a circle, holding hands, they prayed for God's guidance and safety as they drove into a country where they were not welcome.

A few minutes later, sitting quietly in the van, each member of the family was absorbed in their own thoughts. They had heard and read of many negative incidents others had encountered on the Russian border in the past, and though they tried not to be afraid, their hearts beat faster than usual as adrenaline flowed freely. Suddenly Gordon realized he had some papers which, if discovered, could cause problems at the border. Bringing their vehicle to an abrupt stop about one mile from the Russian border, he made a bonfire on the roadside. Watching the flames lick up the paper, he was relieved they were no longer in his possession.

CHECKPOINT

An austere building loomed ahead when they arrived at the border. Several stern officials stood at attention.

This was it! They had been told earlier that if one showed discomfort, they would immediately suspect that one of trying to hide something. So the family was determined not to look nervous!

They stopped the vehicle.

"Get out of your car!" ordered the border guard.

Obligingly, they did.

At this point, the guards took all the passports and examined them thoroughly. Taking suitcases and personal effects out of the van, they carefully checked to see if they could find anything illegal. Would they confiscate the literature?

Meanwhile, in the customs building, Gordon and Esther

filled in the necessary paperwork. All personal valuables, such as watches, jewelry, glasses, and whatever, must be listed individually. If not, upon leaving the country, everything could be confiscated. One of the officers stared at Esther's wedding band, reminding her she must surely record all her jewelry.

Looking outside, Esther shivered as a large, trained German Shepherd dog investigated their van. Well-disciplined and trained, if necessary, he would attack on command.

Then suddenly shaking his head, the official told them they could leave. Gratefully, they re-packed their van and drove on. Was this all there was to crossing a border? They hoped so.

"That wasn't bad at all," said Gordon, when they were out of hearing distance of the border guards.

Breathing a sigh of relief, they settled down in their seats.

Poplar trees bordering the narrow roadway as they slowly drove along, reminded Esther of the Peace River country in Northern Alberta where she and Gordon grew up.

But this was Russia! It was difficult to believe they were here at last. Though the road ahead was unknown to them, it was familiar to the God who had called them to work behind the Iron Curtain. He would guide them every day as they put their trust in Him.

Thoughts of Katy, Esther's mother, flooded her mind. Katy had been apprehensive about Esther and her family going into a country where they could be imprisoned, persecuted, or harassed. But Esther knew her mother was praying and peace filled her heart.

RUSSIAN BORDER

Their feelings of relief came to an abrupt halt however, as a larger, more austere building loomed ahead.

"Had they not been through customs? Now, what was this?" they wondered.

As they stopped, a stern-faced border guard ordered, "Get out of your van!"

This new Volkswagen camper bus interested him. Now what could be inside? He and his colleagues would surely investigate!

Proceeding to unload their suitcases and other belongings, they knew the guards would find the literature. Searching eyes probed into the interior of the van. Sensitive fingers felt the ceiling and sides to make certain nothing was hidden there. Arms lifted the seats out. Every inch of the van was checked thoroughly. The cupboards were opened as officials looked and probed around inside. All their suitcases stood on the ground nearby.

Only the area behind the back seat had remained untouched. "What do you have here?" asked an official. "What kind of reading material is this? Take it out now!"

The official watched carefully as Gordon took the literature from the van and placed it outside with the rest of the things.

They had been so careful in selecting the literature. People were crying for Bibles in the USSR. Would they take them, too?

The face of Jimmy Carter smiled at them from the cover of the latest *Time* magazine. Other current magazines were there, as well. Soon the Bibles and other literature were unpacked and in plain sight to be scrutinized.

Finding the Catalogue

While in Germany, they decided to take a Fall and Winter Quella catalogue with them. Planning on leaving it in Russia, they knew a family who would be thrilled to own it.

Meanwhile, Esther was especially interested because it was in German and helped her review the language effectively.

Esther had left it on the front seat where she had been leafing through the colorful pages.

"Hey, come over here!" called a young official to his colleagues.

Gathering around the catalogue, it proved to be of great interest to the men. Never had they seen a book like this! Colorful literature was not available in Communist Russia. Becoming so fascinated with its brightly colored pages, all thoughts of other literature was forgotten. Turning page after page, they were completely absorbed in what they saw.

They especially concentrated on the women's undergarment section. Forgetting momentarily that the family stood nearby, laughingly they jabbed one another and made comments about the beautiful buxom ladies smiling at them from each page.

Time passed by as the Baliskys patiently waited for them. Taking their time, they continued to turn the pages.

Suddenly, one of the older officials, regaining his composure, straightened up, resumed his stern, official stance, and remarked, "You may put your things back in the car now!"

They couldn't believe it!

Working quickly, Gordon packed the precious Bibles into the back seat. Could they still change their minds? Was there another checkpoint? Could this be all? Quickly retrieving passports they climbed back into the van.

Though they had no idea that a Quella catalogue could be God's way of leading them that day, they knew it had served the intended purpose. The border guards' attention had not been on the family or the literature, but on the Quella catalogue from Germany.

Esther knew that, "God works in mysterious ways, His wonders to perform," but she never realized He would work through an ordinary catalogue!

Destination—Repino

Though they had safely crossed the border, each one had the distinct, uncomfortable feeling they were being watched.

In guard houses and checkpoints placed strategically every few miles, the sentries were always on duty. The shiny steel on their guns glistened in the late afternoon sunshine. Yes, the family would be watched every day, every night, and all the time during their travels in Russia. They were constantly being told to use caution, not only on their own behalf, but for the believers with whom they would come in contact.

Dirt roads, heavy traffic, smoggy air, dust, staring people, crowds, and police would be their companions from the day they arrived in the country to the day of their departure.

The miles crept by slowly as they drove toward their evening accommodations in Repino. Because the officials knew where they would be every day and night, they were waiting for them when they arrived at the campground.

That night, crawling into hard, cold beds, they thanked the Lord again for taking them safely across the border, and for the protection He promised for the future. They thanked Him, too, for the Quella catalogue and the mysterious role it had played at the border crossing.

They were in Russia at last! They knew they were just as safe behind the Iron Curtain, in His divine will, as they would be in their free United States of America.

Resting in His promises, Esther pulled the covers up over her head and went to sleep.

So far, Gordon and Esther had been in Poland and Russia. Teaching for long hours in churches and youth camps, it was always rewarding to see people come to know Christ as Savior, and believers strengthened and encouraged as they shared God's Word.

Trips to Eastern Europe brought a different kind of dimension to the girls' lives than they had ever imagined. Sometimes, when they were not in school, they came with their parents. Their presence added positively to the over-all ministry as they mingled with a suffering people.

Other times, while Esther and Gordon went into these countries, someone stayed behind with the girls. Whenever this happened, Esther left a part of her heart with them. Praying all day for her darlings, she committed them into God's safekeeping. Would she see them again? The question always haunted her.

A Divine Encounter in Kiev—1976

"Have we been invited to attend the church where Georgi Vins pastored before he was imprisoned?" Esther asked, excitement rising in her voice.

Gordon replied emphatically in the affirmative as they prepared to leave.

Climbing into the Volkswagen camper, David (their coworker), Esther, and Gordon prayed that the Lord would help them to encourage this suffering family. They were always concerned that their presence would not endanger the lives of the people, especially those who had suffered for their faith. Realizing they must be wise in all contacts made in this Communist country, kept them in an attitude of prayer continually.

Driving away from the campground, their eyes searched the roadside where they had previously arranged to meet Pastor Jan, superintendent of Baptist churches in Kiev. Gordon and Esther had spoken with him the evening before while ministering in a nearby church, and discovered that he was the brother-in-law to Georgi Vins.

"There he is," pointed David, as a tall, blond man stepped from the shrubs.

"Please come in," Gordon invited their new friend. David and Esther sat in the front seat, while Gordon and Pastor Jan talked in the back. The fervency in the voice of the Russian made them realize it was important for him to confide in other trustworthy Christians.

Esther and David watched the road as they skirted pot holes and stones. "I wonder if we are getting close to the church?" Esther pondered, as they drove past trees bursting with colorful fall leaves. Already many leaves had fallen, making a rich carpet beneath.

Then Pastor Jan spoke up from the back seat. "We will not be going to the church tonight. I decided it would be better if we met at the Vins' home. There we can talk with them on a personal basis."

That's fine with us," Gordon responded.

They parked the van in a crowded neighborhood behind tall trees so as to avoid any suspicion. They stayed, while Pastor Jan went inside to inform the family they had arrived.

"Why don't we unpack some gifts for the Vins while we wait?" said the practical Gordon. So David, rummaging to the bottom of the box, found the clothing and fabric they had brought all the way from the States.

Still Pastor Jan did not arrive.

Esther had read the book, *Georgi Vins—A Testament from Prison*, and knew he was imprisoned because he dared to teach the Word of God. He had been under surveillance and pressure by the KGB police while pastoring a church in Kiev. Though he was warned numerous times not to do so, he continued fearlessly on. He was imprisoned on several occasions. Each time he left a family of five children, a wife, and an aging mother at home. They knew that at this very minute he was in prison enduring hardship and testing for being a faithful witness.

Suddenly Pastor Jan stepped from behind the trees and told them to join him. Quietly they walked toward the house, fall leaves crunching under their feet.

"Nadezda, Georgi's wife, is not at home," he informed them, "but Lydia Vins, the grandmother, is there with two of the children. It is fine if we go in now."

Following the pastor, they walked quietly down the street, past peasant homes. He warned them to be as quiet and inconspicuous as possible, because he knew they were being watched by neighbors' prying eyes. Perhaps there were others watching, as well. They knew to whom he referred.

Dimly the peeks of small houses behind a high weather-beaten fence appeared. Bending down and entering a low gate, they walked along a crumbling sidewalk. Tall, over-hanging trees hid part of the old house. The night was so dark they could scarcely see where they were going, but followed closely behind the pastor. A light appeared from a house nearby, shining from a crack in a partially-opened door. Lydia knew they had arrived.

She was a white-haired woman of about seventy-five years. She invited them in, lead them through a small corridor, and opened the curtain dividing the parlor from the rest of the house. In the interior, as in most Russian homes, there was very little. A couch occupied the far corner, while a table covered with a linen cloth stood in the heart of the room. A few other pieces of simple furnishings were scattered around. Inviting them to sit, Lydia Vins started to open her heart. David and Esther, not understanding all her hurried words, listened as Gordon interpreted, whenever he could get a word in edgewise.

Her face, stained and drawn, peered from a halo of silver white hair. They could see as her dark eyes looked directly into their own that suffering was written there.

"This is the little magazine I write that goes out to all our Christians in prison," she said, holding an illustrated booklet. With a catch in her voice, she continued, "Here is a picture of my son, Georgi, and his latest poem written from prison.... I could be taken to jail at any time because of my work to encourage Christians in prison," she whispered. "I have an unrelenting goal to have my son released and returned to his family and congregation.

"On December 1, 1971, I, too, was imprisoned," she said, while dabbing her eyes with a handkerchief, "and released in April of 1973. The KGB police came to our home one night and arrested me.

"'Lydia Vins?' they asked barging into the house without knocking.

"'Yes?' I answered, my heart pounding in my chest.

"Without explanation, and walking toward me, they commanded, 'Come with us!'

"I couldn't move. My legs seemed frozen to the floor. Whimpering, my grandchildren crowded around me, tugging at my skirt—holding me around the waist. Remembering clearly how they had taken their daddy away they shouted, 'No, Baba, no!'

"The KGB have no heart. All they care about is carrying out orders. Nadezda was not at home, and there was no other adult present. What would happen to the heartbroken children if they took me, too?

"Not heeding their cries of fear, and grabbing me by the arms, they forced me out of the house into a waiting vehicle.

"The sobbing children followed me outside, and watched as the police drove away with me. My spirit broken, I heard their heart-rending cries until we were too far away to hear. Standing in a small huddle in the middle of the road, they watched the car until it disappeared over a hill. I could still hear their weeping in my heart, while I lay on the cold, prison bed that night. What had become of them? Tortured, I, too, cried all night.

"While praying, eventually peace came to my troubled soul. Surrendering them to Jesus, I knew He had promised to look after them and never leave his little ones alone."

Stopping long enough to change her position, Lydia continued, "Georgi was a well-known leader of the Soviet Reform Baptists, so many across Russia and other countries are praying for his release. Please pray with them," she said, her lower lip trembling, while tears filled her dark eyes.

On December 27, at the age of forty-five, in one of the Far East labor camps in Russia, her husband (Georgi's father) ended his suffering and joined his Savior in his heavenly home. There would be no more persecution, trials, or sorrows. He was free at last! Now Georgi, her son, at age forty-eight, seemed to have the same fate as his father. But by faith, she believed he would be released before that happened.

Assuring her there were people in the United States praying that a release would be granted, Lydia was comforted.

GEORGI—IN THE CHURCH

Pastor Jan, sitting on a chair next to David, finally spoke. "Georgi was an engineer by profession. After he was ordained as an elder in the Baptist church, he became very active in various ministries in his church. Teaching, youth ministries,

and preaching began to take prominence in his busy life. 'Please,' encouraged the people, 'we need to be taught from the precious Word of God. He has given you an anointing we have rarely seen before. Effective Bible teachers are needed in Russia. You have the gift, Pastor Vins. Would you please teach us on a regular basis? We are so hungry!'

"Gradually, Georgi began to spend more time away from his job. The officials found out fast, and of course questioned the young pastor."

SUSPECT

"'What are you doing when you are not at work? How do you live? Where do you find money to support your wife, mother, and five children?'

"Suspecting him of teaching his people on a full-time basis, they sought to imprison him again, but Georgi went into hiding. Here he continued to teach the people.

"How he lived during those difficult days, we are not sure," added Pastor Jan. "It was hard for his family, too. Nadezda had a job teaching in a school. Though the salary was meager, this became their sole livelihood.

"It didn't take long before the pastor was found by the authorities, and taken back to prison camp. Once more he was released, but continued fearlessly to teach the people. Again, he was arrested, tried, and sentenced to prison for a much longer period.

"'This time,' they reasoned, 'he will learn his lesson!' But Georgi never did!"

Everyone was startled when the clock on the wall chimed the hour. It was getting late, but Zhenya and Esther had an interesting visit because Georgi's twelve-year-old daughter had some command of the English language.

"I will write to your daughter, Corinne," she said.

Esther told her they were about the same age, and that pleased Zhenya. Eagerly the Russian girl asked if she could have their address. Carefully she tucked it into a private place until there was time to write.

Alexander, their five-year-old boy, was not quite so open toward them at first. While coaxing him to come and sit on her knee, he smiled shyly, but refused. Meanwhile Gordon dug into his pocket and produced two packets of gum—a rare commodity in Russia. This melted the heart of the Russian child considerably and before they left, Alexander, too, was their friend. He held tightly to Esther's hand, begging her not to go away.

Everyone, including Grandma Vins, stopped talking abruptly when they heard someone at the door. Had the authorities caught up with them? Could they imprison the Vins as well as ourselves?

Jumping from her chair, Zhenya went to the door to see who was there. Heaving a sigh of relief, she saw it was her mother. Nadezda, a graceful middle-aged woman, entered the room. Quietly, calmly shaking hands, she greeted them in the English language.

Pulling up a chair for her, Pastor Jan introduced her as Georgi's wife.

Her face looked troubled.

"I was on my way to church this evening, and on my way I stopped at the post office to mail a package to my husband. He had requested a kilo of powdered milk next time I sent a package. I was worried because all day I searched for milk and found none. Our store shelves, as you know, are often bare. This was one of those days. Reluctant to send the package without the milk, I left the post office. How could I find some milk? Georgi desperately needed nourishment to supplement his meager diet in prison."

They saw the unmailed package by the door. She needed milk before she could send it.

"I didn't even go to church, but came straight home. I had no idea we would have visitors from the West, and I don't know why I came home instead of following through with my usual plans."

David and Gordon exchanged glances across the table. They were both thinking the same thing.

"Don't we have powdered milk in our van?" David asked.

"Why yes, we do!" smiled Gordon.

"How much do we have?"

David's eyes opened wide as he replied, "We have exactly one kilo, no more and no less!"

"Praise be to God!" shouted Nadezda. "Now I can send milk to my husband! God knew I shouldn't send the package today! Georgi would have been so disappointed without this needful nourishment."

She had prayed for milk, and received it all the way from the West. It was the exact amount needed, and came in such an unexpected way.

"God had it all planned," smiled Zhenya.

The Lord had this encounter with the Vins family arranged long before the night of September 17, 1976. They just didn't know it.

As Grandma Vins looked on, Nadezda began to tell them about the hardships Georgi was enduring in prison. He needed a heavy coat. Winter was coming, and his threadbare jacket would not be warm enough. How could she, on her meager salary, buy him such a coat? In Russia, a wool winter coat could cost a year's salary. What could she do?

Her voice breaking with emotion, she read Georgi's latest poem.

"He teaches them about faith in God from his prison cell in spite of difficult circumstances," she choked. "The joy of the Lord, though he is separated from loved ones, is with him every day."

Going to the other room, she brought a letter in which Georgi stated, "It is better to be in prison with Jesus, than in liberty without him!"

Like his father before him, he requested, "Tell our dear ones to pray that the Lord will strengthen the brethren and myself here in prison, to be faithful witnesses for Him, no matter how difficult it is."

Looking at her watch, Esther interrupted, "We have been here for hours, Gordon," she whispered.

With a little urgency in his voice, Gordon stood to his feet and said, "We must go now."

In that humble living room in the heart of the Ukraine, they clasped hands while kneeling on the rough, wooden floor. Together, they touched the heart of God. His presence was real and potent as Pastor Jan prayed with compassion. Though Esther and David did not understand most of the words, they sensed an urgency in the petitions he offered up to his Friend. Yes, this family realized their total dependence on a heavenly Father in whom they had learned to trust.

After taking a few pictures, they were ready to leave.

"I have brought some fabric from America. Would you be interested?" asked Esther looking toward Nadezda. She knew that many women in Russia, if they can afford a sewing machine, sew rather than buy their clothes because of the cost involved.

Her eyes lit up.

"Oh yes! Thank you! My children need school clothes." Gladly she accepted the offer.

GOOD-BYE

After saying good-bye, Nadezda and Pastor Jan accompanied them out the door so they could bring back the milk and fabric.

Closing the door behind them, they heard a shriek, "Mama! Mama! Please don't leave us!" sobbed Alexander.

Afraid they were taking his mother just like the men had taken his daddy away, he stood beside the closed door, tears running down his cheeks.

Going back, Nadezda tried to comfort the frightened child, explaining that these people were brothers and sisters in Christ. They would never harm them. Then taking his hand in her own, they walked together toward the Volkswagen camper bus.

Walking slowly, quietly, and close together, they ducked under the trees where the van was partially concealed. In case they were being watched, Gordon and David quickly gathered the promised valuables.

Esther handed Nadezda a beautiful wool winter coat that had been packed in the gift box for someone who needed it "Here is a gift from God for your husband," she smiled.

Nadezda had no words. God had sent a warm coat that would fit Georgi! Praise His name! Her gratefulness knew no bounds as she clutched the kilo of milk under one arm—the coat and fabric under the other—and disappeared with Alexander and Pastor Jan into the night. They went back under the little door in the fence, and into the house to her waiting family. Jan returned in a few minutes, quietly climbed into the van, and closed the door.

Grinning, he pinched himself. Was this experience real? Oh yes, his Father had performed another miracle. He had a great big wonderful God!

After taking the pastor home, each of them were

absorbed in their own thoughts as they drove toward their campsite, marveling at the divine encounter God had arranged, for them to be of some encouragement and assistance to a hurting family. They were challenged afresh to pray for those who determined to follow Jesus no matter what the cost. Their Father planned it all!

From Georgi's cell, undaunted and praising God, he wrote, "I am not alone here. My brothers and sisters in the faith are in neighboring cells. Even within these walls, Almighty God is strengthening the faith and inspiring radiant hope in our hearts. Christ is unconquerable. The faith lives on and grows stronger. The Messiah is with us. Our native Russia needs Him so!"

Georgi's latest poem written from prison:

FAITH

Faith helps ships make it through the storm,
It moves caravans through the desert.
It draws the prisoners of earth
to distant stars in the sky;
Without it, there is no friendship—no love:

Without it, all of life is in a gray fog;
But the faith that we have just been talking about,
you can call only human faith.
But then, only when your heart is visited by a heav enly brilliant light,
Faith flames up with a joyful fire, like a giant lamp of love;
It will break through the silence like an alarm bell
It will not give way to the strength of the storm.
In my native land it is called evangelic faith
That faith will move mountains,

casting them into the abyss
And it shall enter with joy into heaven to participate
in the glory of the beloved Son.

* * *

Back from another trip into the East, the winter days fled rapidly by. Esther wondered why they went so fast. She realized life was slipping by. Charlene and Corinne, kept busy in school, never seemed to have much spare time.

7 God's Timing In The Rain

The rain came down in torrents. Huge drops splashed onto the windows of the Volkswagen camper bus, only to bounce away again. Everywhere cars and buses had stopped as people, removing their footwear, ran for shelter from the deluge. Rivulets ran along the streets of Kiev as dark, muddy water steadily rose higher. The drainage system in Russian cities is so poorly constructed that when it rains, water fills the streets. In the past, water has risen so high that it has spilled over the dashboard into the vehicles.

Visibility was almost impossible, but the windshield wipers fought valiantly to keep the windshield clear. Conversation in the van was scarce as Gordon concentrated on driving.

It was late afternoon when they drove into the beautiful city of Kiev. Located in colorful Ukraine, it is filled with historic landmarks and interesting sights.

Each of them had looked with anticipation to see the grandeur and history of this great city in the heart of the Ukraine. And now they had to wait until the sun came out again—if it ever did! They had never seen such rain! Surely, God was pouring bucketsful from heaven?

Planning to stay in a cabin that night, slowly they drove toward their destination. But would they find it in the rain and fog? Then their thoughts were interrupted.

"Mom," came the call from the rear of the van, "I'm starved!"

When her sister echoed the same sentiments, Esther and Gordon also realized that their stomachs were giving them the same message.

"Yes, I suppose we could stop, but where?" Gordon silently wondered.

Eventually they pulled up on the slippery curb near a small grocery store. Gordon, taking a deep breath, made the final plunge to go out into the rain to find something to eat.

Kielbasa (sausage), *chleb* (bread), and *sehr* (cheese), would probably be their usual Russian dinner again. But tonight, even this simple fare tempted their palates.

Pulling a coat over his head, Gordon ran toward the store. The shop was so crowded, he shoved and elbowed his way, European style, to stand in line. Eventually he hoped to reach the celebrated meat counter.

In Russia there is always a queue. This time was no exception as he stood in line with at least a dozen people all intent on feeding their stomachs. The small shop was steaming and hot. Perspiration flowed freely as the people waited. Would this line ever end? The unmistakable odor of garlic was pungent and strong, but no one seemed to notice.

Finally, one by one, the people paid for their groceries and left the store. It was closing time so the employees were anxious to hurry the process of waiting on customers.

By the time Gordon arrived at the end of the long queue, there were only a few people remaining. He heaved a sigh of relief. He would get there! His family was hungry.

"It is time to close the store," loudly announced the heavy-set woman at the cash register. It was obvious she, too, wanted to go home.

Triumphant, Gordon finally arrived at the check-out counter, and bought his bread, cheese, and sausage.

When the last loaf of bread had been purchased, the remaining customers reluctantly filed out into the deluge. The sky was a dark gray as rain continued to come down in torrents. Splashing on the street below, the raindrops bounced and danced on higher pavement, only to be carried away by water running down the streets of the city.

Eventually only a Russian couple and Gordon remained standing on the steps beside the store. All were reluctant to leave their temporary shelter.

A small awning above them offered temporary refuge from the pelting rain. Standing there, they listened as rumbling peals of thunder resounded throughout the city while lightning split across the darkened heavens.

Suddenly another streak of lightning rent the sky. The little woman standing next to Gordon, exclaimed in awe and wonder, "*Bozimi*!" ("Oh, my God!")

Looking at her, surprised to hear his best Friend's name, Gordon answered, "How come you say that?"

"What do you mean?"

"I have been told there is no God in Russia."

"Where did you hear that?" asked the lady.

"Oh, I heard it in the Leningrad museum, at the Expository, and at the Pavilion. I also heard it in the library. Everywhere in Russia they say there is no God."

The woman was quiet for a moment and looked very thoughtful.

"That may be true in those places," she said, "but God is here in Kiev!"

Excited, they continued this theme of animated conversation for some time. They all wanted to talk at once.

"Would you please come to our home so we can discuss this subject further?" smiled the man.

Gordon was delighted that two people in the heart of a teaming Ukrainian city, in a Communist Socialist country, had a hunger in their hearts to receive more knowledge about this sovereign God. He had allowed them to meet with one of His children from America in the middle of a severe thunderstorm.

Because of the rain, others had fled for shelter, thus allowing only those people of His choice to meet in a preplanned divine encounter. Ever alert, KGB officials had disappeared, only to arrive back on the scene after the deluge was over.

Telling the interested couple he would try to contact them at a later date, Gordon quietly slipped their home address into his pocket.

Just then, the rain stopped. The sky grew a little brighter, as a hazy sun peered through the hanging black clouds. Already the KGB officials were reappearing.

Hastily shaking hands, Gordon stepped out into the muddy street and headed toward his vehicle, *kielbasa*, *sehr*, and *chleb* wrapped in brown paper, securely tucked under his arm.

Their Father who sends the rain, had allowed a storm in His timing to accomplish His divine purpose.

JESUS LEADS

Like a shepherd—tender, true,
Jesus leads...Jesus leads,
Daily finds them pastures new,
Jesus leads...Jesus leads;
If thick mists are o'er the way,
Or the flock 'mid danger feeds,
He will watch them lest they stray,
Jesus leads...Jesus leads.

All along life's rugged way,
Jesus leads...Jesus leads;
Till they reach yon blest abode,
Jesus leads...Jesus leads;
All the way before He's trod,
and He now the flock precedes,
Safe into the fold of God,
Jesus leads...Jesus leads.

Through the sunlit ways of life,
Jesus leads...Jesus leads;
Through the warrings and the strife,
Jesus leads...Jesus leads.
When they reach the Jordan's tide,
Where life's boundary line recedes
He will spread the waves aside,
Jesus leads...Jesus leads.

John R. Clements; Jon. R. Sweney
Favorites Number Five

The Egg Queue—1981

Queue can be defined as file, line, row, series, chain, tier, sequence, string.

Everywhere Esther looked, there were people standing in line for food, shoes, beer, ice cream....

On a busy street corner a heavy-set Russian woman, wearing the traditional *Babushka* stood at her pop machine selling a sweet, colored drink. Rinsing the glass carelessly, she filled it again for the next person in line. Holding out a work-worn hand, carefully she collected the small sum of money charged for each drink, and put it into her soiled apron pocket.

Another anxious woman stood in line for a pair of shoes. Time fled away...still she waited. Finally reaching the end, dully she turned away with a disappointed look on her face after being told there were no shoes. They watched as she slowly walked away, her old shoes tapping on the cold cement. How could she survive another summer with shoes that were worn and full of holes?

Food lines in the Russian marketplace

How often Esther, herself, had stood in these lines only to find that when her turn came, the item she asked for was not available. To her, this seemed like a waste of precious time.

Eggs, she discovered, are a rare commodity in Russia. While driving in the country, often small market places stood beside the road. If there were eggs, Gordon was sure to stop the vehicle and make a purchase. But this happened very rarely, because they were not readily available.

On a cold, drizzly day, noticing an "egg stand," they stopped their van abruptly. Gordon and David (a coworker), joined the group of people waiting in line.

"Omelettes would be delicious for breakfast tomorrow morning," Trish remarked wistfully, while watching her husband from the car window. Karen and Esther heartily agreed. Each of them were yearning for wholesome, home-cooked food. Russian black bread and rounds of fat *kielbasa* had been their daily fare far too long.

They watched as David slipped the camera off his shoulder and eagerly began taking pictures. Wanting to take as many human interest photos as possible, he realized this was another good opportunity.

Gordon smiled slightly as he heard the people talk in the Russian language. Curiously looking him over, they talked about the Americans standing in line with them. No one realized Gordon could speak and understand their language.

"The man taking pictures must be a news reporter," stated one woman. Everyone stared.

"I certainly would have worn fancier clothing if I knew we would be on these pictures," said an older woman, endeavoring to tuck her stray hair into a faded *Babushka*.

An aged grandmother, her front teeth missing, buttoned her old sweater carefully, as crookedly, she smiled into the camera lens.

Having traveled all day, David was dressed casually. A young man standing nearby remarked, "If he was a newspaper reporter, he would be dressed like a businessman."

While this discussion was going on, David was oblivious to the fact that they were talking about him and enthusiastically continued taking pictures.

Gordon, with a little smile on his face, stood by enjoying himself thoroughly.

Suddenly, a young KGB official, weary of standing, boldly pushed his way through the crowd in the line. Shoving and elbowing, passing Gordon and the aged grandmothers who had been there for some time, he triumphantly took his place at the front of the queue near the egg stand.

Gordon, who had been quietly standing and listening, could be still no longer. Looking hard at the official, he spoke in Russian, his voice loud and accusing.

"These women have been here much longer than you. What makes you think you can push past everyone and go to the front of the line? Surely, you don't respect your own mother if you shove in front of these grandmothers like you have just done!" he said.

The people in line looked at him in utter amazement as he spoke to the official in their own language. As he continued to berate the young man, grandmothers listened and began smiling and nodding their white heads, looking quite pleased.

"Yes," they said, "we were here first!"

Gratefully, with respect, they looked at the authoritative American who had taken their side. Meanwhile, the official silently stole away. The eggs he wanted were no longer important to him.

David and Gordon reached the end of the egg queue eventually. The people watched and smiled as the two Americans walked back to their van, carrying several dozen eggs. Gordon had won their hearts!

Workers in the Church Unite

That evening in Odessa, on the Black Sea, was warm and humid. Wiping the perspiration from her face, Esther blew a strand of stray hair out of her eyes.

They had been in the great USSR for several weeks and miraculously God had opened many doors of opportunity to give encouragement to hurting believers there. Now, on their way to a church they had never been before, once again their desire was to help.

"I hope we find a place to sit tonight," Esther said to Gordon as they saw crowds of people standing outside the church.

Russians worship by candlelight

The building was much smaller than others in which they had ministered, but hundreds of people sat in the crowded interior. One of the elders saw them as they slowly threaded their way through the building.

"Welcome," he said. "Will you please come with me?" Escorting them to the front of the building, he encouraged them to be seated on the platform.

Facing the congregation, Esther observed the somber faces below. They reminded her of her forefathers who had worshiped in this country so long ago. She recalled her grandmother saying the services were long, with a variety of songs and recitations. Several pastors sharing the Word of God were oblivious to the clock. No one was in a hurry to go home though they had been in church for many hours. It didn't matter that some were hungry. "Spiritual food always came first," she said

The married Mennonite women sat silent and prayerful like their Slavic sisters, wearing head coverings to show submission. Little girls with shining tresses would some day be expected to have their hair covered, too.

Fathers, heads of households, sitting somber and attentive, would later discuss the lengthy sermons with their offspring. Listening carefully, the children knew they were expected to remember the details.

Esther remembered well, as she watched the people kneel to pray, how, in her Mennonite up-bringing, her family, too, knelt while talking to God. The similarity between Esther's people, who had lived in Russia, and the Slavs themselves, was unique. Little had she realized, as a young woman, how much her parents and grandparents had related to this culture in their worship.

Suddenly the congregation was standing and Esther and Gordon were joining them in prayer. With eyes closed, they worshiped the Lord as one. Oblivious to others around them, the Slavs sang hymns—many of them in a minor key. Every verse was sung reverently, worshipfully.

Looking across the sea of faces, they could see no Bibles. They had learned to hide God's Word in their hearts because there were no Bibles available.

LAMP LIGHT

Suddenly all the lights in the building went out! No one seemed to take much notice. The service went on as it had before. However, to be in a dark, crowded building with hundreds of Slavs, was a unique experience for them.

Esther poked her husband.

"Do they worship in the dark?" she whispered.

Before Gordon had time to reply, a number of people came from the outside doors with small, coal oil lamps. While they carried these to the four corners of the building, the pastor never stopped preaching.

Flickering softly in the shadows, pale lights softened the rugged features of the people who worshiped there.

It was difficult to kneel because of the size and closeness of the crowd, but somehow they shifted to find room. Kneeling on the rough, wooden floor, they raised their petitions to God with one voice and heart. It gave them a special joy to know they all worshiped the same Lord, their hearts united because of their Savior's death and resurrection. They felt insignificant and humbled to kneel beside those who continually faced trial and testing because of their undaunting stand for Christ. Would they be willing to do the same?

Rising from their knees, suddenly they realized Anatoly Desatnyk was introducing them. Gordon greeted the people in Russian as he stood behind the pulpit. Later, asking Esther to share with the congregation, he acted as her interpreter.

Standing before the people in the soft glow of the lamps, she asked God to help her say something that would bless and encourage this suffering, expectant people.

"The same Lord," she began, "is rich unto all who call upon Him. I feel it is a privilege to worship Him together with you. We all belong to this great family of God, whether we come from across the sea or live here in your country."

"Amen!" chorused the vast congregation when she had finished. Tears of gratitude shone in their eyes. Did these people from the West really care enough about them to come and help?

As Esther's fingers touched the yellowed keys on the old piano, she and Gordon chose songs that were familiar to the people. Closing their eyes, they mouthed the words in the Russian language, as Gordon and Esther sang in English. After the last prayer had been prayed, the last song rendered, and the final sermon shared, pastor Anatoly encouraged his people.

"One more announcement before we go. Tomorrow night at six o'clock, we will gather to work on our church. Please come and help. God will bless you for it!"

Responding affirmatively, the people, acutely aware that an addition to their church was necessary to accommodate the overflowing crowds who came regularly on Sundays and weekdays, were willing to do all they could to finish this project. Many stood throughout the entire service, which lasted four hours. Yes, they needed a larger sanctuary.

After church, Esther and Gordon were surrounded by hundreds of smiling people, each desiring to speak to these people from the West.

Knowing it would please the believers, they, too, planned to come and help tomorrow.

Work to Do

The rain came down in torrents as they climbed into their van the next evening on their way to the church where energetic people were remodeling their house of God.

It was a miracle God had sent rain! Not so easily observed because of foggy weather conditions, they slipped through the gate to enter the church property. Having been watched closely by the KGB officials for some time, they always exercised caution so the lives of believers would not be put in jeopardy by their presence.

The people, recognizing their guests from the evening before, greeted them enthusiastically. The women, Esther noticed, were soaked as they worked in the pouring deluge. All were dressed in plain, dark clothing, their heads covered with Russian *babushkas.* They smiled in greeting as Esther and Gordon walked toward them. Not pausing long, however, they vigorously shoveled heavy, wet concrete while the men put it into buckets. They, in turn, carried two buckets at a time to the new addition.

Gordon didn't wait. Esther watched as he picked up heavy pails of concrete and began helping. The men smiled

Workers in the church unite. Women mixing concrete to build a church in Odessa.

their approval. A preacher from the West had never done this before and they were pleased. Yes, this man could be trusted. One by one, they began to ask questions concerning the Bible. None of them had their own precious Word of God. Working together in harmony, Gordon answered as they probed further.

The evening wore on and still they worked. But sharing the Word of God made the work light. What wonderful insights they were receiving! Time went by rapidly.

They were amazed at God's accurate timing. Had the rain not continued to come down in torrents, the KGB officials would have been on the alert. In the fog, visibility was minimal.

In the Kitchen

A Russian woman, waving her hand, beckoned to Esther. "Please come into the house," she greeted.

It was nice to step out of the rain into a warm, dry kitchen.

Entering, a pair of old *touflee* (shoes) were offered. Her feet, by this time, were cold and wet.

"Please, put these on. Your shoes are wet," she smiled.

Coaxing was not necessary. Her feet slipped into the warm slippers while her own shoes dried by the fire.

She took Esther to a high single bed, covered with a clean white sheet. Firm, white noodles, made that afternoon, were drying there for future use.

Pointing to the dough, Esther said, "noodles?"

Her hostess understood. Nodding affirmatively, she said, "*Lupsha!*"

Esther had learned another word.

Smiling, leading her guest to the sofa, she invited her to be seated.

From that vantage point, Esther watched the women in the tiny kitchen make dinner for the crew working outside in the rain.

A mixture of tantalizing aromas filled the house as hot *borscht* simmered on the front burner. *Lupsha* cooked in steaming water, while the typically Russian *kielbasa* splattered in the hot pan. Smoke filled the tiny room.

"*Holidna?*" (hungry) smiled her hostess. Esther rubbed her stomach and nodded her head. She understood.

Suddenly the outside door opened bringing a surge of cool air into the steamy, warm room. Discussing the Scriptures, the work crew still probed for answers from their guest. Working out in the rain had made them ravenous for physical food, as well.

The table was not large, but crowding together, about twenty adults sat down and fell to.

Though everyone was busy eating, still they talked about the precious Word of God. Absorbing the teaching like sponges, it seemed they never wanted to stop. Gladly their guest complied.

The *kielbasa* was too spicy for Esther's stomach, so she quietly slipped it onto Gordon's plate. He didn't notice. Talking with his new friends kept him almost too busy for food.

"Please, eat," urged the women. But the men didn't hear.

JOSH

Josh, a rugged-looking man, pleaded with Gordon to come to his house several miles on the other side of the city. "Please come and meet my wife and family," he begged. "We need Bible teaching." His appetite not satisfied, he was hungry for more spiritual food and wanted Gordon to share with his family, too.

But Gordon and Esther had made arrangements to meet their coworkers at a designated place and hour. Looking at his watch, Gordon realized they were already late.

"I am sorry we cannot come to your house tonight, but we will keep praying for you," he consoled. Registering keen disappointment, tears welled up in Josh's eyes.

Bowing in prayer, they stood and held hands around the table. Several prayed audibly while others talked to God silently. Everyone prayed.

The room by this time was hot and humid.

Men, laughing and talking enthusiastically, shook hands with Gordon and Esther and said good-bye. This had been a wonderful encounter. Each had a sense of well-being because they were satiated with spiritual food and their stomachs were satisfied, as well. Only Josh did not smile.

The Russian women waited their turn. Then, gathering Esther in their warm, motherly arms, carefully they kissed her, first on one cheek and then the other.

Dosveedanya, (good-bye) and *Sposeebo*, (thank you), she called as she followed the men out into the foggy night.

Walking toward their van, Josh was still pleading with them to come to his house.

Perhaps they could go another time? They sincerely hoped so.

It continued to rain as they drove to the other side of the city to meet their coworkers. Parking beside an impressive building, they waited for them to arrive. Rain pelted on the roof of their van while cold wind howled around them.

Something didn't feel right. To their great concern, they realized they had parked outside a police station! Though visibility was poor, they saw men in uniform everywhere. But still they waited for their friends to come. Were they safe here?

Suddenly they froze! Someone knocked loudly on the window. Who could it be? Too foggy to see out, slowly, cautiously, Gordon rolled the window down. Expecting to see a police officer, he was shocked to see their friend, Josh. Water dripped from his nose and a smile of joy lit up his happy face.

"Praise be to God!" he cried. "You have parked near to my house. Please come in and meet my family!"

Incredible, but true. God had led them right to his front door. They thought it would be impossible to visit him, but God had other plans.

After carefully moving the van behind a grove of trees nearby to partially conceal it, Gordon went with Josh. Locking the door, he promised to be back soon. What that meant, Esther had no idea, but someone needed to stay in the van to wait for their friends.

As Gordon and Josh enjoyed this miracle meeting together, Esther felt uneasy. Where were their coworkers? Would they find the van?

An hour went by. Finally, she heard a faint tap on the window. Getting into the van, David whispered, "Don't you know you are parked close to a police station?"

"Yes, I know. I am waiting for Gordon." Then she explained.

Drenched and tired, the coworkers shared individual events of that interesting day. God had led them all in unconceivable ways.

Finally, hearing another tap on the window, they opened to see Gordon and Josh. Smiling, his wife standing beside the men, handed Esther a bouquet of freshly cut flowers from her garden. "*Sposeebo*," she said, gratefully taking the flowers.

"These are beautiful?" The woman beamed her satisfaction in giving the best she had.

The windows were steamed and rain obscured their view, but they watched the couple until they were out of sight.

Cautiously driving their vehicle from its temporary hiding place, they thanked God for protection. Once again, the rain obscured them from the eyes of prying officials, and they drove away safely.

Tired, but grateful to God, who had prepared the way before them, they didn't even mind the rain! He had led them into the interior of the great USSR to a group of believers they had never seen before, and sent the rain so, unobserved by the KGB, they could work to help complete another house of God.

He led them to share His Word, as hungry believers absorbed every word. Here they had united as brothers and sisters in a bond of love and unity.

Praying they would see them again, they drove toward their campground in the pelting rain.

Reunion with Anatoly and Valentina

Never would they forget that memorable night when they helped build the house of God in the rain in Odessa. The congregation had constantly been in their prayers

Seventeen years later, in August 1991, the sun shone on a baptismal service in Seattle, Washington. Russian immigrants, clothed in white robes, indicated they were making an outward sign of an inward change as they emerged from the waters of Haller Lake.

Someone had been watching Gordon during the service, and when it was over, this middle-aged man came, shook his hand, and asked, "Aren't you Wasyl Was Ylovitch?" (Gordon's second name, William, in the Russian language.)

"Yes," he answered.

"Do you remember me?" he smiled.

Gordon scanned the memory bank of his brain and could not quite place the man at first. Why did he look so familiar?

"Was it you, Wasyl, who carried cement bricks in the mud in Odessa? Was it you who shared the precious Word of God while we worked together in the pouring rain? Was it you who helped build our house of God?"

Then Gordon remembered. Anatoly Desatnyk from Odessa!

Incredible! They were meeting again! It was moving to see two grown men embrace with tears of joy running down their faces.

There was so much to say. They stood for two hours on

the shores of Haller Lake and shared their experiences.

Immigrating to the U.S.A. due to religious persecution, many Slavic people arrived in the early 1990s. Anatoly and Valentina were among them, seeking to carve out a new life for themselves in a foreign country.

Gordon offered to help. Gratefully accepting his kindness, many necessary details would be cared for in the immediate future.

Josh, he said, did not come to America with them. Many of his people stayed behind. Perhaps some would come later.

"Josh has spoken often about the time when God brought you together in the great city of Odessa. He will never forget how you shared the precious Word of God with him," said Anatoly with tears in his eyes.

Time stood still as the men talked.

"Come to our apartment. Valentina will serve *Borscht*," smiled the older man.

Reminded of the day she served this Russian delicacy in the steamy, hot kitchen in Odessa, Gordon thanked her for her hospitality—then and now.

"Next time you come, please bring your wife. Yes, I remember when she helped us make noodles in the kitchen so we could feed the hungry work crew!" smiled the Russian woman.

They talked for two hours more. Finally at midnight, Gordon turned his car toward home.

Seventeen years!

The Word of God had born fruit in the hearts of these people and they had not forgotten. From the heart of the great USSR to Seattle, Washington, God had brought them together once again. Only God could do that!

8 To Odessa With The Girls

The hot sun shed its rays across the road as the Balisky family drove into the seaport city of Odessa. Everywhere they looked, vacationers roamed the streets wistfully looking into shop windows, while others bought souvenirs to take back home. Thousands were sunbathing on wide, sandy beaches, enjoying the heat of the scorching sun. Odessa, a popular summer resort, located on the Black Sea in Russia, draws thousands each summer to vacation and obtain their yearly tan.

Gigantic trees lined the roadside as they drove toward the campground. Nestled in this cozy setting was their cabin. It didn't take long to unpack and settle in these new surroundings. Then to their dismay, they noticed that their cabin was filled with flies, spiders, mosquitoes, and numerous other species of insects.

"We can't stay here," Cori wailed. "There are too many bugs!"

"We must," Esther answered, while swatting a fat mosquito. "We really don't have any other choice tonight, so let's relax and get ready for bed."

Reluctantly the girls changed into their nightgowns and crawled under the clammy sheets.

"Put your lights out and close the door," called Gordon from outside. "Bugs and mosquitoes are attracted to light, you know."

When they had done this, he came into the cabin with a deadly spray bomb, and ended the tormentors' short lives forever.

The Bondura We Never Learned to Play

Gordon had an address from their mission, instructing him to locate a group of believers in the city.

Charlene and Corinne asked to be able to stay behind and sunbathe on the sandy beach. So Gordon and Esther left the campground and drove toward their destination. Realizing it would not be safe to take their van all the way, they parked it in a car lot, locked it securely, and hailed a taxi.

"Sir, please take us here," said Gordon in Russian, while showing the man a slip of paper on which he had clearly written the address.

The taxi sped through the crowded city. Vehicles, bikes, and pedestrians were everywhere. Esther gritted her teeth as he barely missed one obstacle after another.

"Now I know why taxis in Russia always look like they need a repair job," she whispered to her husband.

Suddenly, after a long drive, the taxi stopped. After paying the cab driver, they got out and walked toward a crowded little church building. The pastor came toward them. Inviting them to sit on the platform with other pastors, elders, and choir members, made them feel quite conspicuous.

The Bondura we never learned to play. Luba and Anya from Kiev. Taken in Odessa.

Everyone stared. Having foreigners from America was an unusual experience here. In larger places, they are more accustomed to visitors from abroad.

The building was stifling hot. Esther tried to find a comfortable position but found it difficult to sit still. Flies buzzed around her head while heat waves almost suffocated her. Many wiped perspiration from their faces, as they, too, battled the elements.

A Russian pastor stood behind the sacred desk. His suit, worn and shabby, was neatly darned. Smiling broadly, he introduced them as friends from the West. The entire congregation, rising to their feet joined in one voice as they welcomed them to their church. "*Sposeebo*," Esther and Gordon smiled. "We are happy to be here with you all."

"Now," continued the pastor, while gesturing toward the Russian sisters in the audience, "We have other guests with us today." Introducing them as Anya and Luba, he asked them to sing.

Taking a large instrument which had been hidden behind the piano, (they later learned it was a Russian Bondura) the girls began. High clear voices, along with the sweet chords from the beautiful stringed instrument Luba capably played, filled the church.

After Gordon and Esther had ministered in song and word, the service was finally over. Everyone crowded around them. It seemed the entire congregation was there. Esther melting into the bosoms of elderly women who hugged and kissed her on one cheek and then the other, was relieved when this ritual was finally over.

Luba and Anya, however, would always stand out in her mind. "We are from Kiev," they smiled while shaking hands, "and are visiting an aunt here in the city."

"Gordon and I have just come from there," replied Esther. The church they attended in that city, had been pastored by Georgi Vins, who was now in prison for his faith.

"We were happy to have Colonel Irwin, the astronaut

from the United States, in our congregation only a few weeks ago. His visit brought encouragement and joy to our people," said Anya.

This interested Gordon and Esther especially, because their friend, Don Best, from Indiana, had been involved in sending the astronaut to Russia.

Finally, saying good-bye to their new friends, Gordon and Esther broke away from the crowd and went outside to a waiting taxi. A man from the little church was the chauffeur, and often came there after the service to offer a ride to fellow believers. On this particular evening, however, he did not know he was being followed by the KGB police. Gordon and Esther also had no idea until later, that they, too, were being closely observed. Aware that they had just visited an unregistered church made the situation potentially dangerous, not only for them, but for other believers as well.

Getting into the taxi, they proceeded to drive down the crowded streets. They noticed that their taxi driver kept looking out of his rear view mirror. Finally, in a quiet voice he said, "We are being followed by the KGB."

Clearly uneasy now, they wished there was a place to hide. Their fears were not only for themselves, but for the young taxi driver. Certainly they did not want him to lose his job, or worse, go to prison.

After many kilometers trying to lose the official car, he let them off somewhere near their van.

After bidding the taxi driver "God speed," they hurried to their own vehicle. With relief, Esther hung onto something familiar. This was her home away from home and there was a sense of security here! Were they ever really safe from the police?

A Flu Bug

Usually they looked with anticipation toward the Lord's day, because it was then they came in contact with more believers.

Charlene and Corinne rose early, put on their bathing suits, and went out to tan on the gorgeous, sandy beach.

Gordon, buttoning his shirt, was getting ready to leave for the little church where they had ministered the previous Friday.

But Esther was lying on her camp cot groaning in pain. Somewhere she had eaten food that disagreed with her. She had been ill all night and now that it was morning, there was still no sign of improvement.

"Sure you'll be all right, Honey?" asked Gordon as he came to her cot. Not wanting to keep him from church, she gulped and said "Yes," in a quivering, small voice.

As soon as he was gone, however, the realization dawned on her that she was alone in the heart of the great Soviet Republic. One goal they strived for, was never, never under any circumstance, to become sick in communist Russia. But the inevitable had happened. They had no choice. She was ill and all alone.

Picking up her old, black Bible lying on the cot beside her, she began to read. Immediately God gave the assurance through His Word that He would heal her from this affliction. A verse, clearly marked, stood out to the ailing woman:

> *For the Lord your God moves about in your camp to protect you"* (Deuteronomy 23:14, NIV).

"Thank you, God," she sighed. While insects swarmed around her, she drifted into a peaceful sleep. God was there with her and she knew it.

Later that night, after the girls came back to camp, though Esther was still weak and shaky, they went for a walk in the campground.

Their mother was not the only one with problems, however. Faintly she heard a little voice cry, "Mom, I'm burning up!"

They had just arrived back from a restful walk near the beach, and now Cori's woes were beginning. Her legs and arms, burned by the blistering sun on the beach that day, had turned a savage red. Applying wet, cold towels to the affected areas eventually brought some relief. Soon they were all asleep while the giant trees swayed gently in the hot breeze.

Happy Birthday!

A new day dawned on the Russian campground.

"Happy Birthday, Corinne!" Esther called, trying to put some enthusiasm into her voice.

Opening one eye, the birthday girl turned over on her lumpy camp cot. It took a few minutes to comprehend the message her mother was trying to portray to her.

Then she remembered—it was her thirteenth birthday! Before leaving on this trip she had mournfully exclaimed, "Having a birthday in Russia is the last thing I want, Dad—especially my thirteenth!"

Nevertheless, it was her day, and this fate had befallen her. Knowing that in acceptance lies peace, she decided to make the best of the situation. Half-heartedly, the young teen climbed out of bed, wondering what this important day would bring.

Choosing to go to the beach with her sister, they made plans to celebrate together later that afternoon.

Meanwhile, Gordon made an appointment to meet with Luba and Anya. Impressed with Luba's bondura, he made

plans to purchase the same kind of instrument in the dollar store. Luba told him on Sunday that she would be happy to help him do so and then teach them to play.

So expectantly, they set out to the store. Seeing the girls waiting for them in a pre-planned place on the side of the road, they stopped, picked them up, and headed toward their destination. The store was very crowded as they made their way to the music section. Expertly, Luba's slim fingers strummed gently on the delicate strings of the large bondura. Fascinated, they listened to the melodious strains, as the sounds blended harmoniously into one silver-toned melody.

"Do you think this is a good instrument?" Gordon inquired.

"Oh yes, it is much like my own!" Her eyes were shining.

Taking the advice of the young bondura expert, Gordon went to the counter and paid for the beautiful musical instrument.

Suddenly they were proud owners of a bondura! Immediately they made an appointment to meet the girls later for the first lesson. Meanwhile, Esther asked the young musicians to write out the chords for the stringed instrument on paper. Obligingly they did so.

A Celebration

The girls were waiting for them when they returned to the campground.

They knew how much Corinne enjoyed seeing museums and castles, so decided to take her to several that afternoon. Luba and Anya, who were with them, were very informative as they explained historical facts related to these places. Corinne, walking along slowly with her sister, drank in strange historical sights and wonders she never knew existed.

Always interested in antiques and castles, she never tired of exploring.

The afternoon went rapidly. Soon they stopped while Anya and Luba disembarked in an inconspicuous place. Gordon's offer to drive them to their aunt's apartment was met with an emphatic, "No! That would be too dangerous." Thinking of police cars which had been suspiciously following them recently, they heartily agreed.

When Esther was ill on Sunday, Gordon and his friends had been watched carefully all day, and they knew now that extreme caution must be exercised at all times.

Saying good-bye, the girls hurried off toward a side road and disappeared.

"Lord, keep them safe," Esther prayed, as she realized what it must be like for a believer to be haunted day and night by the authorities. How often they had sensed powers of darkness here. "God," she continued, "there is no freedom in this place—only a sense of Satanic oppression and heaviness. Thank You for freedom at home in the U.S.A.. Help them to appreciate it more."

It was exciting to dress up for a birthday dinner. Gordon had made reservations in a well-known restaurant the evening before, carefully ordering ethnic Russian foods they so seldom found in most eating establishments. Either they were "fresh out" or just didn't want to share with them. *Borscht* and *holopsie*, their favorite ethnic foods, would be served for this special dinner.

Flowers are always given for special occasions in Russia, and this birthday was no exception. As Gordon presented Corinne with her first beautiful bouquet, her eyes grew large as she hugged her dad. These flowers went with them for hundreds of kilometers after leaving Odessa.

Customarily in Russia, everyone carries flowers into the

dining room for a celebration, so Corinne shared hers with her sister and mother. The aroma of freshly-cut roses filled the dining room as they entered.

The restaurant was completely crowded, so they were thankful a place had been reserved for their family. Unfortunately, loud dance music sounded to the farthest corner of the building. Couples danced sensuously to the beat as they swayed in the dim light of the room.

In spite of this, their meal was delicious. They ate until they could eat no more. When it was time to leave, each of them fully agreed they were happy in the knowledge that they had a personal Friend to satisfy their longings and desires. There was no need to resort to what they had witnessed with their eyes that night.

A full moon shone brightly as they walked toward their van that warm, dark evening. The girls walked ahead. Corinne had joined the ranks of teenagers throughout the world. What would the future hold for her?

She looked so sweet that night. Big, liquid blue eyes and a girlish white face peered from a crown of freshly-washed golden brown hair.

"Lord, guide her in every decision throughout her life, and keep her always true to You," whispered her mom.

They stepped into their van and drove toward the campground. It had been a good day. Corinne thought so, too!

Trouble

Another new day dawned bright and sunny. Already, they could feel the sun's rays penetrate into their cabin.

In response to a knock at the door, Esther shouted, "Come on in!"

Charlene and Corinne appeared. Putting their bathing suits on in the bathroom, and now on their way to the beach, they carried towels and suntan lotion. Both had turned into golden brown beauties, but still insisted on more sunshine. Already the beach was teaming with hundreds of guests, so the girls hurried to find a spot on the sand.

Informing them they would be meeting with Luba and Anya, and planned to be back to pick them up a little later, they let them go. Tomorrow they needed to pack early and leave their cabin and Odessa.

Luba and Anya were waiting at the side of the road. The previous evening they had taken the bondura with them to tune it. Carrying the large instrument, they quickly stepped into the van. Having promised to give Esther and Gordon a lesson, eagerly they looked forward to their first instructions on how to play a bondura. Esther knew she couldn't make sweet music right away, but planned to practice until she could.

It was imperative to find a place for their encounter, but they realized this was not easy. Finally, noticing a small road that led to the beach, they turned to follow it. They soon realized that here, too, swarms of people were enjoying the warm sunshine. Relaxed brown bodies covered the sandy beaches as far as they could see.

Turning the van around, they continued to search, but where, with so many people around, could they practice?

Anya, Gordon, and Esther walked down a rocky trail following the beach. Looking out over the vast Black Sea, they saw the shimmering water glistening in the sunshine and longed to stretch out on the warm, sandy beach. But they couldn't. Their time was limited.

They knew Luba had left to find a place where they could meet. But where was she? Why was she taking so long? Finally from a trail high above their heads, they saw her silhouetted against the sky.

Presuming she would join them, they walked on a little

farther. However, she did not come back and they began to feel somewhat apprehensive. Walking back down the trail to the van, they waited for her to return. Time stood still as they waited. Still there was no sign of the Russian girl. Anya, becoming anxious, decided to go and look for her sister.

Now both girls had been gone for too long. By this time they were feeling alarm and concern. Why had Luba wandered off by herself? Had she found a place for them to meet?

Why didn't she come back and let them know? Anya, too, was not returning. Where were they?

After Anya left, they tried to be as inconspicuous as possible, but it seemed everywhere people stopped and stared. It wasn't every day tourists from America graced their beaches. While they were waiting, feeling more uncomfortable all the time, Gordon, to his horror, realized they were near a military station. Then he assumed that this was a private beach for military personnel only. They were not welcome in this place. No wonder they were staring!

Still Luba and Anya did not return. Now, really concerned, they knew it was impossible to leave without them. Seriously, they wondered what to do.

Suddenly, very quietly, Gordon whispered, "Look, Honey, there comes Anya with a policeman!" Both she and the officer walked by Gordon and Esther, who were sitting on a bench nearby. The girl appeared fidgety and nervous. There was fear in her eyes

When they walked toward their van, Esther's heart leaped with apprehension. "What do they want?" Esther whispered as they watched them talking beside the vehicle. The conversation was loud and animated. Gordon, too, frowned in consternation, not really understanding what was going on.

And where was Luba? The question remained unanswered for some time, until they saw her with several policemen. With bated breath, they walked toward the girls and officials who were now looking into their vehicle.

"What is the problem?" asked Gordon in Russian. "Can we help you with something?" With a look of steel, one of the men turned toward them and said, "These girls have stolen something from our beach."

This accusation was absurd! Incredulous!

"The girls were carrying nothing. Even their purses are in their van and the vehicle is locked. Take a look," Gordon said, as he opened the doors. Still not finished, he continued, "How could they steal something? What was there to steal?"

Esther's stomach twisted into a little ball of nerves as she noted that the policemen had stiffly turned their backs on them. Cold and unreasoning, they had no intention of listening, no matter how they pleaded. Seldom had she experienced fear such as this before. Now, the cold fingers of apprehension tugged at her heart.

Gordon reached for the girls' purses while the officer carefully looked inside the van. "You get in your vehicle and leave now!" ordered the big officer. Helpless, they looked on as their friends were led away by three policemen. They assumed they would be taken to headquarters where they would be interrogated, perhaps even put in prison.

Getting into the van, they were saddened at the injustice they had just witnessed. They could be of no help whatsoever. Esther shuttered as she thought of the relentless KGB officers who were unyielding toward their pleas and those of the girls. They knew they were there to do their jobs. Grimly they drove from the scene, desperately wishing they could aid their friends. The police car drove close behind them as they left the beach, carrying the two helpless girls.

It shocked them to realize that since that night they had gone to the small unregistered church, they had been fol-

lowed every day. Apparently a police car had trailed them even today, while they drove into the beach area earlier. They knew Anya and Luba were with them.

The girls had not been arrested because they stole something from the beach, but because the system frowns against tourists associating with average citizens, especially believers.

They prayed for Anya and Luba then, asking God to be with them wherever the police were taking them. The promise, "I will never leave thee nor forsake thee," was just as true today as when Paul and Silas were imprisoned so long ago.

They never did receive their bondura lesson, but the beautiful instrument is a constant reminder to them that they must never stop praying for believers in Russia who have chosen to follow Christ, no matter what the cost.

Nerves jangling, and bodies exhausted, they finally found their campground, and crawled into the lumpy, camp cots. It had been quite a day!

Esther, closing her eyes, had visions of KGB police and believers dancing in her head. What would tomorrow bring?

It wasn't long before they realized that they did not leave the KGB behind. They were following closely, and were their constant shadow until they reached Kishnev the next day.

Some time later, they heard that their two friends had been kept in custody and harshly interrogated. After abuse and cruel treatment, the police released them and the girls went back to Kiev. Luba and Anya knew that they must be cautious at all times because "Big Brother" was always watching those who put Christ before Communism.

Weddings: Russian Style

DEDICATED TO LENIN

They looked on in amazement as the bride and groom

walked arm in arm up the cement steps to a towering national monument in Moscow. The family members and wedding attendants stood back while the young couple purposefully and ceremoniously walked to the base of the eternal flame.

The bride slowly bent over and placed a bouquet of flowers there. Then, taking her new husband's arm, walked back to waiting friends and out to the wedding car.

They had not even reached the car, when another couple repeated the ceremony. They saw a continual stream of wedding parties as they stood there, each couple repeating what those before them had done.

"Why are they leaving flowers beside the monument?" Esther asked the friend who was guiding them around the city. Of course, they had never seen anything like this in their own country.

"The bride places her flowers there beside the monument as a tribute to Lenin," their friend explained. "She thus vows allegiance to the State and its cause. This also signifies that future generations will be trained to follow Lenin as well."

This troubled them. These young people had dedicated themselves to the communist government enough to ceremoniously pay a tribute to Lenin at their wedding. They left no room for Jesus Christ in their lives.

Dedicated to Christ

Christian couples, however, make Christ the focus of their wedding and their lives together.

Members of the Moscow Baptist Church invited Esther and Gordon to the wedding of a Christian couple. With anticipation, they entered the church on the morning of the ceremony, curious to see how a Christian wedding in the USSR would contrast with the ceremonies at Lenin's monument.

The service began with singing hymns. This was all done by memory since there were no song books. Emphasizing every word, with eyes closed, the people concentrated on the words as they sang slowly and deliberately.

The choir then sang from hand-copied sheets of music. One choir anthem would never suffice in Russia. There must be at least half a dozen!

"I wonder when the bride and groom will arrive," Esther whispered to her husband.

Later they learned they were in a small room near the pulpit. The parents waited with the nervous couple, probably to give moral support.

Finally, at a word from one of the pastors, the young people walked to the front of the crowded church. Both sets of parents came in at the same time.

The bride, wearing a flowing white gown, carried a bouquet of scarlet flowers. Her girlish face peering from inside a halo of cascading dark hair, she attempted to smile, despite her nervousness.

Esther stretched for a better look as the couple joined hands and repeated their wedding vows.

Then each of the parents prayed for their new life together. The bride, in a wavering voice, also prayed that the Lord would be the head of their household and that God would guide them along life's way, as together they ventured ahead.

Finally the groom concluded with a prayer, asking his Friend and Savior to lead him in this new responsibility.

Women throughout the congregation dabbed at their eyes, weeping for joy. Their head scarves nodded up and down with their heads as they cried into wrinkled white handkerchiefs.

A feast and celebration followed the ceremony, which

surpassed the American cake and coffee receptions, treating the guests to many delicious Russian dishes.

The sharp contrast between the two types of weddings is obvious. Though the way ahead may be difficult for the young couple who have decided to follow Jesus Christ in a Communist society, the dividends will be great.

A Plea for Bibles in Kishnev

While in Odessa, on the Black Sea, Gordon was given the address of a pastor who lived in this Russian city. Though their schedule was filled to capacity, and they had many kilometers to drive that day, Gordon felt impressed to visit the pastor. Perhaps he would need encouragement—or even literature. They still had several copies of the Gospel of John and wanted to give these to someone before leaving the USSR. Bibles, they knew, were a precious commodity and could not be bought there.

Taxicabs whizzed by as Gordon tried to attract their attention. He had been waiting for some time and felt impatient because his time schedule did not allow for such a delay. Finally, a dilapidated taxicab came to an abrupt halt beside him. Informing the driver of his intended destination, Gordon climbed in. Yes, the driver knew where this place was and would deliver his passenger there soon.

Driving through the crowded city, the unfriendly driver sucked his cigarette and swore constantly as he continued his battle through a mob of honking cars, pedestrians, nervous horses, farm wagons, bicycles, and red lights.

Eventually the driver informed Gordon of their arrival at the requested address. A slight smile appeared at the tight corners of his mouth as Gordon paid the fare and gave him several extra rubles.

Walking to an old building behind a high, weathered

fence, Gordon stopped and knocked on a door. Would the pastor be there? He sincerely hoped so. A heavy-set Russian woman opened the door. After carefully introducing himself in the Russian language, she knew she had never seen this man before. Leading him into the parlor, she left the two men alone.

A large man he assumed to be the pastor, sat beside a table slowly, laboriously typing with one finger on an archaic typewriter. It was obvious that painstaking, slow motion would take the man days to complete the task at hand.

Coming closer, Gordon noticed he had several carbon copies, plus the original in the machine. The ink barely came through to the final copy, but he knew all would be used. Paper, too, was expensive and none could be wasted.

Introducing himself, Gordon extended his hand. The pastor, in turn greeted him in the Russian language.

"*Djien dobri*," (good day) he said, holding his big hand out in a welcoming gesture.

"I have only a few minutes to spend with you, dear brother, but felt impressed of the Lord to come and see you," said Gordon.

The pastor's eyes filled with tears.

"Oh, my brother," he replied, "your visit is so very timely. I have been sitting beside this typewriter for days trying to type the whole Gospel of John. Recently, a young man here in Kishnev, accepted the Lord as his Savior. He has been so excited about sharing his faith, that thirty people in turn, have accepted Christ as Savior since his recent conversion! He is now helping to teach these new converts the Gospel of John. That is why I am typing the book for him. It would be so wonderful to have our own Bibles," he continued with a wistful look in his brown eyes.

"I have recently made a trip to Siberia. The churches

there are thriving during these difficult times, but Scriptures are needed desperately. In most churches they have no Bibles. In one church I visited, there were about 500 people in the congregation, and they did not have one Bible available. So many are longing to have the Scriptures. Many smaller churches in our own area express the sincere need to have even a Gospel of John."

Gordon gulped. It was not a mere coincidence that he had copies of the Gospel of John in his possession. God knew his pastor friend had been earnestly praying, and today through this visit, He answered the prayers.

"Yes, brother," replied Gordon, "I have copies of the Gospel of John in my vehicle, as well as other pieces of literature. I also have clothing for you. I will take a taxi back to my van and return with these things. Please wait for me here." Time was no longer a factor. God was at work!

The pastor, though anticipating an answer to prayer, had not expected it that particular day. "Yes, we will wait here until you return," he promised. "There is no place we would rather be right now!"

After reaching the van, Gordon drove toward the church, parked, and walked the last half-kilometer to his destination so he would not attract attention. Caution was always important.

When he arrived at the pastor's house, they were waiting with smiles on their faces. When Gordon gave the grateful man the Gospel of John, his broad shoulders shook with sobs. With tears running down his weathered cheeks, he threw his arms around Gordon, crying, "*Sposeebo*, *sposeebo*! (thank you) God bless you!" His heart was too full to say more. He had prayed so long and waited for God to send Bibles. His prayers had been answered!

The pastor's wife gratefully shook his hand as tears shone

in her large eyes. Yes, they needed clothing, too, and it had arrived all the way from America. She knew no distance was too great for her God. Happily she picked up the clothing and went into the other room to sort through her treasures.

A coincidence? No! Gordon had simply followed the leading of His heavenly Father in response to the sincere prayers of a Russian pastor in Kishnev. The Gospel of John would also light the way for others who were waiting.

9 ONCE AN ENEMY

The year was 1978. They were in Chernevsy, and knew they were being followed. During the Communist era when Christians in Russia were persecuted and imprisoned for their faith, Gordon's and Esther's whereabouts were very important to the KGB. What were they doing in the country? Certainly they were not average tourists.

Russia was not allowing missionaries who came from abroad to preach to their people. After all, religion was the opiate of the people. It was their goal that all Russians be intertwined into the Communist system, and not part of a group who followed the imaginary prophet, Jesus, and claimed to be believers or *verruyuschiye*.

It was evident in the various cities in which they had ministered, that their activities were being closely monitored and scrutinized. On this particular trip across the country, they went to Leningrad, then east toward

Krakow, and south to Odessa on the Black Sea.

It was possible to travel only in areas in which they were given permission by the state. In Russia, during the Breshnev-Gorbechov era, exposure for Western people was very limited to certain routes, and going through check-points was a routing requirement.

There, licenses were verified and the number of people in vehicles accounted for. Checked thoroughly for literature or anything they felt could incriminate the government, they were often kept at border crossings for many hours.

By 1978, Gordon and his family were well-known throughout the countries of Russia and Ukraine. They were watched constantly.

Knowing in advance that they were coming, the border guards were always prepared with ammunition as they rudely interrogated them and meticulously searched their vehicle and persons.

This family was not welcome here, and the authorities made certain they were aware of that!

Meeting with church leaders, ministering in churches, teaching and trying to help and encourage the persecuted church, they put their lives in danger each time they came to this godless country.

Upon arriving in Russia or Ukraine, it was a requirement to check into the local tourist Hotel, and from there, be directed to a place to camp for the night.

Most often the days were long as Charlene, Corinne, Gordon, and Esther, drove from one place of ministry to another. It was physically fatiguing, but the emotional strain was even worse. Would they be imprisoned? Or would the believers be persecuted as a result of finding this family with them?

Always careful, they parked their vehicle a distance from the church or believer's home. From there, they took a taxi or bus, or even walked to their destination. Extreme caution must be taken at all times. With their lives at stake, or perhaps another's, these precautions were absolutely necessary.

"Mom, I'm tired!" complained Corinne from the back seat of the crowded Volkswagen. "Me, too," answered Charlene. "When can we stop?"

Wishing she could answer that question, Esther sighed.

Yes, it had been an enormous day. Skirting holes on dusty, corrugated roads, driving over bumps and gravel, over hills and around curves, while a blistering, hot sun shone into the van, they were ready to camp.

Today they had encountered a rainstorm as well. Huge drops—like the girls had never seen before—hit their van and bounced ferociously against the defenseless windows, while mud flew in all directions.

Thunder rolled, as jagged streaks of lightning lit the entire darkened sky. Then stopping as suddenly as it had begun, the blistering sun came out again. In a short while, dust flew inside and outside their crowded van, as if it had never rained at all.

Camping

But the process of getting to a campground was far from over. Gordon drove toward the Intourist Hotel to do the necessary paper work with regards to checking in, and making reservations in a nearby camping place.

"Why does it take so long?" Esther complained. Perspiring, she wiped her dusty face with a soiled Kleenex. Leaving streaks of dirt, the sight would have been comical—that is, if anyone felt like laughing.

Inside the Intourist Hotel, Gordon was having troubles of his own. A stern, professional KGB officer, tearing a clean sheet of paper from his notepad, took his pencil from behind

his ear, and began to write as he threw questions at Gordon. Frustrated by now, Gordon realized it was evident that he and the other KGB officials in the hotel were well informed as to the whereabouts of their travels and work among the Slavic Christians. Cool and collected, with eyes as cold as steel, they observed the perspiring young man. Making him as uncomfortable as possible was their goal. Would he wilt under the querying pressure? They hoped so.

Silently crying to God, Gordon suddenly felt peace wash over him. Now, looking straight into the eyes that bored into his, quietly, calmly, he answered their questions.

Yes God was with him.

After a lengthy confrontation, clearing his throat, the young man (who they later learned was Arcadi), told Gordon where the campground was located and gave him permission to leave.

Driving out of the crowded, teeming city where thousands of souls made their homes, they arrived at their place of refuge. Or was it a place of rest? Loud, incessant music screeched through a tiny loud speaker as they entered the unkempt campground.

Checking in took another hour. Finally, settling into a decrepit, dirty cabin, they were all hungry.

But what should they eat? The hour was late and they were so weary. Yet, their stomachs gnawed for some kind of nourishment. Going back into the crowded Volkswagen, Esther rummaged through piles of boxes to reach the small fridge. Taking out cold sausage, and a hard loaf of yesterday's bread, she knew this would have to be their daily bread that night.

Too tired to really care, mechanically, the travel-worn family chewed and swallowed. Then they crawled into camp cots fitted with stained, gray sheets. "Have they been washed?" Esther wondered. Perhaps they should use their sleeping bags instead?

"Hey, the springs are hitting my back!" complained Esther's weary husband. The rest of them, having the same problem, endeavored to find a place where the springs did not jut out to puncture them. They were not successful.

But soon, the cabin was still. Even the brassy music from the loud speaker had stopped. Now it was time to sleep—or so they thought.

Esther tried to relax. Bumpy, dusty, corrugated roads, cold sausage, Intourist Hotels, and stern KGB faces crowded her weary mind. "Would their girls be safe in this forsaken place? How would these encounters affect them? Should they have taken them into Communist Russia in the first place?" she worried.

"Mom!" came from the bed in the far corner of the cabin. Apparently Charlene couldn't sleep either.

"Why aren't you sleeping, Dear?" asked the concerned mother.

"Mom, did you notice a car from the Intourist Hotel following us to this campground?"

"Yes, Honey, I did. Hopefully, they are gone by now. Please try and go to sleep!" This statement made her feel like one of Job's comforters.

But the men weren't gone. Parking a short distance away, they had followed. Charlene's observation was right.

Three men stayed up all night to take vigil. Unknown to the family that they were under surveillance by the KGB police, they could sense the intense, chilling, suspenseful atmosphere around them.

The night was wrapped in inky blackness. Why was it so dark and cold?

In a country dominated by Communism, in the natural,

they were not safe, but in God's hands, they knew He was with them. Who could harm them?

Uneasiness grew, however, as they heard muffled voices outside the cabin. Coming toward the van, parked near their window, they heard someone trying to enter. Locks rattled, as the Volkswagen began to shake. Seriously, they were trying to break in.

Gordon jumped out of bed. "Hey!" he yelled, in the Russian language. He looked out of the window, but the night was black. Not seeing anyone, he quickly pulled on his trousers and ran outside.

"What do you want?" he cried.

No one answered.

Three men had just fled into the darkness of night.

Hearing the loud commotion outside, the girls cowered in the corner of the old cabin, horrified. Eyes wide with fright, they waited for their father to come back inside.

But where was he? Esther, looking out, couldn't see anything but suffocating darkness.

Praying out loud, she and the girls waited.

Finally, Gordon returned. He was obviously shaken. This kind of mysterious encounter had happened before. Who was trying to harass them?

The family didn't get much sleep that night, but committed themselves into God's hands. He would keep them safe from the terror that lurked in the darkness.

Morning finally arrived. Eating a cold breakfast, Esther was concerned to see dark circles under the girls' eyes. *Are they getting enough rest?* she worried. And this makeshift meal in front of them was unappetizing, unappealing, and not very tasty.

"Lets go, Dad!" begged Corinne, eager to leave this place.

Once again, loud, tinny music blared from the camp loud speaker overhead.

Eager to begin a fresh, new day, they began to repack the Volkswagen. Perhaps some positive adventure lay ahead. They hoped so.

An Encounter with Arcadi

Gordon decided it was necessary to go to the Intourist Hotel to check out why they were being harassed by the KGB. They had come to their country in peace, and would like to be left alone.

Seeking an audience with the director of secret police, through the Intourist office, once again, he saw the young man whose name was Arcadi. After a lengthy conversation with him, Gordon became more aggressive as Arcadi evaded questions asked.

"I would like to meet with the KGB secret police officer," he informed the young man.

"His office is not for the ordinary public—especially it is not open to foreigners," cautioned Arcadi.

He could not meet Gordon's eyes when he was informed of the harassment they were receiving in their country.

Not wanting to deal with this, Arcadi subtly dropped hints as to where the KGB offices were located.

Deciding to go on the little information he had, Gordon, always observant and very capable in following directions, no matter how vague they were, located the offices.

KGB Headquarters

"*Djien dobri*!" he said, holding out his hand to the official present. Not returning his greeting, the man abruptly turned on his heal and gestured for Gordon to follow him.

They spoke for over an hour. The officer, though cautious, reluctantly opened up to Gordon as they talked.

"We have travelled in your beautiful country many times," said Gordon, nearing the end of their conversation. "Receiving numerous invitations, we assumed we were always welcome. However, it is evident that on many occasions, we are being followed night and day. This, officer, is harassment!

"My family is nervous about this. Why do you frighten them so? What have they done wrong? My girls are young and impressionable. You are making this trip a nightmare for them. Please allow them to enjoy your country in peace. They will go home and tell their fellow-Americans how beautiful your country is!"

Clearing his throat, while his big feet shuffled nervously under the chair, the man did not give a reason. However, it was not long afterward, Gordon learned that he had sent his officers—including Arcadi—to follow and harass them on numerous occasions. Not pleased that they were influencing the Christians to stand true to their faith in God during times of testing and persecution, he wanted them out of his country.

Non-committal, the devious officer bid Gordon goodbye.

Looking Ahead

The year was 1992. The season was spring.

Since their encounters with believers in Russia and Ukraine, many had applied for religious asylum to flee from the persecution. Having recently received permission when the face of Communism changed in Russia and Ukraine, they immigrated to the United States by the thousands.

Knowing that Wasyl Was Ylovitch, (Gordon) lived in Seattle, they proceeded to locate him. Asking for assistance while they began their new life in the United States, Gordon and Esther were constantly on call to help in one way or another.

Sacramento was another city to which many of the immigrants came. Calling Gordon, they asked if he would come and help them give birth to a new Slavic congregation in the Sacramento area.

Complying with their request, he went. Staying with a Ukrainian family from Chernovsy, whose son-in-law had recently come to America, Gordon immediately recognized the young man as someone with whom he should be acquainted.

Time stood still.

Unbelievingly, they stared at each other. Could it really be true that this was the young man with whom Gordon had spoken to in the Intourist Hotel in Chernovsy?

Memories flooded back like a boomerang.

His mouth open, the young man kept staring, too.

Finally finding his voice, he rose from his chair.

"Are you Wasyl Was Ylovitch?" he whispered.

"Are you Arcadi, the KGB officer from Chernovsy?" asked the astonished Gordon.

The two had met again—not on Communist, hammer-and-sickle territory, but here, in America—a free nation under God where the Stars and Stripes waved proudly, and where the Statue of Liberty proclaimed freedom and justice for all.

"But how could it be?" wondered the questioning Wasyl. "Why is he here?"

Arcadi's face, troubled and frightened while in the USSR, was smooth, peaceful, and smiling.

"I remember how you and I spoke in the Intourist office in 1978—so long ago. I will never forget the positive, indelible impression you stamped on my hardened heart," he continued.

"You made statements that I have never forgotten, Wasyl. Other officers talked about their conversations for years afterward, as well. Yes, you spoke about spiritual values, positive thought patterns, and morals, which we were not accustomed to here in our country. Communist values had been heavily instilled into the very fiber of our beings. Having been trained that way, we were living strongly by them." After talking to you, conviction soon made us uncomfortable."

Arcadi stopped long enough to smile at the toddler playing at his feet.

"As a result of our conversation, I seriously began to question the moral and ethical standards of the people with whom I worked. Before you came, I had lived in a small village prior to moving to Chernovsy. Asking me to come, the KGB officials knew I would be more readily available to work with them in the city."

Filling their cups with hot tea, the lady of the house smiled at him.

"We are happy to have Arcadi here. He is now a believer and one of us," she concluded. "Thanks be to our God!"

Reminded afresh that God can do anything, Gordon asked, "But how did this all happen, Arcadi?"

"Hold on, I will get to that," he grinned.

Eager to carry on with the remarkable story, he continued. "The KGB had information concerning various Christian families living in the city, who would have accommodations where an undercover KGB official might live. This would be done in order that they would be arrested for their faith eventually..

"Through God's intervention, though I didn't realize it then, I found a Christian family who agreed to take me in. Renting a room, I constantly watched to see how these people lived. What kept them going? Their walk with God was solid and real. Secretly, I longed to have what they had. At first, the family did not realize that I was an undercover policeman from the KGB, and that I was there to find out about their Christian lives.

"Daily I watched, listened, and took notes. Did they have a Bible? Who and how did they worship? Were they really *verruyuschiye* (believers)? If so, why did they believe in a God who dos not even exist?

"As time went by, observing them, the desire to know God gave me a hunger I could not describe. I was so impressed with their lives that I almost divulged my secret. Respecting them too much, knowing that I would frighten them if I told the truth, I remained quiet.

"Time went on. I desired to have a Bible of my own. So I asked the man of the house one day if he had one.

"Nervously, the man replied, 'No, I don't.' By this time, he suspected my true identity.

"'Can you get me a Bible?' I asked.

"'I'll try,' he stammered, 'but Bibles, of course, are very scarce in this country.'

"Gradually the family came to know the real truth about me and why I was living with them."

The young man blew his nose. With tears welling up in his eyes, he said, "These wonderful Christian people must have been living in terror during the time I lived with them, when they realized I was a KGB official. Yet, they were willing to look for a Bible for me. Of course they didn't trust me. Would you? I was a Communist officer and a traitor!

"What a position in which to be placed! Knowing I

could turn them in, they remained true to their God, never compromising at any time. Never would they recant if given the choice. I knew they loved Him that much.

"Conviction in my heart steadily grew.

"Finally after much prayer and searching, the family found a Bible for me, realizing I was there to report any suspicion. If I was found out, I could be convicted! Miserably, I wanted to read this book, and yet, I was afraid to do so. When I finally started, the more I read, the more convicted I became. What would become of me? Sincerely I wondered. I didn't know—but God did!

"Normally, I would convict, arrest, and imprison people who had a Bible in their home. Of course, I could not convict this family—my conscience wouldn't allow me to do that! I was in a fix. My goal upon arrival had been to find their Christian friends so they could be arrested as well. Everything was so mixed up now!

"Opening the Bible, my eyes became glued to the text. This was no ordinary book, I knew. It spoke out loud to my soul. No other book had ever done that.

"I began to resent the system to which I was entangled. Then I prayed. What? Archadi praying? That sounded ridiculous, even to me. I had, and was, persecuting those who did.

"Seriously, I promised God if He would extricate me from the ungodly system to which I had become entangled, I would serve Him the rest of my life."

Archadi sighed. Sipping his tea, which by now was cold, remembering, he stared into the distance.

"Weary of my difficult assignment which I received from my superior officer, I rebelled against the surveillance to search out Christian young people in the educational system so they would be harassed and eventually imprisoned for their faith. Seriously I wondered, *what can I do?*"

GOD SENDS A MIRACLE

Looking at the cherub face of his beloved Anna, who was helping to prepare dinner for their guests, his heart skipped a beat.

"One day," he smiled, "I met a beautiful young woman in her late teens. Just looking at her made my pulses throb! But she was a *verruyuschiye*, I knew. Visiting her home in the course of time, miraculously, I began to go to church and Sunday school with her and her family.

"I couldn't imagine a KGB officer, out to harass Christians for their beliefs, now going to church himself. I always thought Sunday school was for sissies. What was happening to me? It scared me. Knowing that if a high-ranking officer could see this, I would be imprisoned immediately—and from there—who knows?"

Arcadi was silent for a long moment, as he brought his thoughts together. His wife, coming from across the room toward him, gently took his hand. Brightening, he continued,

"I loved Anna so much, I asked her to marry me."

Her parents were reluctant. There was no evidence in my life that I was born again, though they knew I showed interest in the Scriptures.

I kept pursuing the young woman. I felt I had to have her for my wife. As time went on, her parents firmly, but gently, refused to allow us to get married."

"Well, what happened?" asked Gordon.

The room was hushed as everyone listened. Waiting for the climax, they knew God had fixed his problems—but how?

"I prayed and prayed. The Bible became more of a living book to me than ever. Again, promising the Lord I would give up my job as a high-ranking officer, and leave the system to which I had been entangled for so long, I asked Him to deliver me from this diabolical system.

"Nothing different happened for a while, but one day something took place that I never would have expected.

"God does work in mysterious ways," smiled his wife. Still close beside him, she encouraged Arcadi.

While Arcadi put his head back on the sofa, she took over.

"Arcadi suddenly became ill with a ruptured appendix. Severe complications set in and he became dangerously ill. Paralyzed and unable to walk, as a high-ranking officer, he received the best treatment available in the entire country. Medically, there was no response. Arcadi didn't get well. Therapy did not help him to walk again. Terrified, Arcadi realized that if medicine didn't help, nothing would. Would he ever walk again?"

Anna, seeing her toddler reaching for a glass, stopped long enough to take it away from him. Continuing, she said, "Promising to pray for him, the family with whom he lived remained true to their word, making their friends aware of Arcadi's physical and spiritual problems, and challenging other brothers and sisters in churches to pray as well. They looked for positive answers.

"Knowing this, while he lay on his bed, the Holy Spirit probed deeply into the young officer's heart. How was God planning to work out his problems? Seriously he wondered. Even now, he questioned whether there even was a God. Was the Bible truly His infallible Word? How could one know for certain? Indoctrinated as an atheist, seriously, he questioned God and His Word. The KGB officials, of course, were aware of Arcadi's major physical problems, and officially declared him to be incapable of his duties as a KGB officer. Dismissing him for medical reasons, the young man's prayer had suddenly been answered.

"Remembering he had prayed to a God he didn't

even really know existed, he said, "If You release me from this immoral system, which has entangled me, I will serve You for the rest of my life. God was taking him up on his word."

Arcadi, now holding their toddler on his knee, unconsciously held the little hands in his own. Wriggling to be free, Arcadi put the child on the floor.

"The only way an officer under the banner of the KGB could be relieved of his duties," he said, "was death, or becoming an invalid and released on medical grounds."

God, Arcadi knew, had intervened. He, too, must be true to his promise. "Repenting of sin, I will never forget how I knelt and received Jesus Christ as my Savior from sin. Like the apostle Paul of old, I had persecuted, harassed, and even killed the people of God. Could He now forgive all that? Assured He had, I rose from my knees. Peace, such as I had never known, filled my heart. Now there was no doubt that God not only existed, but He lived in my heart!

"And I didn't have an ulterior motive, either," he laughed, taking Anna's hand in his own. "Receiving permission from her parents, we were married soon after that!

"God miraculously healed me of my afflictions as time went on. Now I can walk as good as I ever did.

"However, having been relieved of my duties, the KGB officers at the Communist Headquarters eventually found out that I was now a born again *verruyschiye*. Hated and harassed for this stand, I applied for political asylum to come to the United States along with many other believers who had been threatened and hurt for so long.

"*Brat* Wasyl," he concluded, hanging his head in shame, "Yes, I was one of the officers who harassed and watched your family constantly while you were in Russia. I,

along with other KGB officers had been trained in criminal law by enemies of the State to harass and kill Christians. Your future did not look very positive at that time! As you traveled from city to city, sharing the good news of Christ, they planned what to do with you eventually. They probably would have imprisoned you, but didn't have the order from higher ranks as yet. Yes, you were in serious danger while working with those who were truly our enemies. Jesus, who they believed to be an imaginary prophet, was their enemy, too. *Verruyuschiye* who followed Him, including you, were also their enemies as they observed your travels from day to day.

Putting his head in his hands, Arcadi began to weep. "I am so sorry for the grief I caused you and your family. Will you forgive me Wasyl?"

Seeing two big men weep, as embracing, they partook freely of God's grace and forgiveness, was a touching experience.

The room was still. Even the toddler playing in the corner didn't make a sound. No one spoke for some time.

With his wife and children around him in their humble home in Sacramento, Arcadi's eyes shone with the love of Christ.

Now there was no more enslavement to an immoral, unethical system of injustice. No longer was he shackled by a heavy burden to a yoke of bondage that had strangled him for so long.

"Thank God, we live in a country where our children are happy and safe. We attend an Evangelical Free Church here in the city where we can freely worship Christ."

Her eyes shining, Anna added, "Joy fills our hearts! Surely goodness and mercy shall follow us all the days of our lives!"

Once an Enemy

Esther wrote a poem, showing the analogy between the Apostle Paul, who, under a tyrannical governmental system, harassed, persecuted, and killed believers so long ago, but saw the light and began to follow Christ (Acts 8:1; 9:1-9)—and Arcadi, the former KGB high-ranking officer in Russia, who was delivered from a system of injustice and bondage like Paul of old, and became a born-again Christian. He, too, became ardent for his God whom he now loved and served.

"Persecute the Christians!" came the stalwart cry.
"Hunt them down—take them all,
for surely they must die!
Fathers, mothers, grandparents, children—
all must face the sword,
For standing up for their Messiah,
they say He's Christ the Lord!"

Saul of Tarsus:

But wait, another shout, a breathtaking,
dazzling light
"Saul of Tarsus! Stop! Release My people—
end your bloody fight!"
Gasping, bowing low before the God
he had despised,
Saul, the persecutor, accepted the Messiah
who opened up his eyes!"
With zealous fire burning within the changed heart of Paul,
Now he won souls for his Messiah, he had heard the Masters' call!

1978 in Russia:

Communism, hammer, sickle, sword…
shedding innocent blood,
"Round up the Christians—bring them in,
for they believe in God!"

Arcadi—1978:

A searing conscience, guilt, depression
now came upon his soul.
An ardent KGB official, he was much like Saul of old.
Yet, he longed to know more of the Messiah,
yes, He could make him whole.
Arcadi, like his predecessor, cried,
"Lord God, forgive my sin!
Dramatic changes—a heart of fire—
Now, others he would win!

10 CHRISTMAS IN RUSSIA

Freezing wind whistles shrilly around the tall buildings in Moscow. Minus sixty degrees Fahrenheit is not unusually cold during the winter months.

Warmly-clad people hurry along the icy streets, small clouds of white vapor escaping with each breath.

Long ribbons of gray smoke curl lazily from thousands of chimneys, disappearing gradually into the cold afternoon air.

Gently falling snow whirls and dances, then settles on the icy earth below.

Braving the severe wind and cold, streams of humanity climb onto the crowded buses. Work has been completed for the day and it is time to go to their homes to prepare for the joyous festivity ahead.

From the great Orthodox Cathedral, melodies portraying the wonderful Christmas message float across the chilled and frosty air. Pious, devout Russians, old and young alike, stand and kneel in the crowded interior of the beautiful old

church, praying silently as they light their candles and listen to the old Christmas story.

Yesterday, they had joined the great Orthodox procession, marching down the chilly streets of the great city. Then slowly, they followed their leader as he walked on ahead, the large replica of the cross of Jesus carried on their shoulders.

Meanwhile, Protestant believers scattered across the land are celebrating the birth of Jesus, their Savior, who left heaven's glory, taking upon Himself the form of a man to redeem lost humanity. Bright-eyed children, too, lisp their thank you's to Jesus who was the child born in a manger so long ago. Many themselves, had recently been babes in their own mother's arms.

Parents around the dinner table in the parlor at home have been faithful in telling and retelling the wonderful Christmas story to their youngsters. The children respond with wonder and joy, so grateful that Jesus loves them enough to care for them as individuals.

For Christians, Christmas is a time of joy and celebration. Caroling is common as children go from house to house in the country, while in the city, they visit the elderly and friends who offer them candy and other sweets.

Church Christmas concerts are carefully planned for months in advance. These include adults and children singing, reciting verses, and acting out Bible stories. Only a few hours are allowed by the Government for group rehearsals and the restrictions placed on children's involvement in religious activities. They all spend time at home rehearsing their parts and practicing alone or together as a group.

A Russian Christmas program is held right before New Year's Day, usually January 6 on our calendars, and lasts as long as two hours.

Christmas in Russia is a time when the Christians often call strangers on the phone during the holiday season, to explain the meaning of Christmas. Some, when called, cry and thank God that the caller cared enough to talk to them. Others become angry and curse and swear.

Parties are celebrated everywhere across the Soviet Union. Often believers, as many as twenty-five, gather for a period of meditation and prayer in someone's small apartment. If the police come to check on them, they say, "Oh, we are just celebrating the New Year!"

While Christians worship the Christ-child and celebrate His coming to earth as a baby, those Soviet citizens who do not know God have an excuse to drink Vodka or watch a special TV program. They are oblivious to the spiritual significance of the Christmas celebration, but observe the Nori god or the New Year. To offset the Christian celebrations, all the Christmas traditions have been transferred to the New Year.

Like some believers, most unbelievers celebrate by trimming a Christmas tree. While Christians are caroling or attending worship services, unbelievers watch TV programs, specially aired by the Soviet authorities during the Christmas season.

Jesus Christ, in their minds, is only a mythical character on the same par as Santa Claus or Grandfather Frost and his granddaughter, the Snow Maiden, who perform in public appearances. Then when the performances are over, the children receive decorated metal boxes overflowing with candy and fruits.

The New Year's observance is circled in red on most Soviet calendars as the most important holiday of the year. Companies throw elaborate parties for their workers, serving a smorgasbord of food and, of course, plenty of Vodka.

Festivities officially begin at 9 P.M., New Year's eve, but

Russians begin preparing for weeks ahead. Russian housewives stand in line at grocery stores for hours to make sure they have everything for a sumptuous feast. They cook foods such as caviar, fancy meats, and potato salad for their guests to eat.

After the meal, the party gathers around the TV to observe elaborate New Year's celebrations in Red Square. After a series of long speakers, all eyes look toward the clock in the Kremlin as it strikes the midnight hour, thus chiming in the New Year. The festivities, however, have just begun.

The Russians continue celebrating till dawn. Drinking is widespread, so they are given a holiday from work the next day to recover.

As the holidays end, Soviets return to their daily routine. Most have not heard the real meaning of Christmas and the wonderful message it brings. Without God, their hearts are empty.

But the message of Christendom rings clearly throughout the ages. Christmas is not about Grandfather Frost, but a risen Savior who loves not only the masses, but also each person as an individual. Only He can fill their empty hearts.

We must tell them that there is hope beyond the grave because Jesus came to earth to become man, then died on the cross to save lost humanity.

God's Intervention in Rovno, Ukraine

"Mom, I'm starved! Can we eat soon?"

"Yes, my dears. I'm hungry, too!" answered Esther.

They had just come from Venetsia and booked into a hotel in Rovno. Having roughed it so long, it was novel to have dinner in the dining room that night. Many of their meals were eaten in the van, in campgrounds, or sometimes in people's homes. Most times they preferred to do their own cooking in the van, however, because food in restaurants was often unreliable. The fat they consumed in one meal there was gastronomical. Slavs love the taste of extra lard or butter, but they didn't.

On this special occasion, they did decide to eat in the hotel dining room. A white tablecloth covered the small, square table, while a dainty bouquet of flowers stood in the center. The unusual cleanliness of the place made them feel like dining. The menu was in English and the native language, so that was helpful. It was not long until a waiter appeared at their table.

"I'd like the stroganoff," said Corinne. On another occasion they had sampled this meal, so felt quite safe in ordering.

Soon four steaming dishes of stroganoff were placed on the table and they began to eat.

Conversation was scarce around the table that night. First, because they were so hungry, and second, they were all weary—exhausted. Eagerly anticipating returning to their rooms for the night, though they savored every bite, they ate quickly.

They were so preoccupied with their thoughts, Esther was startled when a tall, robust gentleman came to their table. Smiling and extending his big hand, he addressed Gordon immediately.

"Are you Wasyl Balisky?" he asked.

Gordon looked shocked.

"Yes, that's my name," he answered hesitantly.

"I am Vonya (John), and have heard about you from relatives in Canada," he said. "I would like to speak with you alone. Could we step outside please?"

Looking into the face of the stranger, they wondered if he was a believer. Was he really a relative of someone in

Canada—or could this be a ploy? They weren't sure.

Wiping his mouth with his napkin, Gordon pushed his chair aside and followed the man outside.

Though they had questions, Charlene, Corinne, and Esther quietly finished their dinner and went upstairs to their rooms.

What does this stranger want? they wondered.

When Gordon did not return, they looked anxiously in the direction where the two men had disappeared. Could it be they were being observed by the KGB?

Time went by. They made preparations to retire, but Esther knew she couldn't sleep until her husband returned.

Finally, she heard a sound at the door. When opening it, she was relieved to see that he did not look troubled or afraid.

"Who is this man?" Esther quietly asked when Gordon walked into the room.

"His name is Vonya and he is a relative of our friends, the Skoworodkos, in Canada," he smiled. "He has very recently been to Canada, and returned home only last week. Perhaps you noticed his Western clothing?"

Esther had observed his Western tie and saw that his clothing was well coordinated.

They agreed this unique meeting in the heart of Ukraine was indeed a divine encounter. How could it be otherwise? They had been friends with Mike and Anita Skoworodko for many years—and now had met with one of their own family members in the USSR!

"Vonya," Gordon continued, "brings greetings from our friends." Incredible, but true, they realized their God works in mysterious ways.

Whispering into Esther's ear, in case their room was monitored, he continued, "Vonya brought a gift of 4,000 Canadian dollars from his family into Rovno. They told him to buy a car so he and his wife could get around more comfortably."

"Is it possible?" queried Esther.

"There are problems involved, certainly, but nothing is impossible," answered Gordon, his brow wrinkled in thought.

"It would be impossible for Vonya to buy the car himself, however," he continued. "Citizens, especially the Christians, are being watched very closely. Many do not make enough money on which to survive from day to day. If Vonya purchased a car worth a lot of money and paid cash for it, he would be questioned immediately. They would ask, 'How can an ordinary citizen have so much money to purchase a car?' He could be accused of stealing the money, or getting it illegally some way. Perhaps, they would even find a way of taking the cash from him.

"If I buy this car for Vonya and pay cash, Vonya could say a friend from the West bought it for him," concluded Gordon.

Now the big Russian was asking Gordon to buy the car for him. Could he please do this favor?

Gordon prayed for hours that night about Vonya's request. If he did buy the car, then he, himself, could find himself in a legal hassle. If he did not, their friend would be without an automobile. He would also disappoint the family in Canada.

"Please pray for me in this decision, Honey," said Gordon. "I am apprehensive about buying a car for Vonya, but I don't want to let him down, either."

Gordon, in thought, was quiet for hours after that. Putting a fleece out before God, he prayed, "If there is a 1978 Volvo, then, God, I will buy it for Vonya. If there is not, I don't want anything to do with it. Please give me wisdom, dear God."

The next day, the girls and Esther met Vonya's wife, Sonya, and their only son, Jan. They immediately felt a kinship as they talked together.

Vonya was anxious to go to the car dealer. Would he soon be driving a new car? He could hardly wait.

Immediately Gordon's eyes were tuned to the vehicles on the car lot. Was there a 1978 Volvo there?

He didn't see one. To make certain, he asked the dealer.

"No, we did have a car like that, but sold it yesterday," he answered.

Vonya's face fell. Did God not want him to have a car? Could he get into trouble if he did have a new, expensive model? There must be a reason, he knew.

"If this decision is not God's will, I don't want the car anyway," he reasoned. Gordon, heaving a sigh of relief, agreed.

But Vonya still had 4,000 dollars on his person. How could he spend it without causing suspicion? He and Sonya talked for a long time that night.

"I have an idea," Vonya brightened. "Because we are in debt financially, why don't we pay that off?"

"How?" asked his wife waiting with anticipation for the forth-coming answer.

"If Wasyl will help us, we could go to the Cashtan store and buy goods there, and then sell them to others at a profit. In turn, we could pay our debtors!"

Sonya smiled. Her husband always had an answer, it seemed.

Vonya and Sonya had been in debt for a long time. With no extra money coming in, though they worked hard, it was difficult to make ends meet. Until now, they'd had no idea how they could pay this large debt.

"Wasyl," he said the next day, "I have another favor to ask."

Now what? wondered Gordon.

His face shining like a light bulb, Vonya continued, "Could you go with my wife and I to the Cashtan store (tourist store) and purchase a number of articles for us with the Canadian dollars I have in my possession? I, in turn, will sell them at a profit, and will be able to pay my debtors!"

The citizens from the USSR are not allowed to buy in these stores. Cashtan outlets are strictly for tourists and they will only take currencies from other countries. The Russian ruble, really worth very little, cannot be used there.

The ordinary citizen must buy in stores for "the people" where there is little variety and poor quality. Then, wasting their precious time, they always must stand in long, endless queues. When they finally reach the other end of the line, very often, the item requested is not available. So they go home discouraged, and "do without." If someone from the West makes purchases for a citizen, as long as there is money to pay, it would appear that he was a rich tourist, enjoying the merchandise from their wonderful store.

"I would be happy to help!" said Gordon.

"I will meet you in the morning at the Cashtan store then," said a grateful Vonya.

"*Dasveedanya*!" smiled Sonya (Good-bye till then).

The couple were excited when they met at the store in the morning. At last, they had figured out a way to solve their indebtedness. Then there would be no more threats and calls demanding payment immediately. Stress alleviated, they could live more normal lives...if there is such a thing in Communist USSR.

Behind a clump of trees, very inconspicuously, Vonya handed Gordon a large amount of Canadian cash. Gordon, in turn, quickly put the money into his wallet. He had never had such a big, bulging wallet before. After a flat purse, this felt good!

It was interesting to see them choose lovely rugs, dishes, and clothing. They, of course, had never purchased such lavish items before. Sonya's eyes were bright, as carefully, together with her husband, they chose the best quality merchandise. Gordon, too, gave as much counsel and help as he could.

When they were finally done, he took the large roll of bills from his purse and paid for the purchases.

"What a rich tourist!" envied the Slavic sales clerks. "It must be wonderful to live in the West and have money like this!"

Store employees loaded the merchandise into the van. Gordon drove to where Vonya's rented vehicle stood. There the goods were transferred from one car to the other. The trunk, back seat, and even the front was packed with expensive articles like few Slavs had ever known!

Sonya and Vonya were so grateful, adequate words failed. At last they could come out from under the oppression and pressures of indebtedness! And later, we learned they did!

Sunday in Rovno

Sunday dawned clear and bright. Anticipating the Lord's day with special joy, they would minister in the church. Meeting with many Slavic believers would brighten their day.

Quickly, Gordon, Charlene, Corinne, and Esther dressed for church. Vonya and Sonya offered to transport them to the church they attended. It was, they knew from past experience, wise to take some other form of transportation other than their van when they met with believers. Their new Volkswagen camper bus, with its shiny new paint, attracted too much attention in a country where most vehicles are old and dirty.

Vonya's smile was broad and friendly as they stepped into the rented vehicle.

"*Dobry dzien*!" he said. "We are so happy to have the privilege of driving you to church."

"Thank you for taking us," Gordon answered.

Though they were crowded and cramped, they realized this was a good idea.

Skirting potholes on the bumpy road, swerving around other vehicles and pedestrians, finally they drove into the churchyard. Though there was a large crowd, not many automobiles were present. Most of the people cannot afford the high cost of owning a vehicle or paying for the gas, so they take advantage of city transportation. The city bus, a widely utilized vehicle in the USSR, is always crowded. Many times in the past, they, too, had stood holding onto the bars overhead, while the vehicle gyrated from side to side. The people, accustomed to crowded, unstable transportation, didn't seem to mind.

Esther and Sonya slipped scarves over their heads, and walked reverently into the congested building. Charlene and Corinne followed close behind. *How long will this service last?* silently the girls wondered. Sometimes they grew weary when they had to sit for hours. Because the language was foreign to them, the time became long, and shuffling in their seats, they often wished for green meadows and wide-open spaces—just somewhere to stretch their legs and run.

Everyone stared as they entered the house of worship and made their way to the front. Already Gordon was on the platform with other pastors.

Are they as curious about our way of life, as we are of theirs? Esther wondered. She knew they were.

This service was long. Following the same pattern wher-

ever they went in Russia, whether it was a large or small congregation, they could anticipate many sermons and a variety of musical numbers. On this particular morning, Esther was particularly moved as two soloists sang. The female, a high, lyric soprano, and the male, a resonant tenor, performed flawlessly. Though she didn't understand all the words, she was blessed by the sincerity that rang from their dedicated voices.

After the service was finally over, the girls slipped out the side door, as their parents stood in line to greet the people. Always warm and friendly, they made many friends.

Are they just curious, or are they friendly because we are from the West? they wondered.

A Dinner at Walter's House

A big Slav shook their hands, and he cordially invited them to his home for lunch.

"We would be delighted to join you," smiled Gordon.

This family too, they were informed, were relatives of their friends, the Filuks, from Canada. What a small world!

Walter and his wife, Katya, greeted them with genuine Christian grace, as they entered their small, frugal apartment.

Asking questions about their family in Canada, they absorbed the information like sponges. How they longed to see them again!

It was interesting to see their friends from the West smiling at them from photographs placed around the apartment. They, too, had visited Russia a year or so before. Incessantly, the family talked about the wonderful time they experienced together then.

Charlene and Corinne, Esther noticed, were communicating with the children.

"Do all these children belong to you?" she asked.

"Yes," smiled the proud mother. "All seven belong to us!"

Ranging in age from six months to twelve years, they were dressed simply but neatly, and were all well-behaved.

While the smaller ones peered from behind their mother's skirts, the older ones were interested in conversation. Doing the best they could in this foreign language, Charlene and Corinne used their skills. Gordon was proud to think his girls, though faltering, could communicate in his mother tongue.

And the children were having fun. It wasn't every day people from the West visited in their home!

"I have been gone for over a week," Walter said. "It is good to be back with my family again." He had a job that required his being away from home some of the time.

How could Katya handle these little ones all alone during his absence? Yet, she was not alone. God was with her when her husband was away.

Bringing up children anywhere is a huge responsibility, and especially so in the USSR where parents are watched at all times.

Esther knew Katya was no older than herself, but noticed her hands were calloused and work worn. Several missing teeth added to the appearance of her wrinkled face. On her head, she wore the traditional *Babushka*, and her clothing was drab and unstylish. But radiating an inward beauty, her countenance shone with the knowledge of her faith in Christ.

Now, the youngest children clamored for their father's attention. Holding them on his knees, he continued, "Yes, we teach all our children about a heavenly Father who loves them," he said. "It is true that this is illegal here in our country because the government wants every child. Regardless, we know it is necessary to teach our families at home, so we read the Bible and pray with them every day. Perhaps, if our family in Canada had not given us a Bible, we would not even own the precious Word of God. Most don't," he added. "Both my wife and I endeavor to instill into their impressionable minds that no matter what happens, they must be true to Christ. They have learned however, at an early age, that it is difficult to be a born-again believer in a country where Jesus Christ is not honored."

Ruffling his youngest boy's hair, he continued, "If the authorities find out we are giving religious instruction in the home, they consider it propaganda and make moves to stop it."

Katya silently wiped her eyes with the big apron she wore, and added, "There is always a danger they will try to take the children from us and put them in a state home where they will be taught to be atheists!"

Esther and Gordon learned that in the Soviet Union, children are separated from their parents whenever a home is judged to be "unfit." The most common reasons are:

1. sanity of the parents
2. the practice of the Christian life
3. the teaching of Christian principles in the home.

One Christian mother wrote, "I am a mother, and as a mother, I also want salvation for my children. I want them to turn to Christ, to strongly believe in and love Him. He is the only source of salvation and joy! I do not want them to be condemned on the day Christ returns. But what mother does not want to shield her infants from degradation and insults? These experiences cannot be escaped if one is a believer—either by me or by them—if they want to follow the Lord."

An atheistic Communist Youth Group – (Young Pioneers)

Katya told about a Christian mother in the city of Kursk, whose two young children, ages four years and eighteen months, were cruelly taken away from her by a court order. Separated from their mother by many kilometers, today these little ones are in a state-owned children's home.

"Still others are threatened," said Katya. "The authorities say, 'If you give up God and verify this by writing it on paper, we will leave you and your children alone. They can stay with you and we will even help you financially.'

"Many believers," said Walter, "are mistreated and ridiculed in school. Forced to attend atheistic club meetings, they often cry from beatings received at school from other students or their teacher. Christians pray daily that their children will not be taken away from them."

Lovingly looking at her brood, the tears fell down the mother's weathered face.

Though the family was keenly aware of this, they fearlessly instructed their children on how to live the Christian life—no matter what the cost.

Walter hugged his youngest child warmly. There was tranquility and happiness evident in that little home. They all noticed it. How could they have such joy when they realized their little ones could be taken away from them? Only Christ was their answer. Daily they clung to Him.

Katya, scurrying into the kitchen, served a beautiful meal. Had she saved the best for them? They knew she had. Bringing to the table one dish after another of delicious Russian cuisine, Charlene whispered to her mother, "When will she stop?" Only the hostess had the answer.

Soon it was time to leave. Putting her arm around Katya, Esther promised she would pray for them all. Gratefully smiling, she pressed Esther's hand.

After ministering in another service that night, their girls longed to go back to the hotel and rest. The day had been long. They were tired. Esther, too, felt the pressures of the day close in on her. At night, closing her eyes, she saw troubled, harassed people who needed courage in the midst of uncertainty and anguish. Praying for them, finally she drifted into a restless sleep.

With her girls nearby, she thanked God daily for freedom to worship unmolested in the great United States of America. How could they be so blessed?

Farewell

The next day they were scheduled to meet Vonya and Sonya at the border town of Lvov before crossing into another country.

Knowing the time had come to say good-bye, Sonya covered her face with her hands and began to weep. Standing in a circle, they prayed for God's hand of protection to be on them daily. They asked that God's love encircle them every day.

Sonya and Vonya waved as long as they could see their van driving out of their sight.

"Dad, why did Sonya cry before we left?" asked Corinne.

"She has an intense longing to live in freedom like others of her family in the West. Harassed for so many years, they are tired of the socialist system which enslaves them. They were reluctant to see us go. I think they feel the confinement more after someone from the West has visited and gone."

"We are so fortunate, Dad," sighed Charlene.

Seeing the concern in her eyes, Gordon reached over and took his eldest daughter's hand. "Yes, we need to thank God every day," he concluded soberly.

Driving out of the dusty, dirty town of Lvov, it soon disappeared in the foggy distance.

With her head on the back of the seat, the verses in Numbers 6:24-26, which had been Esther's father's blessing to her and Gordon on their wedding day, came to mind. As a prayer and benediction, she quoted them on behalf of all the believers in that restless, godless society:

> *The Lord bless thee, and keep thee: The Lord make his face shine upon thee, and be gracious unto thee: The Lord lift up his countenance upon thee, and give thee peace.*

Together, they prayed for peace in the midst of this crooked and perverse society among whom God's children shine as lights in a dark world.

11 THE VINS ENCOUNTER

During their trip in Russia, they looked with anticipation to meeting the Vins family again. Recalling their last visit in 1975, they prayed, long before entering the country, that the Lord would make it possible.

As they entered the ancient city of Kiev, it was raining heavily again. *Does it always have to rain when we come here?* silently Esther questioned.

They had never seem it rain so heavy. Coming down in a mighty deluge, it overflowed the streets and sidewalks. Everywhere people ran for shelter, under the awnings or closest buildings. Exclaiming in awe, they watched the mighty cloudburst unleash it's power.

In a hurry to arrive at their campground, have dinner, and go to bed, they kept on driving while all other traffic had stopped.

"Look what's ahead!" exclaimed Gordon in disbelief.

The main street was totally submerged in water. They didn't know how deep it was, but other cars had moved to higher ground where they were parked until the rain stopped.

Changing into low gear, Gordon stepped on the gas, and the van moved forward. The water was deeper than anticipated, but there was no stopping now. The back wheels began to spin, but the front ones strongly plowed through the murky water and mud, splashing on the windows of the van. It was almost impossible to see ahead, though their windshield wipers were doing a noble job. Thanking God for a vehicle with fuel injection, they drove on. At last they reached higher ground. The worst was past. Later they were told the water was about a meter deep. It had even crept into the van, soaking the rug.

In their cabin that night, they listened to the rain as it pounded on the roof. Secretly Esther hoped it would stop soon.

"Guess what?" Gordon said into the darkness. "I have been praying for rain for a long time!"

"What?" said Esther. "Please!"

"Because of the rain, it will be safer to visit with the Vins without being watched so closely. I will keep praying during the days we are in Kiev," he continued.

Though she had hoped for sunshine, Esther understood.

Prayerful Visit

Arrangements were made to meet Nadezda Vins and her small son, Alexander, in a park nearby. So the next day, in the rain, Esther and Gordon looked for them. It was a relief when they saw the young woman and her son walking out of the park toward them. Smiling graciously, extending her hand, she said, "Welcome! It is nice to have you back with us again!"

Talking softly so as not to attract attention, they walked toward her house.

After greeting white-haired Grandma Vins, and Georgi and Nadezda's three girls, Natasha, Jane, and Elisa, they began to talk.

The minutes on the clock ticked by as the girls showed them photograph albums, explaining the story behind each picture. There were pictures of Elisa's youth group from church who were willing to suffer for Christ's sake, though it meant imprisonment.

"We go out to different places with instruments," she said, "and play for people on the streets. Then we witness to them about our faith in Jesus Christ."

"Are you afraid?" Esther asked, finding it hard to believe they could actually do this in a Communist country.

With a small smile and a nod of her golden head, Elisa replied that she really was not afraid.

"We have been imprisoned many times, but are legally too young to be kept there, so they must let us go. Prison does not keep us from witnessing and telling others about our love for Jesus. After an overnight stay in custody, we are released and warned not to talk about Christ again. But without fear, we go out again the next day to do the same."

They knew that Peter Vins, their grandfather, died in a far off Siberian prison in 1947. A few years later, Lydia (Grandma) Vins, his wife, was imprisoned for her stand for Christ. This happened repeatedly because she circulated a small paper for believers in prison. This, of course, enraged the officials. Threatening her, they warned her again and again to stop. But when she wouldn't, they took her to prison. Again they allowed her to go home, with strong words of warning to stop all involvement with the prisoners. It was on her heart. She couldn't stop!

Each time she was released, she never knew when they would come for her again. In fact, the entire household never knew when the police would search their home. They always did so without warning. Ransacking the house, they took everything of value. But Jesus meant more to them than possessions.

Georgi Vins, the children's father, was in prison because of his stand for Jesus. Peter Junior, their twenty-three-year-old son was there, too. Would he die like his grandfather? They knew he was willing.

"His absence, as well as his father's, is very evident at home. It is difficult to have loved ones torn away. The KGB has harassed us for generations. Will it ever end?" sighed her friend.

With the rain pounding against the windows, they sat beside the table. Nadezda was gracious to prepare Russian *holidettes*, tomato salad, and fresh strawberries and cream. Gordon carefully left a donation under his plate.

Before their departure, eyes wet with tears, they stood in a small circle, holding hands while praying for Georgi and Peter. They also prayed for other brothers and sisters who were suffering the same fate. Wasn't their God always with them? They knew He was.

Georgi smiled at them from a picture on the wall.

"He is always thought of and remembered by a heavenly Father who is love, and though He allows His children to go through deep times of testing, He has a reason. Who are we to question Almighty God?" added Nadezda, looking at her husband's picture.

Filled with mixed emotions, they walked out the door. Grateful to live in the United States of America where they were free to worship, the burden to pray for those who are not so blessed was heavy upon them.

Carefully looking around, they knew there was no one following them because the rain was heavy and visibility poor.

"Yes, Gordon, you were right. The rain has been a blessing," agreed his wife.

God knew exactly when the cloudburst was needed. He was answering Gordon's prayer.

Finding it difficult to sleep that night, Esther struggled to get comfortable on the lumpy, damp cot. Eventually, after talking to God, she went to sleep.

Sunday Worship

A miracle! In the morning, the sun was shining into the dirty windows of their cabin. It was Sunday.

"Time to get up!" Esther called, looking over at her husband's cot. "It's time to get ready for church!"

Sleepily, he crawled out of his lumpy cot and went to the bathroom to wash and shave.

It was sheer pleasure to step out of the cool, damp cabin and feel the warmth of sunshine.

Making their way to the bus stop, instead of taking the van, they hoped to meet Nadezda again.

"Good morning!" she smiled when she saw them.

The bus was crowded and swaying to and fro as they held onto the bars overhead. Finally, after many stops, it was time to disembark. It was only a short distance to walk to the church where Georgi Vins was once one of the pastors.

It was difficult to find a seat because the church was packed. Gordon and Esther were graciously invited to sit on the platform with the other pastors, while Nadezda and Alexander finally found a place in the audience.

Observing the crowd from this vantage point, Esther was moved to see them worship the One for whom they were willing to die.

"Let us pray," said the pastor.

But where could they kneel? Every inch of space seemed to be taken. But the crowd, carefully making room, in close proximity, knelt together. It was an honor to worship with people who loved the Lord with body, mind, and soul. Their hearts beat as one while they talked to God.

Walking to the old piano, Gordon and Esther sang one song after another. The Russians, though they did not understand the English words, nodded their heads and smiled.

"*Sposeebo*! *Sposeebo*!" they cried.

After many choir numbers which consisted of a dozen verses each, and numerous messages and announcements, they walked out of the crowded church into the brilliance of God's sunshine. Taking several long, deep breathes, the air was fresh and invigorating.

Waiting for Gordon, Esther and Nadezda sat on a bench in the church courtyard, in the bright sunshine. When he finally arrived, they said good-bye, hoping to see each other again in the evening service.

The pastor's wife accompanied them in a taxi on the way to her house. Opening her purse, she handed Gordon a tape cassette.

"We enjoyed having an astronaut with us recently. He, his wife, and another brother from the West were guests in our church."

Gordon was interested immediately. "Was the astronaut Colonel Irwin? Was his friend Don Best?"

"Why, yes," she smiled. "Do you know them?"

"We were aware they were taking a trip to Russia and have been praying for God's safety and blessing to be on them while in the USSR."

"Would you like to hear the astronaut speak?" she asked the taxicab driver.

He mumbled an inaudible okay, but it seemed incredible to him that an astronaut from the U.S.A. was in Russia speaking in a church. How could that be? To him it was conceivable that perhaps he would meet with the high officials of the Communist party—but in a church? That was ridiculous! As far as he knew all astronauts were atheists. They did not believe in the God who, the Christians proclaimed, made the sun, moon, and stars. Of course anyone educated or refined knew that this was fantasy. Only uneducated ignorant people believed that.

"Well?" said the pastor's wife. She was not giving up easily. "Do you want to hear or not?"

Interested, but reluctant, he put the tape into his cassette player. The voice of the astronaut immediately filled the car. Speaking via an interpreter, he told about his love for Christ and invited others who did not know Him personally to believe in Him as the God of the universe.

"I could sense the power and majesty of the Almighty as I walked on the moon!" he emphasized.

The taxi driver listened. Could this really be? Yes, he would like to hear more.

The pastor's wife had taken a risk in playing this religious tape for the taxicab driver. What if he decided to report her to the authorities? It would not be difficult, but she was willing to pay the price as long as an unbeliever heard the words of life.

Turning into a small lane, the driver informed them they had arrived at their destination.

"*Sposeebo*," they said. Eagerly he took the cash and tip offered him.

After walking up many flights of stairs, finally they reached the pastor's home.

Putting on a snowy white apron, she prepared a beautiful

lunch. Three Russian pastors who had been in prison for their faith graced the simple home that day. Their eyes revealed deep suffering, but they would go to prison again rather than renounce Christ. There was no question about that!

Earlier in church they had noticed the left coat sleeve hanging loose on the arm of one of the pastors. Soberly they learned he had lost that arm and part of his eyesight through persecution in prison.

They were awed when he spoke fearlessly that morning. Perhaps there were informers in the audience? Could he go to prison again? Would he be released next time?

No cost is too great when one has a love for Jesus such as this.

The meal was satisfying and hot. *Borscht*, dessert, and tea satisfied their appetites.

The afternoon fled quickly as they shared, ate, prayed, and talked. It was time for evening service to begin. They had to leave.

When they arrived, the choir was already singing. Once more the church was crowded and humid. The pastor's wife and Esther slipped scarves on their heads and quickly found a place to sit in the choir loft.

Where was Nadezda? Esther quickly scanned the audience. When their eyes met, they smiled and individually vowed to talk afterwards.

The service went on and on. After numerous choir numbers, messages, and several songs by the Baliskys, they were dismissed. But this was not the end. A youth meeting following the service would last for hours. Could they sit that long?

While Nadezda and Esther sat in the back of the church, the enthusiastic young people Elisa had been talking about, sang and played instruments.

When Gordon was introduced to speak to them in their mother tongue, there was a hush. Yes, they would like to hear what this uncle from the West had to say.

After he had spoken for some time, a hand went up. A young man asked, "Why is it that people think America is so much better than the Soviet Republic of Russia?"

Gordon thought for a moment and said, "When I was a little boy, I often watched my Ukrainian grandfather milk cows. One day he said to me, 'Gordon, cows are really very much like people.'

"'How can they be like people, Grandfather?' I asked. 'Cows have four legs and a long tail. They have a big face and two ears that are so much bigger than ours. I really don't understand how they can be like people.'

"Grandfather nodded his wise old head and said, 'Yes, Son, they are very much like people. When a cow has eaten the fresh green grass in the pasture, she is often not content to stay where she is. Instead she goes over to the fence and kneels down on two legs. Then she puts her head through the wires of the fence and eats the green grass on the other side. It would be so much easier for her to stay in her own pasture, but she does not. You see, Gordon, so it is with people. They have their own country in which to live and grow, and they are not satisfied, so they seek greener pastures!'

"'So,' Gordon said, 'in answer to your question, young man, people say America is better than Russia because they are beginning to put their heads under the fence. They are not satisfied with their own situation. Far away pastures always look greener,'" he concluded.

Satisfied, the young man settled in his chair.

A small *Baba* (grandmother) who watched Esther closely all day, sat close to her during the long youth service. Though their cultures were vastly different and there was a

language barrier between them, they both knew they were a part of the family of God. Carefully she took a piece of sausage wrapped in a clean towel out of her handbag, and put it into Esther's hand. No, Esther had no need for the sausage, and probably could not eat it, but it was a gesture done in love. She was reminded of the widow's mite—"she did cast in all that she had."[1]

"*Sposeebo*," she whispered, putting her arm around the *Baba*. A toothless smile revealed the woman was pleased.

The youth service was finally over at 10:30. Stumbling into bed that night, Esther wondered when she had been so weary.

Gifts of Love for Nadezda

Next morning they woke later than usual. The sunshine gone, the sky was overcast and dark, while rain hammered on the roof.

"Not again!" thought Esther.

Gordon woke up, stretched, yawned, and said, "I'm so glad it's raining again! God does answer prayer. Today, we are going shopping with the Vins and must exercise a great deal of caution. The rain always helps."

Several friends from England had sent money for Nadezda and her family. If she took the cash as a gift, the authorities would probably take it away and question her. If it was spent on necessary items, by someone from the West, it would be different. She decided on the latter.

There are tourist stores or Cashtans in Russia as well as stores where the ordinary people shop. Nadezda was not allowed to shop in the tourist stores which had all the quality clothing. However, if they went with her and bought the merchandise, she could come and choose what she needed. This plan seemed to be a good one.

"Yes, we all need clothing," she smiled, excitement showing in her wan face.

THE PEOPLE'S STORES

These places were usually very crowded while people stood in line for hours. When a customer finally arrived at the counter, the store may or may not have the merchandise for which she was looking. If they did, she then went to stand in another line where she payed for her goods. Then she came back with the slip to prove she had paid, and stood in line again. When she reached the counter a second time, she presented the receipt of purchase and received what she came for—hours previously.

The shops were nearly bare and what they carried was expensive. An average workman made 100 rubles a month (about $150 U.S.). Regardless of the size of his family, which was often large, the money must stretch for their many needs.

But they would not shop there today.

Once in the crowded tourist Cashtan, Nadezda could not hide her delight. "Natasha, do you think these boots will fit Jane? She gets so cold in the winter and has no warm clothing. What about this umbrella for Elisa? I think this warm scarf would be perfect for Georgi, don't you?"

One item after another was taken off the shelves. Soon there was an array of blouses, coats, shoes, umbrellas, socks, and more, piled high on the counter. The sales clerks, naturally very curious, wondered what was going on. Was it possible this woman had enough money to pay for everything?

At the end of a long shopping day, Nadezda's eyes were moist as she exclaimed, "This only happens once in a lifetime. How grateful I am! How grateful we all are!"

After Gordon paid for the merchandise, carrying bulging packages, they left the store.

Gordon and Esther knew when Georgi was taken to

prison, the family was in dire need. How could the mother clothe her family for the cold winter ahead? Often at night, when everyone else was asleep, Nadezda prayed, asking God to show her what to do. Now He had!

The cool weather and busy shopping day made them all as hungry as young cubs. They decided to take the family home and then go to the hotel dining room near their camping grounds for dinner.

Nadezda, however, had other plans. Without their knowledge, she had prepared a large dinner earlier in the day. "Please come to our house and eat with us. Grandma is expecting you!"

They tried to politely decline, but because they insisted, Gordon and Esther reluctantly went inside. How could they say no?

The beautiful cauliflower and egg dish plus other Russian foods were soon on the table.

"Mmm, that smells good," Esther quietly nudged her husband.

Alexander, their youngest child, who had been visiting an aunt in the country, was home again. Sitting across the table, they saw his large eyes follow every move they made. *Who are these people anyway?* he wondered.

Esther smiled at him and, with several front teeth missing, shyly he smiled back.

Later, Gordon took the slight child on his knee and asked, "Alexander, what do you want to be when you grow up?"

With large, liquid eyes, he looked up at him and replied, "I will be a prisoner just like my daddy when I grow big!"

The room was hushed. No one said anything. What could one say? This child knew the agony of being present when the police took his grandma, father, and brother away. Silent and helpless, he had watched them ransack his home.

Someday they would get him, too.

The big clock on the wall chimed the hour. It was time to go.

"But wait!" said Grandma Vins. "I was not in church on Sunday to hear you sing. Please, come upstairs where there is a piano. I will record the music so we can hear you sing in our darkest hours."

Though it was getting late, how could they deny her this small request?

Holding tightly to the shaky banister, Grandma slowly made her way up the long stairs. Her legs and feet swollen and bones aching with rheumatism, finally, out of breath, she took the last step.

From this vantage point, they listened while the rain pounded loudly on the peaked roof. Looking out the tiny window, the night was dark. But inside, they felt the warm glow of friendship.

Esther went to the old piano. As her fingers slid slowly over the yellowed ivory keys, the words of the twenty-third Psalm soon reverberated to the four corners of the attic

The Lord's my Shepherd, I'll not want;
He makes me down to lie
In pastures green; He leadeth me
The quiet waters by.

Yea, though I walk thru death's dark vale,
Yet will I fear no ill;
For Thou art with me, and Thy rod
And staff me comfort still.

Goodness and mercy all my life
Shall surely follow me;
And in God's house forevermore
My dwelling place shall be.

Then, gathered in a circle, they clasped hands and prayed for believers who were suffering in prison—even at that moment—for their faith in Christ.

Esther squeezed Nadezda's work-worn hand.

Tears filled her eyes. "You don't know what this means to us! *Sposeebo*! *Sposeebo*!"

Grandma said, "Amen!" as she clutched the precious tape in her hand.

Another New Day

Looking over at Gordon's cot, Esther knew he was still sleeping. Silently the sleeping bag rose and fell as he breathed deeply.

Rain was still pounding on the roof and windows. Esther wondered when it would stop. Was it always raining in this country? She began to think so.

The sky, dark and foreboding, looked angrier than yesterday. Snuggling down in her sleeping bag again, she was not interested in facing another day at that point. The weather had grown colder and the feel of fall was in the air. Soon she slept. Later they would face this new day together.

It seemed only minutes later, when she felt Gordon shaking her.

"Hey, Honey, are you going to sleep all day?" She had to get up. They still had money to buy other valuable items for the Vins family.

"Let's hurry and have breakfast," urged Gordon. "It is almost time to pick up the Vins family again."

Taking day-old bread from the plastic in which it was wrapped, they began their breakfast. Cold sausage and hot tea added to the plain meal.

Nadezda and her family were delighted to see them again. "Did you sleep well? Would you come to the house later to talk to Grandma?"

So after a few more necessary purchases, they made their way to their home.

Grandma's eyes filled with tears when she saw them coming. "Yes, we are so lonely," she said wiping those tears with a corner of her big apron. "Many come to visit us, but they stay only a short time and are soon gone again. I think they are afraid to stay too long, in case they, or we, are being watched. We love your fellowship. Thank you for coming to see us. Thank you for staying longer and not expressing fear, but love."

Nadezda had picked up her mail earlier in the day. Taking a letter out of her pocket, her face lit up as she announced, "Oh, I heard from Georgi today! He can write once a month to a different family member. This month it was my turn!"

Putting her glasses on, carefully she began to read:

My dearest,
I love Jesus just as much today as I ever did.
Yes, thank you, I am feeling better now than I was a few months ago. That is good! Your prayers are so necessary!

Greeting each member of the family, he assured them of his love and prayers.

It was a letter of hope, as from prison, he tried to encourage his hurting loved ones.

Putting the precious message back into her pocket, she tried to smile. "It is wonderful to hear from Georgi!" she said.

The clock chimed again. It was time to go.

"But wait!" admonished Grandma Vins. "Dear ones," she said, "I am very happy you have come to us. It is not an accident. I feel God has sent you here. These are times when

we are so lonely, but your coming has brought warmth and encouragement to our spirits. It has also made me think of the days when I was young. When my husband asked me to marry him, he said, 'If you marry me, Lydia, you will die in the mud in Siberia. You will suffer persecution for following Christ along with me.' But regardless of this warning, I said yes to his proposal. Part of this statement has come true for my husband. My son and grandson are in prison as well.

"I know God loves and cares for us, but there are times when our spirits become like a desert—so very cold and lonely. Your coming has been in God's divine timing, and not in vain. We are expecting harder times in the future, and times of warmth and blessing such as this prepare us for those days ahead...."

The suggestion to take Alexander to the zoo the next day was greeted with enthusiasm. Regardless of weather conditions, they planned to go. Hugging the young child, they saw his eyes shining for the first time since their arrival. Alexander must not be disappointed again!

Saying good night, they walked toward their van which was carefully concealed under a grove of trees some distance away. They had been warmed by Grandma Vin's talk and would always remember.

The Zoo

"Would you believe it if I told you the sun is shining?" smiled Gordon the next morning.

"Not really," answered his wife, "not until I go to the window and see for myself!"

A hazy sun shone faintly through the clouds. *Will it grow brighter later in the day? Or is Gordon still praying for rain in order to protect the Vins family and their guests from the KGB?* she wondered.

A Divine Encounter in Kiev, 1976. Left to right: Corinne, Charlene, Nadezda, Alexander, Esther.

Later, an excited little boy and his mother emerged from the trees in the park where they had planned to meet them.

He had never had a ride in a big, new van, and his eyes danced with excitement. Piling coats for height in the front seat, so he could look out, the child sat with his uncle from the West. Who could wish for more?

Before they arrived at the zoo, they stopped for lunch. Alexander was too excited to eat.

"We're going to the zoo!" he cried. "We're going to the zoo!"

"Would you like another surprise?" asked Gordon.

"I can't guess, Uncle. What is it?" Jumping on one leg then the other, he waved his arms in the air.

Stopping at the Cashtan, Gordon took him into the

store. "Now, what kind of toy would you like?" asked the uncle while taking him into a world of fantasy.

Pointing to a small truck, he knew this is what he wanted. In a moment, he was walking back to the van, with a package clutched tightly in his hand.

Waving it in the air, he cried, "See what I have, Mama? The uncle from the West bought it for me!"

When eventually they arrived at the zoo, they saw that by western standards it was primitive. However, to the little boy, it was a little piece of heaven.

Gordon, lifting Alexander high on his shoulders, felt the rigid little body relax. He could see everything from here!

Suddenly growing rigid and serious again, he said, "Mother, do snakes bite?"

"Why, yes, Alexander, they do," she replied.

"Well then, I would like them to bite the men who took my daddy to prison," he said.

They were not surprised when he asked to see the snakes. He frequently said, "Mother, are the snakes here somewhere?"

"We will see them soon, Son."

When they arrived at the reptile house, the boy looked long and hard. Yes, he would like the biggest one to bite the men who took Peter and Daddy.

His busy mind relaxed when they bought ice cream. What a treat for a little boy! Licking it slowly so it would last longer, he savored every bite.

The sun began to set behind the clouds. Alexander yawned. Esther was tired. It was time to take the family home and go back to the campground.

Carrying the sleepy child into the house a short time later, they were satisfied that he was content.

Then after a prayer time together, quietly everyone

walked to the van to say good-bye. The ritual of kissing three times, on one cheek, then the other, and on the lips, was over. In the darkness they embraced. It had been a wonderful time of blessing. No one would ever forget!

Nadezda, Grandma Vins, and her children silently turned and walked back toward their house in the pouring rain.

Would they see them again?

Silent and lost in thought, Gordon and Esther drove back to the campground.

The Recital

Back in Germany, the evening of the piano recital had finally arrived. The girls carefully put on long dresses for the occasion, as they felt their hearts beat with trepidation. Many hours of practice had gone into Mozart and Beethoven in order to perform that night.

The room was filled with parents, teachers, and young people when the Baliskys arrived.

"I'm nervous," said Charlene, tightly clutching the music book containing "The Moonlight Sonata."

"Me, too," from Corinne when she saw the crowded room.

Sitting in the front, Esther silently prayed for her girls. One by one, palms perspiring and hearts pounding, the young people played their selections. Jolene Enns, who had patiently taught these students throughout the year, fervently hoped they would do well. She had done her job. Would they do theirs? Conscientious and hard-working, she faithfully sought for excellence in each student.

Now who was next? Glancing at her roster, she smiled.

"Charlene Balisky has chosen "The Moonlight Sonata" for her musical selection.

Esther watched as her daughter played. Nervous prior to performing, now her fingers slid smoothly over the ivory keys as Beethoven's music mesmerized the audience.

Corinne, quietly taking her place on the piano bench, was next. Fingers wet with perspiration, she, too, made her parents proud. The girls had done their best. Some had faltered or missed a note, but they always got back on the right track again.

Jolene smiled heartily, commending her students, relieved that the recital was over.

12 PERSONAL HYGIENE IN RUSSIA

They had been on the road in Russia for days, while the hot sun sent its torrid rays into the dusty interior of their Volkswagen camper bus. Wiping the perspiration from her face and pushing back damp, stray hair, Esther took a deep breath. It seemed there was no fresh air to breath—only humid, sticky, heavy, smog. Diesel smoke, belching out from the big trucks on the pot-holed road, stung in her nostrils.

Gordon's shirt was soaked, while Charlene complained that her blouse was clinging to her.

"We will need a good shower tonight," she sighed.

But where would they find a shower or bath with which to wash off the dirt and grime that covered them? Their hair, damp and thick with dust and dirt particles, was difficult to comb out. Corinne, whose head had always been sensitive, cried out when Esther tried to brush it.

Yes, they all needed a shower.

Finally, near morning, they drove into a primitive campground. Yawning, they stepped out of their bus. Gordon stretching his weary body, heaved a sigh of relief. They were finally here!

"I don't want to go to bed feeling this dirty," he said.

"You all settle in and I will find a shower and privy."

Realizing the sheets on the rough cots inside the cabin were unwashed, they stripped them and put their own sleeping bags on top.

"There's a shower nearby," called Gordon, coming into the cabin.

"Esther, why don't you and the girls go first?"

Slipping damp, gray towels over their shoulders, they headed for the shower—or at least what they thought was a shower.

Stepping into the stall, Esther left her shoes on. The floor was green with algae and slime. Everywhere, the place reeked of bathroom stench, which by now had become familiar to them.

Turning on the water, she let it run. Surely there must be some hot water? But there wasn't.

"Mom, there's no hot water!"

"We will have to wash in cold," she sighed.

"Oh no! They had all forgotten to take the shampoo—and their hair was thick with grime."

"Did you bring shampoo?" called Charlene.

"No," shouted Corinne from her stall, "did you?"

"Mom, we have no shampoo!"

"I'm not going back to the bus now!" Esther said. "Let's just use soap!"

Looking on the floor, she saw green, lye soap lying in a moldy corner of the shower. Grateful for clean, white hand soap purchased while in Germany, she decided to use that.

The water ran and ran…but it remained cold.

Stepping under the flow, Charlene gasped.

"This is so cold!" she shivered.

"Just take a deep breath and wash your hair," instructed her mother.

Gasping, they all washed. Never had cold water seemed so devastatingly cold before.

Heaving a sigh of relief, they stepped out of the shower, their skin tingling with cold. At least they felt refreshed.

It seemed their heads had just hit the pillow, when loud, heavy music filled the campground. It was morning! Had they really slept? How could it be daylight so soon?

Impossible to sleep, exhausted, they climbed out of their hard cots.

"I have to go to the bathroom," said Esther.

The girls hugged their beds a little longer, while Gordon went to the camp offices.

When they arrived last night, they decided to use "John Paul," their faithful chamberpot. The bathrooms in camp grounds were so unsanitary sometimes, they preferred to use their own primitive facilities.

Now, with the family in the cabin, there was really no privacy. Esther decided to go out and find the toilets.

Zipping up her housecoat, she grabbed her soiled towel, and headed toward the aroma—yes, that familiar smell that graces every bathroom in Eastern Europe and Russia. It didn't take long for her nose to tell her where it was.

But what was this? Opening the door, she saw a long hallway. Every few feet there was a hole in the floor. With no walls or doors between them, women of all ages, crouching in a long line, relieved themselves.

"How can I go here?" cried Esther. "There is absolutely no privacy! I can see everyone straining...I can't do it!" she concluded.

But she had to go! Now!

Undoing the zipper on her black one-piece housecoat, she followed the example of all the other women.

Staring at her, they wondered what this woman from the West was doing in such a filthy place. Esther wondered, too. How could she bear to be so humiliated?

While they stared, her tears flowed freely. Longing for her clean, white bathroom at home, she allowed the tears to course down her cheeks.

Quickly zipping her housecoat, she washed her face in icy cold water. Her towel reeked of coal dust and diesel fuel. Hair that was washed only hours ago with hand soap, was still damp, coarse, and unmanageable. Quickly she tried to straighten it with her hairbrush. Kinky and thick, it stuck to her head.

Opening the door to the small, dark cabin, she saw her girls were ready to go through their morning ritual.

"I think it would be better if you used John Paul and washed in the trailer," she encouraged.

It proved to be a good idea.

Finally, after they were all groomed, it was time for breakfast. There was no café, and if there had been, the food, they knew, would be comparable to the atmosphere.

It would be better to rummage through their messy bus, find the small refrigerator, and something to eat.

Climbing over the suitcases and items purchased in Russia, Charlene opened the icebox. Cold, greasy Russian *kielbasa*, and day-old bread came out first. Bottled water was next.

Thirsty, Corinne was ready to drink, when she cried, "Hey, there's something in here! What's this, Dad?"

Looking closely, they saw mosquito or fly wings and other parts of the hapless creature floating around. How could they drink this? Their water from Germany was all gone. Now what would they do?

Silently, while eating the cold, unsavory meal, they longed for home. Even Gordon, who was usually talkative, was meditative.

I will find a good restaurant when we get to the city, and treat my family, he promised himself. That thought comforted him a little, as he took his last bite of sausage.

A BATHROOM IN KIEV

The zoo they visited in Kiev was not interesting. Animals, sloshing around in their own excrement, were locked up in dirty, fenced cages. Reeking of a variety of odors, the air was stale and hot.

One of their girls excused herself. She needed to find a bathroom. But what kind of a private facility could she find in the zoo?

Eventually, the odor to which they had become accustomed, greeted her. Holding her breath, she stepped inside the small, outdoor, wooden building. She couldn't stand to be in there long, so decided to hurry and do what she came for.

But how could she? Looking at the place where there should have been a hole, she saw to her horror, the feces were piled high over it. There was no place to go!

Somehow she found a way. But the degradation of it all made her feel sick.

Unlocking the door, she pushed, thankful for some fresh air soon. Her lungs were bursting with something they had put into the toilet to take out the odor. It hadn't worked—obviously.

She pushed again. The door wouldn't open. Now what?

"I want out of here!" she cried.

She pushed harder.... No response.

"Dad! Mom! Open the door!" she called, thinking perhaps they were nearby. But they were not. Breathing heavily, she pounded harder.

Suddenly the door swung open on its rusty hinges. Almost falling out, she hung onto the side of the old building. Recovering her balance and her dignity, quickly she walked away.

Had someone locked the door from the outside? She would never know. What really mattered now, she was free!

JOHN PAUL

What would they do without John Paul? Esther couldn't remember who had given their chamber pot that dignified name, but it had stuck.

All of them preferred to use this pot or the confines of the woods in Russia, rather than the odorous, deplorable toilets there.

Finding a place to empty him after use, carefully they rinsed John Paul in clean, running water. Then he was ready for occupancy once more.

They had been vacationing in Venice. John Paul was helpful during that time, as well. Instead of going out to the toilets in the campground, they preferred to make use of their little pot.

At the end of the vacation, carefully maneuvering their trailer, Gordon drove the car out of the campground. Leaving the beautiful old city, behind, they drove toward their next destination.

Suddenly, Esther realized she had to go!

Gordon stopped the car, and she went into the trailer to find John Paul. Looking under the bed where he was usually placed after use, she couldn't see him.

Surely, he must be there. He always was!

But on this occasion, he was nowhere to be found.

"John Paul isn't in the trailer," said Esther, coming back to the bus.

Getting out, Gordon stretched, yawned, and walked toward the trailer.

"He's got to be here," he said. "I'll find him."

"Good luck," said Esther, "he's not there."

Coming out a few minutes later, Gordon looked puzzled. "You are right, Honey," he said. "He isn't there!"

They all knew John Paul was a necessary part of their belongings. They decided to drive back to the campground to see if he was there. Perhaps one of them had rinsed the pot and left it outside.

They had only been driving for a short time, so it didn't take long to go back to the campground.

There, clean and awaiting the next customer stood John Paul where they had left him. Corinne jumped out of the car, opened the door to the trailer, and slipped him under the bed. Their pot was home again!

WHERE DID HE GO AGAIN?

This time, John Paul seemed to be lost for good. They scoured the trailer, backtracked and searched, but couldn't find him. Traveling to Eastern Europe or Russia, the bathroom conditions were so deplorable, they didn't want to use them. But now that their chamber pot was gone, they had to. Where, in this country, could they find a pot to replace the one they had? They never did.

After another lengthy trip—lots of teaching, fellowship, and hard work—they headed from Poland toward the border into East Germany.

They drove to a friend's house for the night, before crossing the border, and on to their own home. After break-

fast, Esther and the girls, going into a back room of the house to pick up luggage that had been placed there while the bus was being washed, gasped.

What was this? Could it be John Paul? Corinne closely examined the pot. Charlene and Esther followed.

"This is John Paul," they said in unison.

"It is!" laughed Esther.

Charlene, Corinne, and Esther laughed until they held their sides. They must have left their pot there last time they had visited.

And what do you think was inside their old chamber pot? Carefully packed, it was filled with sauerkraut!

Not taking him with them this time, they knew the family would enjoy the contents that now filled their chamber pot. How could they know what it was previously used for?

They would sacrificially donate him to the cause!

13 THE BORDER CROSSING

Esther rolled over and opened her eyes to see the light in their hotel room still burning and Gordon's bed empty. Looking to the other side of the room, she saw him bent over the table, where he appeared to be working on something.

"What are you doing at 3 A.M.?" she yawned.

Glancing at his watch, he whispered, "I have work to do. Please try to go back to sleep, Honey. I'll tell you more about it in the morning."

She realized then that he couldn't say much because their room was probably monitored. Because the night always seemed too short, though she was curious, Esther turned over, put a pillow on her head and went back to sleep.

Their family had been in the USSR for about five weeks, and tomorrow was the scheduled time for their departure when they would go across the Russian border into Poland. The little town of Lvov, very close to the border, was where

they were spending their last night in this great country.

Lost in the Countryside

Earlier that evening, they had made reservations in a campground. All of them, tired and stressed, were anxious to find their accommodations as soon as possible. They asked several people on the roadside where the camp was located. Receiving different instructions each time, they were soon hopelessly lost in the country. It is strictly forbidden for a tourist to drive off his usual prescribed route in Russia and this, they realized was exactly what had happened.

Uneasy, they noticed a police car speeding up behind them. After ordering them to pull over, carefully they explained their dilemma. Perhaps he thought they were spies or maybe he believed their story that they were really lost, nevertheless after showing their passports and other important papers, he directed them to the campground. This time they finally found it. Though conditions in Russian campgrounds are primitive and crude, they were looking with anticipation to settling down for the night.

Gordon climbed out of the car and asked the usual questions at the camp office: "Where is our bungalow?" and "Could I please have the key?"

Instead of showing them where it was located, a stern-faced matron barked, "You cannot stay in this campground tonight!"

"But we have reservations," objected Gordon.

With no explanation, she all but pushed him out of the office. "No, you must go back into town and stay in a hotel. We cannot keep you here tonight!"

Her mind made up, and knowing there was no way to change it, reluctantly he climbed back into the van informing them they would not be staying there.

"But why do we have to stay in a hotel?"asked Charlene.

"Perhaps they want us to register there. That way they can keep track of us while we are in the country. I don't know any other reasonable explanation," answered her dad.

The cost of the hotel room was considerably more rubles than the campsite, but they had no choice.

The Hotel

The receptionist was anxiously awaiting their arrival when they reached the hotel a short time later, and immediately began her line of questioning.

Gordon, asking for an explanation for their actions, soon found she choose not to divulge that information, but sent them abruptly upstairs to their room.

However, the beds were wonderfully comfortable after sleeping on hard, lumpy cots in camping grounds or in the crowded van. Relaxing, they felt the weariness and pressures to which they had been subjected for so long melt away. It was sheer luxury to have a hot bath and then close their eyes in slumber—that is, all but Gordon, who was working until the wee hours of the morning.

He was serious when he told them to check through their purses, suitcases, and handbags for addresses or information acquired in the USSR. They were careful to do this before retiring. However, Gordon stayed up most of the night sorting through his belongings and papers as with a fine-toothed comb. Taking individual pieces of paper on which he had written addresses of believers in Russia, he carefully tore each one into tiny fragments. However he was still not finished with this important procedure. After pouring capfuls of bleach into a glass bowl, he took the minute pieces of paper and immersed them in the solution until all the writing had been completely erased. Then, and only then, were

they ready to be flushed in the WC. Some toilets in Russia have a "catch all" just for the purpose of holding papers such as these. The Russians don't miss anything, and Gordon realized how very careful he must be.

After these proceedings had been completed, he finally turned out the light and tried to sleep for a few hours. It was difficult for him to forget how they had been followed by the KGB officials for two long weeks. Realizing they were no doubt waiting for him somewhere nearby, did not make him feel better. Tomorrow he would be followed again. What was in store for them at the border? Only God knew, but Gordon was confident that He who had led them to this needy country would also take them out safely.

It wasn't easy for him to forget the two Russian girls, Anya and Luba, from Odessa, who had been taken from their presence and interrogated by the police recently. How could he forget the steel coldness in the eyes of the men as they completely refused to listen to his pleadings on their behalf?

Since that day, the officials had been following them constantly. Sometimes they would lose them for a short time, but they always showed up again. Questions churned in Gordon's mind. "What do they suspect me of doing or being? What do they want?" Obviously there was a reason for observing them closely every day for so long.

Finally, Gordon allowed his taut muscles to relax and fell into a restless sleep. Already, pink streaks of light were showing in the darkened sky heralding the beginning of a new day.

A few hours later, Esther opened her eyes and saw that her family were all still sleeping. "Hey, it's time to get up!" she challenged, crawling out of bed herself.

No one wanted to vacate these comfortable premises, but finally, everyone slowly crawled out of their beds to make preparations for the day ahead. Though the night was short, they had rested well, and praised God for an undisturbed and peaceful sleep.

"Don't forget anything," Esther cautioned the girls as they packed their suitcases. Meanwhile, they performed the usual ritual of checking under the sheets, blankets, and beds.

Positive their bags would be inspected at the border, they packed especially well that morning. Carrying stuffed suitcases, they checked out of the hotel, and began to reload the van which was getting more disorganized as the trip progressed. Having purchased souvenirs and other interesting articles, they all required space in the crowded vehicle. Esther was getting tired of this and seriously looking forward to going home, to get settled, unpack, wash clothes, and clean the Volkswagen camper. The van had been their home during the day and often at night for the past forty-five days. It would be wonderful to stretch out and have some privacy. Their new vehicle was corroded with tar and mud. Yes, it would need a thorough bath and overhaul.

The Russian Border

Illustrated by Corinne Balisky

On the way to the border, they shivered as a purple car followed them every kilometer until they arrived at their destination about 4:30 P.M. The customs building loomed up

ahead, appearing austere and foreboding. Large, trained German Shepherd dogs strained on their leashes to attack upon command. KGB officials, checking on the passengers arriving, looked out of the windows of tall guard houses built for this purpose. Ever alert, they reported every move of suspects. Long, rectangular ditches were built especially so cars parking over them could be checked thoroughly from the bottom by trained mechanics. Yes, there was fear in the very air they breathed.

Closing her eyes, Esther prayed for protection for her family. Their God had promised to go with them. They were not alone.

While waiting their turn in the long line of cars, Gordon saw the purple car that had been following them from Odessa. It was parked by the side of the customs building and soon they found its two occupants waiting inside the building. Gordon had the passports, declaration slips, drivers licenses, and vehicle registration ready when the border guard arrived at the van.

Not too friendly a chap, Esther thought while looking into the unsmiling face of the Russian. His face seemed set in concrete—stern and hard.

"Pull over your vehicle and get out," he ordered in the Russian language.

"Yes, Sir," said Gordon. Parking directly in front of the customs building, they climbed out.

"Carry all your suitcases with you inside," the officer said. "I will now take your passports and declaration slips."

Watching him walk away with all their identification, they couldn't help but feel some apprehension. Fortunately all their papers were in order—Gordon had seen to that.

As he walked toward the customs building, they couldn't help but see a revolver bulging in one back pocket, and a shiny knife handle protruding from the other.

Charlene poked Esther, "I hope he doesn't have to use those," she whispered. "So do I," answered Esther while hugging the slim waist of her daughter.

Gordon, Esther, and the girls made several trips to the van to take all their belongings inside. The officials, eyes sharp as darts, watched every move they made. Previously deciding to look positive and cheerful when they arrived at customs, now their knees were weak. In spite of how they felt, they continued to smile as they carried their heavy suitcases and boxes into the building. The officials scrutinized the actions of all the people coming across the border. If anyone appeared nervous or afraid, it gave them reason to think something had been concealed on their person or vehicle. This would cause them to check everything more thoroughly than ever.

Spreading their suitcases, sleeping bags, jackets, trinkets, Berioska packages (souvenirs and gifts), and shoes over the long counter, the officials went through their belongings centimeter by centimeter, until they had checked everything. Never in their travels had they seen such a thorough job.

During the entire procedure, the purple car remained parked outside the building, while seated in vinyl-covered chairs just a few feet from them, watching their every move, sat the two men who had been following them. What did they have in mind for them anyway? Their eyes, hard and calculating, they watched them like a hawk seeking its prey.

The hours dragged by and still the officials continued to check their belongings. By now everything was scattered across about 30 feet of the counter. Becoming indignant, the girls watched as they poked at every personal item in their suitcases, very carefully picking everything apart. Not one thing did they miss! The girls had bought gum for the

Russian people before going into the USSR, and had a few packages remaining. These the men took apart, piece by piece, wrapper by wrapper. It was obvious they were looking for something, but what? To what length would they go to find it?

Gordon thought he had destroyed all the addresses the night before in the hotel, but realized to his horror, there was still one he had put into a gum package earlier. Esther didn't move a muscle when he left in a hurry for the nearest bathroom. Knowing this was strictly forbidden as far as officials were concerned, he took his chance. If they found this address, it could endanger the lives of Christians who trusted him. He had to take a chance!

"Come back here!" barked a husky official. His eyes were hard and demanding, his voice harsh with authority. But Gordon had already shut the door to the lavatory. The men, now really upset, suspected him of something. One waited outside the lavatory door while Gordon, shaking, tore the gum wrappers into very small pieces and flushed them. This time he did not have Clorox to take out the print, but he had done the next best thing.

Coming out of the bathroom now, the men questioned him even more thoroughly. Why did he go to the bathroom so hastily? Was it because he had to, or was he hiding something? They were sure the latter was true.

Esther, Charlene, and Corinne were afraid to even go to the bathroom now. An escort would have been necessary, but they chose to stay where they were and trust mother nature to help them.

Having purchased a number of Matrushka dolls while in the Soviet Union, they thought they would make nice gifts for friends at home. It was incredible how the officials opened each doll within a doll until they reached the last one which was about the size of a kernel of wheat. Only then were they satisfied that something had not been hidden inside. It took hours to go through all these dolls, but they felt it was necessary.

It was up to Esther and the girls to put all the Matrushkas back together again. Leaving their belongings scattered all over the counter and floor was no concern of the inspectors. That became the family's problem. The inspectors had done their job.

Esther looked toward Corinne who was seated nearby trying to read a book. She had given her daughter her big traveling purse earlier and knew that within this bag was important information. Her heart pounding, she watched an officer go toward Corinne. His heavy cleated boots ringing down the hall, he pulled the bag away. Corinne stared, wide-eyed, as he walked away with the bag under his arm. Esther watched in dismay as the man turned it upside down and poured all its contents on the table. The large diary in which she had written her encounters and experiences while in the Soviet Union, fell with a thud! The officer picked it up and began turning the pages. Now she could be in trouble. Would they interrogate her, too?

Charlene saw the worried look on her mother's face. "Mom," she comforted, "they will only see what God wants them to see, so please don't worry!"

"Thank you, Dear," sighed Esther, trying to regain her composure. Esther thought that if the book was in her purse, perhaps it would not have to go through inspection, but she was wrong. With sinking heart, she saw the men make neat piles of items that seemed important. On that pile was her journal.

A KGB official picked up these things and walked toward an office in the back of the building. Presuming they had an English-speaking Russian who could read the book later proved to be true. Esther prayed earnestly as the hours of the clock ticked by. Finally, about five hours later, they brought articles taken into their inner sanctum back to them. Breathing a prayer of thanksgiving, she clutched the manuscript close. What had they found? Could the information be used to incriminate a believer in their country? Could she, herself, be interrogated? She sincerely hoped not. She had used abbreviations and written in several languages, and was sure this would help. Who could decipher that? Certainly not a person with limited communication of languages.

It was time-consuming to wrap up all the sleeping bags again after each one had been so recklessly taken apart. Squeezing the down-filled material between their fingers, they checked every inch of those bags. It was the same with the jackets. The lining and pockets were turned inside out and inspected thoroughly. What were they looking for?

Esther was saddened when they took her jewelry box apart. Inside there was a locket Gordon had given her before they were married. After they had taken the box apart and broken it, Esther found it later, the locket still inside.

The Kleenexes were taken individually out of their boxes and checked as well. Even used ones were plucked apart by eager fingers.

FILM

While in the country, they had taken many pictures, which included photos of the Vins family, church groups, and others. These undeveloped negatives were also taken into the customs building. By this time the officers were getting impatient. This whole procedure was taking much longer than originally anticipated. They were not finding information or documents with regards to Christians in the USSR like they had hoped. Perhaps the evidence was in these photos. They hoped so. Poking through the films, they continued to shower Gordon with questions. They probed mercilessly.

"What is on the films? Why are you so interested in this country that makes you take so many pictures? Tell me, did you have contact with other people while you were in the country? Name them now!"

Finally, in exasperation, the interpreter said, "We will take these films into our darkroom and develop them. Then we will see the proof of your interest in our country and people." Triumphant, he walked into the room, the films in his hand.

As they continued to interrogate Gordon, the man started to develop the films.

They prayed something would go wrong with the process of developing them. *Help us to be as fearless as Daniel and as wise as Solomon*, Gordon silently prayed.

Unmercifully, they continued to probe him with questions. Seven officers surrounding him, all spoke at once, their faces becoming red with frustration.

Finally, the officer who apparently had some experience in developing pictures, came back into the customs building. Looking puzzled, he scratched his head. "These people don't know how to take pictures, because none of the negatives turned out."

Gordon knew these were color films. They only had the means to develop black and white. Besides, their mechanics were crude and outdated. So, incidentally, the films were not developed!

Relieved, Gordon put on an innocent face and said, "We are not really good photographers. Very few of these films turned out the way we had hoped, I am sure. There is no need to try to develop more today. We will have to learn to take pictures in the future. Perhaps a better camera would help!"

Of course Gordon knew better. The inspectors did not.

Had they been developed as planned, the faces of Nadezda Vins and her family, as well as other Russian brothers and sisters, would have been enough evidence for the KGB to imprison them—and the Baliskys!

God had performed another miracle! Thanks be to Him!

FOOD IN THE ADVERSARIES' CAMP

"Mom, I'm hungry!" whispered Corinne into her mom's ear. Looking at her watch, Esther realized it was almost 10 P.M., and far past their usual dinner hour. When had they eaten last? She couldn't even remember. It wasn't fair to keep the family waiting, but what could she do?

Then Gordon, addressing the nearest officer said, "We are hungry and have not eaten all day."

Nodding toward a few tables and chairs in the next room, the official agreed. "You may go into the cafeteria and eat if you want."

They had found the food in most restaurants in Russia to be unsavory, tasteless, greasy, and unsanitary. More than once they had dysentery as a result of eating there.

"No," Gordon replied, "we have food and can eat right here in the customs building. Charlene, please go to the van and bring back some bread, cheese, and meat."

Suddenly the officer became very obliging, and offered to make hot water for tea.

Charlene had a police escort as she went out to find the food. Coming back into the customs building, she placed it on a big, round table beside the customs desk. Finding a can opener, she opened the meat as Esther cut the bread.

Ironically, they bowed their heads in prayer before eating the simple fare placed on the table. The officers stared. What? Did they dare to pray in a Communist border building? What kind of fearless people were they? Did their God gave them that kind of courage?

In a few minutes a pot of hot water was placed on the table. Thanking the officer, Esther began to pour water into cups. The tea was refreshing and hot. It was amazing how tasty a simple meal could be. A lavishly prepared banquet would not have tasted better.

Corinne, smiling coyly, began to quote a significant verse: "Thou preparest a table before me in the presence of mine enemies."[1]

They all smiled, realizing the greatness of their God.

Yes, these men had treated them as if they were enemies, but suddenly they realized they had no animosity toward these people at all. They were just men who needed a Savior. Jesus died for people such as these. He said that He would have all men to be saved and come to the knowledge of the truth.[2] It is not His will that any of these should perish, but that all should come to repentance.[3] Indoctrinated in a socialist society, they were only doing what they had been taught.

After the dinner dishes had been packed away, Esther sat down in the middle of their scattered belongings. By this time they were all tired and longed to cross the border to a place where they could rest. It was nearing 1:00 A.M., and still the guards kept them. Esther's feet began to throb, her back tensed, and they waited some more.

Suddenly, with a start Esther realized there was an officer beside her. Pointing to their suitcases and boxes, he said, "You may pack your things in your vehicle now. You are free to go!"

"*Sposeebo*," (thank you) she stammered. "We will begin immediately."

While packing the van, Charlene was speaking German

to one of the young men who had searched their vehicle so thoroughly. Was that a smile that played on his plain face?

It was not pleasant to see how they had taken their Volkswagen apart. Gordon groaned inwardly at the havoc created while they were in the building. Pieces of wire had been forced between areas that were not accessible and the paint had been scratched in many places. The hub caps were taken apart to check thoroughly inside. The spare tire was on the ground, along with other parts from the van.

Realizing they had scratched and mutilated his new Volkswagen, Gordon vowed to charge the damages to the Russian government, but he never did. It wouldn't have helped anyway.

It took a long time to repack the van. Patiently they tried to find places for boxes that had fit so tightly before, but now didn't seem to. When everything was in place again, the hour was late and they were emotionally and physically drained of all energy.

Just before driving away, one of the chief officials came to Gordon, extending his hand. "We have looked through your belongings and have not found what we were looking for," he said. "Balisky, you are an honest man. You may come back to Russia any time. You and your family are welcome. Please tell your wife and daughters we are sorry for the inconvenience we have caused."

"*Dasvee danya*," (good-bye) said Gordon as he walked toward the van.

After going through the Polish border, which took more time and red tape, they all heaved a sigh of relief.

Stopping beside the road, each of them prayed a short prayer of thanksgiving to God who had enabled them to come out of the Soviet Union unharmed. They were a little worse for wear, but after rest and good food they would be fine again.

Though they had just entered another Communist country, it was like a land of milk and honey compared to where they had come from. Relieved, they settled down in their seats. They would soon be in Germany again!

"If the border guards had found what they were looking for, Gordon, what do you suppose would have happened to us?" Esther asked.

"I firmly believe they would have put me in jail," replied Gordon. "And perhaps they would have confiscated our vehicle. But worst of all," said Gordon, "they could have put our friends in jail."

How grateful Esther was for a husband who had gone through his belongings and paper so thoroughly the night before crossing the border. Had he not done that, she wondered where he would be at that moment and how the lives of others would have been endangered. And where would Charlene, Corinne, and Esther be?

The lights from their van shone ahead into the darkness. As they drove steadily toward freedom, Esther settled down between their two sleeping daughters in the back seat and breathed a sigh of relief. Then she, too, went to sleep.

14 MAJDANEK, POLAND

After a fruitful journey into Russia, the family settled into a few days of normal home life in Kandern. The girls, busy at school, knew that when summer arrived, they would be leaving with their parents to go into Poland again.

It was Monday morning in Lublin. Sunday had been a very full and active day of ministry, and they were all weary.

Esther turned over in her bed, wanting to sleep a little longer. Gordon and Pastor Joseph were in the kitchen discussing the events for the new day.

Just as she was getting more comfortable, Gordon burst into the bedroom.

"Get up, Esther," he encouraged. "Joseph wants to take us through the Majdanek concentration camp." It didn't take long to dress. They had heard about the atrocities that took place there so many years ago, and were anxious to tour the sight.

Charlene and Corinne were already in the kitchen when Esther arrived. Breakfast over, they were soon on their way.

Dead, brown grass blew in the hot wind, while the hazy sun burned mercilessly. Esther's eyes smarted as she viewed acres of land where thousands of people had been killed and buried so long ago.

This was Majdanek's state museum in Lublin, Poland. It was a monument to the martyrdom of millions of innocent Slavs, Jewish people, and others who perished there because Hitler desired to have a pure Aryan race in his kingdom. His goal was to eliminate, until this plan had been achieved.

The concentration camp was created to serve as a source of slave labor. The chief aim was to create conditions for extermination of millions of citizens from countries in Europe.

Pastor Joseph chaperoned them into a large theater where they saw a movie of this tragedy. Overwhelmed with horror at the bizarre scenes, sometimes they could only turn away.

Prisoners were transported in freight trains, devoid of sanitary facilities. The trains were densely packed with people, for whom no water or food was provided.

Upon arrival, the prisoners were driven amidst shouting and beating, to the place where they would eventually die or be put to death.

They walked on the broken, crumbling sidewalks under the blistering sun toward the barracks, which now housed prisoners' clothing.

"Eight hundred and twenty thousand pairs of prisoners shoes are displayed here," said their tour guide. "These are only a fragment displayed in this camp. There are more in other barracks."

They saw sizes ranging from tiny baby shoes, to men's and women's. They were all there. Years ago, someone's mother and child had walked in these shoes ... now they were on display for the world to see, and the innocent victims buried in the earth beneath their feet.

Scorching wind moaned around the barracks. The large room, in one of the many display areas, was dismal and warm. Esther sat down on the nearest chair and reflected on the desolation of this place. In her mind, she could see thousands stretching out their hands for life, and hear their cries in the moaning of the wind.

"Even yet," said Joseph, "some say they can smell the blood of the victims in the air."

Esther rubbed her swollen feet and then proceeded on the way to find her family. They were standing quietly beside a display of prisoners' clothing which was so thin it couldn't provide sufficient protection against the cold and rain. Wearing additional clothing was subject to severe punishment.

"The prisoners were housed in leaky barracks built with parchment-thin walls. They were always too cold or hot.

Sewage was a problem so it was not surprising that insects became a plague of the camp. There were no washing facilities and there was dirt everywhere."

Alfred Kwiatkwoski recollects, "The lice and fleas soon became unbearable, especially during the night. It was impossible to sleep. The body itched and ached constantly. We spent time trying to crush the creatures to death, but there were always multitudes more," he said.

Joseph informed them that food for the prisoners was reduced to an absolute minimum. The daily ration was equal to less than 1,000 calories. Irrespective of the weather, the food had to be eaten outdoors.

"The starving prisoners," he went on to say, "were forced to do exhausting labor. The work continued from early morning until dark. SS men supervised the prisoners.

Often they beat them with horsewhips, sticks, or bars."

He stopped for a moment to catch his breath. Joseph had been to Majdanek many times, but he never ceased to be moved by the atrocities that were committed in this place.

"Members of the commandos coming back to camp," he continued, "used to drag heaps of dead bodies home. Those who were not dead yet, were led by their arms and when left alone inside the camp gate, they would creep to the barracks, scraping the frozen soil with their hands and feet.

"The horrors of the camp were increased by an organized system of terrorizing and tormenting the prisoners. Some would be crucified, others baited with dogs. Still others were hanged on the gallows. Another frequent penalty was making prisoners stand between live wires.

There were other means of exterminating prisoners, before they began to use gas. These included hanging, drowning, killing with injections of poison, shooting, and plunging prisoners into hot or cold pools. Sometimes they shot masses of prisoners and pushed them into a common grave."

Esther felt more melancholy and grieved as time went on. Corinne, her youngest, came close to her mother. Quiet and troubled, she took her mother's hand. Esther thought of the millions of children who were torn from their parents and brutally murdered. Her eyes filled with tears again as, holding her daughter close, she squeezed her small hand.

The others were ahead, so they hurried on.

Charlene's eyes were large, Esther noticed, as she stood beside life-sized pictures of suffering humanity. Taking her hand, too, they walked along the endless corridors of horrors.

"In August," said their tour guide, "they began to use gas chambers, in which they murdered their victims. Not infrequently, complete transports of prisoners were sent into the gas chambers to be killed immediately after arriving in camp. They usually sent in only those they believed were not fit for work. Prisoners too dilapidated during their stay in camp to represent any value in terms of labor were also killed in the gas chambers. Selections of weak people unable to work were carried out every day.

"The yield of bodies burned daily was one thousand. Within a period of less than three years, by 1944, 360,000 people lost their lives in Majdanek camp."

Slowly they walked into the gas chamber area. The opening in which they placed the cyclone B and carbon monoxide was there. The dangerous fumes would penetrate the shower when they were released to do so. The movie they had seen earlier portrayed these helpless victims as they were dying in the showers. Sometimes it would take up to ten minutes to die a horrible death.

The noise of the tractors around the bath interfered with the desperate cries of those led into the gas chambers and murdered.

By this time, Esther and the girls were ready to leave, but Joseph still wanted them to see the dissecting table. "After the prisoners were gassed, their bodies were laid out on a large stone table where their teeth were extracted, rings removed, and their hair cut. This human hair was later utilized in making mattresses for the German populace.

"After this procedure," Pastor Joseph said, "bodies were taken to the huge ovens and cremated. People in the city of Lublin could smell burning flesh and see smoke billow from the smokestacks in the crematoriums."

When they stepped out of the building, the sun almost blinded them. It still burned mercilessly in the dreary surroundings. Dead, brown grass continued to bend in the hot wind. Wrinkling her nose, Esther wondered if the aroma she detected in the blazing hot wind was the blood of the innocents.

Taking the hands of her two daughters, slowly they walked toward the monument of struggles and martyrdom. It was an enormous structure.

"What is this monument made of?" asked Charlene.

"Powdered bones of the martyrs mixed together with cement," answered Joseph.

Craning her neck to see the top, she could not even venture to guess how many bones were entombed there. She didn't want to know.

Esther's heart ached as she and her family turned around and walked toward the car. They tried not to hear the cries in the wind. Nor did any of them want to remember they were walking on mass graves.

No one spoke as Joseph headed their vehicle toward the city of Lublin. Everyone was acutely aware of the thousands of people who had once lived and breathed and were brutally punished and their lives taken away. For them, there was no hope. It was forever too late.

But the Baliskys were challenged anew to reach the living with the message of the Gospel of Jesus Christ and to tell them there is hope beyond the grave.

Esther bowed her head, asking God to help her witness to others around her and, in turn, lead them to the living Savior. In Him there is hope.

Heroes of Faith—The Polish Women

> *Now faith is the substance of things hoped for, the evidence of things not seen.*
>
> *Choosing rather to suffer affliction with the people of God, than to enjoy the pleasures of sin for a season; esteeming the reproach of Christ greater riches than the treasures in Egypt…* (Hebrews 11:1, 25-26).

Many heroes of faith are listed in this familiar chapter. But the heroes of faith not listed anywhere, and never will be, are women in Eastern European countries who must have faith to survive on a daily basis. Women, unknown, obscure, and living in a different culture than her own, are examples of faith such as Esther had rarely seen. With a heart of compassion, the Father watches, loving and protecting them each moment. He knows their lives are difficult, and without Him it is impossible to meet their challenges and testings, without eventually crumbling.

These women will never be listed as great or famous, as many men and women of old, but Esther has seen children rise up and call their mothers and grandmothers blessed. Like precious gems to them, they will always be heroes of faith and role models of strength. Going forward for Christ, in spite of difficult situations, they have learned to cope.

THE LOCKS

Think of the locks that enable a ship to rise and proceed up a stream that otherwise would be impossible to navigate. When ships travel upstream, they are locked into an enclosed area which is then filled with water. Weighing thousands of tons, they are lifted easily through the floatation power of the water. The lock system enables the ships to sail on and on through higher bodies of water.

So, too, women in Eastern Europe have learned to trust in God to rise above hard times. Floating upward, by the invisible, silent, escalating flow of the Spirit of faith, which only God can give, they rise above the shoals of life that would have grounded them had they not looked to their eternal God.

Faith is taking God at His word and asking no questions.

> *Without faith it is impossible to please him: for he that cometh to God must believe that he is, and that he is a rewarder of them that diligently seek him* (Hebrews 11:6).

Faith is paradoxical. It goes beyond reason. It believes without understanding why.

It sings in prison (Acts 16:25).
It glories in tribulation (Romans 5:6).
It chooses to suffer (Hebrews 11:25).
It accepts all things as God's will (Philippians 1:12).

May our faith be strengthened as I share examples of women of faith in Eastern Europe.

Life on the Farm in Novy Tomysil, Poland

Nadya, short of stature, and amply endowed with rounded contours, is not a woman who, outwardly, would capture one's attention.

Shoulders stooped, she struggles to carry two large, full milk pails in her work-worn hands, as she walks toward the house.

Over her faded housedress, she wears a big, floral apron. Graying hair, covered by an old *Babushka*, is styled in a traditional bun. Held in place by two hairpins, precariously, it barely holds together.

High rubber boots, too large for her, keep droppings and unclean matter from spattering onto her small feet, as she dutifully feeds the squealing, boisterous pigs.

Blowing aside a strand of hair that has escaped from beneath her *Babushka*, she sighs with weariness.

Face covered with dust and grime, she would appear to be black, but after a good wash with homemade lye soap in the crowded back porch, she looks more like herself again. Her hands show broken, discolored fingernails. Though she has cleaned them repeatedly, they are still stained.

Why, then, is Nadya beautiful? Her outward appearance is not elegant. There is no sweet perfume wafting across the air when she enters the room, no manicured, polished fingernails to attract attention, no cosmetologist to give her a facial, and no fancy clothing to distinguish this woman from others.

Inside, she shines with the love of Christ. Her adorning is not outward, but the inward, hidden man of the heart… even the ornament of a meek and quiet spirit, which is in the sight of God of great price.[1]

A living epistle, known and read positively by others,[2] putting her own busy schedule aside, she welcomes her neighbors in for a cup of hot tea, so they can unburden their hearts to someone who will listen and try to understand them. Assured she will pray for them, they leave her house with a lighter heart. Someone cares. So few really do.

People coming from afar, seek out this woman of character and dignity. Strength and honor are her clothing, and she shall rejoice in time to come.[3]

Nadya is always prepared for whomever God sends her way.

ARRIVAL—WELCOME—SLEEP

Nadya's two, big black dogs barked furiously as the van entered the yard. The hour was late. Gordon, Esther, Charlene, and Corinne had traveled all day to arrive at the big farm where they were always welcomed heartily. Time had sort of run away with them, and now the hands of the clock pointed to 1 A.M.

The great farmhouse, in total darkness, came alive as the lights were turned on, one by one. Nadya's bedroom first showed signs of life. She must stop those dogs! They would

wake up the entire neighborhood if she didn't hurry.

Hastily, she slipped on a pair of old shoes, crawled into her husband's big housecoat, and ran outside to meet her guests.

"Hush, Boys! Hush!" She commanded the two big dogs. Realizing by then who had come, the dogs ran toward them, wagging their tails.

Often, after a busy time of ministry in Poland, the Baliskys came to Nadya's house. Here they could rest easy. She always saw to that. Also, her farm was about eight hours from Braunschweig, East Germany—another stopping place they had adopted.

"Nadya!" Esther exclaimed, coming toward the little woman.

"Esther!" She gestured toward the girls and Gordon, and bade them come inside.

Though the hour was late, she put the teakettle on to boil.

"You must have something hot to drink before you sleep," she gently consoled.

Before long, they were sitting around the familiar, big table, drinking the hot liquid. Of course, she added some homemade deep-fried fritters, as well. "Yes, I made these this afternoon. Eat now," she ordered. "You will sleep better on a full stomach than an empty one!"

So they ate.

The boys had joined them by this time.

Accustomed to activity at the Borowka household, neighbors who had awakened were really not upset about the hour, but curiously wondered where the guests had come from this time. Nadya was always ready for everyone who came. She never turned anyone away—not Nadya.

Corinne and Charlene always enjoyed coming to the

farm. Her boys, of course, added to that enjoyment. Long hours of walking, swimming in the lake, talking, and laughing, were in store for them here. Powell, Greg, Richard, and Caju knew how to give these American girls a good time. And they never failed.

Totally exhausted, the Balisky family had given many hours of time ministering across the country, as well as in youth camps. Now they all needed rest. Here, on the farm, they weren't even expected to rise at a certain time. Brunch would be served whenever they arrived in the dining room.

"You are tired," comforted Nadya, when she saw Corinne's eyes falling shut. In spite of the fun she was having with the boys, she could not stay awake.

Because the house was big and roomy, there was ample space to stretch out and really sleep. It wasn't long before Nadya had made their beds. Soft, *pirennas* (quilts) filled with goose feathers from her flock, were made into comfortable beds. Big Polish pillows were fluffed and ready when they came into their rooms.

Esther put her head on the pillow. Totally exhausted, she felt cool, night air come in through the open window. Gently stirring the lacy curtains, it fanned her flushed face.

Knowing the birds would be singing soon, announcing the arrival of a new day, she willed herself to drop off into deep, dreamless slumber.

Tomorrow there would be no pressure, no meetings—only relaxation and fun. Perhaps they would go swimming with the young people in the warm, sleepy lake.

Of course there would be ample food prepared in the farm kitchen. There always was. Nadya saw to that.

Sleep, dreamless and still, washed over Esther's weary body. The two big black dogs slept peacefully. The great farm house, now darkened, would see the light of dawn in a few hours. She sighed, contentedly snuggling under the warm *pirenna*.

A NEW DAY

"Rise and shine!" sang Gordon, as he entered the girls' room.

"Go away, Dad, ple-ease!" sighed Charlene, crawling further under the warm, feather comforter. Morning had come too soon.

Esther stretched lazily. The roosters had heralded a new day hours ago, and were busy scratching for food in the back yard.

Trying to find a dress still clean enough to wear, Esther rummaged through her disorganized suitcase. Washing clothes while in Eastern Europe, was usually not possible, unless one rinsed them out in the sink. By the end of a trip, everything was in disarray. Wrinkled and soiled, Esther pulled a summer dress over her shoulders. Skimming a comb through hair that needed some tender, loving care as well, she headed for the dining room. Nadya, as usual, had prepared a beautiful brunch and gone out to feed her pigs and milk the cows.

Does this woman ever sleep? they wondered. She hardly ever sat down. *Where does she find her endless energy?* She always seemed to be giving to someone or something.

The boys joined them as they ate. Hearing their voices in the hall, Charlene and Corinne threw aside the warm, feather quilt and came downstairs—posthaste!

Leaving for Posnan, a large city not far away, the car carrying their young people left pools of dust behind as it drove away. Waving, Charlene called, "We'll see you later!"

Gordon and Esther went for a long walk in the Polish countryside. Along the way, green grasses clinging to embankments were mixed with field flowers of every hue.

Forming a small bouquet, Esther would put them in water when they returned to the house.

Breathing deeply, she noticed Gordon looked more refreshed than he had for a long time. Holding hands as they walked, quietly, each one enjoyed deep solitude and beauty. Finally they had time to relax. Who could wish for a better place to rest?

The afternoon went by.

Knowing Nadya would have dinner ready, and the girls would be back from Posnan, laughing, they ran down the dusty road toward the farmhouse. Coming closer, the aroma of fried chicken greeted them. They were hungry now. Exercise could do wonders for anyone's appetite.

THE CHURCH

An old building, standing on the farm property, had been used as a church since their Grandpa and Grandma's younger years.

Though crowded, outdated, and needing repair, it stood as a memorial of blessing. The Borowka children attended church there since they were born.

Pastor Adam capably led his flock, but the building—a low, thatched roof, simple cottage—was far too small for the growing congregation.

Charlene decided she wanted to help. Giving her tithe, she told them to use the money wherever it was needed most.

Praying about building a new house of God on another location, the people were happy to receive her gift. How could they make it stretch? They found a way.

Garlic is popular throughout Poland. They would plant a crop of garlic and sell it to help defer expenses for monies needed to buy lumber to build a church.

The ambitious Borowka boys soon bought the garlic

with the money gift, and planted it in fertile soil. Growing well in the warm sunshine, they eagerly looked forward to harvest time to reap the proceeds.

The money Charlene had invested for the Lord, bore dividends as it was used to further His kingdom in Poland.

Later, a beautiful church stood on a property near to the farm. Finally they had a large enough house of God to accommodate all the people who came to worship.

SUNDAY

Esther awakened on Sunday morning after another warm, deep sleep in the big farmhouse. Hearing the roosters crowing—the young ones in their squeaky, little voices, and the older roosters in their wise, mature "cock-a-doodle-doo's"—she knew it was time to get up.

Looking out the window, she noticed it was a glorious day. Flowers growing in the garden beyond, opened to the sun. Grass, green and full, gently blew in the morning breeze. Birds in big trees overhead, unanimously chorused their glad praises to the Creator who fashioned them.

"*Djien dobri*!" smiled Esther, entering the kitchen. Already, the girls and their friends were seated in the spacious dining room. A prepared breakfast was served without the lady of the house. Rising early every day, including Sunday, chores had to be done, breakfast and lunch prepared, and the house tidied. There was rarely a free minute for this busy woman.

Sometimes, Esther noticed her wince in pain when she sat down, but no word of complaint ever came from her lips as quietly, she continued to do her tasks.

Bowing their heads in prayer, Nadya's husband asked for God's blessing on the new day, thanking Him for food He so graciously supplied.

Then Nadya came in to clear the dishes away, so the table could be set for lunch. There would be extra guests again.

WORSHIP

Looking into the distance, they could see people coming to church. The dirt road left tracks of dust behind them as they came on bikes, in buggies pulled by horses, on foot, and in tiny, Fiat cars.

All were dressed simply—the women, mostly in modest, ordinary attire. "Perhaps," Esther reasoned, "they owned only one Sunday dress." The men, wearing old suits that had become shiny with years of cleaning and pressing, led the way, as their families walked into the familiar building they called church.

Stooping low, in order not to bump their heads on the low threshold, they were soon seated in their familiar place of worship. Creatures of habit, they have been in the same spot as long as they could remember.

But always, before sitting down, standing in worship, they reverently bowed their heads, asking for God's blessing on today's service. Pastor Adam could always be assured that he was covered in prayer as he ministered to the people.

There were no church bells ringing across this Polish

A church building sight in Novy Tomysil, Poland. Kaju and Esther.

countryside, like they had often heard in Germany and Switzerland on a Sunday morning. There were no fancy cars or beautifully dressed men and women coming to the house of God. These were simple, country folk, standing in His presence, waiting for a touch from Him. Hearts open and transparent, here they would receive strength to live for another week.

All were oblivious of time, while roosters crowed and chickens scratched in the soft soil just outside their house of worship.

No one, it seemed, but Esther and her girls, heard the cows nipping grass outside the window, or saw the big flies with blue wings, as they buzzed around their heads.

It didn't matter that as the sun shone, it revealed cloudy patterns on the dusty furnishings and windows. They were engaged in true worship. What were a few distractions anyway? These would not detour them from worshiping God in their traditional manner.

Esther quieted her heart, as she noticed the unaccustomed sounds and disturbances. These would certainly interfere with a service at home. She couldn't imagine a cow chewing her cud outside her big city church in Seattle! And chickens scratching in the dirt? Hardly!

The people always loved to hear the Baliskys sing, so while Esther played the old piano, they joined together in worship. Gordon, announcing his text, began to share God's Word. Carefully and prayerfully, they listened. They would put into practice during the week, all that they had learned from His Word on this, the Lord's day.

LUNCH

Mingling in the farmyard after church, the people talked. Today, Nadya had no time to stay. There was lunch to prepare for numerous guests.

Her swollen, calloused feet took her quickly into the kitchen, which she found to be her mission field. Among many other avenues of service for God, this selfless woman spent a great deal of time preparing food so others could be nourished.

Powell, Greg, Caju, and Richard joined Charlene and Corinne as they walked toward the house. Luncheon aromas were sending tantalizing messages to them.

"I am hungry!" emphasized Caju. "Let's hurry!"

"Hey *Mamushka*! What smells so good?" sniffed Powell, upon entering the fragrant kitchen.

"Son, you are always hungry!" laughed Nadya, playfully shooing him out of her way.

Twelve people were soon seated around a table filled with delicacies Nadya had prepared.

Taking little time to sit down and eat, dutifully, she ran from the kitchen to the dining room. Was everyone satisfied? Did they want more? How about a drink?

> *She riseth also while it is yet night, and giveth meat to her household...* (Proverbs 31:15).

Laughter and tears mixed together as everyone shared. These people from America and Poland blended as one, while they interrupted one another. "Excuse me...Excuse me! Now can I talk?" laughed Richard. Everyone smiled and obligingly gave the floor to the tall, handsome Pole. Next, it would be someone else's turn to share a happening or voice an opinion.

Nadya, excusing herself, went into the crowded, back porch, and put on her faded housedress and boots. Milk pails in hand, she walked into the muck and mire of the farmyard. The boys, reluctant to leave the girls, but knowing their mother needed help, soon followed suit.

Problems on the Farm

Farming is not easy anywhere, but in Poland, complications pile up like nine pins.

The pigs Nadya so faithfully fed, were born to die. Only a small allotment of pork will go into her cooking pots.

The government kept meticulous track of every pig raised on every farm. A family could withhold a small portion of their litter, but it was compulsory for the rest to be sold as soon as they were big enough to make a little profit.

When the animals were sold, the farmers received a slip, informing them that they can purchase a necessary commodity for the farm. The Borowka's had needed a new barn for years. In order to purchase cement to pour a foundation, after selling the pigs, the coveted slip would be presented to the buyer. Even after this requirement was met, the promise was not. The old barn, standing in disrepair, had to do for still another season. And who knew how many more? Perhaps the next year when the pigs were sold, there would be cement. This went on year after year. Eventually hopes became shattered, and they learned to make do with the best they had. How can one erect a new building without the necessary cement to make a foundation?

The farmer must keep his word and sell the animals, but it was not required that the government, or buyer, keep his.

"We must sell our pigs," stated Greg, "but we get little for one animal. It costs us just as much to feed a pig for a year. What can we do, perhaps stop raising them? But we need the little pork we get," he concluded.

"If we want ham for dinner, the cost is high," emphasized Richard. "We can't really afford to pay 300 *zloty* for just one kilo of ham, so we just don't buy it. Though we raise hundreds of pigs, we rarely have this delicacy. Three hundred *zloty* is one quarter of what we get for a whole pig," added John, the man of the house. "It is like water, water, everywhere, but not a drop to drink."

"Some groceries are hard to find, too," sighed Nadya. "It tries my patience and eats up my time when I have to stand in line at the store all day. Often, when I reach the end of that line, the item I need is not there anyway, so mostly I compromise and do with what I have. Meat is hard to obtain anywhere. I am blessed to have chickens. They make up a lot of the protein of our diet."

Though the family works long hours to keep order and cleanliness, the farmyard is filled with mud when it rains, and flying dust when it is dry.

Listening to the family share, Esther recalled how, that week, she had gone to the barn to talk to Nadya. Having been brought up on a farm herself, she thought she would be

prepared for what was ahead. But she wasn't. Picking her way, she could not avoid the fact that her feet were sinking deeply into dirty, fecal water. Trying to skirt the puddles, she stepped onto a fresh pile of manure. Now she knew why Nadya changed her clothes and shoes and washed so thoroughly after each encounter in the barnyard.

Rank odors rose from steaming piles on the barn floor. Big flies landing there left their culinary fare to crawl on Esther's face. Waving her arms, she shooed them away, but more immediately took their place.

This barnyard is the place where Nadya spent half her life. It seemed it was always time to milk and feed the animals. Tied down so, it was difficult to go away—even for a short period of time.

This farm was the Borowka livelihood. The sons, strong and healthy, would inherit the investments after Nadya and John were gone.

"The boys work hard on the crops they have planted, but expenses eat up most of the profit. The work must be done again to pay expenses for next year. So the cycle goes on and on," sighed the weary Nadya.

THEIR DAILY BREAD

"I love to cook," she said, her face brightening. The food she prepared was tasty, but like her mother and grandmother before her, fat was always used liberally. Most of the cuisine she prepared was deep-fried. Using either chicken, pork, or beef lard, it was not a healthful way to cook. Often her culinary creations consisted of dough in one form or another. Homemade noodles and potatoes were the staples. Tomatoes, in season, graced the table, but most vegetables came at a premium. Cabbage, the most common, was made into salads or soups.

"*Begosh* (a cabbage and sausage dish) is my favorite," smacks Powell.

Even eggs are deep-fried, Esther noticed as they visited many homes across the country.

"If I see another *kinapke*, I won't be able to keep it down," choked Corinne when they were at youth camp near Lubartow. Charlene, agreeing, nodded her head. Every breakfast consisted of bread with a spattering of tomato and pork on the top. Often the leftovers were left on the cupboard all day, while flies and bugs had their fill. These *kinapke*, along with fresh ones, would be served for dinner, too, not only in youth camps, but in homes across the country.

"Soups I can eat every day" said Charlene. "But mostly, there is too much fat floating on the top. I have to skim it off before eating. I don't like fat," she laughed.

"The whole grain bread," Gordon added, "is much better than American." And his ample stomach grew, as he fed on it each day.

David Ryan, their chiropractic friend from Seattle, who came to Poland on several occasions to give hurting people adjustments, stated that the rate of arteriosclerosis was rampant throughout the countries of Eastern Europe. Not just the older people, but even the young had clogged arteries.

Esther observed, as she picked at her own food, how the boys, ravenous, after coming in from the field, buttered their bread with a generous portion of butter. Dipping this into a plate of fat pork, they added more artery-clogging artillery. The soup, though delicious, was swimming in grease. No one takes any heed of what will happen, health-wise, farther on down the road.

A Polish Kitchen and Bathroom

Esther went into the kitchen to wash dishes one day.

With the sink clogged up with debris, Nadya, gently scolding, told her to go and rest.

There was no disinfectant. Flies buzzed overhead, landing on left-over food and dishes. Plumbing was usually not working, so sinks stopped up and greasy water floated on top. Dishes were washed in cold water, often without soap, and dried with a soiled cloth. Dishrags, rancid and sour, were often used for weeks without going through a washing machine—if they had one.

Esther looked around for cupboard space, but couldn't see any. The little shelf room there was, was filled.

"Where does she put her dishes?" silently Esther wondered. Realizing Nadya would rather not have her in the kitchen, she wiped her hands and left.

The bathroom had odors of its own. Esther usually went in and out as quickly as possible. Happy to breathe cleaner air in the bedroom, opening the windows wide, she inhaled deeply of nature's perfume. But sometimes even that was not possible because barnyard odors got in the way. Quickly, she closed the windows again.

Blossoms reigning in abundance in Nadya's flourishing garden stood in sharp contrast to the crowded kitchen and bathroom.

The girls went for walks. Enjoying nature and sweet, pure country air, away from the barnyard, they inhaled deeply. Cities through which they had traveled, reeked of coal smoke and made their lungs hurt. They often went for walks, taking advantage of the cleaner country air.

A Gathering Place—the Old Bench

Women in Poland did not have an easy lot. In order to rise above their difficulties, they learned to depend on God.

Sitting on an old bench near the house, several women,

A Gathering Place – the old bench. Corinne and Esther with women in Novy Tomysil.

Grandpa (Grandma had died some time ago), and Nadya, enjoyed the sun. Walking past them, Esther realized they were sharing the contents of Sunday's sermon. Jesus Christ was the central theme, as with faces animated, they shared about His love.

This was a favorite gathering place where Nadya comforted those who hurt, wept with those who wept, and gave a cup of cold water in His name.

The other women who came to talk also had their hair pulled back from their faces, and wore the traditional *Babushka*. Many had gold teeth. Others, who could not afford to have dental work done, did not have any. Toothless, with cheeks sunken, they grew old before their time. Unshapely

and overweight, from generation to generation they continued the same lifestyle. There were some women who pursued a different lifestyle, but mostly, it was expected that they keep house, cook for their families, and raise little ones.

Nadya Bids Farewell

Nadya did the best she could in the midst of poverty and discouragement. Many odds were against her, but she learned to trust in God. She learned to rise above the shoals of life that would so easily ground her, but for her trust in a living Savior.

In 1998, Nadya went home to be with her Savior. Cancer was diagnosed and spread rapidly throughout her weary body. The fight was over.

Grieving, Andrew, Powell, Greg, Richard, and Caju, carried the casket containing the earthly remains of a faithful soldier, and buried her in a cemetery near her home.

They will never forget this woman who, in spite of circumstances, did good and not evil, all the days of her life. How could they forget that she rose early in the morning while it was still night, to feed her family and others who were in need, or stretched forth her hand to the poor and needy? She opened her mouth with wisdom, and in her tongue was the law of kindness. She looked well to the ways of her household, and did not eat the bread of idleness.

Surely her husband, children, and grandchildren, rise up and call her blessed. Her husband also praises her.

"Many daughters have done virtuously, but you excelled them all...A woman who fears the Lord shall be praised...Her own works praise her (see Proverbs 31:12-31).

Nadya will never be forgotten. Now, courageously, her boys carry on as they, too, rise above the shoals of life that would easily ground them, if it were not for the Savior their mother loved and served.

15 THE KGB CATCH UP

They had only been home in Germany a few days after about two months in the Soviet Union. The stress and strain of that trip still weighed heavily on their minds. Already, Gordon was in Eastern Europe again and Esther was left at home with the girls.

It was Sunday afternoon. Esther and Corinne had just arrived from church and were sitting at the table having lunch when suddenly they heard a *thump*. Running upstairs, they found Charlene had fainted and was lying on the floor.

"What happened?" Esther cried.

No answer.

After a great deal of effort and frustration, they helped her into bed.

Anxiously, Esther watched while, as the afternoon wore on, Charlene grew steadily worse.

What should she do? To whom could she turn?

The hours dragged by. "Please, God, send relief!" They prayed.

Trying to get up later in the day, Charlene collapsed again. Kneeling beside the prostrate form of her daughter, in desperation, they sought help from the only Source they knew. Tears spilled unheeded down Corinne's cheeks as she pled with her sister to walk again.

By mid-afternoon, Charlene was critically ill.

Charlene, at fifteen, was bright, popular, and beautiful. Gordon and Esther were concerned when they made the long move from Seattle to Germany to be nearer to their work in Eastern Europe and Russia. Knowing it was not easy for their children to be uprooted to begin a brand new life in a foreign culture, they worried. Their fears were soon hushed, however, when they saw both girls adapt to their new surroundings. Thriving in school, they made friends quickly. Active in the local BFA church, they fit in well. The adjustment period was going well when Charlene was stricken with illness.

"Why, God? Why?" pleaded Esther. "Was not the trauma of leaving home difficult enough? Now this?"

Esther felt desperately alone and frustrated on that Sunday afternoon, when Charlene did not respond to her attempts to help. She knew it was difficult to find a doctor who would come to the house on a Sunday afternoon.

Could Esther take her to Lorrach in the car? To help her down the stairs would be impossible because she couldn't walk alone. She tried to call some of her new friends, but it seemed no one was home.

While pain exploded violently in her head, the teenager tossed and turned on her bed. Not able to stay on her feet because of dizziness and fainting, helplessly, she grew worse.

This continued all day. What could Esther do to make

her daughter more comfortable? She had no answers.

About midnight, Charlene collapsed on the floor again. They realized they had to do something! Lying unconscious on the floor, her face was white as chalk, with unseeing eyes staring at the ceiling. Esther had come to the end of her resources.

Just then, God intervened.

Bill and Irma Neudorf, working with BFA, drove into the yard. Running to the window, Esther almost wept aloud when she saw them step out of their car. Having lived in Germany for many years, they knew just what to do.

Running to the telephone, they called the children's hospital in Lorrach, a neighboring city.

Within twenty minutes the ambulance arrived. Oh, blessed relief! With lights flashing and sirens screaming, it turned into their yard.

Running out, Esther told them what had happened. Would they please take over from there?

Capably, white clad attendants lifted the unconscious teenager onto a stretcher and carried her into the waiting ambulance. Numbed, they climbed into the Neudorf car and followed behind the speeding emergency vehicle.

"Thank You, God! Thank You!" breathed the distraught mother in the back seat.

Bill's prayer calmed them as they drove toward Lorrach. Lovingly, Irma offered words of comfort.

In the hospital, the foursome sat in the waiting room, anxious to hear the diagnosis of this illness. The doctors worked fast and efficiently. Could they help Charlene?

First, they did a spinal tap, as all her symptoms pointed toward this. But to their surprise, they found the tests did not reveal what they had suspected. What, then, was the problem? They would have to take more tests.

Charlene spent weeks in the Children's Hospital in Lorrach. New tests were taken daily, while she was observed carefully by the medical staff. Weakness and fainting spells continued. What could they do?

When Charlene's school friends came to visit, she seemed almost indifferent—aloof? Her classmates from BFA sent her a mammoth card, expressing messages of hope and cheer. She vaguely smiled. Spending hours with her in the hospital, Esther tried to give her daughter joy. Special handwork and books lay untouched on the table beside her bed. Losing weight, she pushed away trays of food. Even nourishment did not interest her. What could they do?

Hourly, the medical staff would try to see how long she could stand on her feet, then watched in amazement as, once again, she succumbed to a fainting spell.

Esther watched the color drain from Charlene's face as she stood for only a moment or two. Perplexed and baffled, the doctors had no answer for this strange malady.

They did not hear from Gordon while he was behind the iron curtain and there was no way to reach him. Esther felt he should know, but how could she contact him? All she could do was pray.

Proving His faithfulness again He spoke to Gordon in Romania.

Suddenly, while traveling with his colleagues toward another point of ministry, a tremendous burden filled his heart. Something was wrong at home. But what?

Not knowing what the problem could be, he slipped into the back seat of the van to pray while his partner drove.

"Go home!" Who was speaking? Could it be God?

The urge was so strong, he had to tell his colleague.

"I need to go back to Kandern!" said Gordon. "I just know it! Something is wrong!"

Of course they could not phone from Romania, but when they finally arrived in Austria, Gordon ran to find a phone.

It rang and rang. Where was his wife? His children? What was wrong?

Then he called the Neudorfs, who told him what had happened.

"Esther is in the hospital with Charlene," they said. "Please go there as soon as you can!"

Breathless, he ran toward the van. "We have to go—now!" he cried. "Charlene is critically ill."

Needing no further prompting, he turned the car toward Germany. They drove all night.

In the morning, the unshaven men, with faces haggard and weary with fatigue, and clothing crumpled, walked into the hospital. What would they find, and how was Esther?

"*Ich will, meine Tauchter sehn*," he said when they arrived.

"*Wie Heist deine Tauchter?*" asked the efficient nurse.

"Charlene Balisky."

"*Ya*," she said, "*Kommen Sie mit mir*."

As he walked into her room, he saw his eldest daughter on the bed, her face wan and pale. His wife, looking exhausted, sat close to her daughter's side.

"How are you, Charlene?" he asked, holding her in his arms.

When there was no response, he held her closer.

What a relief it was to have Gordon home! Spending hours in prayer, they asked God to heal their daughter. Why, when she had been vivacious and healthy, was she so weak? No one knew.

It took weeks before the doctors allowed her to come home. Even then, they did so reluctantly. At home, her situ-

ation still did not improve as she lay on her bed listlessly. Nothing seemed to interest her.

The first encouraging spark of joy showing since her illness, was when they took her out into the mountains.

As towering peaks appeared, they knew she remembered special times there. Spending many hours skiing in the exhilarating, fresh air, as she gracefully glided through the snow, it brought back precious memories—how could she forget?

Now it was fall—a beautiful time of year in Switzerland. As they drove, viewing God's marvelous handiwork, they never ceased to marvel at His greatness.

By this time Charlene was able to walk short distances. They watched as she breathed of the clean, invigorating mountain air. Her eyes lit up with pleasure when she saw mountain flowers still clinging to the hillsides. Bending down, she picked an armful and gently carried them to the car.

Gradually, they noticed a little color in her wan cheeks. Very slowly she came back to life, but like the doctors in Lorrach had said, it would take time.

When Charlene was stronger, she decided to go back to school again. But was she strong enough to go full days? She knew she wasn't. Approaching the principal at the Black Forest Academy and asking about special tutoring, sadly he admitted they didn't have enough staff to accommodate this request. She was hurt and disappointed.

As an alternative, they arranged for her to take correspondence from the U.S.A.. Because she was interested in Chemistry and Science, they were fortunate to obtain equipment from Seba Giegi—a firm that specialized in this area. Setting her laboratory up in the basement, she spent many hours in experiments and study. But she was often lonely. She missed the interaction with her fellow students at school.

However, spiritually, her life opened up like a flower

opens to the sunshine. Spending hours in prayer and Bible study, during loneliness and weakness, God was fashioning something beautiful.

Spring arrived and with it, colorful blossoms and beauty covered the land. Charlene still suffered.

One day, while talking to the doctors in Lorrach, perplexed, they advised her to go to the United States for medical help. After seriously praying and discussing this delicate issue, together, they decided to take her to the famed Mayo Clinic in Rochester, Minnesota.

At the Mayo Clinic, once more Charlene was forced to go through grueling days of testing to find the root of this illness. It seemed there was never an end to what she had to endure.

Finally, at the end of that long, exhausting week, a white clad doctor arrived.

"Are you Mr. and Mrs. Balisky?" he asked.

"Yes, Doctor. What did you find?" Anxiety showed in Gordon's blue eyes.

The doctor cleared his throat. "Please follow me into my office," he said.

They followed with bated breath.

"Please have a chair," he continued, while gesturing to several empty places.

"We, as a team of doctors, have made a series of tests," he said, "that would indicate something very unusual. You told us about your work in Communist Eastern Europe and Russia, Mr. Balisky. Our tests show that your daughter was poisoned. We do not see cases such as this very often. It will take a long time for your daughter to get well. Just be patient."

As he went on. Esther's heart pounded under her thin blouse. Eyes filling with tears, silently she sobbed.

Could it be, the KGB had used a viral chemical warfare poisoning—with intent to use it on Gordon, and not on their daughter? Remembering clearly how they had been followed day and night for weeks, while traveling in Russia, she knew now, their intent was to either kill or maim her husband.

Charlene told them later, that when the waitress, in one of the restaurants in Russia, had set their plates of food on the table, a larger portion was set beside her. "Here, Dad," she said, "I'll trade you...mine is too big." So they traded plates.

They realized now that the one set in front of Gordon probably contained a deadly poison. Unaware, Charlene had eaten the portion intended for her dad.

They knew there would be sacrifices involved in working behind the iron curtain—but this?

Soberly walking to their car, everyone was shaken.

Bowing her head in surrender, Charlene asked God to make her willing to follow Him—no matter what the cost. Could she?

It took Charlene years to outgrow the deadly virus—but eventually she did. Now, serving God unreservedly, she works as a nurse in hospice, tenderly ministering to dying patients and relatives. Could it be that same tenderness would not be present in her life if she had not gone through the crucible? Only God knows.

16 CAMP IN THE MOUNTAINS – POLAND

The winter wind wildly beat its fury against the chapel where young people were holding a service. Sitting in a big circle studying the Word of God, they were oblivious to the sound of snow beating against the frosted window.

The weather was cold—so cold one could see clouds of vapor escaping from the Tatra Mountains beyond. Rugged, indomitable, with high peaks ascending toward the sky, they towered above the small town of Yelena Gora in southwest Poland.

In spite of inclement weather, this youth camp had been in session for almost two weeks. Tomorrow the group would reluctantly go back to their respective homes.

Enthused and eager, they listened as Gordon taught. Young people often were receptive, but this year they were unusually so.

Sometimes, sitting for five sessions per day, they drank in

truths from God's holy Word. Rarely, unless they came to youth camp, was teaching such as this available.

On the last morning, it was snowing heavily. Drifts two meters deep covered many of the narrow roads.

Though the wind howled and snow beat against the windows, and continued to pile up in drifts, the young people listened in rapt attention. No one was in a hurry to leave. No one was tired—only enthusiastic. Even those who had not made a decision to follow Christ were attentive. Should they make a decision tonight? Surely, the Lord was working in their hearts.

Gordon prayed every moment. No one had made this important step throughout the camp and that was unusual. Would they come tonight? His heart burdened, he prayed as he taught. At night he stayed awake and talked to his heavenly Father. What was keeping these people from coming into the Shepherd's fold?

"Please bow your heads," he invited, in the last service.

Everyone did. The room was bathed in a holy hush as the Holy Spirit spoke. No one moved at first.

Then one stood. "Yes, I would like to make a commitment to have the Lord change my life," said Jan.

Then several more indicated this, too, was their desire.

Soon, there were fourteen who followed camp leaders into another room adjacent to the chapel, to pray the sinner's prayer.

In Poland, a decision such as this could not be made lightly. How would it affect their jobs, their families, and friends? Would the cost be too high? But those indicating they wanted a changed life were willing to face the consequences—whatever they would be.

Coming back into the chapel to join the others, now they, too, sang the songs of the redeemed. Joy shone on everyone's faces.

Finally, in the early hours of the morning, after great celebration, they put on their coats to leave. Many, staying in their own homes in town, needed to catch the bus.

Walking in the cold air, their breath made white clouds of vapor in the frosty air. Ignoring the elements, they sang as they walked to their destination.

But there was one who still struggled.

Peter was unhappy. Along with the others, he had listened as the Word of God was shared on a daily basis. Was he willing to face the challenge? He had decided he was not ready. Now he wondered, should he? He was dragging his feet while his friends were buoyant and alive with new life, walking toward the bus singing songs of assurance.

Peter knew the Spirit of God had been speaking to his heart. Why was this decision so difficult? What was wrong? Was Satan also tugging at his heart? To whom should he listen?

Dimly through the fog and cold, the image of the old bus appeared. Soon he would be getting on with the others. Would his opportunity to receive Christ be over? He wanted to make the right decision.

Suddenly he stopped. "I'll be right back!" he shouted to his friends.

Turning around, he ran back toward the chapel. Would there still be someone there? Had they all gone home?

His breath came in gasps as he ran faster.

Dimly the church appeared through the darkness. Yes, there was still light there!

"I have to make a decision!" he cried, running inside.

The pastor smiled as he took Peter in his outstretched arms. "Praise God!" he shouted.

Kneeling beside the altar in the still warmed chapel, without hesitation, Peter cried to God. "I am a sinner, Lord. Please make me Your child and forgive my sins. I have doubted You, but I am ready now, Lord."

In the heart of Yelena Gora, situated under the massive Tatra Mountains, Peter gave his heart to Christ.

Laughing, he rose from his knees. Yes, this decision was the right one! How could he have doubted God?

The bus would be leaving soon. After dawning his big, winter coat, and pulling snow boots over his feet, he hugged the pastor once more. Running into the blowing, freezing snow and wind, joyfully he ran toward the bus.

Singing at the top of his voice, the sound carried into the night air. "I am one of God's children now!" he shouted into the wind.

Boarding the departing bus, his face shining like a neon sign, he thanked God for salvation.

There would be challenges to face ahead, he knew, but there was nothing he and God could not handle together.

As Gordon drove to his next destination the following day, he smiled as he maneuvered the van on the narrow road. Surrounded by two-meter snow banks, nothing could hide the joy in his heart. Fifteen young people, now redeemed by the blood of the Lamb, had entered the Shepherd's fold. Directing them to pastors in the area, he made certain they had earthly shepherds as well, who would assist them in their new walk with God.

Shielded from some of the wind because of the high snowdrifts, he, too, sang songs of blessed assurance.

> *As the rain and the snow come down from heaven, and do not return to it without watering the earth and making it bud and flourish, so that it yields seed for the sower and bread for the eater, so is my word that goes out from my mouth: It will not return to me empty, but will accomplish what I desire and achieve the purpose for which I sent it* (Isaiah 55:10-11, NIV).

A Saint is Called Home

Gordon took Esther to the airport early in the morning. Freezing wind and a bitterly cold white world greeted them as they walked out the door that morning. Having stayed in Warsaw at the Bible school the night before, their room had been cold and drafty, and neither of them had slept well. Gordon continued to cough. It was a raspy, hoarse cough that came from deep in his throat. When Esther heard his labored breathing, she worried. It was always complicated and difficult to receive medical help of any kind behind the Iron Curtain.

Gordon still had several weeks to minister in Poland. Esther was leaving for Germany because they both felt it would be wise for her to be with the girls there. Excited to return, she recalled the challenging, grueling, exhausting, and yet blessed times they shared while working together in Poland.

Her weary eyes didn't want to stay open. Her head nodded as the van bumped over frozen streets toward the airport. The weather had definitely taken a turn for the worse.

She and Gordon had driven into Warsaw from a church in which they ministered in Lodz, the night before. It was only with God's help that they plowed safely through the storm. Everywhere on television and newspapers, warning alerts were out.

"Do not be on the road if it is not an emergency!" they warned.

Snowdrifts, three to four meters high, bordered the slippery roads. Visibility was poor as the wind howled, turning the blowing snowflakes into a hazy white blur.

Esther seriously wondered if the airplane would fly on a day such as this. Phoning the airport to inquire, they were

told the plane was still scheduled to leave for Zurich in spite of the inclement weather.

At the airport, after the officials had gone through her luggage, and asked many questions, Esther finally boarded the airplane for home. Gordon and their coworker, Roy (who had arrived in Warsaw a few days earlier), stood at the gate and watched Esther's retreating figure. Then stepping onto the aircraft, she disappeared from their view.

It didn't take long to reach Zurich. There, after a brief stop, she boarded a plane for Basil.

Esther found it refreshing to see the green countryside from the window of the plane. There were no longer endless stretches of blowing snow, but patches of many shades of green throughout the warm countryside.

"What a different world," Esther mused. "Here there is freedom to worship and hold good jobs without fear of them being snatched away because of a stand for Christ." The very atmosphere breathed cleanliness and freedom.

As warm, sweet air greeted her, she stepped out of the craft. It was good to be home again!

A Tragic Surprise

The weeks at home went by rapidly as Esther did her best to catch up on correspondence that had piled up while they were away.

The day for Gordon's arrival finally came. Charlene and Corinne had not seen their father for about a month, and excitement and sweet tension filled the air, as they waited for their familiar Volkswagen van to drive into the yard on Steinenstrasse 1B.

Finally, hearing the honking of a horn, they ran outside to a happy reunion. Gordon was away from home so often, and it was good to have him back. Already, the girls had planned day trips into Freiburg to go to C. N. A.—the department store where we often shopped.

The novelty of having Gordon at home had hardly worn off. Gordon and Roy were at the office in downtown Kandern and Esther was at home, when the phone rang.

"Hello?" said a familiar voice. "This is Dick."

Immediately the time of recent fellowship in Warsaw came to mind. But this wasn't what Dick wanted to talk about.

"Now Esther, brace yourself," he soberly answered, after she told him Gordon was not at home. "Tadeuez Urbaniuk was killed yesterday. The funeral is on Thursday."

"No! It can't be!" Esther protested. "Why, I saw him just a few weeks ago while we worked together in his church and youth camp. Gordon said good-bye to him the other day. He was fine then," she protested, denying the shocking truth. Then catching her breath, she asked, "Whatever happened?"

"He was in a car accident. Lydia and the girls were hurt, too, and are now in the hospital, critically wounded."

Tears filled Esther's eyes. Slowly she wiped them away.

"How could it be that this faithful young man was dead? Would God allow a thirty-year-old Polish pastor, in his prime, to be snatched away from his growing flock?" she questioned.

"O God," she prayed, "I don't understand Your ways, but I know Your thoughts are higher than ours, and Your ways higher than our ways. Surely You have a purpose in everything. Help us to accept this accident as your will. And God," she concluded, "please minister to Lydia and her little ones."

Drying her tears, she quickly drove toward the office to tell Gordon and his coworkers. They, too, had worked in Poland with the young man on many occasions. Gordon, she knew, would receive this information with great sadness.

His eyes grew wide with astonishment, as Esther broke the news.

"Tadeuez Urbaniuk?" he questioned, incredulously. "What happened?"

Telling them briefly the few details she knew, she urged Gordon to call Dick himself.

Before he did, they gathered in a small circle in the office in downtown Kandern, and asked God to direct and heal his wife and his church family who would be grieving beyond measure at the untimely departure of a young man who was well loved.

When Gordon called his friend, Dick, he was not able to relate many more details than he already had with regards to the accident.

"They notified me instead of you," he explained, "because of the fact that this might jeopardize future visits into the country."

"Please call Balisky right away!" they said.

The news traveled across the Eastern block, then spread into the Western world. Everywhere, people who knew Tadeuez were shocked.

After retiring that night, Gordon lay staring into the darkness, unable to sleep. He sensed the need to pray for their friends in Poland like never before.

The next day, after a sleepless night, Gordon approached his wife. "I feel I should go back into Poland for Tadeuez's funeral. What do you think?" he asked. His face was lined with weariness. He had just arrived home, but they both knew he had to go.

"Tadeuez would never know," replied Esther, "but others need comfort and encouragement. I think you should go."

Once more, Esther went into the attic for Gordon's suitcase. She had finished unpacking it just a few days ago. Now, carefully folding his freshly laundered shirts, and picking up his socks, she prayed for strength and comfort for their friends in Poland.

At noon, Gordon left for Warsaw. Once more alone with Charlene and Corinne, she totally focused on them. After they left for school that day, the clock ticked loudly as the day dragged slowly by.

Gordon was in Poland for anther ten days. Driving the blue Granada to Basil to meet him, she was excited. Seeing Gordon come down the ramp, she called his name. The reunion was sweet as, hand in hand, they walked toward the car.

THE ACCIDENT

Taking out his wallet, he removed pictures of the accident in which the pastor and his family were involved.

Esther gasped when she saw the remains of the familiar vehicle that had been their taxi while they were in Poland such a short time ago.

"Please tell me all the details," she said to her husband.

"Tadeuez and Lydia and their two little girls, were enroute to Bedguishk, where a pastor's conference was taking place," he said. "Lydia said that Tadeuez had a burden on his heart for many days prior to his death and seemed to be carrying a heavy load. Not really wanting to go to the pastor's conference, because of heavy responsibilities in his church, eventually he decided it was his duty to go. They were only twenty kilometers from their destination, when they stopped for gas because the tank was almost empty.

"Tadeuez looked around him that day as if he had never seen the beautiful countryside before. This was unusual for him as he commented on the trees, grass, and blue sky. He also talked about his heavenly Father who made them. Then he and Lydia began to sing. She thought it was strange," said

Gordon, "because he couldn't sing. But he asked Lydia if she would sing with him. In a clear soprano and a faltering bass, they sang about a place God had prepared for them in heaven. Asha, in her childish voice, joined in from the back seat. Yerena, safe in her mother's arms in the front, only smiled as she clapped her small hands.

"Suddenly from the left side, they saw a large bus bearing down on them. The children screamed as Tadeuez tried to stop. But it was too late. In a split second, tires squealed, brakes shrieked, there was a terrible thud, shattering glass, and crunching steel. Then all was blackness.

"A Christian family living across the road had witnessed the fatal crash, and ran pell-mell toward the sight. It was not a coincidence that the father was a medical doctor.

"Others, too, came from all directions to see what had caused the sickening *thud*. All were willing and ready to help in whatever way possible. Someone called the hospital. The crowd, ever increasing, gathered to witness the devastation.

"In the distance, they could hear the screaming sirens as an ambulance approached. First, the First Aid attendants pulled Lydia and the baby from the front seat of the wreck. Then, carrying their patients, they rushed to a nearby hospital.

"The men present tried desperately to pull Tadeuez from the wreck, but it seemed to be a hopeless task. He and the Fiat had become hopelessly meshed as one, as he was held tightly in a bunch of tangled steel. Finally, after pulling and prying, they retrieved the bruised and broken body. Tadeuez lay on the road, his body limp as a rag doll. While waiting for the ambulance, they carried the fallen pastor into the doctor's house and placed him on a bed. He still felt a heartbeat, however, he knew Tadeuez was nearing death.

"When the ambulance returned, the wounded man was rushed to the hospital as quickly as possible, but he died on the operating table. It was too late! Tadeuez was gone!

"His heart and lungs, crushed by the impact of the speeding bus against his small Polish Fiat, proved to be fatal for the young man. In split seconds, the car folded like a cheap accordion.

"Had this been a murder staged by the Communist government in order to rid the system of one more Christian?

"Eventually, the men at the scene of the accident found the slight, unconscious figure of three-year-old Asha, wedged between the back and front seats. They had just pried her out when an ambulance arrived. Once more, with sirens screaming, it drove toward the hospital where the child's father had just past into eternity."

"This little one had been her daddy's special friend," Esther observed. "I often noticed as she put her arms around his neck and buried her head in his shoulder. Knowing she was in daddy's arms, the cares of the world seemed to melt away. Asha knew that when she was shy or afraid, this place was a safe retreat."

Gordon continued, "Lydia, still unconscious, did not know until the next day, that her husband was gone. When they informed her, the young woman's body shook with deep, heartfelt sobs. Who can tell the horror of losing a loved one so suddenly? Then, breathing deeply, bracing herself for more shock, haltingly she asked about her girls. No one knew for sure."

"What were the extent of Lydia's injuries?" Esther asked in a whisper.

"Her leg is broken and in a cast from the hip down," he answered. "Her jaws were broken, too, and are wired together. But the pain of losing her companion exceeded all the other hurt.

"When the nurses brought Asha to her mother some

time later, she hugged the little girl fiercely to her breast. How would she tell her children? She knew she had to.

"The bewildered child did not recognize her mother. Lydia's heart ached as she anxiously wondered what was wrong. Asha only stared at her. Finally, after three days of testing and deliberating, the doctors did exploratory surgery on the little girl and found a large blood clot in her eye. Her memory, though temporarily impaired, improved and gradually she could see again."

Though Lydia and her child remained in the hospital for weeks, they knew God was a faithful father and husband. He would be with them in their time of sorrow and adjustment. Bravely the young widow clung to God's promises as she looked toward a future without Tadeuez.

FUNERAL SERVICE

Their pastor friend was buried on a wintry, blustery day. A drab, gray casket was carried to its final resting place by his faithful pastoral colleagues.

Dead, bare branches of nearby trees bent in the freezing wind as the pale sun weakly peered through hazy clouds. Tall, brown grasses moaned as they bent before the fury of the wind. Men, in long overcoats and big overshoes, huddled together around the grave. Women, holding their own little ones, wiped tears of sorrow from their eyes. In spite of this, Tadeuez's friends, church members, and family were singing a song of hope and joy, because Tadeuez was not dead. His body lying stiff and cold was there in the casket, but his soul was rejoicing in heaven. He had seen his Savior face to face.

"Ashes to ashes, dust to dust," quoted Gordon as the coffin was gently lowered into the darkness of the newly-dug and frozen earth. Then he read a precious promise to the grieving loved ones in this, their time of sorrow. In a low and steady voice, Gordon read this message of hope and compassion:

> *But I would not have you to be ignorant, brethren, concerning them which are asleep, that ye sorrow not, even as others which have no hope.... For the Lord himself shall descend from heaven with a shout, with the voice of the archangel, and with the trump of God: and the dead in Christ shall rise first: Then we which are alive and remain shall be caught up together with them in the clouds to meet the Lord in the air: so shall we ever be with the Lord. Wherefore comfort one another with these words* (1 Thessalonians. 4:13,16-17).

REVIVAL—CONFESSION

Tadeuez's comrades and pastor friends from all across Poland attended the funeral. Many had been present at the seminar where he had planned to be the day he was killed.

Grim-faced, in black suits, ties, and white shirts, they stood in complete silence, paying respect to their fallen colleague. Now his body, lying still in the casket, reminded them that time could be short. One never knew when God would call them home.

As they bowed soberly in prayer, suppressed sobs could be heard while God dealt with each one individually.

Everyone, not only the pastors, realized the brevity of life as, one by one, they renewed their pledge to serve God without reservation. Had their hearts turned lukewarm? Realizing their need for God, they dedicated themselves afresh, asking Him to melt, mold, and remake their calloused hearts.

Except for the wind and the rustle it made in the trees, the place was hushed as each one bowed reverently in the divine presence of the One who gave life and who could also take it away. Blessed be the name of the Lord!

Many pastors confessed sinful areas in their lives as the Spirit of the living God continued to deal with them. Truly, God was at work.

Lydia

Here we are with a group of people we taught in Yelena Fora in the heart of the mountains in Poland. On far right are Lydia, Taduish and child. He was killed in a car accident.

Though Lydia was not able to attend her departed husband's funeral, she sensed the presence of the Lord with her in the lonely hospital room. Asha and Yerena, close beside her, were too young to comprehend that their father would never return. But as they clung tightly to their mother's hand, she told them he was in heaven with Jesus. There would never be any accidents or "owies" there. Daddy was better off than he had ever been before.

Confident that God would walk beside them through the unknown future, she smiled and hugged her daughters closer.

17 GOD'S GIFT TO MARIA

They were excited as the huge airliner descended. Anticipating this trip to Israel for a long time, now their dream had finally come true. What made it challenging, however, was their assignment to visit Russian Jews scattered throughout the country. Sincerely they prayed that God would use them to help in some way.

Traveling in a crowded bus from Tel Aviv to Jerusalem, they viewed the sights so often read about in the Bible.

When the twinkling lights of the great city appeared in the distance, Esther was reminded of the Lord's compassion as He stretched out His hands and cried,

> *O Jerusalem, Jerusalem...how often would I have gathered thy children together, even as a hen gathereth her chickens under her wings, and ye would not!* (Matthew 23:37).

"God," she prayed, "give me that kind of love and com-

passion for the Russian Jews living in this area, and cause them to be receptive to the Messiah they have rejected for so long."

Joppa

It was raining heavily the day they decided to go to the ancient city of Joppa. This, they knew, was the place where Jonah ran away from God, his disobedience resulting in a chain of drastic reactions.

Since coming from the USSR, many Russian Jews had made their home in the area. Gordon had the address of an elderly couple who ministered among them, so planning to visit them, they walked in the direction of their home, church, and bookstore.

It was raining even more heavily by the time they arrived at the bookstore.

As they opened the door, a little bell tinkled softly overhead, summoning a smiling, gray-haired woman. Extending her hand, she introduced herself as Mrs. Seth. While she waited on a customer, Esther and Gordon noticed the shelves were filled with Bibles and Christian literature.

"This is an oasis in a desert," Esther whispered to her husband. Nodding in agreement, he continued to check the interesting surroundings.

"Now," said Mrs. Seth, "let's go into our apartment at the back of the shop."

Though the three of them had never met before, immediately they sensed a kinship. Here was a woman whose life radiated her love for the God she served.

Sitting in chairs beside the small table, soon a kettle of steaming water was brought in.

"Let's have a cup of tea while we talk," she smiled.

Sipping the hot tea and telling about the work in which she and her husband had been involved for years, she said, "I would like to share a story with you that shows again that our Lord is just the same today as He was in Bible times when He walked the face of this earth. He has not changed and still performs wonderful miracles today. My little friend, Maria, can prove this."

Maria

Settling into their chairs, they waited for her to go on.

"Maria, a lovely Russian Jewess, lived in the USSR all her life. Her parents, strict Kosher Jews who adhered to the letter of the Law, sincerely sought to bring up their children like their parents and grandparents before them.

"One day, through a divine encounter, miraculously, she accepted Jesus as her Savior. From that time on, she was happier than ever before. Her life completely changed, and others noticed immediately. 'What did she have that was not there before?' they wondered.

"The girls parents thought this was just a phase in her life and would soon pass, so they tolerated it for a time. However, it did not pass, and each day Maria became more in love with her new Friend, Jesus Christ. Joyfully, without reservation, she let others know about the joy that was now in her life."

What Shall We Do with Maria?

"Gradually and hesitantly, her parents and grandparents noticed this change in their daughter was not just a passing fancy. Saddened and frustrated, they began to threaten her. What would their friends say about this disgrace that affected their family? Still they tried to reason with the girl.

"But how could Maria give up her new Friend? No matter how difficult things were at home, she remained true. The joy inside was like a spring of living water, overflowing and abundant.

"'What shall we do with Maria?' sighed her weary father. No one had an answer.

"Finally, in desperation, one day he called, 'Maria, come here!' Glaring at her from under a pair of bushy eyebrows, he said, 'I have decided to send you to Israel. There you will be a true Israeli and forget about your new adventure, and there you will live up to the faith of your fathers. The more I have thought of this idea, the more I have desired to bring it to pass. You will go soon!'

"'Yes, we will send Maria to Israel!' he informed his distraught wife. 'Please begin to pack her bags and I will prepare flight arrangements as soon as possible.'

"His heart a little lighter, he hurried to expedite his mission. On his way to the airport, he was confident that his move was the answer to this plight. What else could be done? His daughter must forget about the man Jesus Christ, who she claimed was the promised Messiah.

"'When she gets to Israel, and comes in contact with our staunch Jewish friends,' he reasoned, 'she will realize it is folly to believe the Messiah has really come.'"

Israel

Mrs. Seth sat her empty teacup on the table and went on. "But when Maria came to her new home, she did not forget. Because she was lonely and her Jewish friends did not understand, the young woman depended on God more than ever. She knew He was always there continuing to give her joy and peace during these difficult times.

"Maria went for walks alone in the ancient town of Joppa overlooking the beautiful waterfront. There she talked to her new Friend for hours. Yes, she was confident He heard."

Oasis

"On her daily walks, she could not help but notice a little shop near to her own apartment. 'I will go in,' she decided one day.

"Opening the door, she heard the little bell tinkle softly overhead. Her eyes opened wide with amazement, when she realized that this was no ordinary shop! Bibles and literature lined the bookshelves. Going closer to the books, her heart beat with excitement as she looked at them and discovered she could read clearly one page to the next. Excited, she looked at the other literature and saw that it, too, was in a language she could read.

"'This is a Christian bookshop!' she cried. 'There must be others here who believe in the same Messiah I do! Oh glory! Can it really be?'

"Her father had sent her far from home so she would not have contact with believers, and here she was next door to a wonderful, Christian bookstore and people who must be of the same faith as herself. Could this really be happening?

"Maria's eyes, filling with tears of happiness and awe, watched as I came toward her. 'Could she be a believer? Oh, yes, she must be!'

"We looked at each other for a moment," said Mrs. Seth, while wiping a tear from her eyes. "Knowing immediately there was a common Christian bond between us, we didn't have to say a word.

"Maria came toward me, and silently, I clasped her in my arms. Weeping she whispered, 'Can this be real? Are you a Christian, too?'

"I knew beyond the shadow of a doubt, that our God had brought us together and sent this young woman to an Oasis in the desert. He had arranged this divine encounter long before we ever knew it would happen. He cares for

each of His children as individuals and always wants the best for them.

"Maria had not only found Christian friends, Bibles, and good literature to read, but now she had a church which was near to her apartment. Here she could grow in the Lord, and be nourished and fed as faithful Bible teachers taught her from the wonderful Word of God. She had so much to learn, and intended to drink in as much as possible."

Their eyes were moist when Mrs. Seth finished her story. In the little shop, in the heart of Joppa, standing in a circle, they joined hands and prayed, asking God to surround Maria with His love. They asked, too, that God would give Mr. and Mrs. Seth patience, wisdom, and understanding as they worked in the midst of a people Christ came to save.

Clasping their hands and thanking them for visiting, she said good-bye.

"Please come again!" she smiled. Assuring her they would try, they stepped out into the pouring rain. Yes, God, who became man and walked these streets so long ago, is still the same today. Countless miracles were performed then, as lovingly He ministered to needy multitudes. Now again, He had performed a modern-day miracle for a young Russian Jewess. God had proved His faithfulness! He always has and always will.

18 CHRISTMAS IN ADELBODEN

The beautiful Black Forest tree leaves, turning to colors of gold and scarlet, snapped under the feet of children as they walked to school. The Balisky family were home again and it was time for Charlene and Corinne to concentrate on their studies.

Summer had fled, as winter stole her bright colors away. With the change in seasons came cooler weather and sharp winds. Snow began to fall on the German countryside, first in small, white flakes melting on the ground, then gathering momentum and freezing, it covered the frozen earth.

Corinne and Miriam stepped out of the school bus into the whiteness of an icy world. In snow too soft and dry to make snowballs, but delightful in which to run and play, the girls chased each other all the way to Cori's house. Cold and rosy-cheeked, they burst into the warm house.

"Mom, I'm home!" called Corinne, taking off her coat and inviting Miriam to do the same.

Charlene and Tim walked slowly, hand in hand, toward the house in the gathering darkness while the snowflakes gently fell. One by one, lights twinkling in homes brought a certain kind of magic to the late afternoon.

A Vacation to Remember

"Mom, I'll make some cookies," said Charlene one day after school. "When we come in from skiing, they will certainly be appreciated."

With Christmas only a week away, the family looked with anticipation to spending this special time of year in the Swiss Alps. Friends owning a chalet in the heart of the rugged mountains offered several rooms on one floor at a reasonable price.

Buying a Christmas tree in Germany, together they tied it onto the top of the car. A small turkey and all the trimmings were put into a roasting pan to cook when they arrived.

"Here, Mom, are the decorations," called Cori from the attic. Not as plentiful as the ones at home, but colorful and festive, they would turn a plain tree into a spectacular thing of beauty.

The house was fragrant with Charlene's Christmas cookies. Capably cutting them into different shapes, she iced the tops with a variety of colors. These, too, would be taken to Switzerland, "to eat when we come in from skiing," said Charlene.

In the frosty outdoors, Gordon started the car. The exhaust sent white clouds of vapor into the icy atmosphere. They were on their way!

As they traveled, Christmas lights shone festively from homes and shops along the way. Last minute shoppers frantically milled around, looking for gifts, while Salvation Army recruiters rang Christmas bells to catch their attention.

Soon the snow-capped mountains appeared. Majestic and rugged, they reached toward a darkening sky. Chalets, nestled in the bosom of the hills, appeared warm and cozy as lights from blazing windows shone on the snow.

"We're here!" chorused the girls as they drove into the familiar village of Adelboden.

The town was ablaze with color everywhere—the atmosphere charged with electricity!

Tires crunching on the ice, their car came to a halt in front of a chalet, which would be home for a fortnight.

Putting the tree in the porch until they could decorate it, gifts, groceries, and suitcases were brought in first. They were thankful for this warm and comfortable place in which to spend their vacation. Who could wish for more?

Ski poles and boots carefully placed beside the door were ready for tomorrow's adventure in the mountains.

Charlene and Corinne occupied separate bedrooms. Enjoying the privacy and quietness, Charlene pulled back the drape and peered outside. A full moon shone in splendor, bathing the white world in quiet beauty. Content, she crawled into bed and was soon asleep.

Corinne, always the bookworm, propped up two big pillows, settled back in her bed, and began to read. Lost in a world of fantasy, characters became alive before her eyes.

Early the next morning, Esther put the turkey in the oven before her family burst into the small kitchen for breakfast.

"Hey Mom, something sure smells good!" cried Corinne, sniffing deeply.

"Merry Christmas!" Esther smiled.

"Now where's Charlene? Let's decorate the tree!"

With four people doing the job, the little tree was soon adorned in festive brilliance. Standing back, each one admired its beauty.

"That's the nicest tree they've ever had," commented Gordon, while scrutinizing their handiwork.

"You say that every year," laughed Esther.

But they were all pleased.

After breakfast, while the roasting turkey sent fragrant aromas into the air, everyone prepared to go skiing.

"When we return, our Christmas dinner will be ready. Now, let's go!" urged Gordon.

The ski lift carried them high up to the top of Engslichen Alp. Charlene and Cori, scarves flying in the wind and faces flushed with cold and excitement, paralleled gracefully down the steep slopes of the mountain. Esther and Gordon, following closely behind, loved the thrill of wide-open spaces as the cold fanned their faces.

Hours later, tired but exhilarated, they took off their skis and headed toward the chalet.

"I'm hungry," complained Corinne as they piled into the car. Everyone echoed the same sentiments. A work-out in the fresh air had made them as hungry as a family of starving cubs. When they entered the chalet, Gordon took off his steamed glasses, threw his coat on the chair, and went to check on the turkey. Done to perfection, he carefully carved the succulent bird while his family watched.

Esther, putting the gravy, dressing, sweet potatoes, and vegetables on the table, told everyone to sit down. Needing no encouragement, they began their feast.

"Wow! This is good!" agreed their hungry daughters. Esther had her mouth too full to answer.

Suddenly the mood was broken when they heard music. Crystal clear, it echoed into the crisp night air.

"Listen!" whispered Charlene, as the singing came closer. The words in German were not difficult to understand.

Stille Nacht, heilige Nacht!
Alles schlaft, einsam wacht
nur das traüte, hoch-heilige Paar,
das im Stalle zu Bethlehem war,
die dem himmilschen Kind
die dem himmilschen Kind.

Looking out the window they saw a row of sleighs pulled by a single horse with bells around his neck. They rang each time he took a step, their crystal notes amplified in the frosty night air.

Inside the sleigh, holiday carolers, faces flushed with cold and their colorful scarves blowing in the breeze, sang Gloria to the newborn King. Warm air, mixing with cold, sent cloudy vapors into the chilly atmosphere.

Slowly passing them by, the music was gradually lost in the night, to be enjoyed by others along the way.

Moved with emotion, they were reminded of the silent, holy night when Christ was born, and reverently they thanked God for sending His Son to earth to take on the form of fallen humanity.

Then Gordon took his Bible from the nightstand. Clearing his throat, he began to read the old Christmas story:

> *And she brought forth her firstborn son, and wrapped him in swaddling clothes, and laid him in a manger; because there was no room for them in the inn.... Glory to God in the highest, and on earth peace, good will toward men* (Luke 2:7,14).

The dishes now stacked on the counter were ignored. It was time to open gifts! Corinne, curiously wondering what those colorful packages contained, gently shook them to find a clue. Finally, the suspense over, the girls went to their

rooms to admire their gifts and contemplate on this wonderful Christmas day.

Colored lights on the tree flashed, casting subdued colors into the darkened living room. German carols playing on the radio softly filled the room with the message of Christmas.

"*Fröhliche Weihnachten*!" Esther whispered to her sleepy husband. In a minute they were both taken captive in a world of dreams. It had been a day to remember!

ADELBODEN

A peaceful place set in majestic mountains high,
Where cool, clear streams reflect the blueness
of the sky.
A place where massive trees stand stately,
proud, and tall,
Leaves changing with the seasons—
winter, summer, spring, and fall.

A panoramic scene I view as I stand high upon a hill
Rugged mountains capped with snow,
my heart with joy is filled!
The fertile earth is covered with grasses
soft and green,
A variety of colors, brilliant shades are seen

I take God's hand, with joy we wander through
the hills and trees.
I thank Him for the world He's made for
His children, you and me
I praise Him for this quiet place, where in
communion sweet,
We walk together, He's my Friend.
I worship at His feet.

Written one day while in the Swiss Alps. I was sitting on a wind-swept hill. The gentle clouds were floating in the blue sky overhead.

There we were alone, just God and I. Peace filled my soul.

—Esther M. Balisky

A New Year's Night to Remember

It was almost time for the New Year to be ushered in. They were in Adelboden, a popular ski resort in the Swiss Alps! Everywhere Swiss chalets tenaciously clung to hillsides bordering the rugged mountains. Above them, stars studded the blue vault of the vast universe. They seemed to hang like great, gleaming diamonds above the treetops. Long ribbons of cloudy, gray smoke curled lazily from numerous chimneys, then disappeared gradually into the frosty night air. The mountains rose, rugged and majestic, beyond the peaceful town, their lofty peaks laden with crusty, white snow. Quiet tranquility filled the peaceful atmosphere. A calm serenity reigned over all.

Gordon and Esther often strolled unhurriedly through the hills of this restful winter paradise.

This was the second year they had come to the Swiss Alps with their family at Christmastime. Rigid schedules for the remainder of the year caused them to look with anticipation toward a short vacation in this relaxing atmosphere. When the time came to leave, they always felt rejuvenated and able to cope with tasks that lay ahead with new vision and motivation.

It was New Year's Eve, and excitement ran like an epidemic through their family chalet duplex.

Cheeks flushed and brows moist, triumphantly they put finishing touches on the heavily laden table for their tradi-

tional New Year's dinner. Reverently they bowed their heads before Almighty God, as together, they gave thanks for His abundant mercy in supplying their daily bread.

They plunged enthusiastically into the tantalizing feast before them. The crisp, invigoration air had made them as ravenous as young cubs waiting for a late meal.

Satisfied at last, they relaxed around the table and began to reminisce about the way their Sovereign God had graciously led them throughout the past year. Familiar verses like, *"Hitherto hath the Lord helped us"* (1 Samuel 7:12), and *"This God is our God for ever and ever: he will be our guide even unto death"* (Psalm 48:14), came to mind. After sincerely thanking Him for His faithfulness, they left the table, one by one.

MUSIC

Suddenly from the ancient church steeple, bells began to peal, their notes resounding crystal clear throughout the little town.

Charlene and Corinne, eager to explore this place and find new sources of adventure, left the chalet and ran toward the sound of the ringing bells.

Esther enthusiastically invited her husband to join her outdoors in this enchanting world of winter whiteness and magic, as well. Donning their winter clothing, they walked out the door and, together, reveled in God's great world, so endowed with varieties of beauty. Hand in hand, they strolled past the old church while the bells continued to toll.

When the bells ceased their melody, the sound of faraway music reached their ears. Running lightly together over the snow-covered road, they laughed with glee at the sheer delight of being alive and well, and able to enjoy the pleasures of this moment.

The harmonious strains of music became louder as they rounded the corner and went past the Hotel Victoria, another old-fashioned landmark in the village.

Suddenly they saw a large group of people congregating around a lamppost, enthusiastically singing Christmas songs. Brightly colored snowsuits, scarves, and hats adorned the joyous throng as they sang Gloria to the newborn King.

Charlene and Corinne, already part of the group and joining in the singing, waved to their parents from where they stood. Joining the group, they added their voices until the end of that song, and then moved on with them as they slowly walked to the next lamppost.

Then, stopping again, they continued to harmonize. The carols were old and had endured throughout eons of time.

The crowd, ever increasing in size, went on to follow the singers until, at the last light, they broke into the final strains of the beautiful Christmas song that Hans Gruber had written many years ago:

Silent night! Holy night!
All is calm, all is bright
Round yon virgin mother and Child!
Holy Infant, so tender and mild,
Sleep in heavenly peace,
Sleep in heavenly peace.

Looking up at the time-worn clock, Esther noticed it was two minutes to the hour of midnight, and the old year had almost run its course. Father time would be ushering in another year momentarily.

HAPPY NEW YEAR

Holding her husband's arm, silently, together, they

bowed their heads, and from hearts filled with praise and thanksgiving, thanked God again for His goodness in the past. They knew He could be trusted to guide each footstep ahead as they embarked into the unknown future.

Suddenly the big town clock chimed twelve o'clock midnight. The silvery sound echoed throughout the little town and across to the towering snow-capped mountains beyond.

Gordon bent over and kissed his wife. "Happy New Year!" he smiled.

Esther returned the gesture and then they began to make their way through the happy throng. Amid the jubilant blast of trumpets and blazing firecrackers, everywhere couples embraced and shouted greetings and best wishes to each other and to others around them.

The air was pungent with a festive merrymaking atmosphere as the joyous crowds made their way to local *Gasthauses* for drinks to celebrate this special yearly occasion. Traditionally, wine would flow freely and the festivity continue far into the night.

Under a canopy of twinkling stars, Gordon and Esther slowly walked toward their cozy chalet. By this time, all around them, gently dancing snowflakes fluttered softly to the frozen earth.

As they opened the door to their vacation home, the warm, tantalizing aroma of freshly buttered popcorn emanated from within. The girls had arrived before them and prepared a snack.

Sinking gratefully into comfortable chairs, they shared their impressions of a New Year's celebration in Switzerland, while sipping hot cups of savory hot chocolate.

When the faithful town clock struck the hour of two o'clock, they were settled snugly under warm feather ticks.

Lights from the town still burned brightly as the Swiss people continued their celebration of the brand new year. Long ribbons of gray smoke still curled lazily from numerous chimneys. The ageless, towering mountains rose majestically beyond, keeping vigil over the residents who had lived there all their lives.

Esther heard the rhythmic, slow breathing of her sleeping husband. The girls in their room spoke in whispers of plans for tomorrow.

Sighing contently, Esther curled up into a comfortable position, and with a prayer of thanksgiving on her lips, drifted off into dreamland.

It had been a memorable evening—truly a New Year's night to remember!

19 WEDROWIEC–1989

Leshak, they were confident, could play almost any instrument. Coming to youth camps across the country of Poland to assist in the music, he always brought blessing to the Baliskys as well as the campers.

Sitting around the campfire, he would accompany them on the guitar, until late at night. Praises filled the air and drifted across the lake to others who listened and were blessed.

Whenever needed, he and his wife, Bozena, made themselves available to be used of God in this special way.

"But," reasoned practical Bozena, "it would be wonderful to have a chorus book in our language. Sometimes the young people don't know the words. A book would be very helpful."

Leshak looked at her and smiled. "We have hymn books—but a chorus book has never been printed to use in our churches," he agreed.

Lysheck

Gordon's mind was already in action. Certain that he could find a printer for these books, he said, "Let's get serious about this project. A chorus book would be a tremendous blessing to many!"

"Bozena and I will assemble the choruses—and you *Wujek* Gordon, can work on getting the books printed," added Leshak.

The gears went into motion.

There were many choruses they had sung throughout the years, and now they must remember them all to put them on paper. They knew it could be done.

Leshak was humming songs at his work, at home, as he drove in the car, and everywhere else. Writing down the titles, very quickly the list grew.

At work and at home, Bozena did the same.

Lysheck and Bozena – a musical couple who helped us in youth camps across Poland.

Bozena was known as the fastest typist in Poland. Her skills would be invaluable once the choruses were chosen. With her speed, it wouldn't take long.

Excitement filled the air. To come to youth camp with completed chorus books would be such a blessing!

"Lord," they prayed, "please give us wisdom, time, and strength to complete this ministry for You. Help Gordon as he looks for the right publisher, too."

They knew God cared, because He is the originator of music.

> *Awake, psaltery and harp: I myself will awake early. I will praise thee, O Lord, among the people: and I will sing praises unto thee among the nations* (Psalm 108:2-3).

Sometimes at youth camp they would sing for an hour before the sermons or seminars would begin—then after church again. Some singing in harmony, were accompanied by Leshak on his guitar. What a sweet-smelling savor to God! They knew He was pleased with this form of worship.

First Book Published

The phone rang in the office in Kandern one day after they had returned from the country of Poland.

"*Wujek* Gordon," said a familiar voice.

"Leshak, my brother, how are you?"

"Bozena and I are excited. We have compiled 128 choruses for the book, but we need a good typewriter for the final copy."

Gordon had already thought this through. "Leshak," he said, "We will pay for the trip if you send Bozena to our place, here in Kandern. The IBM Electric typewriter will be perfect for what she needs to complete the typing."

Schedules and workdays were shuffled as plans were made for her to fly to Kandern. Carrying the precious manuscript in her suitcase, she boarded the airplane.

A few hours later, she emerged, her face wreathed in smiles.

"Welcome!" said Charlene.

"We are looking forward to having you in our home for a while," echoed Corinne.

The Chorus Book we published in Poland with 299 pages and 500,000 copies. It was printed in Lodz, Poland

The next day she went with them to their office on Haupstrasse, where they watched her capable hands fly over the keys.

"At this rate, it won't take long," smiled Esther to herself. And it didn't.

By this time, Gordon, too, had done his work. Finding a reasonably priced publisher in France, the details were negotiated.

Bozena went with them on Sunday to their local Black Forest Fellowship Church. Although unable to speak with anyone because of the language barrier, she found that talking, was not even necessary. Her smile alone made others want to meet this beautiful young woman from Poland.

Something Fishy

While Bozena was with them, they decided to take her to the trout farm in Kandern. Watching the small fish in the pond, darting here and there, Esther almost felt guilty. But they had to eat!

Within an hour from their fishing encounter, the trout were ready to eat. Sitting down at the table in their dining room overlooking the Kander River, Gordon blessed the food and they fell to.

Their book was almost completed. A cover and good title, they knew, are always important factors when publishing a book.

Unanimously choosing an appropriate cover picture, it featured a cross, showing the central theme of the book. The name they chose was *Wedowiec* or Pilgrim.

Eventually Bozena went to join her husband in Poland. She had done a good job and they were pleased.

Putting the precious document into a large envelope, Gordon went to France to take it to the printing house.

When 5,000 copies of the 128-page book were printed, everyone was excited!

Psalm 100, printed on the inside cover, encouraged them, too:

Fishing for Sunday dinner near our home in Black Forest. Bozena, Gordon, Charlene, Corinne and Esther.

> *Make a joyful noise unto the Lord, all ye lands. Serve the Lord with gladness: come before his presence with singing. Know ye that the Lord he is God: it is he that hath made us, and not we ourselves; we are his people, and the sheep of his pasture. Enter into his gates with thanksgiving, and into his courts with praise: be thankful unto him, and bless his name. For the Lord is good; his mercy is everlasting; and his truth endureth to all generations.*

They were pleased. Soon all across the country of Poland, the books were distributed to be used for worship. "This Is the Day That the Lord Has Made," became a favorite among the young people.

Enthusiastically they sang:

DZISIJ JEST DZIEN

Dzisaij jest dzien, dzisaij jest dzien
Ktory dai nam Pan, Ktory dai nam Pan;
Weselmy sie, weselmy sie
I radujmy sie w Nim; i radujmy sie w Nim.
Dzisiaj jest dzien Ktory dai nam Pan,
Weselmy sie i radujmy sie w Nim.
Dzisiaj jest dzien, dzisaij jest dzien
Ktory dai nam Pan.

Second Printing

Time went by. The books became scuffed and dog-eared. Were they running out so soon?

Another printing was planned. There were so many more contemporary and familiar songs that needed to be added. It was increased to 228 pages.

Once again, Bozena worked hard to type the growing manuscript. This time, 10,000 books were published in Helsinki, Finland.

One day, while Gordon was in Poland again, he was walking along a street, when he heard music. Could it be these were songs that were glorifying to God? Where were the sounds coming from?

Walking a little farther, clearly he heard, "*Dzisiaj jest dzien*" ringing from the voices of dozens of young people. Singing enthusiastically, the songs filled the air.

Others had stopped to listen.

Stopping outside the circle of singers and listeners, Gordon realized to his delight that they were singing from the *Wedroweic*! What a way to send the message of Christ to others in the city!

To his astonishment, he discovered the singers were Catholic. Incredible but true! Their little book was not only reaching the evangelicals, but the Catholics, as well.

Silently he bowed his head. The work and expense put into the book was worth it all—many times over, just to hear them sing:

Swieta Krew Jezusa (3 times)
Ona zmywa wzwlki grzech!
Oh the blood of Jesus (3 times)
It washes white as snow!

He knew the message of the Gospel was clearly presented through their little chorus book.

Third Printing

More time went by. Once more, the books became dog-eared and frayed as they ministered across the country. They needed more.

This time they decided to re-arrange some of the choruses and add others to the growing compilation of songs. Once again, Bozena, Leshak, and Gordon went through the lengthy process.

This time, after re-arranging, adding, typing, and locating a reasonable printing house, 299 pages were compiled and 50,000 copies printed in Lodz, Poland.

Standing outside the circle of the large group of young people at one of their youth camps, Gordon and Esther felt tears fill their eyes, as they saw Leshak faithfully accompanying the young people on his guitar. Singing enthusiastically from the *Wedroweic* with hearts full of love to God, the message rang out into the countryside beyond, telling the story of salvation.

Gordon, catching Bozena's eye, smiled, watching tears of joy run down her cheeks.

The hard work was worth it! They knew their Father who had planned it all, was pleased as well!

Gordon and Esther received a call in April 2004, from Lysheck. They knew Bozena had been ill for some time. Diagnosed with stomach cancer, she had major surgery and was forced to take food through a tube. Bravely she coped with this new developement. Young, talented and serving God to the best of her ability, she lived happily with her husband and daughters. Still ministering in the capacity of music, she and Lysheck joyfully continued to work with many people scattered across Poland. Now this?

"Bozena, my sweetheart, passed into the presence of the Lord," Lysheck sobbed the day he called. "She died in my arms a short time ago."

Falteringly they endeavored to comfort the distraught husband. Praying with him across the miles, they knew only God could comfort and console this family. Hanging up the telephone, they too would hold on to the Saviour. Only He could bear burdens too heavy to express.

Laying her to rest, they realized that Bozena had left a Godly legacy behind her. She was with Jesus! What a blessed hope!

20 ISRAEL

Driving through the little dorf on their way home, Gordon made an announcement that pleased them all. "This summer, when school is finished for the year, and we have returned from Poland, let's plan to go to Israel. I have work among Russian Jews there."

Another country they had only read about, would become a reality that summer.

"Can we go, too, Dad?" asked Corinne.

"Of course!" he smiled. And so the decision was made.

Taking a bus from Tel Aviv to Jerusalem, Esther gasped when she saw the city of Jerusalem appear. Great shining gold domes glittering in the sunshine, caused her thoughts to turn toward the heavenly Jerusalem. The upper room and temple areas, the *Via Delorossa*, the shepherds' fields, Bethlehem, Cana of Galilee, the Pool of Bethesda, and finally Calvary, brought vivid memories of stories read in the Bible.

Stepping out of the bus, Esther was reminded of

Moses in the book of Exodus, when God appeared in the burning bush.

"Put off thy shoes from off thy feet, for the place whereon thou standest is holy ground" (Exodus 3:5). This was also His word spoken by the angel to Joshua when he was about to enter the land of Canaan.

God, as Son of Man, walked and talked here with man. Personally he journeyed through Galilee, sought shelter with others in inns, and drank from the same well as other travelers. Here he mingled with the crowd, preaching and healing the sick. He trod the streets of Jerusalem while bearing His cross. He feared, as man, in Gethsemane, and wept on the Mount of Olives as he beheld the city.

In holy places in this land, people heard His mighty words and beheld His miracles—His suffering, dying, and eventually rising again.

As they entered the rich Jordan Valley, extending from south of the Sea of Galilee to the Dead Sea, they saw the Jordan River. Flowing majestically, it curved gracefully around bends in its path, heading, with strong currents, to the sea.

Dry soil covered the valley, but along the banks of the river, colorful plants and foliage grew and flourished in the damp earth.

Baptism

They were reminded of the incident when Jesus, the Son of God, came to John and asked to be baptized of him in the Jordan. The story became real as they stood there.

John said, "I need to be baptized by you, and do you come to me?" Aware that he was the Son of God, John felt small and insignificant as he immersed Jesus in the river.

Then the heavens opened. John gasped as he saw the

Spirit of God descend on Jesus like a dove and a voice came out of heaven saying, "This is my Son, whom I love; with him I am well pleased" (see Matthew 3:14-17).

"Dad, I want to be baptized in the same river as Jesus was," commented the serious Charlene as she watched the gentle flow of the water. Corinne, two and one-half years younger, also expressed the same desire. Thrilled that their children had chosen to be baptized, they made arrangements.

On the day they chose for their baptismal service, the scorching sun, like a ball of fire, burned through them as they walked prayerfully toward the river.

Warren Graham, a long-time missionary to the people of Jerusalem, read the account of Jesus' baptism. Esther sang softly as Gordon walked carefully into the current of the Jordan, with Charlene and Corinne following close behind. Expressing their desire to follow Jesus, the girls had patterned their lives after Him—making Him their role model. Each one was immersed, making a public decision that this was an outward sign of an inward change in their lives. The heavenly Father was pleased because two young lives were in His hands.

"Dear God, please bless my children," whispered Esther as they walked toward the golden domes in Jerusalem and the places were He, Himself, had lived and loved.

From Bondage to Freedom

They returned to their home in Northern Germany, and very soon they left again, in the wee hours of the morning, enroute for Frankfurt. The evening before, they had heard via the radio that the Vins family had been released from Russia, and were staying in a hotel near the Frankfurt airport. Georgi Vins was one of the five Soviet dissidents released from prison several weeks prior, in exchange for two Russian spies. He

was now in America, and having not been at home with his family for years, looked with anticipation to the day of their reunion. Who would have thought it would be in America?

From the cold, dark prison of Siberia, to the class and splendor of the White House was an unplanned culture shock for this soldier of the cross. God had honored his faith above that which he could ever have asked or thought.

The incident, splashed across newspapers nationwide, became a topic of conversation in the East and West. Why did they allow this man to go free when there were hundreds just like him languishing in prisons across the USSR? What made him so special? But God had the answer. They did not need to understand. And Georgi was free!

Though security was guarded, Gordon phoned ahead and made arrangements to meet with their friends in Frankfurt. It was less than a year ago when Gordon and Esther had last visited the Vins home in the heart of the great USSR. They never realized then that God had such a wonderful plan in store for them in the very near future. Their release was an answer to the prayers of thousands of people throughout the free world and Russia. They were witnessing a modern-day miracle and thrilled to see God's hand at work.

Nadezdah Vins was on the phone when they arrived at the hotel. In frustration, she was trying to answer calls that were coming in from various parts of the world. Reporters, curious people, and mission organizations were asking to speak with the family. Nadezdah, almost in tears, breathed a sigh of relief and handed the phone to Gordon when they entered the hotel room. Her limited command of the English language at this point made it difficult for her to understand others and explain her situation accurately.

As tears filled their eyes, each member of the Vins family embraced Esther and Gordon. They had learned to trust the Baliskys during their times together in Kiev. Now Nadezdah leaned heavily on Gordon for support. Together, they praised God for this miraculous release from bondage to freedom. God does work in mysterious ways!

"I can't believe it! I feel like I am in a dream," she whispered.

"But it's real," Esther answered, smiling at her. "You are in Germany and soon you will be in the United States, where there is freedom to worship. There will be no need to hide again!"

Nadezdah, Esther noticed, looked older than the last time they met. Dark circles under her eyes told the story of a lack of sleep during the last hectic days in Kiev.

"I have not slept for a month and a half," she confessed. "The days before we left were hard. Many came from all across the country to bid us farewell. Some, coming from long distances, even stayed at our house. I cooked, visited, cleaned, and packed all at the same time. There were details to tie up everywhere. I had little help.

"Peter, our son, was released from prison a short time after his father, and was at home with us the last few weeks. But the pressure was so great," continued Nadezdah, "because the KGB watched us constantly.

"'If you let Peter out of the house, we will kill him,' they warned. He already had been stabbed in the leg several times and was suffering from physical and psychological wounds. We seriously wondered if we would ever be able to leave.

"It was difficult for me. Peter could be of no help because he was in such trauma after being released, and now he was watched constantly!"

They lived in constant apprehension and their minds were filled with questions. How could they know if they would actually be released? Would they see Georgi again?

Where was Georgi? Was he safe?

Her body trembled.

"That's all behind you now, Nadezdah," comforted Gordon.

"Yes, praise the Lord!" she replied. "We are free!"

The family seemed stunned and in shock the entire time before their departure to New York. Everything had happened so quickly. Could they adjust? How would Grandma handle the trip and changes ahead?

It was nearing 10 A.M. and no one had eaten. Gordon picked up the phone and ordered a breakfast of ham and omelets to be sent to the room. Knowing they would be surrounded by reporters the minute they reached the lobby, Nadezdah and her family did not want to face the publicity they would surely receive if they went to the restaurant.

There was a knock at the door. The omelets had arrived.

Gathering around the table, they all clasped hands and began to sing. At the request of Grandma Vins, Gordon and Esther sang the Shepherd song. Tears came to her eyes as she vividly recalled the evening they spent together in their home in Kiev. Gathering in a small room upstairs, she recorded the song she would never forget.

Fellowship was warm and sweet, the coffee hot and strong, as they enjoyed their meal. But the phone and doorbell kept ringing. Reporters and mission organizations wanted to interview the Vins family. Nadezdah was grateful when Gordon answered, "No, an interview is not appropriate at this time. The family is tired and in culture shock. Sorry!"

When the gentleman from the U.S. consulate came to escort the Vins family to the airplane, everyone was excited. Suitcases and boxes, rechecked for the long flight across the water, were wheeled to the baggage checkout counter.

As their group walked down the long corridor to the

boarding area, reporters and cameras were everywhere. Eugenia, carrying a large bunch of flowers someone had given her, smiled shyly when a photographer took her picture. Peter deliberately dodged them. Curious people looked on. A look of incredible wonder shone from Alexander's face as the unusual procession made its way toward the craft that would be flying to America momentarily.

A bearded reporter handed the microphone to Nadezdah, asking her to comment on this supernatural event.

"I feel as if I am in a dream," she repeated. "We are going to see Georgi, my husband, in America, as soon as possible. Yes, he has been imprisoned for his faith and is now free."

Watching the family walk down the ramp to the airplane, they knew they were walking into a different world and a completely new future. Eugenia, with one last look, turned around and smiled. "Good-bye!" she called, "we'll see you in America!"

Silently praying that the Lord would give courage to adjust to their new country, they looked with anticipation to what He had in store for them.

The large aircraft disappeared into the clouds. They were going to their new home!

Herr Fritz Schick

As the tantalizing aroma of fresh, strong, German coffee wafted down the stairs, we heard Gustel Schick, our landlord's wife, call, in her broken English, from upstairs, "Come up! Have a cup of coffee with us!"

Throwing the dish towel aside, Esther wiped her hands and headed for the stairs while Gordon followed close behind.

We had rented our beautiful, old German chalet from this wonderful German couple before arriving in this country. Though they lived in Freiburg, some distance away, they often came to relax in their suite upstairs. It was fun to get together and talk—and we often did.

"Sit down," she smiled. Taking the only two chairs remaining, we joined them at the small table. Putzie, their small, orange Beagle, sitting content on the floor, wagged his tail in greeting. After a time of fun, our conversation turned to more serious matters.

Taking a bite of the sweet chocolate cake, Gordon looked thoughtful. "Please tell us a little about your life, Herr Schick," he queried.

The stately, dignified man, cleared his throat. He was glad to oblige. "As a child," he said, "I was brought up in a Lutheran home. God had an important place in the life of my parents. I admired my father greatly, but I never really got to know him, because when I was very young, he died on the battlefield in the first World War. My family did not believe in serving in the army, although it was compulsory, so when my father received the call to serve in the *Vehrmacht*, it was very difficult for him to go. But if he did not, there would be serious penalties for him and his family. Reluctantly, he prepared to leave home.

My mother told me later that when he came from the front in France to visit her and his little boy, before he was killed in action, he held me close to his heart." Wiping his eyes, our landlord continued, "She said he wept as he said good-bye just before leaving to go back to the front lines northwest of Lille. Here, in a small graveyard, he was buried soon after being killed on the battlefield."

His eyes brightened as he looked at Gustel.

"Meeting my future wife, soon we fell in love." Pinching

her playfully, she shooed him away, but we could tell she was pleased and thought the world of her husband.

"Though she was Catholic and I a Lutheran, we have made it together all these years," he smiled.

Putting her hand on his knee, for once she was quiet.

So often during our visits we observed that Gustel "wore the pants" in the family. Fritz made sure he did everything possible in order to make her happy. Together with the man she adored, they were happy and content.

Esther looked at the clock. Her girls would be home from school soon. They would be starved.

Thanking the Schicks for the coffee and snack, she went downstairs to prepare dinner.

A Journey Back in Time

"Herr Gordon," called Fritz Schick the next day.

Gordon turned in his tracks.

"I hear you are taking a trip to Billy Montigney, which is near Lille where my father is buried. I have never been to his gravesite. When are you planning to go? Would it be possible for me to come along?"

Our mission had asked Gordon to drive to mission headquarters in France to pick up a shipment of the *Gospel of John*. Would he enjoy Herr Schick's company? Of course he would!

So it was settled. Fritz and Gordon planned to leave soon. Packing the Volkswagen camper bus the night before their departure, the men looked with pleasant anticipation to spending time together. It was a golden opportunity for Gordon to hone his skills in the German language and culture.

"Gordon, your alarm is ringing," yawned Esther as she climbed out of bed to shut off the loud ringer the next morning.

"Is it morning already?" retorted her surprised husband.

"It seems like I have just crawled into bed! Have I overslept? Or have I even slept?" he asked.

Getting up at 5 A.M. was not a routine at our house, but he knew it was time to go.

Driving all day, the men shared about various subjects. The time went fast. Roads, meticulously groomed (everything is always in order in Germany), they arrived at mission headquarters at dinnertime. "Welcome!" greeted Gordon's coworker, Bill Kapitaniuk. "Welcome to our home!"

Introducing Herr Schick, the gentlemen shook hands. "Yes," thought Fritz, "I will like this man." The feeling was obviously mutual as they talked around the dinner table.

The next morning, our landlord was impressed when Bill took them through the large facilities including the church and printing press.

"These *Gospels of John*, which have been printed here," said Gordon, "will be taken to Russia and distributed to people across the country."

Fritz wiped his eyes with the back of his hand. To think someone cared enough to take Bibles into another country, was almost too much for him to comprehend.

"Now, where shall we sit?" asked Fritz as they loaded the bus to capacity. They found room.

Driving toward Germany, the city of Lille was on their route. Fritz Schick was exceptionally quiet as they drove toward the gravesite where his young father had given his life for his country.

Slowly but eagerly he disembarked and stepped onto the manicured graveyard. But where was his father buried? He had to find this resting-place.

Reading names on tombstones, his heart filled with hope. His father's remains were here somewhere. He would find the grave if it took all day! Knowing Gordon would wait, carefully, slowly, he walked from grave to grave.

There it was!

Reverently, thoughtfully, the men stood beside the grave of this brave soldier. But he was not only a soldier, however. He had been a devoted husband and father, as well. His belief in God had been strong.

Quietly standing there, Fritz tried to remember the things his mother had told him so long ago. Vaguely, he could see his father's face before his eyes. With longing in his heart, he was keenly aware of his loss. Silently, Fritz sent up a prayer to God. Would he see his father again? He didn't really know.

Others were present in the cemetery that day. A woman of perhaps his own age, stood silently beside the grave of her departed husband. Fritz, careful not to interrupt, looked her way. She caught his eye.

"*Guten Tag*," she smiled.

Fritz returned the friendly gesture.

These few moments of introduction turned into a full-fledged conversation. Because she lived nearby, Fritz asked her if it would be possible for her to tend to his father's grave when she came to the cemetery to visit her husband's grave.

"I would be happy to," she smiled. "It will be no trouble at all!"

Promising to send money every year to defray the costs, she insisted it was not necessary.

Two hours went by, and it was time to be on their way to Kandern. Bowing their heads in prayer, they thanked God for an opportunity to spend time at the grave of this courageous soldier, husband, and father.

Driving from France into Belgium, they crossed the border at night. As dark shadows covered the inky sky, they were weary. It had been a long journey.

"Let's stop here to get some sleep!" said Gordon.

Fritz heartily agreed. He couldn't wait to put his head down on a pillow.

Flipping up the top of the bus, they prepared to sleep inside that night. Herr Schick crawled up into a bunk and was soon asleep. Because his friend was sleeping toward the front of the crowded bus, Gordon crawled into the back, so his snoring would not keep Fritz awake.

In a quaint German restaurant the next day, Herr Schick began to ask questions. "How do you know that God has forgiven your sins?" he wanted to know.

Carefully, prayerfully, Gordon shared the Scripture:

> *That if thou shalt confess with thy mouth the Lord Jesus, and shalt believe in thine heart that God hath raised him from the dead, thou shalt be saved* (Romans 10: 9).

"I have believed in Jesus all my life," he said, "but I have never confessed or told anyone. Though I have gone to church all my life, and talked about religion, I've never confessed Him."

"Why don't you tell God that, too?" asked Gordon. "Do you want to ask Him to come into your heart and forgive your sins?"

Without any further prompting, Herr Schick asked Jesus to forgive his sins. Then, thanking him for sparing his life, they wept together.

After a busy day of traveling, they went to the van and crawled into their bunks. Hearing the night birds calling, Gordon heard another sound, as well. Herr Schick was praying the Lord's prayer in the German language while he lay quietly on his bunk.

The next day dawned. Another story followed as they drove toward Germany.

"While I served in World War II, my colleagues and I were ambushed by Ukrainian partisans or Communist vigilantes near to Vinitsa where Hitler had his headquarters (code-named *Wervolf*). As Lieutenant, my orders were to facilitate the return of 28,000 soldiers from Kiev to Berlin, which was under seige. These men were expected to help fight the Allies who were nearing Berlin, the Jewel of Germany. Running into the swamp during the ambush, we quickly tore reeds from their stems and held them to our mouths so we could breath under water. Pulling the roots over ourselves, we dug our feet into the mud below and did everything possible to conceal ourselves. Lying motionless in the swamp water for five days, we could hear the rattle of machine gun, rifle, and cannon fire overhead and in the water. As blood of dead comrades colored the swamps, we took shallow breaths through the hollow reeds so we wouldn't choke and drown. After the ambush, out of 28,000 men, only 78 came back to tell the story. I was one of them," whispered Herr Schick.

Sharing one story after another as they traveled toward home, he told of how the German people suffered during the war. Most of the soldiers did not want to serve under the Hitler regime. However, they had no choice but to follow orders. Otherwise, said Herr Schick, "we would have been killed by the Gestapo and treated as shamefully as the Jews had been.... That was a horrible experience—to know what was happening and not to be able to do anything about it," he sighed.

"I am so grateful to God to be His child. Surely He saved me from the jaws of the lion's mouth so I could serve Him all my life."

The *dorf* of Kandern, nestled in the hills, appeared before their eyes. As they saw the lights twinkling from the

various homes, Gordon stepped on the accelerator. They were almost home!

Before driving into Steinenstrasse 1B, the grateful man added, “We, as Germans, are so thankful to the Americans, Canadians, and British—the Allies—who freed us from the debauchery of Hitler’s regime. We will never forget.”

Stepping out of the van, Herr Schick walked upstairs to the apartment where Gustel was waiting. Putzie barked long and loud. His master was home again!

21 Camp Ochweika – Poland

Esther thought the rain would never end! It beat against the van, as the windshield wipers labored faithfully to keep vision clear.

Gordon, squinting his eyes, and wrinkling his nose, carefully watched the road ahead. Fog, rain, and darkness covered the land. He hesitated momentarily when the camp sign appeared ahead. Cautiously, he turned the vehicle down a narrow, muddy path leading to their destination.

They plowed forward, the van veering from side to side while the wheels sank deeply into the fresh mud. A heavy mobile home followed reluctantly behind.

Growing very quiet, each of them breathed a prayer, committing the remainder of their journey into God's hands. Would they make it through the heavy gumbo and torrential rain?

Finally, in the hazy distance, a grayish-blue lake appeared. Dilapidated buildings and a few soggy tents

assured them they had arrived at their destination—Camp Ochweika, Poland.

A few young people, sloshing through the mud, ran to meet them. Smiling in welcome, some of the young men pushed the muddy vehicle and trailer in through the gate to the camp. They had arrived—and unscathed, too! Thanks be to God!

It wasn't easy to find a place between the dense trees where their mobile home and van could park for about two weeks. Eventually this task was completed and their "home away from home" nested snugly among the foliage.

"At least we have a warm, dry place to stay," commented Corinne, looking in the direction of the young people's soggy tents. "Wouldn't they be cold—or even wanting to go home?" Later, they relaxed when they realized these people were accustomed to roughing it.

The Big Tent

Most of the campers were in the big tent where an evening service was in session. Hastily, the Baliskys and their helpers all ran through the pouring rain, ducked under the tent flap, and stepped inside. Charlene complained when Gordon picked her up and carried her piggy-back style through the mud and into the brightly-lit tent. He deposited her carefully on a backless bench. Everyone smiled. Then he, too, sat down and proceeded to concentrate on the message of the evening.

Esther, shivering in a light summer jacket, tried to keep her sandled feet dry on a little plateau where they would not get wet. Little rivulets of water ran into the tent, under their feet, soaking the earth beneath. Loud, incessant rain pounded on the roof above them. Gusts of chilly wind blew the sides of the canvas tent, so it billowed out and then in toward them.

The speaker, battling with the noise of the elements, almost shouted to be heard. Esther's back became increasingly weary and rigid from sitting on the backless bench.

"Will he ever be finished?" Charlene whispered.

Finally, after many announcements and a few more songs, the long meeting was dismissed. Campers stretched their legs, and stomped water from their shoes. Then, gathering around the family, the campers greeted them with enthusiasm and warmth. Being several days late for camp, they were grateful they had finally arrived—safely!

Mr. and Mrs. Bulloch

The next day was cold and sunless, as Esther awakened to the peel of the breakfast bell. "Wake up! It's time to eat!" she informed her sleepy daughters. Rubbing her eyes, Corinne wanted to know why the night had fled so rapidly.

Laughing, ambitious, and hungry young people walked briskly past their mobile home. In a few seconds, Charlene, Corinne, and Esther squeezed into jeans, pulled warm sweaters over their heads, patted unruly hair into place, and joined the group in the warm, humid dining room. How could they be so cheerful? After all, outdoors it was dark, cold, and rainy.

Already they were heartily singing their thanks for a meager breakfast. Generally *S'niadanic* (breakfast) consisted of strong, black, boiled tea and open-faced cucumber and meat sandwiches, often made the night before. That's fine for a few days, but when it continued on for the entire duration of camp, Esther's stomach began to rebel. But what choice did she have? She either ate the food or went hungry. She chose to eat.

Before they sang a thank you hymn of praise at the close of the meal, heavy drops of rain could be heard once again on the roof. This didn't seem to bother the campers very much, however, because they were already damp and wet. A little rain never dampened their enthusiasm. After all, they were together at camp! Esther felt guilty for complaining, because she and her family slept in a dry place.

After breakfast, Esther smiled as she watched stately Mrs. Bulloch, a visitor from Hollywood, California, pick her uncertain way toward the unconventional outdoor bathroom—trying in vain not to slip on the narrow planks which, by now, were green and slippery. In one hand the woman held tightly to her bulging handbag, and in the other, she carefully clutched a roll of American toilet paper. Her nose wrinkled in distaste as she neared the unsavory destination.

Though she was laughing inside, compassion filled Esther's heart, as she tried to be sober again. Silently she prayed for her. "I'm sure she has never encountered facilities quite like these, but she'll make it!"

Bill and Mildred Bulloch had been corresponding with the Baliskys from their home in Hollywood, California, for some time with regards to the possibility of coming to Europe and traveling into Poland together. Gordon told them about the ministry to which God had called them. Interest was sparked immediately. When invited, they actually came.

They had met the Bullochs in Israel for the first time, and felt it was a divine encounter. Immediately they sensed in them a warm, caring couple who put Christ first in their lives.

When they left Poland a few weeks later, with tears in the eyes of this businessman, he remarked, "We often prayed for your family while you were in Eastern Europe, but now we know how to pray far more effectively. We had no idea of the tremendous strain under which you work, or what a gigantic work schedule you carry. Now we really know what to pray for, and you can be assured, we will always be your prayer supporters!"

Seminars

The gong sounded again, echoing across the lake into the countryside beyond. Quickly, Esther closed her Bible and slipped a warm sweater over her white blouse to go to the morning seminar. She had been studying all winter on the subject she planned to share with the university girls at camp that year.

Once more, sensing the responsibility, she bowed her head and asked God to give her liberty. The girls in youth camp always had a myriad of questions on diversified subjects. Esther counted on the Lord to help her deal with these in the right way, wholeheartedly depending on His wisdom and freedom to present the material the way He would share it with others. Though she had studied hard, without the anointing from the Holy Spirit, her lectures would be dull and dead.

"Good morning!" sang Dorota, the camp director's wife, who was also Esther's capable translator and interpreter.

As they walked into the tent where the girls were waiting, she innocently informed Esther, just ten minutes before the second bell would sound, about the subject matter the girls had chosen to hear. Esther had worked all winter on material she felt God wanted her to present. Now what was she to do? The requested subject was vastly different.

"What do they want to hear?" she asked, trying hard to remain calm and collected.

"They want to learn about God's will for their lives. What could the future hold? What did the days ahead hold for them with regards to a life's mate? How could they know if they were in love with the man of God's choice? How could they know God's will with regards to service for Him in the future?" Dorota answered.

Esther's brain began to work overtime. With the few minutes remaining before class, she went back into her mobile home, put her carefully prepared notes away, and sought the Lord for ideas from His Word to help her answer questions that could mold the entire life of a young person.

She knew this was from God, because verses from Scripture stood out boldly as ideas began to take shape. He was faithful and did anoint his humble servant. She and the girls had many profitable learning hours together during the duration of camp. Coming to each session with transparent, teachable hearts, they waited to hear from God's Word and received answers to their questions and frustrations that throbbed within.

Between sessions, Esther prayed and gathered new material from His Word to pass on to these eager, young lives.

As the days went by, they sincerely thanked their leader for helping them see the need to spend time in His Word.

Confident that if they allowed Him to have first place in their hearts, they knew He would show them the path of life.

"He wants the highest happiness for each of His children," Esther said. "He may allow you to go through deep waters and unfamiliar places in the process, but He will never let you down. With the end result in view, He knows what is best for you and is the most capable One to run your life."

Day after day they came to hear. In the evenings, services lasted for two to three hours. The singing was always hearty, the testimonies genuine, and many decisions were made for the Lord during the camp.

Each day, the rain pounded on the top of the flimsy tents. Even this and wet clothes did not dampen the enthusiasm of the young people.

Day after day they sat with Bibles open, listening to Gordon and Esther share the Word.

Esther always sensed her own inadequacy when a young woman, coming to her with a problem, would pour out her heart through an interpreter. Esther sensed the Spirit of God within her own heart as He faithfully gave counsel to her to pass on to the inquirer. Then, with hope in her heart, the new friend began to apply the enlightened Scriptures to her personal situation.

Faithfully, the Holy Spirit gave words and wisdom to share, while He gently probed deeply into hungry hearts.

Breathing a prayer of thanksgiving, Esther placed one after another on her growing prayer list.

A Birthday Party

"Mom, it's my birthday tomorrow," sighed Corinne. Esther looked into the eyes of her beautiful fifteen-year-old and tried to speak positively. They had usually held birthday parties for her at home, but the last few years she had been in

Eastern Europe or Russia for that important day of her life.

Wistfully, she looked out the foggy trailer window toward a dark, angry sky. Watching the rain splash on the water-logged soil, she desperately longed to be home. Realizing she was really homesick, Esther felt like one of Job's comforters. "Just wait and see what tomorrow brings. We will try to make it a special day for you, Corinne."

Gordon told a few of the young people about Corinne's birthday. Excited, Anna, and Peter began to make plans for the next day. No one told Corinne.

The morning of July 17 dawned rainy and cold. Shivering, they put warm coats over heavy winter sweaters and hurried to the dining room for cold sandwiches and boiled black tea.

All morning, while Corinne tried to keep warm in the trailer, Peter, Anna, and others prepared for a birthday party that would be unique and different. They ordered ice cream cakes. Bill Bulloch supplied Cokes for everyone. Green plants and simple decorations hung from the low ceilings in the dining room, giving it a festive appearance. White cloths covered long tables, while bouquets of colorful field flowers graced them with fragrance. Corinne loved wild flowers.

Finally, the anticipated evening arrived.

"Corinne," said Anna, "please come into the dining room. I have something to show you!"

Reluctantly entering the dining room, Corinne was completely surprised as everyone began to sing "Happy Birthday."

As she was escorted to the head table, Corinne had no idea what a Polish birthday party would be like. She soon found out!

What a celebration they had! Never in their lives had they attended a party such as this. Tears of laughter running down their cheeks, they were introduced to one Polish game after another. Stately Bill Bulloch slapped his knees as tears of laughter ran down his face. The Polish sense of humor is beyond description.

Peter, leading the five-hour party, spoke broken English and his native language intermittently. Corinne was given a few written sentences in the Polish language. "Think of a familiar tune, and use these words," said Peter. They rocked with laughter when her pronunciation of their language was uniquely Americanized.

Everyone forgot about the rain or that it was getting late. Inside, the atmosphere was fun and friendly. Corinne said she would never forget her Polish birthday party.

Her spirits were greatly lifted when she walked back to the trailer to sleep. It was the best party she'd ever had and certainly the most unusual.

Fever

Esther went to the trailer feeling chilled and shaky after the session the next day. Had the weather suddenly turned colder or why was she trembling so?

Crawling into her damp bed, she pulled the covers over her head. Tossing and turning, there seemed to be no way to get comfortable. Drinking often from the lukewarm bottled water they had brought from Germany brought no relief. Her stomach was churning, her head throbbing, and her teeth chattering, as she pulled the covers even higher.

When Mildred Bulloch came into the trailer, she put her hand on Esther's head and exclaimed in alarm, "My dear, you are burning up!" In this camp, she knew, cleanliness was not next to godliness. What kind of germ did she pick up? Was it the *Kinapke*? She wouldn't be surprised. Mildred almost gagged when she thought of it.

But what could she do for the sufferer? No one knew.

When dysentery reared its ugly head, Esther tried to make her way to the odorous outhouse in the rain, but she couldn't make it. This is when John Paul, the family chamber pot, came in handy. During the next few days, the pounds fell off, and her clothing hung loose and unfitting. There was no doctor. If there were, he would not have had a solution, she was sure of that. Not in Poland.

Dorota knocked gently on the door. Painfully raising her head Esther whispered, "Come on in—the door is open!"

It was thoughtful of her to bring a cold Coke. What a luxury! "Esther, please put your housecoat on. The cook would like to help you," she offered. "Would you please come into the kitchen for just a moment?"

Please, just leave me alone, was her first silent response, but wanting to oblige, she said, "Just a moment. I will come." But what kind of remedy could a cook have for her? Probably some Polish concoction.

Shaky, Esther pulled on her housecoat and walked toward the unsavory kitchen just beside the dining room.

"I know how to cure dysentery," smiled the cook.

"Here, I have cooked some hard boiled eggs. I want you to eat as may as you can." Saying this, generously she sprinkled heavy, black pepper over the top.

Flies filled the crowded kitchen. Cooked food standing on the cupboard was invaded by crawling insects. The floor, difficult to keep clean in the rain, was covered with mud. Unwashed dishes spilled over the sides of the sink while tea towels, damp and soiled, lay on the unwashed counter.

How could Esther eat hard boiled eggs? Not wanting to offend, carefully she took a few small bites, and a few more. Then, stumbling back to the trailer, she couldn't wait to crawl back into bed.

Perhaps the cook's remedy helped however, because Esther grew better soon after that.

Glory

The atmosphere was hushed during the last evening service in the big tent. Surely those who had not made the decision to follow Christ, would do so tonight?

Gordon had spoken on how vital it is to know Jesus as Savior. When all eyes were closed and most of the young people were praying, he challenged those who wanted to make this decision. "If you are serious, please stand now," he encouraged.

Without the least bit of hesitancy, several responded. The seed had been sown during the weeks at camp. Now they were ready to yield to the prompting of the Spirit. Kaju, the camp director, and Gordon took them into the dining room for prayer while the rest of the group stayed in the big tent to sing and pray.

The glory of the Lord filled the simple dining room that night as several lives were transformed.

John, a university student from Kiev, prayed a simple prayer for salvation. Then saying, "Amen," he raised his hands upward and began praising God. His little brother beamed, as he, too, came through to victory and the joy of salvation.

The group in the tent continued to sing. No one was in a hurry. They were rejoicing with the angels over each sinner as they repented.

Late that night, guitars were still strumming praise choruses in the big tent. This time, John and his little brother sang with them—rejoicing that they, too, belonged to the family of God.

Looking at her watch, Esther saw it was past midnight.

Charlene and Corinne silently left for the trailer. They all slept well that night, because they had seen the miracle of new life. This always gave them joy.

Fun and Games

Besides being fed spiritually, the kids were having fun. Playing ping pong, volley ball, and other forms of recreation, plus boating in the lake, kept everyone active most of the day.

"We can't believe the skills your daughters display in all of the games," grinned the boys. The Polish girls, not interested, looked on. How could these American girls enjoy boys' games?

Charlene scored one point after another as she hit the ball over the volleyball net. The boys eagerly took turns playing ping pong with the girls. Usually Charlene or Corinne were the winners. The boys were impressed. There was a slight communication gap, but it proved to be no problem. It became a common sight to see the young people gathered around their girls, each exchanging the others' language. After saying the Polish word, it was repeated in English. Everyone who wanted to take part saw benefits in learning a language this way. When the sun peered from behind a cloud, which wasn't often, the enthusiastic young people quickly ran to the shore of the lake to have a boat ride. Of course all vied for the attention of the two girls. Both had many boat rides.

The day Esther went with Gordon, the sun was shining and the water was clear as crystal. Dorota and Kaju skimmed across the water next to them. After all the rain, it was refreshing to soak up some sunshine.

Farewell

It was raining again on the last day of camp. Everything was bathed in a black, dismal fog. As drops, large and cold, splashed to the ground, boards were strewn on paths to the tent, dining room, and lavatories. Mud was everywhere.

In spite of this hindrance, the young people worked all day to prepare a big banquet. This was a pleasant ritual at the end of each camp, and this time was no exception. Through the soggy weather they carried chairs, tables, and food from the dining room to the big tent. Careful not to slip on the boards, they slowed their pace.

That evening as the rain poured, they crowded into the steamy tent. Each place was taken. There were visitors from Holland, Africa, different parts of Poland, the United States, and Canada! What a grand time they had as singing, testimonies, fun, food, and fellowship were all included in the long program. There must have been twenty special musical selections, including the Baliskys' contribution.

The celebrations lasted so long that by the end, their feet were cold and wet. Rain had soaked the sides of the big tent as running water covered the muddy floor, but everyone agreed they had a wonderful time.

Realizing they would not be seeing some of their friends in the morning because they were going to their respective homes early, they went to various individuals to say good-bye. Each time, there were tears, hugs, and smiles. Corinne and Charlene, having made a lot of friends, did the same, promising to keep in touch by letter or telephone.

The next day, the campers who were still there gathered alongside the van and mobile home as Gordon and Esther and the girls drove out of the grounds. "God be with you till we meet again!" echoed across the countryside as they drove away to their next point of ministry. The campers watched until the van disappeared over the hill. "*Dovejenya*!" they called after them.

In spite of the rain, mud, and other inconveniences, the

camp had been one they would long remember in a positive way. They rejoiced that some had come to know Christ for the first time, while others made re-commitments to follow Him at any cost. Though they had to say good-bye, they were reminded of One who never does. For He promised, "Lo, I am with you always" (Matthew 28:20). He would go before these young people to be their Guide in a world filled with uncertainties and unknowns. They knew He would. He had promised!

Meeting Needs in the Countryside

Gordon, Charlene, Corinne, and Esther had been in the city of Lublin for several weeks. Most often, there were people who needed their attention. Gordon, especially, was always ready and willing to help.

One afternoon they made plans to drive 60 kilometers out of Lublin to bring groceries to a couple and their family who were living in poverty. Relatives in Wasau, Wisconsin, had sent money to buy food for their distant kin in the country.

"Dad, Cori and I want to stay here, and take a hike into the old city. We still have *zlotys* to spend, too, so we would like to go shopping," said Charlene. The girls had done so much traveling, they wanted to be alone.

"OK, just have some fun," answered their father. "We will be back later this afternoon."

After driving through the congested city, they were finally in the Polish countryside. Sitting in the back of the car alone, while Pastor Joseph and Gordon talked in the front, Esther's thoughts turned toward the people of Poland. She realized that 97 percent of the population is Catholic. The Communists and Catholics were not friendly toward one another. This, in turn, caused the Communists to be more lenient toward believers. Some children were even being taught by Protestants, and this was not frowned upon by the government.

Yesterday, Esther had asked a believer if it was difficult to live in Poland as a Christian. "Not really," she replied. "If one does not talk against the system, there is no problem."

Suddenly, they were stopping, interrupting her thoughts. Joseph and Gordon got out and filled the car with gas. Coming out of the station a few minutes later, they were both smiling.

"You look like the cat that swallowed the canary," Esther said. "What gives?"

"Forty-two liters of gas just cost us a pound of coffee, plus 3 dollars in cash," laughed Joseph. "Rather an inexpensive way to travel, don't you think?"

It was difficult to make good time. Esther thought they would never reach their destination. Horses, bikes, trucks, careless drivers, cows, horse-drawn wagons, and even mothers pushing baby carriages, caused them to stop over and over again.

They drove past houses, children playing on the streets and in playgrounds, chickens and geese scratching for grubs, people talking across the fence, sunflowers ready to be harvested, and tobacco growing in fields. Some tobacco already picked, was draped on entire sides of buildings to dry in the sun. There were feather beds hung from open windows to air out, apple-laden trees, fields of hops, and thatched roof cottages, as they traveled along the bumpy roads.

Meanwhile, the hot sun beat down, causing Esther to wipe her brow many times. Joseph and Gordon, engaged in conversation, didn't seem to notice.

Eventually, they came to a farm, located in a sort of courtyard. The dilapidated buildings, brown and weather-beaten, had not been painted since they were built years ago. As they entered, chickens, feathers flying, ran off the road, squawking loudly. Cats scattered and dove under a nearby shed, while cows with great liquid eyes, just stood and stared.

Arrival

An elderly couple came out of the house when they heard the commotion. The woman wore a large apron covering the stains on her floral housedress. Big bosomed, with a scarf on her head, she looked the other way when they held out their hands to shake theirs. The man, also, ignoring their gestures, wore old coveralls, and his mouth was sunken and hollow, because most of his teeth were gone.

An awkward silence followed till Joseph introduced them. Were they not going to talk? Was this even the right family?

Suddenly, an attractive daughter of about thirty-two years of age appeared. Though still young, she had several gold teeth. Two younger women followed. They stood and stared at them. Who could these strangers be? What did they want? Their questions were soon answered.

"We have some food for you," said Gordon, in Polish. Your kin from Wisconsin (he named them) asked if we would bring it for you."

Suddenly, they smiled and wanted to shake hands. This gift sounded good to them.

Still not really certain if they were at the right farm, Joseph asked for their passports. Obligingly, after searching in the house, they showed them that, indeed, they were the people for whom they were searching.

Inviting them into the drab, dark house, they asked them to sit down. Being strong Catholics, their walls were adorned with pictures of saints and Mary, the mother of Jesus. Statues also stood on a table nearby.

By this time, the woman, conscious it was her obligation to be hospitable to these people who were bringing gifts, went into the small kitchen and began to make lunch. Not having much variety with which to cook, she prepared the best she had. Cold meat and bread are the usual fare in Poland, and this time was no exception. Strong, hot tea, almost scalded Esther's throat as it went down. Gradually the burning went away.

Esther's stomach, which had been uncomfortable even before they arrived, lurched when she saw big flies with blue wings on the pink meat. Buzzing loudly, still others landed on the hard, dry bread. She could see that the *maslo* was already speckled with something. It wasn't hard to imagine what it was.

She could smell the scent of cow dung as it came in through the open door.

"Where is the toilet, please?" she asked, suddenly aware of her need. By this time, Gordon, too, was feeling the same.

"It is outside,"gestured, the old man. Not bothering to get up, he continued chewing his food with the few teeth remaining in his mouth.

Excusing themselves, Gordon and Esther went outside. They walked past pigs, cows, horses, and chickens. Careful not to step on unwanted matter, they gingerly made their way. Where was that toilet anyway?

A different kind of aroma gave them the answer. Following this scent, they soon found it. Behind the barn, they saw a shabby little building—a typical Polish outhouse. Flies swarmed around them as they entered. The interior was dark and unsavory. But it was a place to go.

GIFTS

When they came back to the house and presented the food gifts, the family didn't have words to express their gratefulness. The big-bosomed woman took Esther into her ample arms, not once or twice, but repeatedly. Kissing her profusely on both cheeks, as well as her hands, weeping she cried, "Yak-o-you! thank you! Yak-o-you!" Gordon was receiving

the same response from the grateful man.

They stood in the yard, held hands, and talked to their heavenly Father. The family was responsive as tears continued to roll down their cheeks. Wiping them away with a work-worn hand, the farmer cleared his throat.

As they drove out of the yard, once again the squawking chickens and roosters scattered. Running to the other side of the road, they continued their search, scratching for grubs in the soft soil.

The family continued to wave and threw kisses as the car disappeared in a cloud of black dust.

Skeptical at first, but gradually warming up to the message of the Gospel, they hoped that this family living in the hinterlands of Poland, would accept Jesus as Lord of their lives because someone cared enough to bring a gift of love.

A River Turns Savage

Back in Germany, the thunder rolled as lightning streaked across the darkened sky. Rain came down in torrents! They wondered if it would ever stop.

The Kander River, near their house, usually so placid and calm, was angry and swollen as it fought its way through a mass of foreign objects in its path.

People came from the *dorf* and watched their once-friendly river as it thrashed and foamed like a wild animal. Holding her umbrella tightly so it wouldn't blow away in the fierce wind, Esther stood with her neighbors. Trying to move to a place where she could see better, she was amazed to see how savage the river had become.

Suddenly everyone gasped as part of the steep bank above the river broke loose and vanished into the churning waters below. Trees, shrubs, and flowers were washed away instantaneously, only to become a part of the raging torrent.

Torn earth showed brown and ragged where, only moments before, it had been covered with greenery and flowers.

The people gasped again. An old barn on the opposite bank from where they stood was rudely snatched from its foundation by the icy fingers of the angry torrent below. Groaning heavily, reluctantly tearing away and breaking into pieces, it, too, was gone.

The next day, it was a relief to see the sun peer through dark clouds that had been there for so long. The storm over, their town was peaceful and still again.

The Kander River, still running wild, was beginning to slow down. Their town was washed and clean after the rain. Raindrops, catching rays of the sun, sparkled on watered grasses and shrubbery.

Relieved, people from the *dorf* were happy to see the storm was past. Children would soon play on the banks of a placid river once more. Everything would be normal again.

22 MOVE TO AMERICA

Gordon and Esther were aware that the Slavic Gospel Association were changing some of their policies and structures.

The President called one day; "Would you," he asked, "be willing to move back to the United States to represent our mission here at home? This would include travelling to various churches and raising money so we can operate more freely. This is a big decision for you, but please consider it prayerfully."

This, they knew would entail leaving Kandern. Were they willing to do that?

Gordon prayed long into the night hours for weeks, asking for God's direction. How would the girls react to this new development? Would they be willing to leave this place they had learned to love? Travailing in prayer and waiting on God, both Gordon and Esther carefully considered this proposition.

Fortunately they had not sold their home in Seattle, and

it could become their headquarters there.

Finally, realizing God was in control, they surrendered and decided to begin this new endeavor.

"Girls," said Gordon one morning, "Mom and I have prayed a lot about a decision we have made to move back to the States to resume our work with the mission. You will soon be ready for college as well and will need to find a place of higher education."

Both were quiet as they contemplated this new developement. "It would be nice to be home again," they reasoned, "but it will be hard to leave our friends here too..."

The family dearly loved their small town. Having made many friends, it was difficult to say good-bye. Would they ever see them again? But packing began in earnest. Esther always dreaded this procedure, but rolled up her sleeves and went to work.

Frau Schick, rarely showing emotion, felt tears flow down her cheeks, when she bid them farewell. Often Gordon and Esther had gone to their apartment upstairs, following the fragrance of freshly-brewed coffee. Together with the fun-loving couple, they often laughed until tears rolled down their cheeks. But there were times of sober, meditative moments, too, when God's Word was shared around the table in the kitchen. Herr Schick, praying aloud, asked God to protect them on their long journey home.

That night, exhausted, Esther crawled into bed. The Kander River continued to make melody as it smoothly slid over the rocks. A gentle wind blew around the house, quietly rustling the loose shutter on their bedroom window. Gordon, snoring beside her, had dropped into bed and went to sleep immediately.

A crack of light showed under Charlene's door. Esther realized she was probably talking to God. Often during her illness she had made this her practice and it would remain with her for the rest of her life.

Pulling the curtains together to shut out the light of a big, golden moon in the sky, the room became dark. Finally Esther slept. It had been a big day, but their suitcases were ready, and everything was prepared to leave their house on Steinenstrasse 1B. This chapter in their lives was almost over, and a new one in Seattle would be the next.

The morning dawned perfectly clear. Birds sang shrilly in the trees on the big yard by the river. Getting into the car, enroute for Frankfurt, where a flight had been booked, Corinne looked longingly at her little town. Knowing every nook and secret hiding place, she knew she would miss her life in Germany. Already having said good-bye to Miriam, the girls promised to write faithfully. Soon her friend, too, would be leaving Kandern, for a college of her choice.

With all the suitcases and boxes on board, the family slowly climbed into the airplane. The large, silver bird thrusting upward, soon vanished into the clear blue sky and disappeared from sight, carrying God's precious cargo.

Home

It seemed normal to move back into the house on Fremont Avenue North. It was also a disappointment. The carpets that had been clean and thick when they left, were now threadbare and soiled. Walls that were white and clean were now marred and streaked with dirty stains. Everywhere there were signs of people who had rented this home, not caring how they looked after the place.

Esther found it difficult to believe that folks who called themselves Christians, could desecrate her home in which she had taken so much pride.

Remembering clearly how difficult it had been to leave

when going to Germany, she had asked God to look after their place. Leaving this to Him, peace came as she closed the front door on Fremont Avenue North. This was God's house, she realized, and He had only loaned it to them for a time.

A group from their church came and helped paint the soiled walls. Carpets were removed and replaced with new. The furnishings which had been stored, were put into original settings.

The kettle boiling on the ceramic counter-top stove, the refrigerator humming, and Max, the cat, contentedly purring on the chair, reminded the family that they were home.

Charlene and Corinne resumed a daily schedule of going to school. Mountlake Christian School was full of young people whose desire was to achieve in life. Making friends again who would prove to be true, the girls easily settled into life in the United States of America.

Corinne sometimes thought wistfully of her friend, Miriam, at BFA, but Julie, her new friend, filled the vacancy that had been left in her heart. The young teens were inseparable.

Esther, happy that her girls were settled again, breathed a sigh of relief. She would now look forward to many long trips to Eastern Europe and Russia as well as travelling in the United States and Canada. It would be time-consuming, but rewarding.

The house on Steinenstrasse 1B, was rented by another missionary couple, so Esther and Gordon purchased a house trailer which proved to be an adequate home away from home.

A New Developement

Shortly after arriving in the USA Donald Best, International director of East Europe Evangelism/Marshall Foundation, (a ministry into Eastern Europe and Russia) approached the Slavic Gospel Association to loan Gordon and Easther to this mission. When this process was being considered, Mr. Best suddenly became ill and passed away soon afterward.

At this time, the board from East Europe Evangelism/Marshall Foundation, asked Gordon to become the International Director of their mission. Another vital decision must be made! Once more the Balisky's asked their Heavenly Father for an answer. Should they consider leaving SGA and working with another mission organization?

The decision was made! They accepted the invitation, and have been with this mission to the present day.

In 1982, the year Charlene graduated from High School, the family all went back to Europe for the summer.

The journey to Poland was one they would never forget. Youth camp ministries always delighted Esther. To teach a group of young people through the duration of a camp, see them accept Christ as Savior of their lives, and watch them grow in faith, was rewarding and challenging. Who could ask for more?

Andrew Finds His Voice

Near Camp Konev, in Poland, was an orphanage. The director decided to send a few of his orphans to the children's camp. He brought them to the camp one sunny afternoon, not really realizing that some would come to know Jesus as Savior, or that there could be positive changes in their lives.

Andrew, a skinny, introverted little boy stepped out of the old Lada and looked around him.

He liked what he saw. While Lake Konev shone in the sunshine, and tantalizing aromas came from the kitchen, he grinned. *I think I will like this*, he silently calculated.

Too shy to communicate with anyone on a one-to-one basis, he slowly followed the children to his cabin. Would the others make fun of him? Insecure and speechless, he settled into his primitive quarters.

Born into a Polish home in the area, how could he forget the abuse and loveless home from which he came? As far

back as the eight-year-old could remember, after his mother died, beating and cursing was all he knew of his abrasive father. Growing up with loud voices raised in anger and accusations toward him, the child felt he did everything wrong. If it wasn't his fault, why did his father always beat him? Why was he always angry at him? What had he done? He blamed himself for it all. After many beatings and tears of frustration and fear, the child ceased to speak. There was no one with whom to talk at home. He was too shy to communicate with anyone else. Why not just draw into himself and be still? This is what he did. Soon he couldn't speak without stammering. Then others laughed at him as he struggled to articulate his faltering words.

"I just can't talk," he cried into the darkness of the night. "I won't even try anymore. It isn't worth the ridicule." Becoming insecure, timid, fearful, and alone, the boy tried to hide from others. Would *they* hurt him, too?

Andrew then lived with his grandmother for some time, but she, too, showed no love toward him. Keeping all his nervous frustration inside, mechanically he ate, slept, and went to school.

"Does no one love me?" he wept. Silently the answer mocked him. No one loved Andrew. He was alone—all alone.

Through divine intervention, a Communist orphanage, run by the State, heard about the little boy. Happy to be relieved of her burden, the aged grandmother watched her grandson leave her home. Yes, he would be better off in an orphanage. Her meager widow's pension was not sufficient to support herself and the child as well.

Heaving a sigh, and walking into her dilapidated apartment, she shut the door with a flourish, relieved, the burden of feeding one more mouth was gone.

The large orphanage housed 3,000 children. Pulling

into the yard, the director stopped the car. Leading the frightened child into his new home, he left him in a room with other boys.

Very soon they realized he couldn't talk. Taunts and laughter stormed his troubled heart, as they, too, jeered at him.

The staff, trying to bring him out of his shell, tried to show love to Andrew, but he resisted. It was better, he reasoned not to be vulnerable enough to open his heart to anyone. Perhaps he would be hurt again. He was not ready for that! Never again!

But would he enjoy the time at Camp Konev? He doubted it. How could he be happy anywhere? Yet, secretly he longed for friendship and love. He looked yearningly toward the beautiful lake. Perhaps he could go swimming here? He would like that.

With a ray of hope, the defeated boy walked toward the kitchen from whence the delicious aromas came.

As the days went by, it was incredible that no one laughed at him here. Gradually, allowing himself to listen, he heard the story about a man called Jesus. Did this man love him enough to die for him? It couldn't be! No one loved him—he knew that!

But slowly he allowed himself to trust again. "Be careful," his heart cautioned, but he knew something positive was happening. Daily he heard the Gospel. Could it be possible to love again? Did he dare open up his frightened and fearful heart?

The big, handsome camp leader invited him to go boating on Lake Konev. "Would you like that, Andrew?" he smiled into the boy's blue eyes. Did he see a glimmer of hope written there?

Shyly the boy, following his leader to the lake, stepped into the canoe Uncle Gordon had sent from the U.S.A..

In the past, he only saw pictures of such a wonderful con-

veyance. Now here it was, in front of him. Could this be true?

Skimming over the clear, smooth water, the camp leader spoke to Andrew. He noticed the boy's mouth gradually curve into a smile. Silently he thanked God. Could they get through to this broken-hearted child? He knew God could.

The big gong sounded for dinner. Andrew raced across the grass toward the dining room. *Wow, that food smells good!* he thought. Running faster, he wanted to be the first one to fill his plate. He arrived in time to do just that. Forgetting his inhibitions, he wolfed the food down. Not even realizing it, he took a second helping. *This food sure tastes better than the food at the orphanage!* he thought.

Andrew listened to the Bible lessons every day. Slowly his heart softened toward the message of the Gospel. The staff noticed that when he was completely engrossed in the lesson, his face softened and his taut body relaxed.

Was this child really singing along with the others? Learning the words quickly, he was singing! What a transformation was taking place! Could he ever be free from inhibitions that had characterized his entire life? Was it possible?

Gradually the haunted look on Andrew's face disappeared. Speaking with a faltering tongue, he told the leader he, too, wanted to ask Jesus to be his Friend.

Amazed, the leader led Andrew to the Lord. He now had Someone to love him. He, too, expressed his love for Jesus.

Slowly his faltering voice returned. As the child drank in more love and care from the group at camp, he began to speak freely. Stammering diminished as his eyes shone with light and hope.

They were amazed to see Andrew laugh and play with his new friends. Almost tripping, speeding toward the ball in the air, he caught it! Everyone clapped. The little boy's face glowed.

When the director of the orphanage came to pick up the

children, he couldn't believe the transformation in all of them—but most of all in Andrew.

Pleased, he drove back slowly, with serious thoughts. Could God really change lives? The answer, he knew, came in the laughter and conversation he heard in the back seat.

Later he said to Gordon, "The children who attended Camp Konev come back here so changed. Much easier to handle, they are well-behaved and obedient. Even some of the unruly children are changed." With 3,000 in the orphanage, he was happy to see a difference in some lives.

"You, *Pann* Balisky, can be sure whenever a camp is in session here, I will give these children full permission to attend!"

Because this was a Communist orphanage run by the State, they knew the camp was a testimony of how God can change lives.

Shaping Generations through Radio

Pastor Joseph's small white Simca purred steadily along the Polish country road. Having lived in the Lublin area all his life, he knew every bump and curve ahead.

It was evident he was in a hurry. Joseph always was. Esther watched the speedometer as it climbed precariously

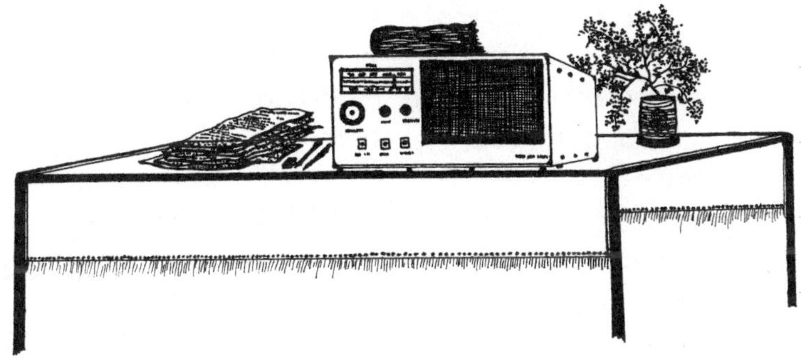

high. Her heart quickened as the needle steadily continued to rise. She had to relax!

Doing her best to settle down, she put her head on the back of the plastic seat, took a deep breath, and watched the golden countryside slip by.

Sheaves of grain, standing proud and erect, would soon be harvested and gathered in for the long, cold winter ahead. As they gathered in the grain each year, the many hours of work all spring, summer, and fall were rewarded. There would be food in abundance for their children. Was this not a cause for rejoicing?

Suddenly Pastor Joseph began to sing:

Surely goodness and mercy shall follow me,
All the days, all the days of my life.
And I shall dwell in the house of the Lord forever!

Joining in, Gordon beside him in the front seat, and Esther in the back, harmonized together for many kilometers. It seemed Pastor Joseph knew many of the contemporary choruses they were singing in the U.S.A.. This surprised them a little. It does not take long for music of all kinds to penetrate—even behind the wall of the Iron Curtain.

FOUR GENERATIONS HEAR THE GOSPEL

As the last notes of the "Alleluia" song died away, they came to a small town. Slowing down, Pastor Joseph pulled over to the side of the road and stopped. Seeing a number of people there, Esther presumed they were acquaintances.

An aged grandmother, her wrinkled face wreathed in a toothless smile, and wearing the traditional *Babushka*, waited with anticipation. Could this be Pastor Joseph? She hoped so.

Looking into her happy face, and greeting her warmly,

he placed his strong, young hands over hers and spoke words of encouragement.

The middle-aged woman, standing beside her mother, smiled broadly as Pastor Joseph, in turn, shook her hand.

A young mother nearby proudly pointed to her bright-eyed youngster in a baby carriage. Gently ruffling the baby's hair, Joseph commented on how much the little one had grown since their last encounter. The mother's broad face beamed as she conversed with the pastor. It was obvious she respected him a great deal.

Bowing their heads in prayer, even the little one seemed to sense they were talking to Someone special. Their Father was there.

Before they drove away, the ladies, coming closer to the car, curiously peered inside the window for a better look.

"*Dovee Jenya*!" (hello) Esther smiled while extending her hand in greeting from the interior of the car.

Gordon, talking to them in their own language, won their hearts immediately. Yes, they would love to hear him preach sometime. "Can you preach like the men on the radio?" they wondered. Pastor Joseph would tell them where to go to hear him and they planned to be there.

"These ladies," said Joseph as they drove away, "are born-again Christians representing four generations. The grandmother, her daughter, grandchild, and great grandchild were all there. Years ago, the elderly grandmother began listening to the radio station from Monte Carlo. Her soul was touched as the Holy Spirit gently stirred her heart. Hungry, she eventually accepted Jesus as Savior of her life."

Joseph blew his nose and continued. "What great joy she experienced as her whole life changed. The lot of the Polish woman is not an easy one, but the change added a new depth, peace, and reality to her once shallow life."

"Each time the broadcast came on," continued Joseph, "she listened eagerly, desiring to know and learn more about her new Friend and Savior. Of course, she encouraged her family to share this good news. It wasn't long before her daughter, after listening to the broadcasts, accepted Jesus, as well."

"Then her granddaughter became interested as she, too, heard the Word of Life coming to her through radio. It was apparent that there had been a change in her grandmother's and mother's lives. This gave her a hunger for the new life they experienced."

Stepping on the accelerator, the car lunged forward. *Is this man always in a hurry?* wondered Esther.

Oblivious to her discomfort, he continued, "Each one of these women have become converted through the power of the blood of Jesus and are now living testimonies in their community as to what God can do. The baby is still small, but they trust that she, too, will receive the words of eternal life when she is old enough. I'm sure the women will share stories of Jesus with her," Joseph smiled.

They hoped many more generations from this one family would crown Jesus King of their lives—all because faithful missionaries heralded the truths of the Gospel over powerful radio transmitters to those who have no other way of hearing.

Joseph, encouraging, mentoring, and teaching, while Gordon, in turn, taught him, was just part of the chain of events that had changed the lives of these women.

Now they had something worthwhile to live for. Like sheaves of golden grain which had been gathered in, they, too, were taken in to be used by God to glean in the great harvest field. Jesus was their Friend. He had made their burdens light.

23 KATOWICE

Doctor David Ryan wiped the perspiration from his face as the sun shone mercilessly into their car as they traveled on dusty, pitted roads.

They didn't see the small Polish Fiat at first, but when they realized the driver had pulled up next to them, they were uneasy. With three cars driving side by side on the narrow country road, they held their breath. All of a sudden, the car crashed into their trailer. They were disturbed when, just as quickly, he drove away. Their home on wheels had been damaged, but they couldn't keep up with the hit-and-run driver. He was soon lost in the dust and fog on the rough, Polish road.

"Thank God it wasn't worse," sighed Gordon. Now he would need to have the trailer repaired. But where? They could only wait.

Entering the city of Katowice, they had to hold their breath. With the smog from coal-heated homes, and factories

Doctor David Ryan giving a treatment to a patient in Eastern Europe.

belching out poisonous fumes, they thought their lungs would burst.

How could they be here for two weeks of ministry when they had trouble getting their breath? How did the people who lived here manage? "Well, if they can," Gordon reasoned, "with God's help, so can we."

Parking their vehicles in the big churchyard, they were

soon settled and ready to begin the ministry to which God had called them.

The church was large and beautiful. What a joy it was for Esther to play the big piano! Sometimes her fingers ached to glide over the smooth ivory keys of an instrument like this, while they were traveling. They sang several duets. The people loved this. While Gordon preached, they were hushed and attentive. How long could the Americans stay with them? they wondered. Would the doctor give them the promised adjustments? The spiritual and physical needs were great. Could they help?

It was the first day of May in Katowice. There were people everywhere, festively celebrating this national holiday. A long parade was heralded with enthusiasm and high spirits. Loud music filled the streets.

While Gordon went to minister in another town, David and Esther went for a walk in the city. Observing the festivities around them, they felt foreign—unattached—out of place. The people continued to celebrate. Forgetting their duties and responsibilities, they indulged in liquor and food. Tomorrow was another workday. Today they would indulge themselves!

Monday dawned hot and dry. The air, smoggy and dark, settled slowly into their congested lungs. How long could they take this?

After breakfast, David was busy for hours. People arriving from Givitz, and other surrounding areas, waited in line for this gifted chiropractor to touch their bodies. Gratefully they shook his hand. "*Dzie kuja*," they said with tears in their eyes. Truly, God had sent these people to minister to their many needs. Thanks be to God!

Pastor Stephen took them to Krakow Aushwitz concentration camp in the afternoon. Dark and depressing, the hot

wind blew, causing dust and dirt to settle everywhere.

Esther, holding a Kleenex over her nose, silently hoped for a breath of fresh air—but there was none.

The film they saw in the cinema depicted thousands of innocent victims who were murdered there so long ago. The horrors shown were incredible. Esther remembered how she and her family had spent a day at Majdanek concentration camp in Lublin, a few years ago. She saw a lot of similarities between the two camps. What atrocities had been committed in these places! Happy to leave, they went for a bite to eat.

While they were having a wonderful meal, Ella, Esther's interpreter, arrived from Warsaw. How could Esther teach the seminars which would soon take place without her capable interpretation? Handing her the material, Ella began to study for these important lectures. Yes, she would do the best she could to help. Esther was grateful.

Not staying in the trailer because there was a big, clean room prepared for them inside, Gordon and Esther relaxed. With a piano and organ in the sanctuary nearby, how could she complain? This was an added blessing from God.

WEDNESDAY, MAY 4

Today Ella and Esther worked on translation of the material Esther planned to present in the church. They thought it would be helpful for each woman to have a copy in her hand. Bowing their heads, they asked the Lord to bless them and minister through them.

Wonderful aromas from the kitchen greeted them when they had finished. The little cook made *mockowiz.* Along with fried chicken, green salad, and small potatoes, the meal went down quickly.

David, wiping his face with a napkin, exclaimed, "This is real home cooking! Thank you each one."

That night in the two-hour service, the heat was insufferable. Esther wiggled cramped, swollen feet in her shoes. But Gordon preached on and on. Playing the lovely piano again, their voices blended throughout the large congregation. "Amen!" they chorused.

Though it was getting late, David treated the people as, one by one, they waited their turn. Grateful after an adjustment, invariably they would feel better.

SEMINARS

The seminars starting the next day were well attended. As Ella and Esther entered the room, they were surprised to see many women. Quietly, expectantly, they waited to hear from God. Would He, through these Bible studies, alleviate some of their pain? They sincerely hoped so.

When they thought everyone had arrived, still more people came. Even after they started the service, others quietly entered the crowded room.

Esther knew she could not give these lectures without Ella. They worked together like two hands in a glove. Silently, Esther thanked God.

The women prayed, sang, took notes, and listened carefully.

The hours went by rapidly as they moved in the anointing of the Holy Spirit. When they thought it was time to stop, the women asked for more.

Finally, four hours later, at 8:00 P.M., they ended this session in prayer.

Both Ella and Esther were excited, but exhausted.

Meanwhile, Gordon was teaching the men with the same response. Doctor David was in the side room giving chiropractic adjustments. God was working everywhere. And they were grateful.

The pastor came up to Esther and Ella, smiling.

"These words from the Bible are exactly what our people need at this time. We are all so blessed, and look with anticipation to the sessions ahead."

That night, however, Esther felt her stomach churn. And the air was so thick with smog she felt her lungs burning. How long could they work in this stinging, polluted atmosphere?

David, too, was totally exhausted as he tossed in his bed across the hall. Esther heard him cough several times. The smog was making him miserable, too.

"God, give us strength!" she prayed. She knew He would, because it was He who had called them to Katowice. They would be fine.

"Good morning!" called Gordon, as he opened the door to Esther's bedroom the next day. Steam curled from the hot meal he carried on a tray. "Here, I've brought breakfast," he smiled.

Breakfast in bed before a busy day in Poland? This was a treat for his wife. Perhaps her lecture had taken root? Propping herself up on pillows, slowly she indulged in scrambled eggs, crisp fresh rolls, and *chi* (tea). The food went down well and she was grateful.

Going to the sanctuary where seminars would begin once again, she greeted her colleague, Ella.

Both were excited to begin this day with teaching from the Word of God. What could be better?

Again, some ladies were already seated while others continued to come. With Bibles open, notepaper, seminar material, and pens ready, they waited to hear from God again.

Esther told Gordon later, "Ella is an exceptionally capable young woman. We work together so well. If only she would be my translator all across the country." But that, she knew, was not possible.

The seminar lasted for another four hours. By the time they were finished, their throats were dry. The smoggy air coming in from the open windows, burned in their chests. But Ella didn't seem to mind. Were the people already acclimatized to pollution? Though many had lung problems, others seemed to survive without illness.

"This seminar was even better than yesterday," came the report from one of the women. "Thank you, dear sister Esther, for helping us with our problems. We knew the Word could solve them, but didn't know how to apply it. Thank you!"

The evening was warm and humid, Gordon and Esther, strolling hand-in-hand through the city of Katowice, knew they needed exercise. Sitting most of the day, their limbs and muscles were stiff.

Another profitable day had come to a close. Gratefully they closed their eyes to sleep. They knew God would give strength and anointing again tomorrow, so they looked with anticipation to see what He would do.

Would the women continue to come when they had other responsibilities at home? The answer was always in the affirmative. Joining the others, still more came to the next session.

After two hours, they broke off their lectures, and joined with the men in another room where Gordon had been teaching. The room was filled with expectancy—anticipation.

Calling Esther to the podium, Pastor Stephen announced she would be speaking jointly to men and women about a subject they all needed to hear.

The material she chose was a little lighter than usual. Sharing seventeen points on how a man should treat his wife, the women nodded in agreement. Sometimes the material was humorous and everyone joined in laughter. Other points were serious when men realized they had not been giving their wives the rightful place in their lives. Were not most pastors and laymen so involved in the work they took their wives for granted? They knew this was true and silently vowed to change. Quietly the women resolved to be better wives and stand behind the priest in their home.

After a short break, Gordon shared with the group. Time went by quickly as everyone listened attentively. Yes, God had sent these people to pin point the needs in their lives.

Crawling into bed that night, Esther held her breath. The sheets had the same distinct odor as the air outside. Dark and rank, it permeated their bedroom. Now she couldn't even put her head under the covers to hide from the terrible smell. Holding a Kleenex over her nose, she tried to think other thoughts.

Meanwhile, David was experiencing difficulties, as well. Working hard every day, he was not getting the exercise to which he was accustomed. His lungs, too, burned with irritation. Could they all endure this and stay for as long as they had previously planned? God was working in the lives of the people. Now they asked Him for strength to bear with the situation.

Quickly the days went by. Each day, the people coming for adjustments and blessings, were sorrowful to realize soon this precious time would be over.

The last Sunday arrived. The large church was packed as, once again, they shared in Word and song.

After Esther spoke, the president of the ladies group presented her with a bouquet of red roses. Burying her face in them, Esther inhaled the aroma of their sweet fragrance.

Leaving words of encouragement and Scripture with her, the grateful women embraced. Others in the congregation had tears in their eyes.

After Gordon shared about Christ's sacrifice, the room

was hushed. While elders passed the elements of communion to the waiting congregation, Esther was grateful she and Gordon were sitting in the front, because a large communal cup was shared by all. Being the first to drink, she remembered that, though this cup represented the blood of Christ, on several occasions she had contacted a virus from others who had sipped before her.

It was a three-hour service. Though everyone was blessed, they were grateful when it was over. More events were to follow in this busy day. Arching her back, Esther stretched her taut muscles. Trying to stifle a yawn, David carefully stretched his long, lanky body, looked at her, and smiled. Soon he would be leaving for his busy chiropractic practice in Seattle. This time of commission was almost over. Shaking hands and greeting people, slowly they made their way through the crowd—to eat another meal. Already potent aromas were drifting toward them.

Posnan, Poland

The countryside was gorgeous as they motored from Katowice to Posnan. Patches of yellow mustard fields contrasted with the black furrowed soil along the way. Big trees with new, lettuce-green leaves lifted their branches proudly toward the azure blue sky. Lacy apple blossoms, in full bloom, interchanged with other colors from nature to accentuate the beauty.

As they drove, the putrefied, smoggy atmosphere gradually gave place to pure, clean air. Esther breathed deeply, filling her lungs.

David had already left for Warsaw, where he would fly on to Seattle. He had taken time from his busy practice at home to bring relief to a hurting people. They knew God would bless him.

"When can Doctor David come back?" was the unanimous question. They could not answer until David rearranged his schedule again. Happy to give of his time, he thanked God for the privilege.

Gordon had made previous arrangements to meet the pastor of their next church at the train station. Following his little car, they drove to the church. What a beautiful building! Built in 1917, with a solid brick exterior, it reminded them of an historic, museum artifice.

Parking their vehicles in the pastor's yard, Gordon maneuvered and experimented in parking the trailer. Finally, after many suggestions from the men there, he was satisfied.

"We welcome you to stay in our living room on the couch," smiled Bagoosha, the pastor's wife.

Looking around her, Esther realized these were the sort of accommodations they had before purchasing their wonderful home on wheels. "Thank you," she answered, "but we have our own beds."

She was grateful for that. To sleep on the hard, small couch in the middle of the pastor's living room was paving the way to complete exhaustion. People coming and going, phones ringing, and food being prepared were already prolific there.

"Help yourself," smiled the pastor as he passed the plate filled with homemade sugared doughnuts to Gordon. Along with the hot *chi*, this was a fitting snack.

The next day, while Esther was still sleeping in the trailer, Gordon burst in. "Guess what? I locked my keys in the trunk!"

Esther woke with a start.

"Can someone help you get them out?"

"No, they have worked for an hour already! No one knows what to do!"

Distraught because he needed the car, Gordon wrung his hands.

"I will help," said the good-natured pastor, "but first, I have to go on an errand. Just wait here!"

The day wore on and on, but where was the pastor?

Finally, just before the seminars were to begin, his small car hurried into the yard. "I'm sorry I am late," he apologized. "Now, let's see what we can do!"

While others stood around, he tried to jam open the trunk. Nothing worked. No one could help.

"Come on in and eat," encouraged Bagoosha. "It is almost time for church to begin."

What could they do? Obligingly, they followed her into the house.

"I have made perogies," she smiled. "Help yourself!"

Trying to let the fat drain off, Esther speared the doughy perogie with her fork. "These are good!" she exclaimed after her first bite. *Fattening and filled with cholesterol, but good*, she added to herself.

SEMINARS

Running back to the trailer for her Bible and notes, she then walked toward the chapel. "Lord, anoint Your servants tonight," she prayed. They always sensed a responsibility to be used of God to help these people.

Ella was not there to translate, so the pastor had arranged for Bagoosha, a young woman from the area, to help.

Would she be capable? Without a good translator, it would be difficult to bring across the message she wanted to convey.

Though the young woman tried, she had a terrible time translating the English words into Polish. Stammering and stuttering, beads of sweat stood out on her forehead.

Esther repeated the phrases over and over again. The girl tried harder, but it didn't work well.

Mothers were distracted because their little ones, in the make-shift nursery next door, kept poking their heads into the room to see what was going on.

"God, please help us?" prayed Esther. She, too, was sweating. In a hot, humid room filled with distracted women, a poor translator, and children crying, it was hard to get the message across.

But the women showed interest. Yes, they wanted to learn more about Spirit-controlled temperaments.

"Tomorrow," assured the pastor, "we will put the children in another room away from the sanctuary, and I will try to find another translator for you," he promised.

The next day, the Mercedes dealer came to the pastor's home. "Someone here has a problem with keys locked in the trunk?" he asked.

Happy to see him, Gordon led him to his car.

In five minutes he held the cherished keys in his hand! Now they could drive to appointments scheduled for that day. Relieved, they drove to Olga's house for lunch. Other important commitments followed all day as they patiently ministered to the needs of the people.

By the time they returned to their home on wheels to change into different clothes, it was time for the seminars to begin.

The room was filled with women when Esther entered. Quietly waiting to hear from God, their Bibles were already open to the passages listed in the notes she had given them the evening before.

There were no distractions, because the children were in a room on the other side of the church.

Smiling, the pastor came to the podium. "I will translate for you," he offered.

Knowing he had a wonderful command of the English

language, Esther gladly agreed, and began the seminar.

The subject that night was, "How to be Filled and Controlled by the Spirit of God."

The women listened carefully, intently. Bowing their heads, many prayed audibly for His work to be more evident in their lives. With no interruptions and a capable translator, the women were able to concentrate, and many were moved to a deeper walk with God.

"Could I photocopy this material?" asked the pastor after the lecture was finished. "I, too, have been blessed. We need this kind of teaching."

Esther was encouraged. "Ella will be here tomorrow," he said. What more could she hope for?

It was difficult to sleep in this place. Though the trailer beds were comfortable, the noise outside was insufferable. Gordon got up every morning at the crack of dawn. This, of course, woke up his wife, who was trying to get a little extra rest. How could he keep going without stopping? Just when she was drifting back to sleep, a large truck lumbered into the yard and awakened her again. Banging and talking loudly, work crews in the area made their presence known. People on the street nearby talked in loud, harsh tones as they walked by. At night, Gordon snored. When would she finally sleep?

With a schedule filled to capacity, and no sleep, Esther began to feel sick. Blessed and encouraged by the Word of God, however, she continued to teach. If one is not controlled by the Spirit of God, life can be so complicated. Every day she prayed for refilling. Yes, He must control her life in order to help others.

On Saturday, both men and women gathered in the sanctuary to hear from God. No one wanted to leave when finally, both Gordon and Esther were finished sharing what

God had given them to pass on. Esther, aching for privacy and rest, was tired all the time.

Sometimes, longing for her children and home, tears threatened to spill down her cheeks. Amazingly, God gave strength and encouragement day after day. She knew it came from Him. She was too weary to go on in her own strength. Daily she repeated God's words to her. How true she found these words of encouragement to be!

> *My grace is sufficient for thee: for my strength is made perfect in weakness. Most gladly therefore will I rather glory in my infirmities, that the power of Christ may rest upon me.... for when I am weak, then am I strong* (2 Corinthians 12:9,10).

A PROFITABLE SUNDAY

Morning service started at 10 A.M. Walking toward the chapel from the trailer, though weary, Esther felt her heart fill with gratitude. Joyful singing coming from the chapel made her realize how blessed they were to minister to people who received the message so eagerly. God had chosen them to convey His Word. How could they be so blessed! Walking into the sanctuary, she found a seat near the front beside Gordon. Everyone smiled as she walked by.

After a long, effective message by Gordon, they went to the beautiful piano and sang several songs. The people, always asking for more, seemed to receive their music with joy. God had added this dimension and blessing to their ministry, even before they were married.

"Sister Esther," said Pastor Stan, "we want to present you with a small gift, showing our gratitude in a small way. Please come forward."

Handing her a big bouquet of red roses, the people

smiled and nodded their heads in approval. Ella, standing next to her, received flowers, as well.

Though honorariums in the form of cash were not given because the people did not have enough even for themselves, they often received other gifts of love.

"Thank you," the two grateful women replied.

"Brothers and sisters, there is food in the dining room for everyone," Pastor Stan concluded.

The room was full. An abundance of food was served. And another bouquet of flowers, a large crystal bowl, and a Bach recording were given to them as a gift of love from the congregation. Fellowship was rich. Bonding was strong as they talked around tables filled with food.

"When will you come again?" asked the people.

"We will see what the future holds," replied Gordon. He hoped it would be soon.

Radoosch to Warsaw

The next day, many of the church people came to say good-bye. Standing in a circle, Pastor Stan took off his hat and prayed for protection for them as they drove toward Warsaw. Others joined in. Gordon and Esther, sensing they were enclosed in a circle of love, thanked each one for coming. When would they see them again?

Assisting Gordon as he maneuvered the car and trailer out of the small yard, the men shouted suggestions on whether he should turn right or left—east or west. As they drove away, the circle of Christians standing in the driveway waved as long as they could see them.

The journey to Warsaw was uneventful. Both Esther and Gordon were exhausted. They figured if they parked in the forest in Radoosch, just out of the big city, perhaps they could rest better.

Short tempered, and tired, they didn't talk much that day. Wasn't it about time they saved their voices? Regardless, if they talked too much, perhaps some of the tension they held inside would burst.

Gordon, wiping the perspiration from his face, felt hot and pressured. Though the car and trailer were a wonderful combination, it was difficult to maneuver them through Polish traffic and bumpy roads. As they neared the city, it grew worse. Horses and wagons, pedestrians on foot, small Polish Fiats, chickens on the road, and other distractions, caused him to concentrate heavily. This always produced stress. He didn't want to collide with whatever was on the road. He always exercised extreme caution.

Esther, sitting quietly beside him, prayed for strength and wisdom for her husband. Stopping in Warsaw before driving on, he met with pastor Martin Piacsecki, of the Baptist church, while Esther waited in the car. How long could she sit? It was getting late.

But they talked on and on. Horns honking, people talking—always talking loudly in the Polish language—children screaming, dogs barking, many curious onlookers staring at the car and trailer, made Esther feel even more weary and conspicuous. Where was Gordon?

Finally, he arrived, and they drove toward the country. Their pastor friend drove ahead of them, to help them find Radoosch. Breathing deeply, she watched dark shadows play across the road ahead. It was night and time to be asleep in her own bed. Turning off the main road leading to Radoosch, they heard the big dogs bark. Their pastor friend was stuck in the sand. Gordon, leaving their car, tried to help him. But the wheels wouldn't budge. How would they make it through with their big contraption? Thank God, eventually, they all did!

Hearing the rustle of the big trees overhead instead of the usual irritating sounds, breathing the fresh, pure air, and relaxing, both Gordon and Esther slept like they had not slept for a long time! This was "what the doctor ordered" and they were grateful.

Eva, the pastor's wife, worked in Warsaw during the day, so Esther welcomed time alone for a change. Gordon was involved in some form of ministry that day. She wished he would rest before the seminars started in Warsaw. But he seemed to be most contented when he could help someone.

It was time to go to Eva's for lunch. Together they entered her house. Always greeting them graciously, she welcomed them to a table filled with food. Salads, potatoes, vegetables, and chicken soon filled the empty spot in Gordon's stomach. He had been too busy to eat before.

Driving back to their trailer in Radoosch, it was time to prepare for the seminars.

Once again, the sanctuary was full. Would these people respond like others had? They sincerely hoped so.

Men and women met together for the first hour, then separated into different rooms.

About seventy women waited in expectancy for Esther to share from God's Word.

Ella was not present, so a doctor translated. Fluent and easy, he made Esther feel relaxed—anointed.

The lecture was wonderful. Seeing the ladies faces change from, *I wonder what this is all about?* to *I need this!* she knew they were very receptive. And responsive.

"Thank You, Lord!" she breathed. With doctors, therapists, and many educated people in the audience she was not intimidated in the least! Expressing gratefulness and encouragement, they asked for more help in their spiritual lives.

Craving a deeper walk with God, they listened intently as the seminars were presented.

On Friday, however, Begoosha arrived to translate for Esther again. What? Why did they send someone who did not have a good command of the English language? Esther's heart sank. But all she could do was trust God to help.

The women waited for them to begin, expectancy filling their hearts.

But Bagoosha had a terrible time! The terms in the lectures were far too difficult for her to understand—let alone translate.

During the break, Esther prayed for her. Why didn't the capable doctor translate for her again? Later, she learned that he could not be there that night.

In spite of an inadequate interpreter, God used the seminars for His glory as lady doctors, therapists, housewives, teachers, pastor's wives, and lab assistants, listened with respect, longing to know Jesus more intimately.

Gena, one of the doctors, so blessed by the material, came to Esther later and humbly presented her with a gift. "Thank you! Thank you for your ministry!" she smiled.

On Sunday, the pastor came to Esther with a request. "Would you be the speaker for our Sunday night service?" he smiled.

Men sat at attention while she spoke on the priestly role of the father in the home. Women nodded and smiled. Yes, this is what they longed for in their homes. Fathers must take time to be with their wives and children. Challenged, a doctor sitting in the front row of the church came to Esther afterwards and said, "This is what we, as men, really need to hear. We know it is our responsibility to be priests at home, but how often we fail! Thank you for sharing with us!"

Esther felt humbled, awed, and a little nervous speaking

to so many men. In the past, women were not encouraged in the pulpit. Now, here she was—sharing with men in many different vocations in life.

"Thank You, God," she whispered, "though I feel so unworthy, you have made me worthy!" Her heart filled with peace, she closed her sermon and sat down with her husband in the front row. Squeezing her hand, he was encouraged Esther had found a niche with his people! She fit in! She was needed!

Eight doctors meeting at the pastor's home, requested to talk to Gordon and Esther. Asking questions, they shared for hours. What a time of learning and fellowship! Their hearts were bursting with gratefulness to God. Opportunities like this were not always available. God was opening doors like they had never anticipated!

Moving to Warsaw

Hearing the birds sing in her little sanctuary the next morning made Esther realize that was the day they were moving back to the city. Scheduled for more seminars there, they found it difficult to drive back and forth. Because their trailer would be staying in Radoosch, now they wondered where they would sleep. Not to worry, a place had been prepared.

Pastor Martin and Erena Piasetsky were beautiful people. Living in the big Bible School building in the Baptist church, they were always available for their growing congregation.

Erena graciously escorted Esther and Gordon to their room on the second floor. This would be a change from the comfortable beds in the trailer, but it was more convenient.

Esther missed her home on wheels when, in the morning, she was awakened very early to doors slamming, loud, high talking, and rusty locks turning in doors. A chain saw buzzed somewhere in the near vicinity, while early risers, conversing loudly, walked by on the street below.

SEMINARS

Compared to other places where they had given lectures, this church seemed to be the most unresponsive at first.

"These people," apologized Yerena, "are all very busy. They don't even know what a seminar is because they have never had one. If they could hear what you have to say, I'm sure we would have a packed church!"

While speaking on worry and anxiety caused by not really trusting their heavenly Father, twenty-five women listened carefully. Later, the men joined their group and both Gordon and Esther shared for a few hours. Interest grew.

As the days went by, the people began to warm up. Soon, the people asked them not to take a break between seminars, because they didn't want to waste any time. What this couple was teaching from the Word was important. They planned to put the principles into action.

MOTHER'S DAY

On Mother's day, Gordon and Esther entered the big church. Already filled to capacity, the people joined in worship.

From their seats, mothers carefully wiped red-rimmed eyes as their children sang in the lengthy service. Smiling through their tears, they watched their own with pride and love in their hearts.

While Gordon preached the morning sermon, Esther's eyes, too, clouded with tears.

Thinking of her own mother, Esther loved her unreservedly. *When was the last time we spent Mother's day together?* she pondered. Silently she asked God to bless her on her special day. She knew He would.

"I hope my children are thinking fondly of me today. It

is Mother's Day," yearned Esther. Longing to see them, she bowed her head to hide the tears.

"Tell Mother I'll Be There," is a melody sung in various languages. Today in the Polish Baptist church, the congregation joined in singing this old familiar hymn. Esther's mother, Katy, seemed to be near. Was she looking on?

After the sermon, Gordon called on Esther to sing. Walking to the piano, she sensed the presence of God as, closing her eyes, she worshiped while singing. Their Father who was with her family at that very moment, also graced this sanctuary today.

After church, people gathered around Gordon and Esther. Friendly and responsive now, they pleaded with them to come back again soon. Martin and Erena, standing nearby, heartily agreed. Would that time come soon? They too, hoped it would.

Ella, Esther's capable translator throughout the week, stood beside her after church. Talking animatedly, they never seemed to have enough time to be together. What a friend she had become to Gordon and Esther! Depending on her to translate material for many seminars, she had been faithful and accurate.

Suddenly a delegation of women arrived. Carrying bouquets of fresh flowers, crystal, linens, and perfume, lovingly they presented these gifts to Esther. Embracing the teachers, they thanked them profusely for the positive input into their lives.

Already in the service, they had received more flowers. What could they do with them all? Perhaps they'd give them away? Meanwhile, they planned to enjoy their freshness and fragrance.

It seemed unusual not to have seminars scheduled.

Moving back to Radosc, Esther savored the sound of the birds as they prepared to sleep. Waking early, because the

cuckoo birds were singing, at first, she thought she was at home. Was that throaty, loud song her cuckoo clock in the kitchen in Seattle? The sound was identical except the real cuckoos were louder.

Fully awake now, she realized she was in the Polish forest again. Grateful it was against the law to shoot cuckoo birds in Poland because they were becoming extinct, she savored the sound. From one end of the forest to the other, their cries reverberated. Answering calls did not stop their song. It went on and on.

Finally they had a little time for themselves. Going shopping in Warsaw was fun! Because their dollar was worth so much, they carried a lot of *zloty*. To suddenly feel rich was a new feeling, as thousands of *zloty* graced their wallets.

Now what could they buy? Gifts for their girls and other loved ones? Leather, crystal, and other commodities were inexpensive with their dollar. Careful of what they purchased, they knew the goods must be transported to Seattle, as well. With a few packages under their arms, they hurried to Piasetsky's for dinner.

"Welcome!" smiled Martin. Yerena came out of the kitchen and placed her culinary art on the table. "Please eat," she said. The fellowship was rich and sweet.

GORDON'S BIRTHDAY

It was June 5. Could it be possible Gordon was turning fifty years old? Where had the years gone? A half a century? Unbelievable!

Graying at the temples, with hair curling around his ears, he was looking more mature, but a young man still. Esther looked lovingly at the man to whom she was married all these years, and loved him intensely. Had they not been through many victories and trials together? Yet, they always stood united. *What would the next year hold?* she wondered quietly.

Today was also Sunday. Once again, the Baptist church was full as people came to worship.

"Today," announced Pastor Marin, "is Brother Gordon's fiftieth birthday. Gordon, please stand, so those who are not acquainted with you, can meet you after church. You will enjoy him," smiled the pastor. "We do!"

Flowers and gifts were showered on him. This was an important day. Gathering them up, they walked toward their car.

Eleven people, including Greg and Donosha, the Piasetsky's, and Ella joined together for a real birthday party in a restaurant nearby. Turkey, fish, chicken, and a variety of vegetables, made them all feel overfed.

Everyone heartily sang "Happy Birthday" while the waiter brought cake with a big candle on top. Others in the restaurant watched and smiled.

What a party! What love! Everybody saw it!

"Happy Birthday, Gordon!" Esther, adding a personal touch, put her arm through his. Walking to their car, she hoped they could spend some time alone.

"Would you please come to our house?" asked a couple.

The hours fled by. Before they knew it, the hands of the clock pointed to 3:30 A.M. So much for being alone with her husband on his fiftieth birthday. Maybe next year? She couldn't count on it.

24 A DIFFICULT SITUATION

The youth camps had been blessed of God. Home again, they prayed for the follow-up and guidance the young people would receive in Poland.

Katya came to camp that year with a desire to know God better. Hungry to learn more about His Word, and with a longing heart, she cried with the Psalmist:

> *As the hart panteth after the water brooks, so panteth my soul after thee, O God* (Psalm 42:1).

She must receive a new glimpse of her Lord in all His fullness and glory. Longing for a revival in her parched soul, she told her husband, Yuri, about her plans to go to camp.

His response was negative. No, he didn't think she should go this year. Money was scarce and there was work at home. But Katya couldn't forget—she had to go!

With mixed feelings filling her breast, trembling, she stepped onto the crowded bus enroute for the camp in the mountains. Pulling her threadbare coat around her, shivering, she sat down in the primitive conveyance.

Why, oh why did Yuri not go with her? Though she knew they could not afford to go, somehow, she knew God would supply their needs. He had in the past, and He would again. But Yuri wouldn't budge in his decision. Not only did he refuse to go, but forbade Katya as well.

How terrible to disobey! Shoulders sagging, she was haunted by his response as the old bus lumbered along the frozen road.

"Please God, forgive me!" she cried. "I long to study together with leaders at camp. There are so many truths in Your Word I do not understand. Open the eyes of my heart and Yuri's, too, Lord. Amen."

She was not disappointed. As the Word of God was opened every day at camp, she drank from its fullness. She bathed in the forgiveness Christ offered. A revival filled her parched soul and caused her to cry for more of Him. Drinking deeply, her soul was being filled with Christ's satisfying peace.

Assured that Yuri, too, would experience a fresh touch from Him, she prayed. Now the Bible was more alive again. Truths she had not understood before, were carefully explained to her. God was opening the eyes of her heart. What assurance and joy filled her soul!

It was time for the retreat to end. But her heart was so full—she knew her joy would never end.

Stepping off the bus, she hurried home to tell her husband about the change in her life. At first, Yuri was sullen. She realized that by disobeying him, she was the cause of his anger and frustration. What was so important to cause her to do that? It must be very special!

Time passed. Working at her job, around home, and everywhere she went, Katya sang. On her face was a glow that could melt a longing heart.

Now Yuri was longing for something—Someone. If Katya's life could be changed like that—could his? In spite of the fact that she had gone to camp without his approval, Yuri forgave her.

Kneeling beside the bed, with hands clasped, the young couple prayed. As they shared from the Bible, the Word of God became new and real, too. Why didn't he see this sooner?

Joyfully inviting Christ to be Lord of his life, now he, too, was eager to share his faith with others.

Together, they did just that. In a domino effect, others came to know Christ as a result of a couple whose lives shone with the love of God.

So shall my word be that goeth forth out of my mouth: it shall not return unto me void, but it shall accomplish that which I please, and it shall prosper in the thing whereto I sent it (Isaiah 55:11).

A Moody Science Film

"Hurry, the film starts soon!" Esther challenged her husband, as they made their way to the banks of the Odra River where a movie was scheduled to be shown in a few minutes.

It was a lovely evening. The sun was beginning to set as vivid colors of scarlet and gold spread across the darkening sky. Campers emerged from their quarters and eagerly walked toward the coming attractions, which drew them like a magnet.

They had been in Poland for about two weeks, ministering to university students. At the beginning of the camp, many were just a blur of faces. Now they had become individuals, each one unique and precious.

Their camp was located a kilometer from the East German border. In only a few short months, Martial Law would dominate the entire country of Poland. No one knew what the future held, but each of them could sense tensions and unrest every day. The vultures would strike soon and plunge the country into total chaos and uncertainty.

Meanwhile, soldiers stood in readiness, awaiting a possible attack from the Russians. Each day police came to the youth camp to check activities there. Sonic booms and military machinery passing by shook their trailer night and day. Many times they awakened from a sound sleep wondering what was happening. Had the Russians arrived to claim the country?

In spite of all this, young people came together from various parts of Poland to learn more from the Word of God. With keen anticipation, they eagerly looked to this event each year.

As they drew near to their destination, many campers were already seated on the banks of the Odra River, waiting until dusk when the film would begin.

Several had guitars and were singing choruses. Enthusiastically they joined in. Just across the river was the East German border. Esther was reminded, once again, of the oppression and sadness these people had endured throughout the years. Her thoughts were rudely interrupted, however, when hoards of hungry mosquitoes decided to have dinner. Eagerly attacking their victims, everyone fought them off. Their young people ran to nearby trees to cut big, leafy branches to use for weapons against these hungry invaders.

Still they all continued to sing, the music echoing across the vast countryside and on into the village beyond.

Drawn to the sound, curious people left their simple peasant homes to join the group. By the time dusk had fallen, the crowd had slowly and progressively increased.

Peter, their projectionist, beamed the picture onto a crude homemade screen and, in a moment, all eyes were intently fixed on the movie.

Translated from English to Polish, several Moody Science films would be shown here. What a novelty these young people were witnessing! It was a rare privilege for films of this caliber to be shown behind the Iron Curtain. Everyone present was fascinated at the miracle they were witnessing. As the greatness of God was portrayed through the opening of an exquisite flower to the miraculous wonders of a working bee, even the biting mosquitoes were almost forgotten.

Service Disrupted

Suddenly, the silence was broken when a rowdy group of young men, wearing black leather jackets and riding motorcycles, roared into their little sanctuary. In a cloud of dust, they came to an abrupt halt, disembarked, and stood at the edge of their circle—swearing, laughing, and mocking.

Their goal was to disrupt the service. No matter what it took, they intended to carry out this plan. Talking disrespectfully, and laughing loudly, the boys deviously approached the young ladies in their group. In vain they tried to attract their attention, but the girls ignored them.

Lighting cigarettes and blowing smoke into the night air seemed to enhance their pleasure.

A Miracle

However, slowly, gradually, their laughter turned to silence. Throwing their cigarettes to the ground, they stomped on them with the heals of their heavy leather boots. Their eyes drawn to the film, they gradually became absorbed in the miracle of creation portrayed there.

As time went on, they forgot the original reason they had come to join the group. Though none wanted to admit it, a desire to know the God of creation in a personal way filled their hearts. They secretly longed to have the joy the young people had so enthusiastically been singing about earlier.

At the close of the evening, a modern-day miracle took place. These young men, formerly rebellious and obnoxious, indicated a serious desire to make Jesus Christ Lord of their lives!

A decision such as this is not made lightly or flippantly in Poland. Knowing there would be a cost involved, perhaps persecution or the loss of a job, this choice is weighed very carefully.

After prayer and counseling, they now had a new Friend. Peace reigned in their hearts as, by faith, they were made pure and clean in the blood of Jesus. These young men, now free from the bondage and doubt carried so long, were willing to face whatever was ahead.

Reluctantly, the circle broke as the young people walked back to camp. In the darkness, in awe, they whispered about the miracle that had just taken place.

Changed young men climbed on their bikes and quietly rode out of the hallowed spot where they had just met Jesus. With hearts full of joy, they drove home to tell loved ones about their decision to follow Christ.

The sovereign God can change the vilest sinner and make him clean because He is the God of miracles.

MORE FRUIT

The story did not end there. They were aware the mother of Janic, one of the young men who made a decision to follow Christ, was the mayor of the village where the youth camp was held.

They had taught the university students from the Word of God faithfully each day and watched them grow in the Lord.

Originally, Janic's mother did not condone such activities because she was a staunch Roman Catholic. However, when she saw the change that had taken place in her former unruly son, her attitude toward them changed. Happy that her boy was so different, she gratefully spoke to Gordon one day.

"You may have a youth camp here in this village any time," she said. "If Janic can be changed by the message you have presented here, there must be something to it. You are welcome to come back and continue what you are doing!"

A DOMINO EFFECT

As time went on, Janic brought others to youth camp and some of them accepted Christ, as well. Still others in the village observed. New hope and interest was born in their hearts. Eventually they came to the services. Truly, through the miracle of one new life born into the kingdom of God, many others came to know Jesus, the Light of the world, in a dark Communist country behind the Iron Curtain.

Loneliness

Esther wrote this poem in the summer of 1981 while on a ministry trip to Poland. Illness made her feel a little blue and extremely lonely. Tensions were prevalent as Russian military machinery roared by. Sonic booms shook their trailer and soldiers stood nearby with guns slung around their shoulders, just awaiting a possible takeover from the Russian army. Martial law was imposed in the country just a short while after they arrived home in the United States.

Loneliness possessively presses my heart
with fingers clutching long and cold,
Molding me into it's presence—
sinister—despondent and bold.

Loneliness determinedly clutches my heart
while dark evening shadows fall.
A tolling bell peals in the distance—
I hear the night birds call.

Loneliness persistently eats at my heart,
the sun slowly sinks in the West
My heart is aching, heavy
and filled with great unrest.

Loneliness stubbornly gnaws at my heart,
I retreat into a world all alone.
This language and people are foreign to me,
so the emptiness steadily grows.

Loneliness stubbornly knocks at my heart
for loved ones I cherish most dear
Remembering them across the sea—
with yearning intense, for them here.

Loneliness despondently squeezes my heart,
powers of darkness enfold—
Encircling, covering, binding.
I see multitudes outside the fold.

Loneliness deliberately eats at my heart,
till my ear is attuned to a sweet gentle voice
Saying, "I am with you always, My child—
for Me you have made your choice."

Still loneliness stubbornly claws at my heart,
until in surrender my head is bowed low.
"Lord, when I'm lonely—You are my all.
Help me through testing to grow."

Then loneliness silently, gently retreats.
The cold, empty void steals away.
A serene, quiet peace replaces aching inside—
and I venture ahead unafraid.

—Esther M. Balisky

A Rewarding Picnic

Looking out the trailer window that lovely summer morning in Poland, Esther could see it was a clear, beautiful day. Sunshine sparkled on the lake as trees gently swayed in the warm breeze.

They had all hoped for good weather because today was their youth camp picnic. It would be different in the fact that all the campers were planning on being ferried across the lake to the other side where they would have their festivities.

Stepping out of the trailer, Esther noticed that the air was pungent with the aroma of cabbage and onions. She walked to the kitchen where, fascinated, she watched the cooks make enormous quantities of *Begosh.* (Cabbage laced with meat, onions, and pork fat.) Yes, she had been at picnics where hot *kielbasa* (Polish sausages) and bread, were served, but never *Begosh.*

The cooks finally finished and put the thick mass into enormous aluminum cooking pots to be transported across the water.

The campers, inside their cabins and tents, were preparing for this long-anticipated event. Eventually, the girls appeared in light, colorful, summer dresses, with bathing suits and towels draped over their arms.

It was growing hot. The light summer breeze had stopped and not a blade of grass moved. The sun shone mercilessly from a cloudless sky.

Already, a large group of young people stood at the shore of the lake, waiting to be transported to the other side. One by one, the boats were filled. The kids waved and sang as they skimmed over the sparkling water.

It wasn't very long before the boats returned to pick up the next group.

Esther watched as large pots of *Begosh* were loaded onto a small boat. Concerned, she observed the laden craft sink deeper into the water. Instead of stopping there, they continued to load dishes, cups, saucers, bowls, and flatware, adding to what was already in the boat. It sank still farther. When only a few inches showed above the water, they gestured for them to come.

"*Wujek*! *Ciotka*! (Uncle, Aunt) come on in! There's lots of room!"

There were still three of them waiting, and two already in the boat. Esther hesitating, suggested, "You go ahead! I will wait for the next boat!"

"No, it will be just fine!" they insisted.

Finally, but not really convinced, they reluctantly stepped inside as the overloaded boat sank even farther.

The water, ever rising, appeared like a bottomless pit to Esther. "How deep is this lake anyway?" she asked, looking over the side of the boat. No one answered. No one knew.

It was not difficult to visualize *Begosh*, bread, butter, and the crew, floundering in the water! No such event took place however, as the craft bravely plowed forward.

She wasn't certain if they would reach the other side, but no one else seemed to be worrying. So holding onto the boat, she tried to relax.

SAFE ARRIVAL

Eventually the tree-lined shore came closer and closer.

They had made it! The young people were waiting there, laughing and beckoning them to hurry. After all, they knew they had most of the food!

Esther heaved a sigh of relief when the big *Begosh* pots were lifted out by eager hands. The boat immediately rose higher.

Stepping onto the dock, they joined a host of young people. They escorted Esther and Gordon into cool, green woods, away from the blazing sun. Many were sitting under the shade trees, while others played ball or went for a swim. Everyone was having fun. On the side, stood a number of long tables laden with the *Begosh* pots and all the other tempting foods the cooks had prepared.

When everyone decided to eat, the food disappeared rapidly. Hurrying, Esther joined the end of the line and put the long ladle into the pot to sample the savory cabbage dish. Unfortunately, there was only a small amount of *Begosh* left at the bottom of one of the pots. Everyone, apparently, had been hungry.

After all the ravenous appetites were satisfied, they gathered around to sing. Gradually it grew dark. The men had gathered logs and sticks to make a fire. They continued to sing as they built it high. Esther watched the sparks as they flew overhead—blaze—then fall to the ground and die.

BEARING FRUIT

Then the testimonies began. It is always encouraging to hear the young people tell of what the Lord has done in their lives as a result of the hours of teaching, counseling, and praying. Many had already been challenged to a closer walk with God.

After Gordon had shared from the book of John, everyone became still as the ever-faithful Spirit of God began to deal with souls. They could hear the crackling of the orange flames—nothing else—as the young people reverently bowed their heads. The forest was dark around them. Overhead, stars hung low in the darkened sky.

When Gordon gave an invitation for those who wanted to follow Christ, nine lives were transformed as they asked the Lord to be their Savior.

Ella was one of them. Her eyes, large and dark, looked into Esther's as she expressed her intention to follow Christ, no matter what the cost. She knew the cost would be high.

"God has given me sweet peace like I have never known," she said, as they rose from their knees.

They knew the angels in heaven were rejoicing because now the young people were aware of the joy salvation brings. Burdens lifted and with a spring in their step, they walked back to the boats that would transport them across the lake.

With lights softly reflecting on the water, each in turn, stepped into an available boat. This time there was no *Begosh*, no bread or other foods—only full stomachs, empty pots, dirty dishes, and happy hearts.

Open Doors

Camp was almost over. Though the results had brought blessings, Esther heaved a sigh of relief. Perhaps soon she could finally get some rest!

Visualizing a quiet place away from people where she and Gordon could relax, made her load feel lighter already!

They had been on the shores of beautiful Lake Konev near Lubartow, in Poland, for several weeks. Before that, ministering in churches along the way, there seemed to be no break. Giving seminars all across the country gave Esther real joy, but she needed a break. Here at camp, too, the young people clamored to hear while Gordon and Esther shared the Word. They were on call daily. The results were phenomenal, but even Jesus needed to get away for a while when He

worked with people while He was here on this earth.

Their trailer, parked near the Konev Hotel (which Joseph had named for the small cottage where some of the campers slept) was too close for comfort. Unable to rest, with so many energetic campers around, they clearly heard all the laughter and talking which often went on into the small hours of the night. In the morning, first thing, conversing loudly, the campers walked past the trailer on their way to the dining room for breakfast. Usually this fare consisted of *kinapke*—sliced bread with cucumbers and cold meat coupled with strong, black tea. They never seemed to tire of this daily regimen.

Sometimes Esther and Gordon were hungry for eggs, coffee, and toast—but they knew this was like longing for the leeks and garlic in Egypt.

Sometimes Esther chose not to have breakfast, but stay in her trailer to study, pray, or try to relax. But always the noise went on and on....

With her bones aching and unable to sleep, somehow, God gave strength and joy to carry on teaching.

The last weekend of camp, people would be coming to Lake Konev from all across the country of Poland for a closing conference. With anticipation, they all looked forward to this wonderful event. Some would come to take their young people home. Others who were interested included pastors and their wives. This was a time they could be fed spiritually. The chapel, they knew, was too small for everyone to be seated inside. There would be a need for some to sit on chairs outside, they were certain. Microphones would enable them all to hear.

Finally the weekend arrived. Esther was excited when she came into the crowded chapel. There were people everywhere! Outside, too, they sat in the glaring sunshine. Coming from across Poland, England, and America, all came to listen while the Word of God was shared.

Esther was the last speaker. By this time her feet were swollen and her back ached, as she felt the perspiration trickle down her forehead. As the heat unmercifully penetrated the crowded chapel, she felt weak and exhausted. Now it was her turn to speak. Could she get through?

She argued with God, "I can't stand on my feet for hours. I am too tired!"

Suddenly, the idea came. Why not sit behind the long table in the front of the building while she shared? Others had done it before—why couldn't she?

Waiting in expectancy, the people opened their Bibles, while Esther and her interpreter sat behind the big table. Spreading her Bible and notes in front of her, she began to speak. Time fled into eternity. People stopped squirming, as they listened intently to what God had to say through His humble servant.

Forgetting the swarming flies and the oppressive heat, she carried on. Words came easily as she sensed the anointing of the Holy Spirit. This, she knew, was the Lord speaking through her. Strength renewed, she felt freedom, joy, and exhilaration. The Word was powerful as it penetrated into the hearts of those present. Everyone sensed it.

Pastors present, taking out their notebooks, wrote down truths that especially spoke to them from the Bible. The chapel was hushed—anointed—as they studied together. Time seemed to stand still and yet Esther continued to share as she and her capable interpreter worked together as one.

"Amen!" the people chorused, after she had prayed the closing prayer. Subdued and quiet, they filed out the door to have *kinapke* and strong black tea.

But many pastors lingered in the sweltering chapel. From Bialostok to Posnan, Warsaw, and Katowice, invitations came to Gordon and Esther to minister in their churches.

When could they come? Now the pastors were pleading.

"We would like you, sister Esther, to share what you have given us from the Word of God today," they said.

Esther felt humbled. Knowing God had given her the material to present and then spoken through her, she felt small in the presence of her Savior. For months, she had struggled in this country to be more effective for Him. Not able to speak the language fluently and not knowing the culture or customs of the Slavic people, she longed to be used of God, but there seemed to be so many obstacles in her path. Gordon, brought up in a Slavic home, spoke Polish freely and easily. Knowing the culture and ways of the people, he felt at home. During the first while, Esther did not. She often had not felt a oneness with the people to whom she had been commissioned to work.

Many times, while conversing around a table, when falteringly she tried to voice her opinion on a subject matter, Gordon would correct her feeble attempts in the Polish language and others would stifle laughter. She tried so hard. Why was this language so difficult? Slowly learning, she still made too many mistakes.

It was a well-known fact that women were not allowed to speak to men in seminars, or behind the sacred desk. This had never been done, and as far as the men were concerned, it never would change. But now, the men were impressed. This woman, who had just shared from the Word of God, had something to say!

She not only shared, but sat when she did so. In her weakness and exhaustion, Esther had chosen to sit, and they liked that. Humbleness was a virtue they extolled in a woman, and in their opinion, this woman showed humility and deference.

To stand and teach in the presence of men would have

made them feel inferior and subordinate, but because she sat, they approved.

In her weakness, God had opened doors far past anything she ever expected. From then on, she was accepted by everyone!

God, in His faithfulness, provided a few days' relaxation after camp was over. With renewed energy they began again. God always gave special strength when they needed it the most and He had opened new avenues of service. His grace was sufficient.

An Effective Witness

Later, back at camp, the night was moonless and shrouded in total darkness. Ominous clouds hung low in the sky as a cold breeze blew in from the lake.

Esther sighed gratefully as Gordon came up behind her and wrapped a warm, woolen blanket around her shivering body. There was no support on the wooden bench on which she was sitting, and her back ached with weariness. Heavy exhaustion enveloped her body like a vice.

They had been in Poland for about a month and the strain was beginning to take its toll.

Ministering at a youth camp about one kilometer from the East German border, Polish soldiers guarded the border area just awaiting a possible attack from the Russians. Russian machinery stood in readiness. It was only a matter of time before Martial Law would be enforced in the great country of Poland. No one knew what course the future would take, but uncertainties and questions ran rampant.

Many of their friends in the United States had warned them not to go to Poland during such a crucial time, but they knew God's direction in spite of loving admonitions. And here they were!

Looking around at the young people seated in a large

circle at an outdoor meeting, Esther's heart was warmed. They had gone to nearby towns during the camp, and invited villagers to attend the services at the campsite. Their efforts had not been in vain. Many of the townspeople had come, and they, too, were sitting around the campfire. Some, unaccustomed to being in a church meeting, stood nearby in the shadows, or listened from afar.

A toothless grandmother seated near the fire, her eyes shining with renewed hope, listened as the group of believers sang about a Friend they called Jesus. Her heart hungry to know more, she listened carefully.

A young mother holding her new baby, looked wistfully at the young people. Her two small children, their eyes wide and alert, hovered nearby.

Still other villagers listened with interest and respect as the Gospel was presented that night.

A hot fire crackled and spit in the center of the circle. It was continually fed by some of the boys in the group.

By now it had become so dark, Esther could just faintly see the faces around her, illuminated by the light of the flames. Many had become dear to her throughout the years. Now these young people had a purpose for living. Their joy was in Jesus Christ.

Reminiscing, Esther was reminded of how Bozena came to know Jesus at camp. The firelight played softly on her radiant face as she listened intently. They had witnessed a consistent growth in her spiritual life, while she drank deeply from the Word of God. Others they had seen at camp from year to year, told about trials and testing endured since they made the decision to follow Him. But they always testified that Christ meant more to them than anything or anyone else in the world.

Breezes still rustled through the tall trees behind them, as water from the lake lapped on the shore. The boys added more wood on the dying fire, and it glowed vibrantly once more.

As the service progressed, Janic, their camp leader, began to share with regards to principles the young people were taught at camp. Several young Poles had already made a profession of salvation that year and were experiencing a new joy and freedom they'd never had before. One by one, they testified about the change Christ made in their lives.

MUSIC AND A CROSS

But what was that music faintly heard in the distance? They listened. Everyone became still. Yes, they did hear muted singing—so faint it could scarcely be heard. They could not even recognize the direction from which it came. Gradually it became louder and more distinct as it came closer. The familiar strains of "The Old Rugged Cross" rang out into the cool evening air.

The night was so dark they could see only the cross outlined with lights, and an illumination of that cross mirrored in the obscure water below.

Few had realized that the young people had devised a wonderful plan to witness to those living around the shores of the lake. A raft, crudely constructed of driftwood and logs carrying the rugged cross, floated in the foreground. The young people, attaching candles to the cross for illumination in the darkness, placed it in the raft and floated from house to house proclaiming the message of salvation. Villagers, living in the vicinity, who were not at the meeting, saw the cross, too, and heard the young people sing about their best Friend. Smaller boats containing singing teenagers followed the larger craft, their voices and guitars blending together in worship. As the musical strains echoed clearly across the countryside, everyone listened and heard.

Esther was absorbed and utterly fascinated as the music went on. Each song contained a message about the cross and

atoning blood of Jesus shed on Calvary. For the first time in their lives, many villagers heard the message of salvation.

The floating procession gradually came nearer to the shore where their campfire burned brightly. All eyes were fastened on the illuminated cross, as strong, young men lifted it from the raft and carried it to the center of the large circle where they sat. Then the young people from the boats joined their group and they all resumed singing around the central theme of Christ's sacrifice.

Later, as Gordon shared from God's Word, everyone listened in rapt attention. The fire continued to crackle and spit, sending live sparks flying into the night sky. Even little children were hushed, their eyes focused intently on the flickering candles. One by one, however, the flames went out, but the spirit and atmosphere of the evening did not die. This effective visual aid had an impact on everyone present and no one would ever forget it.

The breeze, now a cold wind, continued to blow as large waves beat against the shore. The night was still moonless and cloaked in total darkness, while heavy clouds hung low in the sky. But in their hearts there was a warm glow. Many of the villagers had heard the message of salvation for the first time. The seed had been planted in the hearts of the people. They had faith to believe it would germinate and new life would spring up within.

Thoughtfully, prayerfully, the people walked to their respective homes. This story about the cross had touched their hearts. Yes, God was really alive!

The campfire had died and the candles gone out, but a witness for Christ had been effective that night. There will be lasting results on into eternity.

25 GOD'S PROVISION

During the difficult years under Communism, Christians gathered for fellowship as often as they could. However, these meetings were always under the scrutiny of the Department of Religion and Cults.

Permission had to be secured for even large family gatherings, especially in cities and villages. In farming areas, the local *Soltice* or government appointed policing agents, personally knew the people of the community. But if the family was having guests, they would have to inform him who the guests were, where they came from, and how long they would be visiting.

It was in this type of atmosphere the children and youth ministries were born in Central Eastern Poland. Pastor Joseph Sizek, a young man in his 20s, attended a Bible training school in Warsaw, where he met Christians from other parts of his country. Here, after praying together, ideas of

outreach and evangelism were shared and put into practice.

In 1975, Pastor Joseph graduated from his pastoral training and moved to Lublin, where he organized youth camp ministries about 70 kilometers from the city, near the Russian-Polish border.

The Gospel message was broadcast via shortwave radio into the Communist world from Trans World Radio in Monaco during the post-WWII years, and many were converted to Christianity.

These believers met for prayer and fellowship in a large family room provided by a Christian farmer and his family. Here, church services were held in the fall and winter when the weather was cold. In the summer months, the families met in the hay barn. It was turned into a meeting hall for church, as well as youth and children's camps and summer Bible school for the community.

Water was drawn from the well for cooking and laundry once a week, and put into a 55 gallon barrel. If it rained, sometimes they would be able to swim in a pond or stream located about 2 kilometers away.

Makeshift cabins were built out of inexpensive material where six or more children or young people would sleep on hay-filled mattresses. Sometimes these primitive beds became favorite sleeping quarters for field mice, as well. Of course these visitors caused quite a stir!

For years, the people thanked God for the provision of these facilities, but during times of house searching and questioning by the police, they realized a permanent location, under the umbrella of the local church instead of on a private farm, was necessary.

Together with Pastor Joseph, the people prayed for God to provide a youth camp property in the country near to the city.

The need was presented to churches in America. Pastor Murray Marshall, from the First Presbyterian church in Seattle, decided to meet Gordon in Poland. He wanted to inspect a piece of land that, hopefully, in the future, would be available to Pastor Joseph's congregation on the shores of Lake Konev, 22 kilometers north of Lublin.

Pastor Marshall, though realizing renovations were necessary, was impressed with the spacious camp site located in this scenic and practical location. Together, he and his congregation in Seattle, prayed that if they purchased this property, God would bring many children and young people to the Lord. And they, in turn, would go out and share the good news with others in their country.

Pastor Marshall's visit was an encouragement to Joseph and Gordon as they pursued the vision for the purchase and development of the camp.

The Purchase of Camp Konev

"Could this beautiful piece of property belong to the Polish believers some day?" Esther and Gordon wondered.

Flanked by Lake Konev, it seemed to be the ideal place where youth camps and conferences could be held all summer long. They were told it was for sale. Would the purchase be possible?

Pastor Joseph from the Lublin Baptist church was excited when he talked about it. Would Gordon, Esther, and their American friend drive out with him to see it? Only a few kilometers from Lublin, it would be relaxing to drive in the country.

"Yes," replied Gordon. "Let's go!"

Perhaps the Lord has a special plan? But where will the money come from? silently wondered practical Gordon. *Could someone in the United States provide the large sum that would be required to purchase the land?*

Not wanting to "count his chickens before they hatched," he turned his mind to the pleasant trip.

The air was filled with the scent of blossoms as they drove toward their destination. Occasionally, an overloaded truck belched out its poisonous fumes as they drove past. As they turned down the side road to Konev, there was even less traffic. After driving through the old gate, they disembarked at the campsite.

They noticed a few dilapidated buildings, scattered here and there. "These," planned Joseph, "could be renovated and made into a chapel and kitchen." Some smaller buildings were scattered randomly around the property.

"These could be the sleeping quarters," suggested Esther. As the men walked around the property, she went to the lakefront. As tall, stately trees gently swayed in the breeze, the waves from Lake Konev lapped softly on the shore. The water, she noticed, was not gray or dirty like other lakes she had seen in Poland, but clear and clean.

Sauntering along the shore, she saw small Polish cottages flanking the lakefront. While chickens scratched in the soil, beautiful white geese proudly walked single file toward the lake. Women, wearing the traditional *Babushkas* and big aprons, carried pails of milk from the barn to the house.

Excited, she joined the men. Yes, this land would be a perfect place where young people could have fun—but most of all to study and learn about God.

"Many of the young people in this area do not have the money to travel to other youth camps held in various parts of the country, so they cannot attend. Here, even our own youth from the church could come without worrying about the expense involved," said Joseph.

Sitting on a log outside one of the old buildings, they prayed, planned, and talked.

But was this land really for sale? Joseph had heard that it was.

"We will go and talk to the owner," suggested Joseph.

"Have you met him?" asked Gordon.

"We have spoken briefly," he answered.

A farmer and his family lived on part of the land. To sell would give them some equity on which to live. Most people lived on the edge of poverty in Poland. The land he owned was valuable. Perhaps he and his family could live on the proceeds for the rest of their lives. But who, in Poland, had the money to buy it?

A Visit

They talked about the property all the way back to Lublin. They knew God could make a way for them to own it if He wanted to. But how?

A few days later, Pastor Marshall and Gordon drove out to the property to talk to the owner. While they drove, they prayed. Somehow, both sensed that someday this land would be used for young peoples' camps, and many would come to know Christ. With clouds of dust blowing around the car, they drove to where the man was working in the field with his horses and plow.

In the distance, the farmer, shielding the sun from his eyes with his hand, saw them coming. *Who could that be?* he wondered as they drove toward him. Stopping, Gordon climbed out and introduced himself.

"And this," he said, pointing toward Pastor Marshall, "is my friend from America."

"We have come to talk to you about your land because we heard it was for sale."

"Yes," said the farmer, looking interested.

"How much do you want for it?" asked Gordon.

The amount he quoted came to several thousand American dollars. Was this too much to ask?

Gordon and Murray smiled. Certain they could raise the money at home, they felt God would supply the necessary funds.

Hope shone in the man's eyes. Yes, he needed that kind of cash. Weary of working so hard, perhaps then he could rest.

"Why do you want this land?" he asked.

Explaining they would like to run youth camps and other functions there, his eyes filled with doubt. "You mean, this is a religious outfit?" he said, raising his voice.

"Not religious," said Gordon, "only people who love God."

"You do, do you?" he stormed. "How do you know there is a God? No, I can't sell my property to those who say they love a God who does not even exist!" He spat on the ground at his feet.

They were so certain God wanted them to have this property, but at the moment it seemed their faith was getting smaller.

"Please think about it," said Gordon.

"There is nothing to think about. I will not sell to you!" he cried.

Getting into the car, Gordon and Pastor Marshall quietly drove away. Looking back, they saw the man raise his fist in the air. He was positive they would not have his land! Never!

What did God have in mind? They had assurance many would come to know him at camps held here. Now what?

A few days passed. The land was still on the market. "Let's drive out there again," ventured Joseph. Certain God had a plan, he pursued his dream.

A group Gordon and Esther taught at Camp Konev. Joseph on the far right.

When they arrived, the farmer saw them coming. This time, though they pleaded, he cursed and swore at them. Ordering Joseph and Gordon off his property, his face was livid with rage. "No I will not sell to you!" he stormed. "And that is final! Now get off my property and don't come back!"

Was this really final? They didn't believe it.

God works in mysterious ways, it is true. What happened next, is not what they planned…or ever thought of.

News travels fast in Poland. They listened incredulously as someone told them the farmer was dead. He had been plowing in the field with his horses, as he was on the previous visit. The family found him under the plow—the reins wrapped around his cold body.

What happened? Perhaps he had a heart attack? A stroke? Only God knew. Never before, in all his years of farm-

Michael Siczek with his quitar was led to Christ by Gordon. Now an evangelist and church planter in Poland and throughout Europe.

ing, did he have an accident—and suddenly this? No one had an answer.

His wife and family, knowing they could not run the farm by themselves, decided to sell the land and move to a smaller place. They needed the money to live. How else could they eat, pay bills, or even have a car?

Now they were willing to sell the property. The farmer's wife, though grieved at the loss of her husband, was relieved when the transaction went through.

God supplied the funds miraculously, as well. The First Presbyterian Church in Seattle, having a burden to reach the Poles for Christ, sent a check to cover all the costs.

Many young people came to know Christ as a result of attending camps at Lake Konev. Here they learned to study the Bible and pass the Good News on to still others who would come to know Christ, too. When sale of the land seemed impossible, God stepped in. Surely their Father planned it all!

Charlene's Decision

The girls went with them on their next trip to Poland. On their way home to Seattle, the family stopped off in Switzerland and stayed in Adelboden for a few days of rest.

One day, while standing together under the majestic Alps, Charlene made a startling comment. "Mom and Dad, I have decided to stay in Europe and go to university in Freiburg."

"Are you sure, Charlene?" asked the concerned parents.

The young woman who had suffered so severely was ready to stay in the country the doctors had advised her to leave. "Yes, I'm sure! Among other things, I want to go to the University of Frieburg and learn German more fluently."

Gordon cleared his throat. Corinne shuffled. Esther just stared. "Maybe you should sleep on it, Charlene," she suggested.

"No, Mom, I have thought about this decision. I want to stay."

Gordon heard himself say, "We'll stand behind you and help all we can, Charlene!"

"Thank you," she smiled.

Several days went by. Esther would never forget the hour when they had to say good-bye. Vowing not to weaken in front of her eldest, courageously she honored the young woman's decision. Then she said what she had heard her own mother say to her so often, "God bless you, my dearest. May His presence go with you!"

Pulling away, Esther climbed into the waiting car.

Driving down the familiar road from the *pension* to Germany, she strained her eyes for a long, last look at her daughter.

Charlene stood alone on a windswept hill, her blonde hair and blue skirt blowing in the mountain breeze. She looked so small, so vulnerable, standing against the blue ridge of rugged mountains. Like Henry and Katy before them, Gordon and Esther had given their child to God. He would look after her now.

While Charlene was in school in Freiburg, God's plan continued to unfold in her life. Esther and Gordon saw glimpses of why God had allowed such a bitter experience of pruning in her young life. She had become a confident, joyful young woman, living each day to the fullest with happiness that only Christ can give. Exuberance and excitement filled her many letters. She wrote of how she was witnessing to her classmates in the university until several had accepted Christ.

Yes, she was where God wanted her to be and they were glad!

26 DOMINIQUE CONQUERS

Gordon and Esther, along with Kristin and Terry Robson from Zoar Church in Inman, Kansas, were at Camp Konev in Poland. They were happy to see children from different parts of the country attend camp for ten days. Each day they were taught lessons from the Bible. Listening attentively, the leaders prayed that the Holy Spirit would prepare the hearts of these children to accept Christ as Savior.

Kristin and Terry had never been to Poland or youth camp before, but the children were delighted to have them there. With God-given wisdom, they faithfully shared their lives with the little ones.

Esther was especially drawn toward Dominique. He was an appealing, bright child. The dark-rimmed glasses he wore seemed to be the cross of his life. He would often remove them and misplace them. During these times, she watched him squint and then finally put them on again.

Dominique was one of the five boys who came to camp for the first time. Becoming excited when he was told there would be stories, games, and other interesting things to do, he eagerly anticipated spending time with the friends who had invited him.

Not knowing what to expect, and realizing this camp would be vastly different from the State camps, reluctantly his parents consented to the pleadings of their youngster and allowed him to go. Being staunch members of the Communist party all their lives, they silently wondered what he would learn, and if there would be a benefit in sending him. They doubted it, but felt it would do no harm.

I Can't Learn

Dominique came, but at first he was downhearted and discouraged. The uncle from the West had promised a reward of chocolate to the children who learned portions of the *Gospel of John*. Chocolate is a rare commodity and expensive in Poland, so they eagerly memorized Scripture.

Chocolate—what a rare treat! Dominique could almost feel the delicate smoothness in his mouth. He had not tasted a chocolate bar for so long! He watched the other children in his cabin each open their own copy of the Gospel of John and memorize long portions of Scripture. Excitement filled the atmosphere.

The next day was very hot. His friends, standing in a long line, waited their turn to quote the verses they had learned.

One by one they were admitted into the chapel and when they went out, Dominique detected the delicious aroma of chocolate on their breath. But he found it so difficult to memorize! Choosing to play the new game the Americans were teaching them, Dominique was miserable.

Why couldn't he memorize like his friends?

One day he came to Gordon with tears running down his cheeks.

"What is wrong?"

"I can't learn the verses," he sobbed. "But I would love to have some chocolate like the others."

Gordon gently encouraged the child to try to learn at least one, but Dominique walked away, the tears still coursing down his cheeks. Meanwhile, he left his glasses on the table.

These children were very active. Though they sat quietly during the lessons, recreation time was different. All their young energy and vitality was released as they ran and played.

The camp, located on the shores of a lake, offered them opportunities to go swimming, boating, or hunting for small creatures in the water. And what fun they had when their leaders taught them how to play ball! Never had they played in a game like this! Terry and Kristin, wiping perspiration from their faces, played with the children until they were weary, but the youngsters never seemed to tire of the sport.

Appetites were also enormous. When the dinner bell rang, the children scampered into the crowded dining room and were soon seated at long tables. The talking and laughing quieted down long enough for them to shovel in large quantities of food.

An Invitation is Accepted

It was lesson time again. The children quietly took their places in the chapel as Terry and Kristin directed craft time. They were learning Bible stories from the Old Testament about how God had created the wonderful world in which they lived.

Pencil crayons moved carefully over the pages as

Dominique and the other children drew and colored pictures of the creatures that went into Noah's ark.

They listened eagerly when Esther told a story. While presenting the plan of salvation, gradually the room became hushed. Individuals, lost in thought, clearly heard, as a still, small voice spoke to them. Some of the children had never asked Jesus to be Lord of their lives.

Eyes were misty as Esther gave the invitation to make this important step. Would they respond? Dominique was the first to indicate this is what he wanted. Four other children, all from Communist homes, did so, as well. The leaders prayed with them a few minutes later in an adjoining room. They realized that not one of them had ever prayed before! Prior to coming to camp, they had never even seen a Bible, the precious Word of God.

Esther asked them to fold their hands. Then they prayed the sinner's prayer after she had carefully explained again what was involved in this important decision. Voicing the words, eagerly they prayed after her, asking Jesus to be their Friend and Savior from sin.

Joy reigned in the camp as the happy children embraced leaders and friends. Jesus had taken their burdens and filled them with happiness! Soon they would go home and share this good news with their parents.

"I Did It! I Did It!"

"I did it! I did it!" cried a very excited Dominique, as he ran toward the uncle, waving a Gospel of John in the air.

"What did you do?" smiled Gordon.

"I memorized as many verses as my friends!" he beamed.

Though memorization had been difficult for him before, now there was a new interest born in his heart. Jesus, his new Friend, had made it possible to learn. He couldn't believe it!

His face shone with joy as he took off his glasses, closed his eyes, and quoted all the Scripture verses to Gordon from memory.

Walking away with part of a chocolate bar clutched in his hand, he was smiling from ear to ear. God had helped him hide His Word in his heart! Dominique was satisfied.

The Boy's Parents

But what would the child's parents say? Would they punish him? As a group, the leaders prayed for the children who had just accepted Christ.

Instead of the opposition from Dominique's parents that they expected, Gordon and Esther were greeted in a friendly manner when they saw them some time later. They learned that Dominique's father was the editor of the largest Communist newspaper in the Socialist State of Poland. Cordially, they invited their visitors into their home.

Later, Gordon and Esther prayed that he and his wife would come to know Jesus, too. Perhaps the little boy with the dark-rimmed glasses would be the one who would lead his parents to the Savior. They sincerely hoped so.

27 MOTHER

Esther didn't know how rapidly her mother was deteriorating physically. Reflecting on the unconditional love her mom had always shown her, she penned this poem.

Your eyes, soft and brown, mirror sweet depths of love,
Your life prayerfully patterned to your Master above.
Yourself, a sweet radiance—chastened and polished by Him
Your heart full of tenderness—washed and cleansed
from within.

The hours that you labored on—long into the night...
Soothing my fevered brow—till early morning light.
The many times you cradled me—secure within your arms,
Keeping me safe from earth's dangers and harm.

The times when with childish problems to you I would run
You gently wiped my tear-stained eyes with your big apron.
You took me in you arms and soothed those childhood woes
Saying that you loved me… you'd kiss my upturned nose.

Many times I heard you pray—I remember clear one night
I walked into the garden… the stars were shining bright.
I heard you praying to your Father who knew all about
your needs.
You asked Him for your children… that each young life
He would lead.

Your precious prayers have followed them as they've
lived each day,
Even though your children have grown up and gone away.
There is always confidence in knowing that your prayers
Are heard by the Lord Jesus—their names are
mentioned there.

Have all the hours of toil and hardship been worth the
pain you bore?
Because of all you've done for me… I love you even more.
Your sacrificial spirit, your dedication true,
From a heart full of gratitude—dear Mother, I love you.

Your eyes, soft and brown, mirror sweet depths of love,
Your life prayerfully patterned to your Master above.
Yourself, a sweet radiance—chastened and polished by Him
Your heart full of tenderness—washed and cleansed
from within.

—Esther M. Balisky

A Visit with Katy

It was a special hour. Esther was visiting with her mother in the Pioneer Lodge in Grande Prairie, Alberta.

When she entered Katy's bedroom, the curtains were drawn. Her mother, looking tired and drawn, had aged since their last meeting, and Esther silently wondered if she would see her alive again. The thought haunted her, but she decided to put it aside and enjoy the last few hours with her instead of dwelling on the inevitable future.

Having dinner together in her room, the evening went by too rapidly. After the dishes were taken away, they turned the lights down low. A street lamp, shining in her window, illuminated her room with a soft glow.

The conversation was stimulating as together they reminisced about highlights in their lives.

"Mom, tell me what you remember about the day I accepted Christ," said Esther.

"You were only eight," she smiled. "You always had a desire to put Christ first in your life. Yes, I remember clearly, when you went to the front of the old auditorium at Bear Lake Bible Camp after an invitation was given, and you asked Jesus to come into your life. Dad and I were so proud. There were tears in your eyes when you came to give us a hug. You had found peace with God."

Other important events followed in the lengthy conversation. One of the most meaningful, however, was when Katy shared about what Christ meant to her during her long sojourn on earth.

"Yes, without Him, sometimes I could not have coped," she sighed, "but He never has left or forsaken me."

Suddenly Katy began to sing. Although her voice was weak, the words came through unfalteringly. The song centered around Paradise, her heavenly home. Clearly singing all five verses in the German language, her memory was keen and sharp.

With every few words she stopped to catch her breath—then continued on:

Las mich gehn, Las mich gehn
das ich Jesus möge sehn;
Meine Seel ist voll Verlangen,
ihn auf ewig zu umfangen
und vor seinem Thron zu stehn
und vor seinem Thron zu stehn.

Süses Licht, süses Licht, Sonne,
die durch Wolken bricht,
o wann werd ich dahin kommen,
das ich dort mit allen Frommen
shau dein holdes Angesicht
shau dein holdes Angesicht?

Paradies, Paradies,
wie ist deine Frucht so süs?
Unter deinen Lebensbaümen
wird uns sein als ob wir traümen;
bring uns Herr ins Paradies
bring uns Herr ins Paradies!

Let me go, let me go—that I might see Jesus.
My soul is full of longing
To be with him forever
And to stand before His throne.

Paradise, Paradise, how is your fruit so sweet?
Under the tree of life, it will be as if I am dreaming.
Bring me, Lord, to Paradise.
Bring me, Lord, to Paradise.

When Katy finished singing, the room was still. Mother and daughter sensed that the quietness seemed to be a "hush from heaven."

Then they heard the old grandfather clock, that had

stood in the family home for years in Clairmont, strike the hour of eleven. As chimes echoed into the hallway, Esther knew it was time to leave so her mother could rest.

Katy, placing her hand on her daughter's head, prayed for God's blessing on her life. Clinging together, they knew it was time to say good-bye.

Wiping the tears from her eyes, Katy, leaning on her cane, stood at the door and watched Esther go down the hallway to the elevator. Esther turned and waved one last time before the doors closed behind her.

Wondering when she would see her mother again, she brushed fresh tears from her cheek.

The Inevitable

That question was answered very soon. At home in Seattle once more, the phone peeled into the night. Answering it, Esther heard Martha's voice.

"Esther," she said quietly, "are you sitting down?" Weakly, she sat down on the nearest chair. "Esther, Mom has gone to glory. She died a few minutes ago."

Breathing deeply, Esther went to tell her girls. Gordon was in Poland, alone, because Esther had not felt physically well enough to go with him.

Charlene and Corinne, whose eyes were brimming with tears, hugged their mother and vowed to stay close. Charlene, recently arriving in Seattle from Germany, was grateful to be home for her grandmother's passing.

Katy had reached Paradise. God granted the request she had sung so recently.

> Let me go that I might see Jesus…
> My soul is filled with longing
> to stand before His throne.

Harold, her eldest son, was at her side when she breathed her last.

Katy, at peace, knowing she was going home, was conscious and alert to the end. Several of her grandchildren soberly gathered around her bed. Putting her hands on them, she earnestly prayed for each in turn, asking God to prepare the pathway of life ahead.

As patriarchs in the Old Testament blessed their offspring, so Katy blessed her own, committing them into the care of her faithful Creator.

GRAND CORONATION SERVICES

A grand coronation service was held in the Alliance Church in Grande Prairie, where she and Henry had attended for many years. A large *faspa* followed. Many people came, paying their last respects to a woman of prayer and power.

Family members then took her body back to the West Coast where she would be interred alongside her husband in the Hazelwood Mennonite Cemetery.

Esther and Edna, living on the West Coast, had not attended the first service. Walking softly into the funeral parlor, they saw the other family members there. They embraced their grieving sisters and brothers.

The casket, and dress Katy wore, were soft pink in color. Her silver hair was carefully combed away from a waxen face.

Putting her hands on Katy's, Esther found them to be icy cold. Remembering how often those hands had massaged her tight muscles, fashioned garments, prepared meals, cleaned, and lovingly cared for her family, Esther felt hot tears brimming her eyes. "Mom, your hands are so cold," she whispered. But Katy didn't hear.

Beyond illness, care, and worry, she had reached the glory land. Heaven was her new home, and her heavenly Father was there.

SECOND SERVICE AND BURIAL

The second service in Abbotsford was beautiful, too. Once more friends and relatives came to honor a woman well respected and loved. At the graveside, Harold, seeing the grief in his sister's eyes, asked, "Esther, would you like to see Mother's body again?"

"Yes," she whispered softly.

Family members stood transfixed beside the open casket. Katy's face was radiant with an ethereal glow. They all saw it. She was in a place filled with light because there, the Lamb is the light.

The guests made room as the immediate family shifted themselves to hold hands around the coffin. Then they began to sing in the German language. Esther's throat was so choked up, she found it difficult, but her older brother and sisters sang one of the old hymns Mom and Dad had once loved.

Take Thou my hand, dear Father, and lead thou me,
Until I end my journey and heaven see.
Alone, I would not wander a single day.
Be thou my true companion and with me stay.

Lord, make my heart responsive and stir my soul
Until through all the darkness I reach my goal.
Then take my hand, O Father, and lead thou me
Until I end my journey and heaven see.

It was time to leave. The sun was setting over the hills, casting soft colors of violet, pink, and rose across the landscape. Taking her daughters' arms, Esther, Charlene, and Corinne walked away to continue their own journey without their mother and grandmother.

Looking back one more time, Esther wondered if Katy and Henry were watching from their new home. Did they see

their family sing around the casket today? Were they singing with the angels now?

One Moment Here—the Next with Him

One moment I am here below—
 the next one with my Lord,
Oh, the peace and happiness
 this wondrous thought affords.
One moment in this troubled world,
 with earthly toil and care,
The next, in that heavenly land—
 What joy beyond compare!

One moment I have an earthly body
 that will groan and die,
The next—transformed and changed
 like my Father's own on high,
A body that will never die,
 but live forevermore!
One moment pain—the next release,
 as I meet Him on that shore.

One moment I have never seen
 His blessed, holy face…
The next, what love and tenderness,
 on His dear face I gaze!
One moment I have never seen
 His nail-scarred hands and feet,
The next—my hands are placed in His
 to make my joy complete!

One moment I have never seen
 those mansions He's prepared…
The next—I stand in awe and wonder

to know that I am there.
One moment I have never seen
those pearly streets of gold,
The next—I breath of purest air,
and glories there behold!

Why should I fear the thought of dying
when it brings release?
Forever with my Lord in heaven—
in sweet harmony and peace?
One moment, in a twinkling, transformed,
I shall be like Him
My last breath taken, I'll rise to meet Him—
forever free from sin!

—Esther M Balisky, July 25, 1974

Read to Henry, Esther's father, on his death bed.

The Sisterhood

WHAT IS THE SISTERHOOD?

When Esther wasn't in Eastern Europe and Russia, or wasn't travelling in the US and Canada, her soul was nourished as she chose to attend a weekly prayer group of women they named "Sisterhood." This was a place where she could unburden her heart. It was a sanctuary where people could share their hurts and blessings.

The room is hushed. Several women of all ages are praying. The clock ticks slowly—its pendulum swinging back and forth. Oblivious to all else, they are agreeing as one while they talk to their heavenly Father. Interceding on behalf of others is their burden.

The Sisterhood began with two dedicated women. Desiring fellowship, Jean and Florence met from week to week, and the bond grew stronger between them.

This was too good to keep to themselves. Inviting several other women to join them, the bond widened and continued to grow as women from various churches in the greater Seattle area were hungry for more of God. Where could they go to find deeper life? Where could they pray as a group, and really touch the heart of God? Women from all walks of life came together—career girls, housewives, missionaries, writers, and speakers. There was no respecter of persons at Sisterhood. Everyone was important as an individual.

Usually, their time together began when a pianist went to the piano and began to play. The group, singing one hymn after another, enjoyed this beautiful expression of worship to God. Many of the older women in the group had memorized entire hymns of the faith as they praised God from hearts full of love.

The younger women learned fast as they joined in the worship. Some contemporary songs were sung, as well. Everyone concentrated on the words of the song as they became a message to hungry hearts.

Then Scripture was quoted. It fell like rain on a parched and dry desert. Hearts were opened to God like soft petals in the early morning dew as they prayed together. Deeply satisfied, the women drank from the well of life. Then refreshed, renewed, and revived, they were ready to face another week. But they would not face it alone. They had heard from God and He had restored their souls.

Strong black tea and refreshments beckoned them all to the table. Laughing and sometimes crying, they shared with one another while they ate.

Soon the hands of the clock pointed to 11 P.M. They

were reluctant to go even then. But realizing everyone needs their sleep, they put on their coats. Next week will come quickly. Then they will meet again to share their burdens and joys and pray for others. Sharing answers to prayer, too, will strengthen their faith.

Often they would come to Sisterhood weary and discouraged, but go home rejuvenated and ready to face another week. They had been with God!

Answered Prayers

Awakening early on that balmy, warm day, he pulled the drapes aside. The sun, shining in all its glory, made Lyle happy to be alive. Little birds, joyfully flying from one treetop to the next, sang songs of thanksgiving to a heavenly Father who cared for them every day.

Lyle Lush's paintings hung like watching sentinels in the art gallery he had created, but daily, these works of art interested him less. Wearily he put down his paint brush for the last time. These days, when a food tray was brought to him, he would wave it away, and say he wasn't hungry. Now the pajamas his wife, Jean, had bought for him, hung like loose threads on his impoverished body.

"I think this would be a good day to die," he exclaimed in a voice that was surprisingly strong.

Concerned, Jean looked at him, pleading with her eyes. *This won't be your last day, so soon, will it?*

That night he breathed his last breath while family members stood around his bed. The next moment, he was in glory—a place where there is no more death, pain, or crying. He was finally home!

Immediately the phone rang at Florence's house.

"Can you come over?" whispered her friend.

It didn't take long to drive to her house. Pouring her

heart out to a woman who really cared, Jean's face was wet with tears.

In days to come, the loss of her husband was like a raw wound in her troubled heart, but she knew the Sisterhood were praying. Sensing the everlasting arms of God underneath and around her during those difficult days of adjustment, quietly she trusted in Him. But does one really ever become adjusted to the death of a loved one?

As peace filled her heart, she rested in the fact that her friends were praying for her.

* * *

The lump on Joyce's neck throbbed with pain. Burying her head in her hands, she prayed for a special touch of healing. Tomorrow was the dreaded doctor's appointment. Tomorrow the verdict would come. Did she have cancer? The word sent cold chills down her spine. Others had the dreaded disease, and so often she had prayed with them. Was it her turn now? Family members tried to comfort and console, but she had to walk through this dark valley alone.

The diagnosis was cancer. Soon she was enduring radiation treatments, followed by weakness and nausea.

The phone at Florence's house rang. Would the Sisterhood please pray?

Standing together, they prayed. Following the developments and progression of her disease, from losing her beautiful hair to weakness, exhaustion, and wonder, they watched as her trust in God grew.

Much later, Joyce, tears rolling down her cheeks, praised God for healing, and thanked the Sisterhood women for praying. Together, they had seen a great God take over as they held to His almighty hand!

* * *

A communist border, guard dogs, sharp eyes of border guard officials, rifles protruding from bulging jackets, were all common sights now for Esther and her family who had been ministering in Eastern Europe and Russia for years. The car was thoroughly searched inside—every item removed and pulled apart.

Purses were emptied to spy on contents, and probing questions asked in hours of interrogation and stress. Heart pounding, perspiration forming in beads on worried brows, they wondered if they would be able to cross the border to minister to needy people.

Then came the peace and calm. It was like a soft, warm blanket wrapped around a shivering body. Someone was praying. Was it the Sisterhood?

Then Esther, home from Russia, knew the Sisterhood women were praying. God had kept her and her family safe as they shared His Word with spiritually hungry people in that great land where the name of Jesus is dishonored.

UPDATE

As the years fled by, several of their group, including Jean, went to be with their heavenly Father. Others joined the group until sometimes sixteen churches were represented. Pressing burdens were released, as by faith, they laid them at His feet.

Now, going from home to home, they meet less often, but the quality of Sisterhood continues to grow as they talk to God together.

28 CHARLENE COMES HOME

Charlene, having arrived in Seattle a few weeks before the funeral, grieved for the loss of her grandmother and friend—but a glow shone in her blue-gray eyes that Esther had never seen before.

Steve, a young man who had briefly courted her before she moved to Germany to go to university, had come to the airport to meet her when she returned home. Clutching a bouquet of flowers in perspiring hands, he waited for a glimpse of the lovely young woman whose heart he hoped to win.

Carrying bags, with a huge smile encompassing her face, Charlene came toward them. "Hi, Mom and Dad!" she grinned. After hugging them warmly, she asked, "Where's Corinne?"

Corinne walked up to her sister. Embracing, both agreed it was good to be together again.

Steve waited his turn. Finally she saw him. "Hey, Steve!"

Uncomfortable, he put his arm around her and gave her the flowers.

Shyly walking hand in hand toward the baggage pickup, Charlene coyly glanced at the handsome man who had come to meet her.

WEDDING PLANS

The circlet of diamonds on Charlene's finger glowed brilliantly, but this did not compare with the radiance on the face of the young bride-to-be.

"Mom, Corinne, lets go shopping for my wedding dress!" she suggested one lovely, summer day. With only a few months left to plan for her big day, they knew there was work to do.

The Spiral Staircase was filled with bridal gowns, but there was only one gown for Charlene. She looked them over carefully, and took a few to try on. But all along she knew she liked this one best.

Corinne, wide-eyed, stared at her sister as she came from the fitting room wearing the wedding gown. A tiny waistline, accented by a flowing satin skirt, made her look like a princess.

"What do you think?" queried Charlene. "Do you like this one?"

"Yes, it's perfect!" They felt it had been made for her.

Wedding invitations were sent to about 400 people. It would be a big wedding. There were so many friends. Where does one draw the line?

On the morning of September 3, Charlene looked out of her bedroom window. The day dawned without a cloud in the sky. She had prayed for this, and God had answered!

Charlene had awakened long before dawn. This was her special day and she planned to enjoy it to the fullest.

"Charlene!" called Corinne, bursting into her tidy, blue room. "Today you will change your name! Aren't you excited?"

Charlene's eyes had a faraway look. Having had a time of devotions, her Bible and notebook lay open on the bed. Yes, she was making the right step. She loved Steve for many reasons. He was handsome, with broad shoulders on a muscular frame, and that was good. But mostly, he had his priorities straight. The couple planned on putting Christ first in their new home.

"Corinne, let's go downstairs and make sure everything is in order. We will have to get ready to go to the church soon!"

Corinne, her maid of honor, and Esther, had made certain all the last-minute touches had been applied. Today, Charlene would have a wedding she would remember with joy for a long time afterward.

With three wedding showers behind her, as well as a boat cruise, she and Steve would never forget these times of joy and celebration. Charlene knew this wedding would be the ultimate!

Hearing Grandpa and Grandma Balisky, some of her aunts, uncles, and cousins from Canada, as well as guests from Kansas conversing downstairs, Charlene went down to greet everyone. Then, driving to the church in a white Cadillac with her parents and sister, she felt like a queen being summoned to a royal ball!

At the church, Corinne and the other bridesmaids, careful not to ruin her coiffured hairdo, helped her put the lacy gown over her head.

Bending down and smoothing the big, hoop skirt for her sister, Corinne looked up and said, "Charlene, let's always be friends?" Tears filled her big blue eyes.

Charlene hugged her sister and agreed they would always be buddies. It was time to go!

Steve, in a smart, white suit, took his mother-in-law's arm and walked down the aisle of the crowded church. Soft lights glowing, and music filling the church, they walked to the front pew.

Esther felt confidence in knowing that family members and friends had come for the wedding, and were sitting directly behind her. Supporting and loving, they, too, had prayed this day would be blessed by God.

Esther caught her breath when the notes from the "Trumpetair" filled the sanctuary. There, framing the door of the church, stood her beautiful daughter on her proud father's arm. Slowly walking toward her future husband, Charlene almost had to pinch herself to believe this was a reality.

When Corinne's beautiful voice filled the church with a rendition of "My Treasure," it was difficult to keep the tears back, but Esther swallowed the lump in her throat. She vowed this would be the best day in Charlene's life. She would not spoil it by blubbering.

Thinking of Katy, who had been through seven weddings, bravely committing each couple into God's keeping, Esther smiled through her tears. She would do the same.

"Do you, Charlene Krista, take this man to be your lawfully wedded husband?" asked Len Kaegler, her pastor.

Glancing sideways at Steve, she whispered, "I do."

Giving her bouquet to her sister, and kneeling with Steve at the altar, Gordon prayed for his daughter and new son-in-law. Communion followed. Gordon shook with emotion.

"I now pronounce you husband and wife!" said Pastor Len. Now they were one!

In the foyer, Steve put his arms around his new mother-in-law. "God bless you, Mom!" he smiled. Gently she hugged him, joy filling her heart.

The reception was a luncheon, catered by friends of the

family, set on long buffet tables. Round tables, covered with white cloths and flowers, were soon occupied by hungry guests. Everyone laughed and talked as they ate. The air was filled with festivity.

The hours fled as a lengthy program took place. One by one, family members and friends had something special to say about the young lady with stars in her eyes, and her handsome husband.

Sounds of music filled the room as a carefully chosen band played love songs during the entire reception. After much singing and celebration, Gordon tenderly sang, "Sunrise, Sunset" from the motion picture, "Fiddler on the Roof."

Not many, who knew what it was to have a child leave the nest, had dry eyes during the singing of this song as Gordon's strong, tenor voice carried throughout the large room.

Where had the years gone? Katy had often commented that her children had grown up so fast. Now, Esther understood.

This reception was followed by a family dinner at the China Passage. Once more, ties were linked as they talked around tables loaded with Chinese food. What a spread! Holding her stomach, Esther knew she couldn't eat one more delicious bite. Others echoed the same sentiments.

After the reception, the wedding party, including the bride and groom, went to the Space Needle downtown.

It had been a day to remember! Esther was filled with mixed emotions as she put her head on the pillow that night. Tomorrow their new son-in-law and his bride would be airborne to Europe for their honeymoon. Charlene had many memories of the places she would soon be sharing with her new husband.

Content, Esther went to sleep in her husband's arms.

They had not lost a daughter—they had gained a son!

Charlene andSteve's wedding in 1984.

TO THE BRIDE AND GROOM

Today we saw you Charlene,
in shimmering satin gown
Walk slowly down the aisle,
your countenance with joy was crowned
Your eyes were softly glowing
as you went to meet your Love
And peace reflected on your face,
as gentle as a dove.

We've also witnessed Stephen—
his eyes gazing on his bride
As she walked in on her father's arm—
to be united at Steve's side.
With pledges firm—unwavering

they repeat their wedding vows
And promise to be true in times
of sunshine and dark clouds.

The years have fled so rapidly—
earth's span but a short day
Those joyful carefree years of childhood
have quickly slipped away.
It seems but yesterday I held you Charlene,
as a babe within my arms
Prayerfully as a mother—
shielding you from earth's alarms.

You were born on a winter day
in nineteen sixty- two
A squirmy little bundle—
soft and cuddly and brand new.
Our hearts were filled with joy supreme
as we gave you back to God
We knew He had a plan in mind
for this miracle He had wrought!

Our prayers were answered when
our firstborn asked Christ into her heart
We were confident He would be her guide—
never to depart
He used her life at home—abroad,
in supernatural ways
From childhood to a young adult—
and on to this her wedding day.

As the years sped along
a life's vocation she chose
To help others in pain—
often occasions arose

So she enrolled in college—
  to become a nurse in white
To work with those who suffered,
  to help alleviate their plight.

Those fruitful years she lived in Europe
  were special ones indeed
When Charlene let her light shine
  and gladly sewed the seed
Through trying months of illness
  she came closer to her God
When he gently drew her to Him,
  under his chastening rod.

What joy reigned in the Dittoe household
  when their first-born son arrived
In sunny San Diego,
  on loving care he thrived
With tender forethought God had chosen
  another child to be his own
The King of Kings who reigns supreme—
  eternal on the throne.

Even as a little boy
  he had the urgency to share
So he called his friends to his garage
  and when they were all there -
He raised his voice and preached to them
  about a Friend he'd learned to trust
One strong desire was within—
  to be like Billy Graham was a must!

Scripture memorization became
  a major part of Steve's life
Long before he was interested

in finding himself a wife!
The Word of God implanted
so deep within his soul
Was always there to draw upon
as he pressed toward his goal.

When he became a young man
the strong challenge to serve
The great God who'd created Him—
never once did he swerve
To have a profession,
crystal clear came the call
So Stephen went in training
and gave to it his all!

Today this couple dedicated—
stand before the Lord
A union joined, a new home founded—
based upon God's Word
With misty eyes and joy combined,
we wish you all the best
And pray that Christ will crown your lives
with joy and happiness!

All my love,
Mom

Dusty Rose

"I brought something for you, Charlene," called Dee, the new bride's mother-in-law. "I hope you will be pleased!"

Charlene, loving surprises, bounded down the stairs to the sound of her voice. *What could she have for me?* she wondered.

Carefully opening the box on the kitchen cupboard, she

saw two very large, round eyes peering at her. With a fluffy coat of gray covering the little body, the cat was beautiful.

"Ah, come here, Kitty," she consoled while gently lifting her from the temporary shelter. Yes, this was a good match. The cat was where she liked to be. This felt like home.

Charlene named her Dusty Rose. The two became inseparable.

Some children had found the cat, alone and vulnerable, in the school yard where Dee was teaching. After asking around, no one made a claim to her. Many stroked her soft fur and shared their lunches, but Dusty, after having been abandoned by her owner, really never had a home.

Contented now, she finally felt that this was where she belonged. She grew quickly with good food, shelter, love, and protection. And yes, she was pregnant! With so many stray Toms running around, it was no wonder. Day by day, her abdomen became larger. How many kittens were there anyway? Every day they wondered. How many could such a small cat carry?

Gordon, Esther, and Corinne were preparing to take a trip to Eastern Europe and needed someone to live in their home for a few months. Charlene and Steve, looking for a new living arrangement, found this to be convenient until they found something more to their liking.

Dusty, the lady-in-waiting, enjoyed the atmosphere and space, where she rested, played, and ate.

THE NEW ROSE FAMILY

One day Charlene found Dusty giving birth to five kittens in the guest closet of the house. Eagerly they suckled at their young mother's breast.

"Steve, come over and look! The babies have arrived!"

"I'll be right there! How many are there?"

“Would you believe it? There are five!”

Steve, pulling the closet door open, laughed when he saw orange, gray, and striped fur balls cuddled close to their proud mother. Eyes closed from birth, instinct instructed them where to find the nourishment they needed to thrive and grow.

Charlene picked up a tiny gray kitten with a small, wet nose. Watching her, Dusty had no fear. She trusted her new owner.

The kittens grew bigger every day while basking in their mother’s love. Dusty was a wonderful mother. Proudly, tenderly, she inspected and groomed each one in turn.

“You have what?” asked Gordon on the phone from Germany when Charlene called one day.

“Dusty has five kittens, Dad. Yes, they are all growing and contented.”

“Is everything all right at home?”

“Sure is, Dad!”

“We will be there soon. I love you….Bye!”

Corinne, who loved cats, looked with anticipation to seeing the new Rose family.

Upon their return home, it was time for Charlene and Steve to move away. They knew the kittens had to be separated eventually.

Corinne, delighted at the prospect of having pets, selected Pumpkin Rose and Fritzy Rose. But until they grew a little, Charlene took them all to her new apartment.

Later Esther, a lover of cats all her life, felt her heart melt as they chose the two kittens to leave Dusty and come back to the big house to live. Dusty’s big, liquid eyes seemed to be filled with tears when she realized some of her kittens were not staying with her. Fritzy, cuddling in Corinne’s arms, had a special affinity with his mother.

Too young to realize what was happening, he and Pumpkin nestled close.

Fritz was special to Corinne. He grew to be a large, beautiful cat. Tenderhearted, knowing when they felt sad, he had a way of comforting. Gently muzzling, quietly purring, he seemed to say, “Everything will be all right. Remember, I am here if you need me.”

Eventually Corinne moved to Los Angeles to pursue her career. Esther was left with the cats, who really had become a part of the family. Corinne silently wondered what she would do without those two lively companions who came bounding to meet her every day when she returned home. Reluctantly she removed these thoughts from her mind. She had to go!

During the early 1990s, when thousands of Slavic immigrants fled to the U.S.A. from Ukraine and Russia, due to religious persecution, many came to the Balisky home to seek shelter, visas, green cards, food....

A young couple from the Ukraine moved into the house to stay for several months during this traumatic time. The Baliskys did everything possible to help during the time of transition.

29 A LIGHT FOR THE WAY

Gordon, Esther, and Corinne were in Poland again.Reaching Warsaw, Gordon began to realize that the generator of the car seemed to have less and less power. The lights were dimming fast. As they continued southeast, soon there were almost no lights at all.

Then the storm began. While lightning flashed, rain pelted on the roof of their car. At this rate, how would they reach the camp?

"Father," Gordon prayed, "please light our way till we arrive at our destination." Esther and Corinne agreed.

The car lights were almost out by now, but as lightning flashed wildly across the heavens, Gordon followed the muddy road. *The wise men so long ago followed the star to where baby Jesus lay. They, too, were guided by light from above*, thought Esther, as the heavens lit up in front of them.

Gordon breathed a sigh of relief when, about midnight, the buildings of Camp Konev loomed in the darkness.

Driving up to the new gate, he climbed out of the car. Pushing and shoving, he wondered why it wouldn't open. In vain he tried. Not wanting to waken the campers, he stood there in the pelting rain. What should he do?

He had no choice. Beeping the car horn loudly, the piercing sound echoed across the countryside.

Everyone was asleep. Soggy, wet tents and weather-beaten buildings silhouetted against a dark sky were hidden until a flash of lightning directed their eyes to them.

No one heard the car horn as it blasted into the night.

Gordon, knowing he must conjure up some other kind of method to awaken someone in camp, looked around for a hole in the fence, or some way he could get in.

Then he found it! A small opening that needed repair. By this time his clothes were soaked. He crawled through the fence and knocked at the door of the building where Joseph usually stayed while at camp. Finally, he was able to arouse someone.

Disheveled and sleepy, Joseph answered the incessant knocking. Coming out with a big flashlight, he directed as Gordon drove their vehicles into the campground.

The next day they put up a *forecelt* (awning) in front of their trailer. Even in the rain, they could sit there and eat, or even have seminars.

"Should we eat the food at camp this year?" they asked each other. Bringing canned food from Germany, they thought perhaps this would be safer. Radiation, spread widely throughout the country after the Chernobyl reactor had blown in Kiev some time ago, could have a devastating effect on everyone here.

Bojenna and Lyschek, two campers they had taught for years, said, "When we came to camp earlier, we knew there were dangerous levels of radiation present. The grass was covered with a layer of white powder, which did not disappear until it rained later."

Eventually, as camp progressed, they decided to eat in the dining room with the others. How can one eat canned food for weeks at a time? Leaving the problem with God, they could only trust Him to help.

Everyone listened during the evening service, as Gordon shared principles from the book of Nehemiah. Taking notes, the campers wrote as fast as they could. A Moody Science film, shown later, revealed the wonders of God's creation. Since films were a novelty in Poland, the young people were awed at what they saw.

SEMINARS

The seminars started the next day. Esther had studied the material she planned to present carefully and prayerfully, and hoped it would be what the campers needed.

Day after day they came. Rain or shine, they opened their Bibles and followed along. What God gave them through His servant would ring in their hearts all year. Eagerly they planned to put into practice what they were learning. In the afternoon Corinne taught English. This proved to be a very popular class.

After the long day was over, Corinne and Esther often walked in the cool of the evening. Twinkling in the dark sky, stars studded the vault of heaven. Seeing the Milky Way, they tried to count them. Of course this was impossible. Lights shining on the lake were mirrored in the water below while night birds softly called to each other.

Invigorated by the clean air, they walked quietly toward their trailer, where they snuggled under the covers and went to sleep. Each tomorrow always proved to be filled with activity.

The next night, during the evening service, though camp had just begun, the pastor's son and the daughter of one of the leaders, accepted Christ as Savior. Everyone rejoiced! Their lives, they knew, would be changed forever.

Corinne, teaching the English class, was encouraged, as simultaneously, she was learning the Polish language. Seeing a big group of Poles flocking around her daughter because they, too, wanted to learn another language, made Esther smile. Yes, Corinne was an excellent teacher.

This gift, coupled with her music, was a blessing to everyone. She and Esther sang together night after night. One of their favorites was:

Love is gentle, love is kind
The sweetest flower that e're was new,
But the only love never waxing cold
Is the love He offers me and you!

Their clothes were getting soiled. The water, never sanitary, didn't clean them well. Sometimes when it rained, they had clothes hanging on the line in their trailer for days. When finally dry, they were hard and still soiled. When they returned to Germany, perhaps they could wash them properly.

Piling into cars one day, the young people went to Lublin to see a castle. Paintings, gilded with gold, icons, centuries old, and antique furnishings, fascinated Corinne. Always interested in history, she stood silently at each display, admiring the beauty.

As they walked, her class, in heavy Polish accents, tried their best to speak English. Sometimes she answered in Polish. She was having a good time!

Paul Tomlinson, from the East Europe Evangelism Board, and his family decided to join them at camp. Arranged at an earlier date, everyone watched excitedly for their arrival.

More Americans would be welcome at youth camp—they always were!

Carefully putting sheets on beds in an extra cabin, Elizabeth (Joseph's wife) prepared to make them comfortable.

The time spent at camp would always be remembered by their American friends. Teaching the young people to play softball proved to be popular. A lot of cheering and yelling went into this sport as everyone teamed together to make this an exciting game.

After seminars and evening service were over, everyone went to the lakefront to have a wiener roast. A big moon hanging in the sky, and stars shining in all their glory, made the evening seem almost magical. Waves from the lake gently washing up on the shore, only to recede and fall back, caught the moon's gentle rays. A path of gold spread clearly and softly across the dark water.

After the wiener roast, the young people sang enthusiastically as Leshak led them in contemporary choruses. Their voices echoed across the lake. They had the joy of knowing Jesus in their hearts. No one could take that away.

Well after midnight, they walked to their sleeping quarters. They had all been with God and no one was tired.

Day by day, the seminars went on. Hearts were touched. God was at work.

Before the Tomlinsons left, they decided to make a spaghetti feed for the campers. Going into the kitchen, stoking up the fire in the old camp stove, they prepared the noodles and sauce.

Watching them, the cooks asked, "Is that all the fat you need? Why don't you cook the noodles longer?"

It all seemed too simple when these Americans cooked.

Wearing big aprons, they peeled onions and sliced pepperoni and garlic until they cried. With tears running

down her face, Corinne went out for a breath of fresh air.

The campers were all talking about this meal being prepared by the Americans. Delicious aromas wafted across the grounds.

"I'm really getting hungry now!" smiled Bozena.

"What is in those pots anyway?" said another.

"It smells delicious!"

The dining room held a special kind of excitement as the campers filed in. This culinary delight was different from the usual Polish fare. The food disappeared quickly. Everyone, filled to capacity, wondered how they would sit through the evening service.

The next day, gathering around the car, the young people came to say good-bye to their guests, the Tomlinsons. Though they had been there only four days, already, they had wrapped themselves around the campers' hearts.

"Good-bye! Good-bye!" they called, as the car drove out of the yard, leaving a cloud of dust behind. This would be a time to remember. Perhaps they could come back soon?

Wind and dust filled the air when they awakened to a new day. Big trees overhead, swayed dangerously from side to side, while waves lashed onto the shores of Lake Konev. They were having a storm! This, however, did not stop the activity.

At seminar time, Esther asked, "What qualities would you look for in a future husband or wife?" Asking the boys to leave, so the girls could give some input, they discussed this delicate matter. Eagerly participating in the subject, they wrote down many important points. Though adults, the young men mischievously tried to listen outside the closed door.

Stifling their giggles, they heard everything. Then bursting through the door, as one, they literally fell into the room filled with girls. Everyone roared with laughter, knowing this was a practical joke. Eventually the seminar resumed, and they became quiet again.

The English classes went on day after day. The attendees were slowly learning English, and gradually, Corinne's command of the Polish language improved. This gave her satisfaction. It really was getting easier to speak in their language now. What progress and encouragement!

Sometimes, going into town with the boys, they treated her to Polish ice cream. Big, succulent *koogles* went down fast, as they vied for her attention.

On the last evening of camp, a banquet was prepared. The candles and colorful napkins they had brought from Germany were carefully placed on each decorated table. The room looked festive and inviting. The cooks worked hard on making this last evening a culinary delight the campers would not forget.

After leading several songs, accompanying them on his guitar, Leshak asked everyone to write a favorite Scripture on a piece of paper. Passing the papers around, each read the verse seriously.

The Scriptures always encouraged! This night was no exception. Reading Proverbs 31: 26, Esther was touched as she read, "she openeth her mouth with wisdom...."

"Now, Bozena, would you read the verse that was passed on to you?" asked her young husband.

Opening the paper, her face changed color.

"What is the verse?" he asked.

Reluctant to read it, she said, "Proverbs 6:6."

Finally she began, "Go to the ant, thou sluggard. Consider her ways and be wise."

Everyone roared! The serious part was over.

During the final service, the boys built another big fire by the lakefront. The weather was clear and warm, as quietly sitting side by side, everyone sang. While a big moon peered from the star-studded sky, the trees around them gently rustled in the warm wind. No one wanted to go! The presence of the Lord was potent as one by one testified of what the Lord had done for them during the last few weeks at camp.

Esther's eyes filled with tears. She knew these young people had wound themselves around her heart.

Sometimes while in Eastern Europe, the days were long and difficult—drinking warm, unsanitary water, eating food laced with lots of fat and dough, seldom having enough sleep, and all the dust, dirt, soiled clothing, fatigue, loneliness, illness, driving on terrible roads, diesel-filled air as they tried to breathe in the big cities, being with people all the time, no privacy, dirty toilets, often no bathing facilities, flies, bugs, and so many uncomfortable amenities. But looking around at the shining faces of the young people, she knew it was worth it all!

Esther walked back to the trailer deep in thought. Tomorrow would be another big day.

A Mysterious Malady

Corinne and Esther had a cold. Or was it a cold?

Day and night they were coughing and choking until they couldn't breath. What could they do?

Kindly offering advice, the Polish people tried to assist, but none of their remedies helped. Going to a doctor in Eastern Europe, they knew from past experience, wouldn't work either.

Coughing until their throats were raw, they gasped for air. Impossible to talk or sing because of choking, they didn't know what to do. Where could they turn?

Eyes rimmed with red, pale and shaky, they endured each new day. "Surely," they thought, "this illness will run its course." But the situation didn't improve.

As days went by, they grew increasingly worse.

Finally, leaving Poland, they looked with anticipation to seeing a doctor in Switzerland. Believing he could help gave them encouragement and hope. With advanced medicine, there must be something he could do.

Finally reaching Switzerland, the Hari's from Pension Hari told them about a doctor they were sure could help. They quickly made an appointment.

Giving them both some white powder, they took it diligently. But what was it? Not only did it taste terrible, but worse, though they took it day after day, there was no improvement.

When they went back to Germany, there seemed to be no help there, either. "What is wrong with us?" they worried.

Finally the day came to fly back to America. Getting on the plane, they were both weak and shaky as huge spasms of coughing spells choked them. The journey seemed long—never-ending—as they tried to rest. This seemed impossible as they fought for air.

Passengers, turning their heads away from them, wondered what kind of bug these people carried. Certainly they didn't want to catch it!

It was good to be home again! Pulling the covers back, they gratefully slipped into familiar beds. Now, at last, they had privacy. Maybe they were just tired? Here they could rest!

Getting a referral to a throat specialist in Seattle from their general practitioner, they went to see him as soon as there was an opening.

Putting a stick into Corinne's mouth, he said, "Please say 'awwww!'"

"Your throat is badly infected, Corinne," he said.

"I will give you a massive dose of antibiotics. That will do the trick in about ten days. Don't forget to take it as directed, though!" he ordered.

Since Esther had the same condition, he prescribed identical medication. Now, perhaps, they would finally get rid of this terrible condition.

Every day they hoped for improvement, but they continued to cough and choke.

Finishing the antibiotics, they tried resting and suppressing their cough. That only brought on more choking.

What could they do? Where could they turn? What was this terrible illness? As they went from doctor to doctor, it seemed no one could help. They prayed—still they coughed!

A terrible realization dawned upon them, as they thought back to what might have happened.

Eating soup made with green grass that had been covered with radiation some time before—could it be that radiation had entered their bodies? Living so close to where the nuclear reactor had spewn its poisons across the Ukraine, Poland, and other countries, perhaps they had not escaped the devastating effects it could bring.

People with goiters as large as baseballs, kidneys resembling long string beans, enlarged hearts, and other terrible long-term effects, were becoming more common across various countries in Europe. And they had been so close. Could it be that this was their problem?

Asking doctors, no one could refute the fact that they were probably filled with radiation. Coughing for weeks, and on into months—for a year or so they suffered. Gradually the symptoms retreated and they were finally able to talk and sing again. With numerous speaking and singing engagements across the U.S.A., Canada, Europe, and England, they needed their voices.

When Corinne and her singing friends formed a group some time later, she practiced until her voice became normal again, but it had taken a long time to achieve.

Suffering another onslaught in July of '98, Esther had the same symptoms once again. Lasting a long time, after therapy at the University of Washington hospital, she was taught to speak correctly once more. After many hours of therapy and patience, determined, she plowed through, until finally the symptoms began to disappear.

Even to this day sometimes she suffers. Determined not to let this detour her ministry, she speaks and sings—depending on God to work through her to bless others. He is always faithful and gratefully she gives Him the glory.

Is she still willing to say, in spite of the odds against her, "Let me be faithful to my trust, and use me for Thy glory?" She answers yes, because God is in control.

A Summer in Poland

This time Esther was on her own. Gordon and David Ryan, their chiropractor friend, already in Europe, planned to meet her in Holland in a few days.

With Gordon's last-minute details unfinished at home, plus her own to do, it seemed the work piled in front of her was insurmountable. Would she have strength to do everything alone?

Finally, her goals accomplished, she awoke to a beautiful day. Soon she would be leaving for the airport for the long flight to Holland.

After David's wife, Joanne, dropped her off with all her luggage at the Sea-Tac airport, she stood in line with dozens of other travelers. Leaning against her biggest suitcase, she heaved a sigh of relief. In a few hours she would be in the Shiphol airport in Holland. From there, she could lean on her husband for support and transport.

The flight was soon filled as 350 passengers climbed aboard. Grateful to find an aisle seat, Esther put her head back and relaxed.

The hours went by slowly. She read, watched TV, and prayed. Thinking of Corinne at home brought a lump to her throat. It was hard to leave family, no matter what age they were. There were always adjustments to make for everyone. This seemed to be the story of her life.

"Please fasten your seat belts," announced the stewardess. "We are nearing Shiphol airport, and will be landing in ten minutes."

After pulling her carry-on luggage from under the seat, patiently she stood in line while passengers disembarked. Waiting around the carousel for her luggage to arrive, she carefully scrutinized each piece as it went by.

Lifting the heavy suitcases into the cart, she pushed it to the bus, which would take her to the Golden Tulip Hotel.

It was blissful, after not sleeping for twenty-nine hours, to pull the clean white sheets over her head and drift off at 5 P.M. Tomorrow she would see her husband!

Hours later, she woke abruptly, wondering,"Where am I? What time is it?"

Suddenly realizing someone was knocking on her door, she called, "Who is there?"

"It's me, Gordon!" answered a familiar voice on the other side. He and David had arrived!

After not eating for nineteen hours, the breakfast smorgasbord in the dining room tasted wonderful!

Was this only the beginning of great dining experiences? In Poland, whether or not the food was greasy and doughy, the people always fed them royally. She would have to watch her weight!

BRAUNSCHWEIG

There was no time to stay in her beautiful room and become adjusted to the new time change. This would be a long traveling day as they continued on to Poland.

Braunschweig, a town near the Polish border in East Germany, was their place of refuge for the night. The Rostenbach's always welcomed them into their home. There was room in their spacious yard for their trailer, as well. This was something they always needed to take into consideration.

While Gordon and David talked in the front seat, Esther slept. The long, dusty hours slowly crept by. Traffic was incredible like it usually is in Germany. Sometimes they climbed out to stretch, but still her feet and back ached. It seemed they would never arrive. Was the time going so slowly because she was so weary?

It was a relief to drive into the familiar yard and park. Ruth looked fresh and neat as she came out of the house.

"Welcome to our home!" she said in German.

Esther, feeling cramped, sweaty, and uncomfortable, climbed out of the back seat and extended her hand in greeting.

"I have dinner ready for you," Ruth welcomed.

Usually German cuisine is delicious, but that night she served the "Braunschweiger Special."

Raw, minced hamburger mixed with onions and garlic, shimmered in a large bowl on the spotless table.

"Please help yourself," she encouraged.

Gordon took a portion and placed it on his plate.

David looked at Esther. Esther looked at David. Could they eat raw meat? Passing the tender cuisine to him when it came their way, gracefully he declined. At least there was some other food, so that was a blessing.

Their trailer was a mess. It seemed Esther was always cleaning up after her man. Couldn't he be a little more tidy? She cleaned and organized until midnight. Then they both crept into clean beds and were asleep immediately.

Meanwhile, David went to rest in the big house. He, too, was exhausted. Tomorrow would be another big day as they drove on into Poland.

Esther's body told her to sleep, but she was wide awake. What time was it in Seattle? Would she be getting up about now?

Breakfast, Germany time, eventually arrived—about when she would have been eating dinner at home. The time change was always difficult, but she knew this adjustment would pass in a few days. She would be fine.

After breakfast, David and Gordon went into town to purchase necessary items for their trip. The hours crept by. They should be leaving, but where were the men?

Was she ready to put up with the waiting, unending travel, questionable food, dusty and dirty conditions, a culture so different from her own? Was she willing to be away from her family? Could she put up with exhaustion day after day? How about the language? She would have to struggle to put her words into correct sequence again, while Gordon talked on and on.

The words of a song learned long ago came to mind.

Lord, Thou hast given to me a trust,
A high and holy dispensation;
To tell the world, and tell I must
The story of Thy great salvation.

Thou might'st have sent from heaven above
Angelic hosts to tell the story;
Yet in Thy condescending love
On men, Thou hast conferred the glory.

Let me be faithful to my trust
Telling the world the story.
Press on my heart the woe,
Put in my feet the go;
Let me be faithful to my trust
And use me for Thy glory.

Knowing God had called her, quietly she whispered, "I am willing, Lord. Just give me strength."

Later, the Rostenbach's backyard was cluttered with necessary items to take to Poland. Packing carefully, they managed to put everything in its rightful place. More time went by.

After many hours, they heard Ruth call, "Please come in for dinner. You must be hungry!"

Sitting at the immaculate table, once again Esther couldn't make herself indulge in the cuisine. Heavy pork sausage, swimming in lard, caused her stomach to revolt. When it was passed her way, carefully she put some on her plate. When the hostess was not looking, even more carefully she tucked it into Kleenexes and hid them in her purse. The Borowka dogs would love this treat.

Novy Tomysil

It was already getting late when they left Braunschweig. They still had eight hours to travel before they reached their destination. The late afternoon soon changed into the darkness of night.

Suddenly, the car turned too sharp, and the stabilizer on the trailer hitch snapped! Now what? Perhaps they could limp along until they reached Novy Tomysil? What else could they do? Slowing them down considerably, they knew they had to be patient.

Roads in East Germany were similar to Polish roads. Esther felt each bump in the crowded back seat. The overloaded trailer, following too closely behind, jarred each time the car hit a pothole. Would everything hold together?

Fortunately, they didn't have trouble at the Polish border. The car in front of them was literally taken apart as border guards searched through personal belongings.

"Thank You, God," breathed Esther when at last, they were on Polish soil again. God was with them.

It was almost time for the sun to rise when they turned onto the road leading to the Borowka farm. Running toward them, the dogs barked and wagged their tails in greeting. One by one, the lights in the big house came on as the family made their way downstairs.

Soon, while the roosters crowed the advent of a new day, they were fast asleep in the big house. Oblivious to farmyard sounds, they had a sense of peace and quiet. God was leading each step of the way.

Because the trailer hitch had to be repaired, they stayed for a day in Novy Tomysil. This was a blessing. Quietly, peacefully, Ether relaxed and enjoyed the calm, uncluttered countryside.

Going for a long walk in the afternoon, she and David

marveled at the beauty around them. Spacious green fields, spring flowers, and budding trees seemed to be rejoicing in their creator.

People from the surrounding area began coming to the farm for chiropractic adjustments about seven that night.

"This man can perform miracles!" smiled a little lady. Though she had been stooped and in pain, now she could walk straight again.

Another couldn't believe how a quick adjustment took all his pain away.

The people left, exclaiming with wonder and gratitude.

"When can he come back?" they asked Gordon. "Please bring him soon. My aged parents need help! Please come back!"

On Saturday, it was time to leave. With Kaju and Greg guiding the car and trailer, Gordon drove cautiously out of the yard. With the elderly aunts and uncles sitting on the rickety bench outside the house, and the Borowkas standing in the yard waving as long as they could, they drove to their next destination.

The big, friendly dogs, cocking their ears and watching them, were still tasting the delightful sausage from Braunshweig. Now they were really Esther's friends. Maybe she should bring some treats next time, too. There would probably be lots to spare in the days to follow.

An Unexpected Problem—September 19, 1987

Another fruitful trip to Poland was over. Deciding it would be best for Esther to go back to Seattle, she and Gordon drove toward the Shiphol airport in Holland.

He had already made plans to return to Poland to minister in churches there after her departure.

Reluctant, but wanting to go home, Esther thought of her girls. When they were small, how often she wept, won-

dering how they were, while she and Gordon were behind the Iron Curtain. With no way to contact her little ones, sometimes she wondered if she would see them again. Believers were being imprisoned and persecuted for their faith there. Could this, too, become their fate? Sincerely they hoped it would not!

Making certain to put a clause of guardianship in their will, they knew Esther's brother Bob and his wife, Shirley, were prepared to care for the girls in case something unexpected happened to them behind the Iron Curtain.

Even though the girls were grown now, and Charlene was married, the same familiar throb of loneliness filled her heart. It would be wonderful to see them again!

And her cats! Often Pumpkin and Fritz crawled into her suitcase while she was packing for another trip. Did they know she would leave them with someone else again? They seemed to.

After roughing it in Poland, to stay in a hotel in Holland would be bliss. Driving to the Shiphol airport, Gordon had made arrangements for them to stay in the luxurious Hilton hotel the night before her departure. True elegance awaited them as they walked into the foyer of the historic structure to check into their room for the night.

Big, spacious and comfortable, the room was unlike any sleeping quarters they had stayed in anywhere. Leisurely they prepared to go out to eat.

The airport van drove them to the train station and from there they took a train to the Sea Palace restaurant. As they entered the spacious dining room, they were escorted to their table. Seeing it was filled to capacity, they were happy there was a table reserved for them.

They dined in elegance amidst the splendor of big crystal chandeliers, high quality china, and good food. Soft music filled the room, while refined people softly conversed at linen-covered tables.

The Chinese food they ordered, Esther vowed, was the best she had ever eaten. Gordon wholeheartedly agreed.

After dinner, taking her husband's arm, they walked to the train that would transport them back to the Hilton.

Looking out over the city made them realize once again, that it was large and filled with history. Esther, whose ancestry had its roots in this country, remembered some of the stories her parents told about her great grandparents when they lived here.

Looking with anticipation to a good night of rest in the lovely, big bed, Esther undressed to shower before retiring.

The water, in sharp contrast to the cold water in which she had so often showered in Poland, was hot and refreshing. Holding her face up, she felt the water running down her body and through her hair. She felt clean—really clean. What a wonderful change!

But where was her soap?

She cautiously stepped one foot out of the bathtub to reach for it. Suddenly she lost her balance. She felt herself fall, and the next instant, she was gasping for breath. While the shower kept running, she lay on the bottom of the bathtub, trying to call Gordon.

Sharp pains filled her chest. She struggled to breath. Couldn't he hear her calling?

The water kept running.

"Gordon!" she called again.

Perking his ears up, Gordon thought he heard something. Because the TV was on, the sound he heard was faint. Was Esther calling his name? What was wrong?

Jumping up from his chair, he hurried to the bathroom.

"Esther, whatever is the matter?" he cried in alarm.

There lay his wife, in the big bathtub, unable to get up.

Turning off the water, he helped her to her feet.

Groaning in pain, she held her chest.

While driving through Eastern Europe, through Communist countries, and across border crossings, they had never had an accident. Now, in beautiful Holland, where the roads were paved and everything was comparatively safe, Esther had a fall!

Helping his wife into bed, he wondered how she would travel alone to America tomorrow.

She did get some sleep that night, but to turn over in bed made her gasp with sharp pain. Could she have cracked or broken her ribs? She guessed this had happened when she hit the bathtub.

In the morning, Gordon discovered that the flight was five hours late. So he ordered a leisurely breakfast from Martinair, their travel facility, and brought it to their room.

The food was delicious, but Esther wasn't hungry. Knowing she had to conjure up some strength for the long flight, however, she dutifully ate the toast, sausage, and eggs. Hot coffee, which is always delicious in Western Europe, went down well.

The next major item on her list was to dress. To bend over and put her stockings on was almost impossible. Rolling them up over her toes, she winced as pain filled her chest. Gordon helped her into her clothes, took her arm and assisted her to the wheelchair Martinair had provided.

The line of people waiting to buy their tickets was enormous. Easily, carefully, Gordon wheeled her past everyone. After checking in, they were ready to go.

In a few minutes, Gordon wheeled her onto the big aircraft. Being in a wheelchair was a place she would rather not be, but it did have its advantages. Others were still standing in line, while she was already in her seat, ready for departure.

Seated in the front, she could stretch her legs and move around comfortably.

Seeing Gordon leave brought a lump to her throat, but thinking of seeing her girls again, she felt a wave of excitement. She would soon be home!

The flight across the water seemed to pass quickly. Perhaps she could sleep on the plane—at least she hoped so. But whenever she moved, sharp pains filled chest. So she chose to sit quietly as much as possible.

Finally, feeling the wheels of the huge airliner hit the pavement in Seattle, Esther knew she was home. Wheeling her through to customs, the attendant helped her with all the details.

Then she saw Corinne! After collecting the luggage, Corinne carefully wheeled her mother to the car. "Welcome home, Mom!" she grinned, while giving her a big bear hug.

To walk in the front door of their home on Fremont Avenue North, and see that her daughter had cleaned the house meticulously, brought tears to Esther's eyes. Though she had a busy schedule, the 6,000 square foot house and big yard were well kept. Swelling with pride, Esther thanked her.

"Hi, Charlene!" she said on the phone, after settling in.

"Mom, it's good to have you home! Are you in a lot of pain? Please, go and see Doctor Anderson tomorrow! You need to have a check-up!"

Dutifully promising she would, Esther winced with pain when she tried to crawl into bed.

In the morning, after a restless sleep, Esther was concerned when she found blood in her mouth. She called Doctor Anderson.

"Is there someone there to take you to Emergency? I think this situation needs to be checked out!"

"I will take you, Mom. Let's go!" answered Corinne.

The hospital was not far away. The doctors in

Emergency checked her thoroughly. "The cartilage is damaged, Mrs. Balisky. Also, you have cracked two ribs and possibly three."

Giving her a rib belt, she was told to wear it and take life easy. The pain, they said, would eventually subside. That night, with Pumpkin purring on one side, and Fritz on the other, contented, she went to sleep. She was home again!

As time went by, her ribs healed. She could not sit idly by when there was work to do!

30 ANNA MAKES A DECISION

...greater is he that is in you, than he that is in the world (1 John 4:4).

On the next trip to Poland, Gordon went first, expecting Esther to come at a later date. Esther and the girls spent quality time together while he was away. LeRoy and Marvel Cotterill, friends from Seattle, decided this would be a good time for them to help minister in a youth camp there. They were excited to join Gordon.

RESENTMENT IN THE CAMP

"Two—three—four—hut—hut!" commanded the former army major, as the young people fell into place. Reluctantly stretching, bending, jumping, marching—many wished they hadn't come to camp this year.

Usually youth camp was a highlight in the lives of young

people across the country of Poland. All year, they talked about what they would do when they arrived. They remembered blessings received from past seminars and sermons. Many lives had been changed forever.

But this year was different. Pastor Joseph had been camp director for so long, they couldn't remember when he hadn't been there. He had generated respect and kindness. He was also a lot of fun. Laughing became an important part of their daily diet at camp, and Joseph was the ringleader of it all.

Alex, a sober, regimented Major, tried to pattern his life after the older man, but he did not have Joseph's buoyant personality.

When Joseph asked him if he would be leader of Camp Konev that year, he eagerly accepted the invitation. Enjoying young people, he believed the job would not be a big challenge.

He was wrong.

Anna, a college student from Warsaw, had been to camp before. She, along with her friends, looked with keen anticipation to coming back every year. This was a time when they could become saturated in the Word of God as it was taught morning, afternoon, and evening. A few hours in the afternoon were designated for free time, when they played ball, went canoeing or swimming, or walked around the lake.

The day when camp was announced to begin again, Anna and her friends came. Excited, she waited for others to arrive. Perhaps Janic, a college student from Posnan, would come, too? Her cheeks became flushed at the thought of seeing him again.

Lake Konev shone in the sunlight, gentle waves lapping against the shore. Recalling how she loved to swim there, she could almost feel the cool, refreshing water on her bare skin, as she unpacked her suitcase.

One by one, the campers arrived. Succulent aromas from the kitchen wafted toward their cabins, and they knew it was dinnertime. No invitation to run across to the dining room was needed.

Quickly they came from their cabins and tents, sat down, and began to eat. Tonight, the cuisine consisted of red beet *Borscht*, a traditional soup made with cabbage and beets. Of course, the usual *kanapke* (open-faced sandwiches) accompanied this fare.

Getting caught up on news from all across the country was fun. Anna blushed when Janic smiled at her across the table. Together, they shared last year's victories. Together, they looked forward to what God would do at camp this year.

Realizing that Gordon would arrive in a few days also added to the anticipation in the hearts of those present. But some were sad that *Ciotka* Esther would not arrive until later, due to pressing details at home. Meanwhile, Alex would be their leader, and they wanted to respect him, too.

As everyone joined in, Pastor Joseph looked on with joy. His young people had returned! He, Alex, Gordon, and Esther had sincerely prayed for revival and blessing.

RULES AND REGIMENTS

But Alex's rules were too strict. Usually everyone was relaxed and happy. Now it was different. In the dining room, a large poster filled with rigorous regiments was posted for all to see. Every camper was expected to adhere closely to them.

"This reminds me of being under the law, not under grace," commented Anna. The others agreed.

Bedtime at 10:00 P.M. was not accepted well, either. In the past, Anna remembered how they sat beside the lake and sang. Accompanied by guitars and accordions, often they sang until midnight. No one stopped them as fellowship con-

tinued. A 10 o'clock curfew was too early for teenagers and young adults. They did not want to go to bed so early.

Anna was displeased. All year long she had worked hard. College homework, a job, and other duties kept her active. Here she wanted to relax and enjoy God's great outdoors and soak in the wonderful Word of God as it was taught by capable leaders. No one wanted to do exercises. They had enough activity around the campgrounds, swimming and going for long walks around Lake Konev.

"Let's go talk to Alex," suggested Janic. "Maybe he will decide to be more lenient, and let us relax a little."

"Yes," agreed the others, "Let's go!"

"Alex," began spokesman Janic, "we don't have enough time to relax. Could we just forget about the exercise time in the morning as well as other regimented activities? Could you treat us like grown-ups and not children?"

Alex frowned. He was not sympathetic to their suggestions. He felt that this camp should be run in a regimented way. He would not change the rules, and it was up to the campers to abide by them. Period. Alex knew the young people were dissatisfied, but he would not budge.

They talked to Joseph, too, but he was dealing with some serious problems and was leaving for Lublin soon. Although he was concerned, he could not help. This was Alex's jurisdiction, he thought.

Frustration and disappointment ran rampant throughout the camp.

As days went by, frustration turned to resentment. Small groups gathered outside the chapel. There was no joy on their faces now. Some stopped coming to sessions while others sat in chapel and moped. No one showed up for scheduled exercises in the morning, but stayed in bed until breakfast. Then they shuffled joylessly to the dining room.

Finally, Anna felt she'd had enough. "I'm packing!" she told her astonished roommates. She was tired of Alex's demands. Wrong attitudes (including her own) were eating her heart like a cancer. This was no fun! Going home would be a welcome change.

Other campers considered leaving as well.

Alex knew the situation was serious. Joseph had already gone to Lublin, and Gordon and Esther were not there yet. Did he have to bear this burden all alone? Yet, he did not change his mind about the rules. Never had this kind of problem surfaced at camp before. Usually days went by too fast. No one wanted to go home, and when they did, there were tears of sadness.

Alex was relieved when Gordon finally arrived. Perhaps the situation would improve.

JOSEPH'S PROBLEMS

But Gordon felt he needed to go to Lublin immediately after arrival, to help Joseph deal with his problem. Leaving the disgruntled campers, he quickly drove to the city. Driving past Lake Konev, it sparkled like a thousand diamonds in the sun. His heart should have been light. All year both he and Esther looked with anticipation to coming here for camp. Why was he so downcast now? Knowing that Satan had disrupted the camp, and Joseph was having a severe problem with depression, Gordon prayed aloud as he traveled down the dusty road. Realizing his utter dependence upon God, he sincerely prayed for wisdom.

Joseph was not the usual, jovial, laughing man Gordon had known. Morose, sullen, his head bowed, he looked up when Gordon came into the house. After hours of counseling and prayer together, the two men, who were like brothers, clasped hands and claimed victory in

Pastor Joseph and Elizabeth from Lublin Poland. Very active in the youth camp at Lake Konev.

the name of Jesus, the resurrected Savior.

There was a slight smile on Joseph's face when Gordon left. Reminded afresh that "greater is He that is in them, than he that is in the world," he firmly grasped onto that promise. But the battle ahead would be long and hard, and for years, this man of God would suffer.

When Gordon returned to camp, lights in the chapel burned brightly. Some had come to church that night, because they knew Uncle would be there. The air was heavy and oppressive when he entered. There was no singing and joyful sharing. Usually when they came, they were eager to hear what God would teach them. Sometimes singing and sharing would last for hours before the message. But tonight, it was not that way.

Alex had tried to make the young crowd enthusiastic, but had failed miserably.

More campers reluctantly came into the chapel. Bowing his head again, Gordon asked God for wisdom as he addressed the depressed group of young people.

Opening his well-worn Bible, words flowed freely as he spoke on disciplines Christians should have in their lives.

No one wanted to listen. Anna solemnly sat in her chair, tuning out. Beside her, others nervously toyed with their fingers, or shuffled their feet. Eyes downcast, no one could meet the uncle's. How could everyone seem to forget that God was there?

REVIVAL

Gradually, some words caught Anna's heart… "good soldiers of Jesus Christ…" How could she become a good Christian soldier? The Holy Spirit began to speak, softly, gently, to her heart. At first she tried not to listen to His pleadings.

"Alex was wrong, wasn't he? Why couldn't he just bend a little?" she reasoned. In spite of rationalizing on her part, God's Word kept getting through to her. She knew God was speaking.

Gradually, her friends stopped their shuffling and began to pay attention, as well. Their eyes were turned toward the uncle now. Yes, what he said was true. Beginning to follow along as they looked up verses in their Bibles, slowly conviction was born.

First they listened reluctantly, then gradually a little more and more, until finally they were listening with their hearts.

The leaders sincerely rebuked Satan in the powerful name of Jesus, and prayed that this situation would turn around to the glory of God. The campers were beginning to respond. God heard and answered prayer.

Gordon had spoken for over an hour. Outdoors, the moon shone, making a silvery path across Lake Konev. A gentle wind blowing the grasses and trees, softly rustled pages in well-worn Bibles. Night birds chirping in their nests basked in the warm, balmy evening.

The sermon was over. No one moved. Sitting quietly, many bowed their heads in prayer. The hearts of the young people were not still. A battle raged, as the Holy Spirit gently showed them their sin.

The stillness in the room was broken when Anna stood to her feet and began to pray so all could hear. "God," she began, with tears running down her cheeks, "Please forgive me for my wrong attitude. I have put the blame on regimented rules, but I am wrong. Forgive me for unkind words spoken, and for this sinful attitude." Covering her face with her hands, she continued to weep. She had barely said "Amen," when another girl stood and poured out her yearning heart to God. One after another, young men and women stood up, and with tears flowing freely, asked God for forgiveness. Truly repentant, they fell on their knees and cried to God.

Soon the young people found it hard to wait for their turn to confess and talk to God out loud. Everyone was touched by the Holy Spirit. A revival had begun!

One by one, they asked God's forgiveness for wrong attitudes. Then going to their leaders, especially Alex, they apologized. Alex put his big arms around each person as they came to him. Realizing his own attitude had not been right, he asked for their forgiveness, too.

Each person was truly repentant as the Holy Spirit continued his work that night.

Those who were born-again Christians led the way as they cried to God to do a new work of grace in their hardened hearts. Weeping and embracing, everyone was making right the wrongs that had been there.

There were a few in the chapel that night who had never made a commitment to follow Christ. They were now asking Him to be Lord of their lives. One by one, the others knelt around them as they made the initial step to believe on the Lord Jesus Christ and be saved.

Then the testimonies began. No one wanted to stop telling about the new peace God had given. Now, instead of tears of self-pity and resentment, the young people, who had been so rebellious, talked of victory.

Anna's friend, Mike, strapped a guitar around him and began to play. Everyone joined in and sang with the same fervor, and even more, that in previous camps.

Love flowed like a mighty current, as they had fellowship with God and each other. Then unanimously, kneeling to pray and praise, burdens kept being released as they gave them to God. No one looked at the clock. The hours fled by as night turned into rosy morning. Still no one was tired.

Now, sober-faced Alex smiled from ear to ear. Anna laughed when roosters from nearby farms began to crow, heralding the coming of a new day. This was not just an ordinary day. How could it be, when they sensed God's presence in their midst so mightily?

Janic took special note of this day as he skipped to his cabin for a little sleep. Birds sang in leafy trees overhead, and even the grass looked greener than it had yesterday. Everywhere he looked, the world seemed washed and cleansed. Was it because his heart was clean?

One by one, the campers went to sleep with peace in their hearts. Lake Konev, gently washing up on the shoreline, seemed to be smiling, too.

A baptismal service, signifying an outward sign of an inward change

BAPTISM

Anna crawled out of bed and walked over to the suitcase she had packed only a few hours earlier. Hanging her clothes back in the small closet, there was no desire to leave now. She only wanted to drink in more of God. So did the others.

But camp was almost over. The next group would be coming soon, but no one wanted to go home. The atmosphere all around was one of excitement, glory, and victory.

Alex told them that if they didn't want to take part in the exercise program in the morning, they didn't have to, but most of the campers came. Now they bent, stretched, and marched to a different beat, without a resentful thought.

Alex smiled as he shouted, "Two—three—four—hut—hut!" What joy to work with such willing campers!

Anna and some of her friends asked Alex and Gordon if they could stay for the next camp. Arrangements were gladly made. Most of the campers would have to stay in tents, but that didn't seem to be a problem.

They eagerly looked forward to the next session. Intermingling with others who came for the new camp, excitement was contagious—the atmosphere electric.

The leaders discussed the possibility of having a baptismal service in Lake Konev. Those who had recently accepted the Lord as Savior were eager to follow Him in this way, along with others who had never taken this important step.

The date set, Anna suggested to her friends that they make posters to advertise the baptismal service, place them in Lubartow and other surrounding villages. The Communists often advertised in this way when they had an important event. Stapling announcements on telephone poles for all to read, caused quite a stir in the community. The townspeople, wondering what a baptismal service would be like, decided they wanted to find out. Yes, they baptized in the Catholic Church, but certainly not in the lake! Coming to see for themselves would be the answer.

Most had heard of the camp at Lake Konev, and knew that something special took place there several times every summer. What did they do all day, every day, for two weeks at a time?

Meanwhile, the excited young people took their guitars and accordions and went to surrounding towns to testify and sing.

Wistfully, the people wondered what it was that made these people so happy. Perhaps they would find out when they came to the service. Yes, they would not miss that!

The day of the baptismal service arrived. The sun shone, warm and friendly, while Lake Konev sparkled like a thousand diamonds.

People from every direction made their way on foot or drove in cars. Nearby neighbors walked. Curiosity ran rampant as people walked toward the baptismal site.

A large crowd of Catholics, Atheists, Communists, and Protestants stood on the shores of Lake Konev, as young people sang enthusiastically of their love for Jesus.

Anna, standing tall and erect, was lost in the moment, as her white robe fluttered in the warm breeze. She planned to serve God with all her heart. Joyfully she testified again of what He meant to her. Others in turn followed, each giving testimony of their faith.

Anna's burdens had rolled off her shoulders. She knew Jesus was carrying them now. She would never have to walk alone as long as He was beside her.

As the waters closed over her head, she gave herself unreservedly to Him. One by one, her friends walked into the waters of baptism, showing they were serious about this step of obedience.

Janic was reminded of Jesus, God's Son, who walked into the waters of the blue Galilee. The spirit of the Lord descended upon Him in the form of a dove and His Father cried, "This is my beloved Son, in whom I am well pleased" (Matthew 3:17). Perhaps the Father was smiling now with tender affection as he looked on these joyful young people who were following Him in this important step of faith.

"Look how happy they are," said a buxom, Polish woman, as she wistfully nudged her husband. He was too busy watching and didn't even hear her.

After the lengthy service, neighbors went to their humble dwellings on the shores of Lake Konev. Strangely quiet, their thoughts were turned to a living God who could give joy and peace such as they had just witnessed.

In many hearts, a hunger burned—for what or whom,

they were not quite certain. But these young people really had something they did not have—or was it Someone?

Anna was smiling and radiant. She had just been baptized—and Janic had asked if he could see her in the future! Clasping hands, Anna and her friends began to laugh for joy as they ran to change into dry clothes.

Satan had tried to defeat everyone at the camp and he had almost succeeded. But once more, the campers had experienced that

> *...greater is he that is in you [the Lord], than he that is in the world [Satan, the deceiver]* (1 John 4:4).

Satan was defeated once more! He had to run away while God did His work in His way.

Another Trip to Poland

The following spring, they again turned off the road at Lubartow, to drive on to Camp Konev where they had spent so much time at youth camps in the past. Soon they could see Lake Konev, shimmering and dancing in the sun.

Esther felt a tug at her heart. Many had come to know the Lord as Savior at this place throughout the years. Keeping in touch with most, they wondered how the others stood in their walk with God.

She also thought of Corinne, who had been faithful in teaching young people in this camp. Some day, Esther expected to hear the Lord say to Corinne, "Well done, thou good and faithful servant." Corinne had done her best.

Stepping out of the car, they saw a group of people, including Joseph and Elizabeth. Soon summer would be here and with it, youth camps would convene. Today the volunteers were cleaning the grounds and buildings so everything would be in order to begin again.

"Welcome!" smiled Pastor Joseph,extending his hand. "We're glad you came!"

Elizabeth, standing nearby, looked older, more serious and mature than their last meeting. Quietly she and Esther embraced.

Lunch was on the way. Big loaves of bread standing on the camp kitchen cupboard must be sliced. *Kinapke* would soon grace the tables. Was this not usual fare at Camp Konev? Everyone grew hungry as they worked faithfully in the cold air outdoors.

Esther cut and sliced bread until her arms were sore. "Could they really eat so much?" The cooks smiled and said yes.

Soon the usual canned pork and mayonnaise graced the *kinapke.* Fresh doughnuts and *chi* completed the simple meal. Eating outside at a long table, Esther remembered times in the past, when they had sat with campers in this very place. Today, fellowship was warm and sweet as they became re-acquainted.

Battling flies and bugs, they wondered how many had already sampled some of the food served that day. Esther, reminded of the many times her stomach had reacted here, was careful not to eat too many *kinapke.*

Carefully scrubbing the dirty, wood floors, the women worked all afternoon to make this place presentable. When dishes were finally washed and other jobs completed, it was time to eat again.

Making green soup from a plant on the grounds, carefully they added onions and spices. Putting the ladle up to her mouth, carefully the cook sipped a little. It needed just a touch of salt—otherwise it was perfect. Gordon said a prayer, and they all fell to eating.

Victory

Parking their trailer at Camp Konev was a safe and accessible place to be. From there, they ministered in Lubartow and Lublin.

They visited with Pastor Joseph and Elizabeth. Trials and hard times had come their way. Joseph had never taken steps to relieve the problem taking precedence in his life. Could Gordon help him?

Spending a lot of time with Joseph, Gordon prayed that he would admit his sin and make it right with God.

The wind was blowing hard on Sunday morning. Esther shivered in her summer dress. After putting a warm sweater over her clothes, she and Gordon made sure all the buildings around the camp were locked.

Entering Pastor Joseph's church in Lublin, they saw immediately how much smaller the congregation was than it had been before. Then it had been filled with a joyful congregation—including many young people. Now, looking around, they saw there were two young people present. Their hearts ached for the problems they faced. But some familiar people greeted them when they walked in the door.

Joseph was still pastor, but he looked defeated. Elizabeth rarely smiled anymore. Somber and old, she sat quiet and unresponsive during the long service.

There was no musical instrument, so Esther played a small accordion while they sang. While Gordon preached, the congregation listened. Could he help them heal their broken hearts?

After church the women kissed Esther on one cheek, then the other. Gordon received the same symbol of friendship from the men.

Joseph's aged mother stayed home to make lunch for them. What a feast they had! Chicken, perogies, and a variety of salads went down quickly.

The afternoon slowly went by, as Gordon counseled with

Elizabeth, praying sincerely that God would solve the problems.

Joseph was having a tremendous struggle. Then, with tears in his eyes, he began to weep. "Please, Elizabeth, will you forgive me for my inadequacy? I know I have sinned, and I am sorry!"

Then he turned to Gordon and Esther. "I want to apologize for the sin that has tainted my life and as a result, the lives of some of my congregation. I will, with God's help, try to do better. Please forgive me?"

The four of them went for a walk into the woods. Birds, singing in the branches overhead, seemed to be bursting with joy. Flowers, green grasses, and other lacy, green finery made them realize afresh how their great God, who made the world, can help solve problems by His mighty power.

They talked for a long time while sitting on an old log. It was good for Joseph to confess and make his heart right with God. Then they all stood in a circle. Weeping, they held hands and prayed. Though rain drops were falling, no one cared. Oblivious to everything else, they talked to God.

Soaked with rain, they walked back to the house together. This time everyone was smiling. They knew God had heard their prayers. Joseph, in God's strength, would change his ways.

After a cup of *chi*, they embraced and left for Camp Konev. It had been a profitable day.

HARVEST TIME IN POLAND

Fields of golden grain are gently rustling in the wind,
Ready to be harvested, then to be gathered in.
With a scythe, reapers labor as grain falls to the ground,
While others gather it together, to be securely bound.

In neat formation, sheaves of grain stand row by row.
The laborers go home to rest as the sun sinks low.

Those hours of toil bear fruit as the harvest is brought in,
It will not be long before winter winds and cold begin.

Trees along the countryside are losing summer's dress
Bright, the leafy green they wore is each day getting less.
The master artist mixes shades of gold, deep red, and brown
And one by one, each rustling leaf falls gently to the ground.

Rows of sturdy apple trees are heavily laden down
Arrayed with apples golden, and autumn's festive gown.
Rows of produce from the garden—God's miracle to grow,
Gathered in before harsh winter winds begin to blow.

'Tis harvest time—great multitudes of people throng the street
Wandering aimlessly in unrest, disturbance, and defeat.
'Tis time to gather in the harvest before it is too late—
O Reapers, hasten to the rescue! They can no longer wait!

—Esther M. Balisky

After the Rain in a Polish Forest

The sky frowned, dark and angry, and though it was early in the afternoon, it seemed to Esther that evening had already arrived. Wiping perspiration from her face, she wondered how much longer she could bear this stifling heat.

The birds had ceased to sing hours ago. Often calls from the cuckoo birds filled the dense forest, but now, they, too, were still. Not a blade of grass moved. Not even one leaf stirred on the massive trees overhead. All nature seemed to be waiting in expectancy for rain to quench the overwhelming thirst and dryness that had grown all summer.

Taking deep breaths, Esther tried to shut out the ominous stillness and oppressive atmosphere which hung like a heavy, damp blanket over everything and everyone.

Suddenly she jumped as a loud clap of thunder hit her

little home on wheels. Then instantly, as lightning spread its jagged finger across the angry sky, the rain came—blessed, sweet rain. Splashing in big, cool drops, slowly the water soaked into the dry, parched soil.

Gordon and Esther had been in Poland for over a month. A heavy schedule of ministry had resulted in fatigue and strain. After an intensive time of teaching, they needed to be alone. Where could they rest for a few days before beginning again? Deciding to go into the Polish forest, they parked their trailer. Here, perhaps, they could refuel, relax, and pray.

Again Esther jumped as thunder rolled across the forest like a mighty army truck. Another bolt of lightning seemed very close as it filled the shrouded trailer with light. The place was like a sauna as drops of perspiration rolled down her body in rivulets.

Carefully she had closed all the windows to make certain their home would remain dry. But now, opening the door just a crack, relieved, she felt cool, refreshing air pour in. Now she could breathe again. Heaving a sigh of relief, she thanked God for His goodness in sending the rain, and with it, cool air.

Birds, safely tucked away in their nests in massive trees overhead, waited in expectancy. There would be food to gather when the rain was over.

Two big dogs crawled into a shelter to stay out of the deluge. Everyone had a place to hide.

While darkness covered the forest, the only sound was the pounding of the rain on the trailer roof.

Cooler now, Esther relaxed. It rained for several hours. When the storm gradually diminished, she opened the door wider. She was pleased to see a clean, washed forest. Water still glistened on the leaves, and dripped noisily from the large trees overhead, but the rain was over.

Suddenly the sun came out. Esther was certain the entire forest seemed to be smiling.

She couldn't stay indoors any longer! Slipping into a pair of sneakers and sturdy jeans, and taking her umbrella, she walked into the newly cleansed forest.

Then the birds came alive. Singing as if their throats would burst, they, too, were released from the ominous stillness that blanketed the forest a few hours ago.

Dogs, coming out of their shelters, wagging stubby tails, came toward Esther as she walked on the wet soil.

Puddles a foot deep, filling crevasses and cracks, were everywhere. Fog rising from the warm earth, creating a hazy, greenhouse effect, filled the living forest. Water, dripping from overhead, fell in droplets into the dirty pools, making rings which widened as they spread.

Esther perked up her ears. Yes, the cuckoo birds were singing again. Loud and throaty, their calls echoed throughout the forest. Other cuckoos, answering, made the forest reverberate with their calls.

A variety of birds chimed in a grand crescendo all around. Little sparrows trilled, black birds warbled, while crows, the scavengers of the forest, cawed and scolded. The forest rang with music. Everything and everyone was alive.

She smiled when a red-headed woodpecker scolded her. After all, she was an intruder. This was his home. Little ants and bugs scurried away as Esther walked on the grassy, wet, earthen floor.

A few small homes, she noticed, were scattered in the dark recesses of the forest.

Proud parents watched their little ones as they splashed and played in pools of water. Oblivious to those around them, joyfully, screaming with laughter, the children responded to the living forest. They, too, seemed to sense an absence of pressure in the clean air.

Suddenly everyone was quiet. Who was this stranger walking into their forest? Everyone stared and the children stopped their play. Finally, one of the fathers greeted her in Polish. Esther answered and quickly went on her way. In the distance she heard laughter as the children resumed their play.

The rain was still dripping from the trees as she walked down the path toward her home. She joyfully raised her voice, and joined in the chorus of the birds. This was an orchestra like no other. Could a trained maestro lead a more thrilling and organized chorus? She doubted it.

Breathing the pure, sweet air, she thanked God for a cleansing rain in the Polish forest.

Home

The potent word, *home*, rang clearly in Esther's ears. They would be flying back to the U.S.A. soon, but with mixed emotions. There were many needs in this country, and they had many dear brothers and sisters in the Lord here, but there were also duties to attend to in their home and office in Seattle, and their girls to see.

As always, she and Gordon would be part of this great family of God—whether it was in Eastern Europe and Russia or in the United States of America. What a privilege to belong!

31 MORAVIA

After travelling throughout the United States and Canada in a myriad of churches, sharing God's work of grace in the lives of the people to whom they ministered, they were in Eastern Europe again.

"Could you come and help alleviate the load by sharing the work of God?" asked the people from headquarters.

They had been asked to speak in beautiful Moravia. Lying in the middle of Czechoslovakia, between Bohemia on the West, and Slovakia on the East, is a flat, fertile farmland. Almost all the people of Moravia are Czechs, a Slavic people who speak the Czech language. Most belong to the Catholic Church. This, too, was a mission field.

They drove their bus through the beautiful countryside. Rugged mountains, rolling hills, green velvet fields, and pine trees covered the luscious terrain. Esther's eyes feasted on the beauty of this ancient country. She pinched herself to believe that she and Gordon were actually there. Excited, they asked

The conference center in Moravia where Gordon and Esther gave seminars.

God for a fresh anointing to share with these hurting people. Without His power flowing through them, they knew their time there would be wasted.

Driving into the conference grounds, the aroma of delicious food filled the air.

"I'm hungry," smiled Esther.

Agreeing, Gordon rubbed his ample stomach.

Several of the leaders came out to greet them, and invited them to eat with them. Walking into the spacious dining room, they saw it was filled.

They had never met these people before, but they greeted them not as acquaintances but as friends.

"Please help yourself!" smiled one of the cooks.

They did. The food was delicious.

"I will show you to your quarters," smiled Jan. "Come with me."

Walking down a grassy slope, they stopped at a chalet. Esther couldn't believe it when they walked in. Never, in all of their travels in Eastern Europe, had they been treated so royally.

Large windows, overlooking the incredibly beautiful countryside, were sparkling and clean. This, in itself, was a change from the conditions they often encountered in these countries.

There were two large rooms on the ground floor. A spiral staircase led to an upstairs bedroom. It looked like they would finally be able to sleep without being disturbed. And if they slept separately, Gordon's snoring would not bother her so.

Oh joy, this was a welcome change! And so spacious, too!

After hurriedly taking their suitcases and bags into the chalet, they prepared for the first service.

Christian leaders, nationwide, were present. All were longing for a deeper walk with God. Gordon and Esther sensed a wonderful opportunity to encourage a suffering people.

Impressed to teach on the subject of how to overcome depression, Esther tucked her notes and Bible under her arm as they walked to the church.

Men and women from across the country, sitting quietly in their seats, waited to hear from God.

Later in the service, they divided the congregation, and Esther taught the women as Gordon ministered to the men.

She noticed a young pastor's wife who sat in the front row during the seminars. Asking intelligent questions, she had a sharp, keen mind. Later, she learned that her name was Grezena.

Many pastor's wives wept as, one by one, they shared with Esther. How could they cope? With little privacy in their homes, many spent very little time with their pastor-husbands because

Gordon and Esther in Morovia with one of the christian leaders.

they were too busy helping others. During prayer time, they opened their hears to the Lord, as tears ran down their cheeks.

At the end of the seminars, many told us that their burdens had been lifted. Now they could go home with joy. They would rely on God to help and give wisdom to cope during trying situations.

Esther, feeling humbled, thanked God sincerely that she had been the first woman to be honored to speak in this needy country since World War II. What a privilege!

Walking back to the chalet after seminars each night, while the large moon shone in all her glory, and stars studded the vault of heaven, she praised their Maker. Weary, but content, she entered the roomy chalet.

"God is so good!" Esther whispered as she snuggled under the feather quilt. The fresh, invigorating mountain air helped them both to relax and go to sleep immediately.

Their Father planned this divine encounter long ago, and they were grateful.

Prague, Czechoslovakia

Invited by the leaders from the evangelical headquarters in Prague to give seminars at a Christian Workers' Conference, Gordon and Esther gladly accepted. Economic pressures—the cost of food and other commodities—had risen sharply. The people were depressed and anxious, wondering how they could cope.

"Please come and share with us," pleaded the president of the evangelical churches in the historic city of Prague.

Gordon, Esther, and David, the chiropractor from Seattle, had been in the country of Czechoslovakia for about a month. Invitations from far and wide kept coming to them. From city to city, from small towns to country, they poured out their strength and energy to help these people. Before they finished in one place, another invitation would come.

On this special occasion, Esther was asked to speak in a deaconess ministry conference to women from all over the nation. She would be the first woman to speak here, also, since World War II. Gordon would concentrate on the men's ministry there.

As they entered the ancient city of Prague, the air was darkened and it was difficult to breathe. Smokestacks from the chimneys of a million houses plus industrial factories, belched out their poisonous fumes, causing them to choke and cough.

Coal is the major fuel used to heat the homes in Eastern Europe, and it produces enormous amounts of toxic pollutants. Wherever they looked, long blackened tongues of smoke curled into the already polluted air.

Daniel and Naomi and family in Prague, Czech.

Prague, the capital of Czechoslovakia, is an important center of culture and learning, and one of the oldest and most beautiful cities in central Europe. Called the City of a Hundred Spires, they could see why. Numerous churches, ancient castles, and historical mansions, dotted the landscape as they drove along.

Excited to minister in this beautiful place, they looked forward to sharing God's Word with those who were hurting.

"There's the church, Honey," said Gordon, pointing to an ancient historical landmark. Wide steps led to the enormous front doors of the huge building.

Daniel, the pastor, had been waiting for them to arrive. Holding out his hand in greeting, he invited them inside.

Immediately after walking through the front doors, they were led upstairs to where the pastor and his family lived.

Naomi, the pastor's wife, hugged Esther, as she welcomed them to their home. After a cup of hot tea, Gordon asked if it would be possible for them to go to bed right away.

BEDTIME

Traveling for many hours that day, they were all weary. It had been another long journey, and they eagerly welcomed privacy, a bath, and sleep.

But where will we sleep? Esther wondered. Looking around, she saw only a very small parlor and kitchen. Most pastors' homes in Eastern Europe are "Grand Central Station," as parishioners come and go. They longed for some privacy, but where would they find it?

Gordon had called Naomi a few days before their arrival, and told her he had a problem with snoring. "Could Esther and I possibly have separate quarters so we can rest?" She knew, as well, that David was coming, and he needed a private room.

David had ministered to many across the country, as he gave adjustments to those who were hurting. Most had never had a chiropractic treatment before. Miraculous things had happened before their eyes as people felt their pains go away.

Pointing to a small couch in the living room, their hostess said, "Esther, you can sleep here." Horrified, realizing that this room was always occupied with people and activity, she knew rest and privacy would not be her luxury.

Suddenly, Esther was startled as the phone rang shrilly into the night. It was beside the couch that would be her bedroom for the duration of their stay in Prague.

She wanted to complain, "Hey people, I need rest!" Having such a rigorous schedule, teaching many hours, counseling, visiting with people, and traveling, she needed time out alone—badly!

"God," she silently prayed, "help me!"

As she contemplated her situation, Naomi led David to an adjoining room. "Here, brother David, you can sleep in this room." It wasn't beautiful, but he would be alone, away from jangling telephones, shill voices, doorbells, and people walking through the house and other interruptions.

"Brother Gordon," added Daniel, "You can sleep downstairs on the floor, next to the street."

Gordon was about to follow Daniel, when he suggested that Esther take that bedroom instead. He would sleep on the couch. Esther sighed with relief, but was concerned about her weary husband, who had just given up his right to privacy and rest.

"Are you sure?" she asked. "What about you?"

"Yes, I will be fine," he answered, not so sure himself.

Esther knew the couch would be much too small for his large frame, but what could she do? What could he do?

Following Naomi down many flights of stairs leading to the bedroom, they walked through dark hallways and various rooms. She thought the stairs would never end. "What have I gotten myself into?" she wondered.

Her knees felt weak with fatigue and the bag she carried seemed heavier than usual. Finally they arrived to see a large room filled with enormous, uncovered windows. All across the big room, curtainless windows yawned wide into the dark night.

With no privacy but the glass between Esther and the street, she shivered, not only from cold, but fear. Anyone could look in! With absolutely no amenities, the room was cold, bare, and unfriendly.

Teeth chattering, in a small voice she asked, "Where is the bathroom, please?"

"Oh," answered Naomi cheerfully, "it is down at the end of the hall. There is no light, so be careful when you go there."

"And where is the bed?"

The pastor's wife led Esther to a far corner of the big room. There on the floor, a bed was made—or was it a bed? A few thin blankets covered threadbare sheets on the floor.

"This is your bed, Esther. I hope you sleep well." With that, she said good night, and was gone.

Making her way down the hall to find the bathroom, Esther kept close to the cement wall. Eventually, the odor of a typical Eastern European bathroom greeted her quivering nostrils. For once, this odor proved to be a road map and a blessing.

The big room was cold. Switching off the lights, she shivered while putting on her small nightgown. Longingly she thought of her warm, flannel pajamas at home. *Home*—what a magical word. Nostalgia hit her like a wet blanket. Her clean, warm bed there was empty!

Trying to shut out the blaring street lights, and crawling under the threadbare blankets, she pulled the thin covers over her head.

The bed was narrow. Remembering the passage her teacher at Bible College often spoke about concerning short beds and narrow covers, she felt quite biblical! (See Isaiah 28:20.) The makeshift bed was so narrow, she couldn't turn without falling out, and the blankets so short, she had to bend her knees to keep covered.

Shivering with cold and weariness, she stared into the unfamiliar darkness. Maybe she would rather be upstairs by the jangling phone after all… but it was too late!

Finally her eyes closed in sleep. It seemed only seconds later, when she was rudely awakened by shrill voices outside

her window. People were walking down the street—some going to work and others on their way to the shops for bread.

Looking at her watch, it showed 7:00 A.M. Had she really slept? She wasn't certain. Her weary body told her she had not. Joints aching, body trembling, she pulled herself out of bed. The room was bright as the sun, and those walking by could easily look in.

After putting her clothes on, she made her way to the odorous bathroom, then (hoping she could find the way) upstairs, to the small parlor. It was already filled with people. Gordon, fully dressed, sat on his couch bed, his eyes pools of weariness.

David, a little more refreshed, was having a cup of tea.

SEMINARS IN THE PRAGUE CHURCH

This was the day they had anticipated with joy for a long time. Christian leaders from all across Czechoslovakia were coming to hear the Word of God. They were Christ's vessels, and had prepared both spiritually and mentally for hours of teaching and fellowship in God's Word.

They had prayed earnestly that God would give them liberty and freedom as they spoke, and that He would prepare the hearts of the Czechoslovakian people to hear and apply the truths of God. Many were going through times of testing and difficulties in their own lives. Could Esther and Gordon help? They sincerely hoped so.

Entering the large sanctuary, Esther saw the seated people waiting expectantly. "Dear God," she prayed again, "meet their needs through Your servants. Make us vessels through which You can work."

Prague is known for its beautiful churches. The one they had just entered was old and dignified. Dark brown pews matched the color of the ancient woodwork. Enormous stained glass windows rose majestically to the tall ceiling. She had a strong desire to hear the pipe organ played at that moment. She could just picture the grand finale, as music rose and fell, reaching to the high ceiling, and ending in a great crescendo of praise!

They were being introduced. Pastor Daniel called Esther to the front to speak to both the men and women. Later, they would break into sessions.

Standing behind the dark wood pulpit, she felt unworthy to be sharing God's Word with a suffering people.

The room was hushed. Everyone waited in expectancy. What did God have for them in their hour of need? Surely, he would use these Americans to help alleviate their pain.

Esther began, "I want to speak on the benefits of suffering in a believer's life."

Pages rustled, as the people turned in well-worn Bibles to the text she had chosen in Hebrews 12:1-2.

"It is inevitable that you, as God's children, should suffer," she emphasized. "Your Savior, Himself, ascended by the pathway of suffering to the eternal throne. There are gains or profits for you, as God's children, if you allow Him to exercise or train you in His way, during times of suffering. Pain can cause you to know God in a more intimate way...."

Quoting from Philippians 3:10, she added,

> *That I may know him, and the power of his resurrection, and the fellowship of his sufferings...*

"Pain can lead you to a deeper prayer life, and pain can make you more like Jesus as you allow Him to exercise or train you," she said.

Tears dropped on open Bibles, handkerchiefs came out, as people allowed the Holy Spirit to speak. "So suffering could be profitable if we allow God to train us?"

"Help me to allow You to do in my heart what You need to do," wept a little Baba in the front pew.

A man nearby cried unashamedly, as he hugged his wife beside him. Others throughout the building dealt with God. No one spoke while God tenderly comforted his hurting people.

They were hungry to hear more. After Gordon had shared for almost two hours, they looked with anticipation to the next sessions that would follow soon.

Entering another large room, Esther saw tables covered with white tablecloths, and set with lovely Czech dishes. A traditional European soup, delicious and hot, was served to hundreds of hungry people. It was good to be fed both spiritually and physically.

Friendly and talkative, they shared with Esther, Gordon, and David as they ate. Making many lady friends, Esther looked with anticipation to their sessions together.

THE BIG ROOM DOWNSTAIRS

After sharing all day, Gordon, Esther, and David were weary. Even the big room with the gaping windows didn't bother Esther as much. She just needed rest! To crawl in anywhere, just as long as she could sleep, was a dominant desire.

After hastily preparing for bed, and using the bathroom down the hallway, she crawled into her makeshift bed. She had expected to nod off to dreamland as soon as she hit the pillow, but such was not to be. Lying there with the bright lights from the street shining in her eyes, she couldn't sleep.

Why are they blinking on and off like that anyway?

Is the outside door (so near her own) *locked at night?*

Uneasy now, she began to hear strange noises not heard last night. Suddenly she froze in her bed.

Shuffling and scraping, something, or someone, was trying to get in. She cowered against the cold, hard wall.

What was going on? No one would hear if she called. She was alone, all alone!

She jumped straight up in bed when the doorbell chimed—loudly, incessantly. "Now what should I do?" she gasped. No one was paying any attention to it. Was it ringing only down in this big, dark area of the church? Could they not hear it upstairs?

Lying motionless, covers pulled up over her head, and heart beating against her ribs, she thought, *Maybe if I am quiet enough, the ringing will go away!*

But it didn't. She froze when it chimed again—only this time with more urgency. Then all was still. Then suddenly she heard her door open.

In an instant, bright lights flooded the big room, and an enormous man stood beside her. She stared back.

What does he want? This can't be happening—but it is! This person is not a mirage or a figment of my imagination!

Sitting up in her makeshift bed, Esther pulled the thin covers around her shivering body.

He watched her closely, as she tried to crawl into the corner as far as possible. But she knew there was no place to hide.

"Oh God, help me!" she cried from deep inside.

Minutes seemed like hours. The room was deathly still, and no one moved.

Hearing her heart pounding under the thin cotton nightgown she wore, vaguely she wondered if he could hear it, too. Did he realize how scared she was?

Head down, she felt his piercing eyes boring into her. After what seemed like a long time, daring to look up, their eyes met. Still, no one spoke. Fear, wrapping its cold, tentacles around her, made her want to scream, "Get out of here! I am God's child. You can't hurt me!"

Just as quickly as he had come in, the man shut off the light and stepped out into the darkness.

Little sleep came that night. Body rigid and mind alert, she wondered what could happen next. The outside door obviously was not locked. Anyone from off the street could come in. Frantically, she called on God for protection.

Outside the gaping windows, lights from the street shone into the big room. Occasionally cars passed by... sometimes a pedestrian. But mostly, it was still now.

After a very long night, gradually the sun came up and shone into her eyes. Esther was actually happy and relieved to get up and go upstairs. There was safety, and her husband was there.

The aroma of fresh coffee greeted her as she entered the small kitchen. David and Gordon, sitting at the breakfast table, smiled at her.

"How did you sleep, Honey?" asked Gordon.

"Not so good—and you?"

"It was a little noisy up here, but I managed," he answered, with his mouth full of bread.

Washing cups of hot liquid down her throat, gradually the tensions of the long night wore away, and she felt better again.

Naomi entered. "Esther, I am sorry for all the commotion last night. Did you hear it?"

"Yes, I heard it. What was going on?"

"A psychiatric patient escaped from the hospital and was roaming around, trying to find a place to sleep. Of course, coming to the church, he thought he would have a bed. Yes, we found a place for him to stay—just for the night. He is gone now!"

Silently Esther wondered if he would come back again. He was not welcome in her room! She would have to ask for a key, if there was one. She discovered there was not.

SHARING

After a busy day of productive, profitable seminars and chiropractic adjustments, Naomi and Daniel, David, Gordon and Esther sat around the table in the small parlor. Hot tea, always relaxing and beneficial, filled their cups as they shared. Speaking English well, Naomi told them a story that moved Esther's heart.

"Thousands of young people," she said, "met to commemorate the death of a man shot down by the Nazis in World War II. They requested permission to meet in the well-known Wenslessness Square downtown, after the ceremonies at the memorial sight. But this was denied.

"When the service was over, the young people, mostly students, made their way from the church where plain-clothed policemen herded them onto the square. When they were inside, the men locked all the gates to the entrances so no one could leave. Carefully barricading every possible means of escape, they began to shoot. Of course, the students panicked. Trying to hide or run away, many were shot in cold blood."

Tears filled her eyes as she said, "So much for freedom in our country!"

They were saddened to think that these young people were killed so needlessly. Where was the justice to which they were entitled?

FOOD

"Yes, Czechoslovakia is now supposedly a free country, but that does not solve all our problems," continued the pastor. "Food costs have risen 300 percent, and most find it difficult to buy even the necessary food they should have."

It was quite evident that fresh vegetables, proteins, and fruit were expensive, as they were not usually on a table.

Most often they ate something prepared with flour. Dough, fried or baked, and served instead of potatoes or made into a dessert, was eaten every day they were there. Malnutrition, causing extended stomachs and fatigue, was seen throughout the country. Before leaving, they, too, were beginning to add a notch to their belts. Was this due to the lack of proper nutrition, or eating too much dough? They didn't know.

They were all excited when a lady, who had a small garden, offered them a head of lettuce. Not having had one salad during their stay so far, Esther prepared the greens. Able to buy a container of yogurt that morning, she made a tasty dressing to go along with the lettuce. They eagerly consumed every bite. What a treat!

Sometimes people invited them to their homes for meals. On one occasion, they sat down to a beautifully set table. Seeing only bowls, Esther presumed they were having soup. Soon their hostess brought soup in a china tureen from the kitchen and, with a flourish, ladled a large portion into Esther's dish.

"What's in this red soup, anyway? It certainly wasn't *Borscht*. She enjoyed that. But this?"

David, looking across the table, had misgivings, too, as he swallowed his first bite.

"Mmmm, what kind of soup is this?" asked Gordon in German.

"I found some liver in the store yesterday. I was so blessed!" replied their hostess.

Never, even if liver was fresh, could Esther tolerate the strong taste. Now, here it was fashioned into soup with tidbits floating across the top—and it was made with second grade pork! Trying to be grateful for God's mercies and this family, she took her first bite. She had to eat it, and with God's grace she did!

"Would you like more?" smiled their hospitable hostess.

Both David and Esther declined, apologizing that they were really satisfied.

That same evening, Sasha and Olga invited them to their home for dinner. Hungry for something green, they hoped there would be vegetables.

Esther's positive anticipation was short lived as, smiling, the hostess placed a dish of greasy pork cutlets before her. The meat, blackened and burned, was deep fried in lard in a thin batter of grease and breadcrumbs. Esther's stomach turned.

Peter, their small son, yearningly looked at the generous portion on the lady's plate. He was still hungry, after eating only a small amount. For the guests, it wasn't rationed, but there just wasn't enough to go around for everyone.

Happy to share part of hers, Esther put it on his empty plate. Gratefully he shoveled it in as fast as he could. Esther went away hungry—craving a giant salad.

More Sharing

Leaning back in her chair, Esther relaxed. Another day of teaching was over. Hot tea went down easily, while she and Naomi sat at the table.

"Tell me a little about yourself, Naomi," Esther said.

"There really isn't much to tell. I was brought up in a loving home. My parents, who are devout Christians, taught us how to live godly lives. My father is a pastor in a small church just out of Prague, so they don't live very far away from us," she continued.

"Because of my busy schedule, I don't see them as much as I would like, but we often visit by phone...."

Esther understood why Naomi was proud of her parents. She, along with Gordon and David, had visited this delightful couple earlier on their trip, while driving from a conference in the mountains where they had ministered. With genuine love and hospitality, they had made them feel special. Sitting down at a table laden with dough and pork, prepared in a variety of ways, they had talked about the Lord. He was the strength and source of their lives. In everything, they gave Him thanks. It was an evening they would never forget!

"My parents love Daniel as their own son," Naomi smiled. "Standing behind us all the way, since we ministered in our first small church, until now, we sense their prayers and support."

"We made many dear friends during our first ministry," she recalled. "The people have been close to us during the years since we were there, and always will be. Our children, Naomi and Daniel Junior, loved school and church in that area and also made many friends."

Handicapped Children

The teapot was empty. As Naomi rose to add more hot water, she said, "I completed a degree in Pedagogy as a physical therapist in childhood education." Swallowing a piece of doughnut she continued, "God tenderly opened avenues of service for me to work with handicapped children in the area where we lived. I was delighted. Sensing I was obeying the voice of God, this ministry flourished.

"Our own children grew as eight years rapidly sped by. We were so happy and fulfilled in this place, where we knew God wanted us to serve Him.

"When a call came to pastor a large city church in Prague, I was not happy at first," she confessed, "and neither were the children. How could we leave all that was so dear to us here? We sought the face of God for months, then finally we resigned, and obeying His call, left for the city.

"We found this big church interesting, but so different

from the beloved country church and congregation we had just left. The children found it difficult to adjust to their new surroundings, too."

When Esther asked Naomi Junior, if she liked school in Prague, reluctantly she shook her head and in quiet, little voice answered, "Yes, but I liked it a lot better in our other place."

Naomi went to answer the phone. When she returned, she sighed. "Among others, I missed little Jan with his severe speech impediment. The children were all doing so well, and loved and trusted me unreservedly."

Tears welled up in her green eyes as she added that she still prays for them all the time.

After the family arrived in their new parish, Naomi immediately went to work to start a school for handicapped and deformed children there.

"No one really cares about children with problems such as these," she added. "In past years, when a mother gave birth to such a child, the parents would take him to the forest and leave him there to die. With no food or water, left to battle the elements, and perhaps even wild animals, it didn't take long for the child to succumb. Winters in Czechoslovakia are always cold and long. How could the handicapped child survive? Totally helpless, the little one suffered until death."

"Why, Naomi, are there so many handicapped children here?" Esther wanted to know.

"We are not sure, but there is a lot of pollution in the air, and also in the food. The fields are contaminated with pesticides and poisons. Sometimes green pools of chemicals lie on the soil after a rain. Then gradually, they soak in again, polluting the growing food beyond repair."

Gordon came into the room just then, and heard what

they were talking about. "How severely does the Chernobyl disaster affect everyone?" he asked.

"Many have been affected by the nuclear reactor that went off in 1983, and have suffered devastating damage because of it. Even today, these children are not in hospitals. We have little modern technology and there is no medication. No one knows where to turn or what to do. Some of the children are at home with their parents. Entire families have been affected in various areas, as they suffer the effects of radiation, chemicals, polluted air, and bad food.

"No one knows how to stop the reactor that is, even now, spewing out its deadly poisons, thus further endangering the lives of countless people. Meanwhile, there are new babies born with malfunctions, and more stressed and hurting families don't know where to turn. They don't have money to move away, or begin again, so they stay here, just hoping things will improve."

The room was silent for a moment. Naomi blew her nose and continued, "I just couldn't stand it. Daniel and I talked about starting a school here in the church for these unwanted children. Church members were supportive and said they would help, too."

Concentrating primarily on crooked limbs, speech defects, and mental deficiencies, Naomi and her staff competently cared for these children. Besides loving them unreservedly, they had a trained therapist who worked with straightening crooked limbs and broken bodies.

"X-rays showed children with organs such as lungs, liver, kidneys, and hearts, which are totally deformed," she said. "Kidneys resemble string beans rather than the normal shape. Lungs fill an entire chest cavity, hearts are greatly enlarged, bone structure is malformed, while blindness, headaches, and fatigue are common. Each child is an individual and needs to be treated with love and respect. Our school tries to show Christ's compassion to these little ones no one else wants."

Therapy School

"Would you like to see our therapy and school room?" asked Naomi the next day. Having a keen interest in children, Esther readily agreed.

After walking down many flights of stairs, she wasn't surprised to realize the school was not far away from the big room where she slept.

"If only we had funds to make this place more convenient and contemporary," thought Esther, as Naomi proudly showed her around. Books, educational help, and toys were almost nonexistent. Just a bare minimum was all they could afford, but it seemed to suffice, along with a lot of tender loving care and therapy. The children were happy there.

Later, praying together, Gordon made a request to God. "Please bless Naomi as she heads this program in working with children no one else cares about. Give her and the staff wisdom and strength and the daily supplies they need. It is You who graciously said, "Suffer the little ones to come unto Me, and forbid them not, for of such is the kingdom of heaven."

Naomi and her staff continue the job their Father gave them to do. Oh, that there were more Naomi's in this world!

Television

Shortly before Esther and Gordon arrived in Prague, Naomi's group of children were visited by a local TV station, which was then run by the Communists. The children were asked to sing in the closing minutes of the program. Three and one half minutes is not a long time, but their performance was one that will never be forgotten by the people of Czechoslovakia.

Excited, they lined up to sing.

"Ready?" said the program director.

"Ready," answered Naomi. Face flushed, and heart racing, she directed the children as they sang. Little ones, with shiny hair and rosy cheeks, joyfully sang with all their hearts.

I don't know why God made me like I am,
but He made me!

They also sang a song of testimony on how God created some of his living creatures. Among them was the beautiful butterfly with its colorful and transparent wings.

The Butterfly Song

If I were a butterfly,
I'd thank you Lord, for giving me wings.
And if I were a robin in a tree,
I'd thank you, Lord that I could sing.
And if I were a fish in the sea,
I'd wiggle my tail and I'd giggle with glee.

If I were an elephant,
I'd thank you Lord, by raising my trunk.
And if I were a kangaroo,
you know I'd hop right up on you.
And if I were an octopus,
I'd thank you Lord for my fine looks.

If I were a wiggly worm,
I'd thank you Lord that I could squirm.
And if I were a Billy goat,
I'd thank you Lord, for my strong throat.
And if I were a fuzzy-wuzzy bear,
I'd thank you Lord for my fuzzy-wuzzy hair.

But I just thank You, Father, for making me *me!*
You gave me a heart and You gave me a smile,
And You gave me Jesus and You made me Your child,
And I just thank You, Father, for making me *me*!
—Brian Howard

Grateful for love and care, uncomplaining about their lot, the children's faces glowed, because they knew Someone really cared.

The closing statement on national TV in that Communist country, with Communists directing the program was,

> *This kind of Christian endeavor has a place in Czechoslovakian society.*

The social health department, soon afterward, met with church leaders and gave them land for building a special treatment and training center for the handicapped children from Prague.

Naomi's school gave her incentive to carry on. Strong in spirit, she never gave up for a moment. While others were complaining how difficult it was to live in a Communist country, and other pastor's wives were weeping, Naomi would say, with a smile on her face, what a privilege it was to serve God. No matter how busy her household was, or how many guests she had, or how many times the phone rang, day and night, she had a positive attitude.

"Vanya, a handicapped child, calls me every day," she said. "I know it is Vanya when he lets the phone ring only once and then hangs up. I call him immediately, and he senses my love across the line."

Not able to enunciate clearly because of his handicap, only Naomi understood him.

Many times she would be accommodating guests, but if the phone rang only once, she knew who was calling. Quietly excusing herself, she knew Vanya's call could not be put off till later. Her guests would wait while, patiently, lovingly, she communicated with her little friend.

Vanya would be so lost without her encouragement and support.

DANIEL

"My husband has been harassed by secret police on numerous occasions," said Naomi. "As a minister of the Gospel, he is vulnerable. One time, he was involved in a serious car accident staged by secret police."

Getting up, Naomi refilled their coffee cups. Bringing a plate filled with doughnuts, she made sure they had enough to eat.

Sitting down, and taking a sip of coffee, she continued, "This accident resulted in a serious back injury. As time went on, his back deteriorated to the point where he was forced to have major surgery—in December, 1992, in a hospital in Prague. The operation seemed to be a success at the time."

"And what happened then?" asked Doctor David with concern.

"After he returned home from the hospital, he was doing quite well, until one of his vertebrae disintegrated. This resulted in excruciating pain and immobility."

Speaking with Naomi a few days later, they learned her husband was back in the hospital on the verge of more surgery. Totally immobile, and confined to bed, his muscles had atrophied so he could not walk.

In spite of these physical setbacks, she informed them that they still were planning to have a handicapped children's youth camp the last weekend in June—and a second one in August.

Daniel was well enough to assist Naomi in the camps on which she had set her heart.

"It was great to meet new faces and those we knew had accepted the Lord at other camps in the past. The change from depressed and hopeless parents, to that of hope for the future is encouraging. As parents attend the camps with their children, they, along with their children, can see how refreshing God's love really is," beamed the young woman.

KATRIN

"After summer was over," she continued, "we were surprised when suddenly one family took Katrin, their handicapped child, out of school. Having been with us for two years, the little one was contented. She was always smiling, and was the example of a happy child in spite of a severe handicap. Each time I held her in my arms, love flowed from my heart to hers. Looking up at me with big, blue eyes, I knew she was trying to say, 'I love you too, Teacher.'

"After the family moved her, they entered their child in a State day care center. It was not long before they were told she could not stay there due to some complications. They put her in a special home for mentally handicapped children in another town, where she deteriorated. Almost every day, her family could see how much weaker she was becoming, until one day, after six weeks, she closed her eyes and quietly passed on."

Naomi looked away, trying to hide the tears that ran down her cheeks. "You can't imagine, Esther, how we grieve for that little one. The only thing that helps us, is knowing she is safe in the arms of Jesus, and nobody can harm her now. Please pray for her family," sighed Naomi. "It has been very hard for them."

Giving Naomi a hug, Esther said good night and went

downstairs to her big bedroom for some much needed rest.

FAREWELL

Seminars, talks around the table, praying and working together, would soon become history for another year. It was time to leave for the next city where they were scheduled to speak. They had to say farewell to Daniel and Naomi, as well as many others they had grown to appreciate.

Earlier that day, Naomi was excited when she saw the outline for seminars Esther was asked to give there the following fall. "Spirit-Controlled Family Living," she said, "will be a timely subject for us. There are many family-related problems in our country. We do look forward to you coming back again!"

Invited a year in advance, their hosts had ample time to advertise, pray, and anticipate. It also gave Gordon and Esther space to wait on God and study their material.

Already, Naomi and Daniel were asking God for help to arrange the details for this anticipated event.

Tabor, Czechoslovakia

They arrived in Tabor on a chilly, fall day in October. Brisk, cool bursts of wind rustled the leaves still left on the ancient trees. With each new gust, gold, yellow, and red leaves fell to the brown carpet below. Crunching under their feet as they walked, already most were broken and crushed, as they mingled with the dead grasses.

"Please come in!" greeted their hostess. "It is cold outside, and you must be hungry!"

"Yes, we are hungry," Esther smiled, inhaling the wonderful aroma of homemade soup.

Entering Daniel and Grezena's flat, which was on the top floor of their church, Esther was reminded of a page in a *Good Housekeeping* magazine.

It didn't take long to realize this gifted, young woman was an artist. Dark antique furnishings graced every wall in the spacious apartment. Adding a class of elegance, pictures she painted were framed and designed in the same dark wood. Needlepoint and oil paintings, all crafted by Grezena, tastefully covered the walls. Dried arrangements of flowers decked antique dressers and tables, while lace cloths gracefully draped to the polished hardwood floor. Every color, from dishes to knickknacks and flowers, was matched to perfection.

Just a few weeks before, in Moravia, Grezena's husband, Daniel, had invited them to minister in his church. They were delighted to be in this lovely, old city, 80 kilometers from Prague. Alive with history, already they had noticed the rustic, artistic beauty as they drove to the church.

In the course of their journeys, especially in Czechoslovakia, they had seen a thick blanket of smog everywhere.

Entering the city of Tabor, smoke curled upwards from thousands of chimneys and major industries, belching out poisons. Fortunately, being a smaller center, the fumes were much less than in the larger centers. Here they could breathe a little more freely.

"Please sit down and rest. I will have dinner on soon," promised Grezena.

True to her word, in a few minutes, a delicious meal was spread before them.

"The soup you make, Grezena, reminds me of my own mother's recipe," smiled Esther.

"I learned from my mother, too," she replied, refilling their bowls with the steaming liquid.

China dishes, white tablecloth and napkins, silverware, and crystal glasses, did not go unnoticed by Esther, who enjoyed these finer touches.

Watching Grezena as she refilled their tea cups near the end of their lunch, Esther decided this young woman was perhaps thirty-four years of age. A mother of three, she took great pride in her husband, children, and home.

The apartment, though lovely, was not large enough to accommodate them. With three small boys in the family, one just a toddler, they knew from past experience how weary they could become.

Thankfully, they had their trailer with them this time. Gratefully, Esther crawled under clean, white sheets in her home on wheels. Sometimes this home away from home was a blessing to everyone.

SEMINARS

Morning arrived after a refreshing sleep. Esther awakened to the sound of wind in the big trees overhead.

"By now," she said to her waking husband, "surely all the leaves will have blown to the ground. Listen to that wind! Winter must be coming."

After morning service, where Gordon preached, they enjoyed a quick lunch which Grezena had prepared. Then they were ushered into the big church downstairs to give seminars to an expectant people.

"God," Esther prayed again, "give us wisdom to help alleviate the pain these people suffer, as they share Your healing work."

They couldn't believe it! The large church was packed when they entered. Still the people continued to come.

Grezena, the pastor's wife, sat in the front pew again. There she was sure not to miss anything. Longing for a fresh touch from God in her life, and in the lives of her people, she listened attentively.

She had told me earlier at the conference that there were

many in her country who were downcast and depressed. There was really no one who knew how to deal with these problems. "Perhaps you and Gordon can help," she said, hope shining in her blue eyes.

Now Esther knew why she had prayerfully studied this particular subject. Opening her Bible and announcing the text, she spoke on "Causes of Depression." Everyone listened. The room was completely still. No one moved.

Was it God who gave Mrs. Balisky this topic to share with us? wondered a medical doctor in the congregation. *It sure is applicable here!*

Later, speaking to Esther, he assured her that depression was, indeed, a major problem in their country.

As the days went by, God impressed her to share on "Steps to Victory over Depression." Ending on a positive note, many were encouraged.

"God is now giving us wisdom to deal with these problems, and He will help us," said the doctor. Others agreed.

PROBLEMS

"My grace is sufficient for thee: for my strength is made perfect in weakness," read Grezena from 2 Corinthians 12:9, in the well-worn Bible she held. "I need this promise every day," she confessed.

Her life was not easy. Like Naomi, the pastor's wife in Prague, as well as other wives in ministry across this vast country, there was no privacy in the home. Incessantly, the phone and door bell rang. There were always people in their apartment, making it necessary for her to be ready for all things, at all times. Her house must be in order, her children clean and neat.

"It is always important that food be prepared, so I can feed those who are hungry," she added. "Often I cannot spend enough time with my boys, because so many demands are made of me."

It was assumed that the pastor's wife clean the church, too. They had seen Grezena, with a dust cloth, bucket, and brush, enter the large sanctuary to scrub the floor and dust pews and furnishings.

"But why can't a church member clean the church?" Esther asked. "Surely, there must be someone?"

"No, it is not convenient for others. It is assumed that the pastor's wife, who lives in the building, should do it," she said, looking down at the floor, so Esther wouldn't see the tears welling up in her eyes.

Finally, brimming over and falling down her cheeks, she shared a story. This experience was a much larger burden than cleaning the church!

NO TIME

"Daniel was so busy a few months ago, he didn't have any time for the boys and me. Besides pastoring this big city church, he was responsible for seven others during the week. On Sundays, he ministered here in the morning and evening. The other days were taken up in travel, preaching, and counseling.

"Very concerned for my husband, whom I love dearly, I tried to help all I could. Keeping up with the house and children, as well as cleaning the church, and ministering to peoples' needs, I was busy, too. Often when our apartment was filled with people, I too, gave of my time to minister to their needs. There was just no time for our family to be alone. Daniel and I slowly drifted apart.

"When he was not in a church speaking somewhere, he was studying. So many sermons had to be prepared. All his spare time, he spent in books.

"At night, he came home totally exhausted. Crawling into bed beside me, it would have made no difference if I was there or not." She was sobbing now. "As time went on, we drifted still further apart.

"The children cried for their daddy often, but he had no time for them, either. Daniel was too busy to listen to me. I would plead with him to notice them, but he didn't even hear me.

"'The boys are growing so fast, Daniel!' I said. 'Please spend more time with them.' But his work had become his total priority and consumed his days, evenings, weeks, and months.

"Helping his parishioners in all the churches was important to him as a young pastor. There were so many needs and everyone pleaded for help. What could he do? Where could he turn for help? Demands were overwhelming!

"I just couldn't stand it anymore. While packing a suitcase, tears fell on the tiny garments of my sons. What would the future hold for them if I left Daniel? What could it hold if I did not?"

Calling her parents to tell them she was coming home, Grezena left her apartment one rainy, overcast day. Longingly, she looked around, and realized how much love and time she had invested in this place—her home—their home.

But for now it was over. She had tried to keep the family together. Perhaps Daniel would realize how important his family really was to him when they were gone. Would he wake up?

"Each day, coming home from an exhausting day of ministry, Daniel was accustomed to my home cooking," Grezena continued. "That night there was none. The flat was hauntingly empty and quiet as he walked around, calling our names. 'Grezena! David! John! Adam!' he cried in despair.

What had he done? With remorse and shame, he bowed his head and wept before his God. How vacant their home was without a loving wife and the pitter patter of little feet and happy voices!

"Daniel was determined to find some help. He wanted his wife and children at home where they belonged. His face turned toward God, he begged for relief. 'Please, send me a helper, Lord!' he cried.

"Miraculously, God did just that! A young pastor called to say he wanted to work with Daniel. 'Could you use me?' he queried hopefully.

"'Could I use you, Brother!' shouted Daniel. 'Yes, God has sent you! Come right away! I need your help now!'"

Daniel drove to Grezena's parents' house. Swinging his boys high in the air, he shouted and laughed for the first time in months.

Grezena agreed to come home. Unpacking their things and putting them back into drawers, she had mixed feelings, but was happy to be home. She hoped desperately for a change.

And change obviously came!

While visiting in their home, Esther noticed Daniel and his children playing games together. Tossing a ball around beside the big church, the boys laughed with glee. Begging for more, they were rewarded. Now they had a daddy again!

First thing in the morning, the father, now taking full responsibility of priesthood in his home, read the Bible and prayed with his family before leaving for work. Loving looks exchanged with Grezena did not go unnoticed, either. They had a second chance, and this family was happy again.

"My husband has changed!" said Grezena. "Now he realizes the importance of family life. I support him all I can in his busy schedule," smiled the young woman through tears of gratefulness.

A BABY

"After all this, we realized we were going to have another baby! It was really unexpected. We wondered if this child would be a boy or girl? A girl would be nice, I secretly thought."

"With apprehension and excitement coursing through our veins, we waited for this baby. However, there was a cloud in our joy. It was a difficult and risky time to have a child," she continued, "because the nuclear reactor had just blown in Kiev, Ukraine. Other women, who had been exposed to the disaster while pregnant, were worried, too. Would we have a handicapped or deformed child as a result of being exposed to radiation? Could our marriage, so recently healed, withstand the stress of that? I doubted it!"

CHERNOBYL

"The Chernobyl disaster affected hundreds of people in the Prague area in a negative way. Mothers worried about their unborn children.

Many of their concerns were founded because some children were born with severe handicaps and deformities. Distressed, the parents didn't know where to turn. How could they cope with a child such as this when there were already so many hardships?

Many didn't allow God in their lives so they had no place to turn or go for help and comfort.

"I became pregnant during this time," said Grezena. The young woman looked down. Slowly she continued.

"Radiation was everywhere. There was no place to hide. The ugly truth was that we were in the middle of a life-threatening problem, and we had to face it!" Esther put her arm around the young woman. How would she have coped, if this had happened to her? She really didn't know.

"My abdomen, large with child, we could only wait and see what would happen. One morning, I awakened to find a dramatic rash, sensitive to the touch, all over my body. Red and itchy, it horrified me. Realizing it was a direct effect of radiation, while I felt our little one move within me, I started to cry.

"'Look Daniel,' I said. Trying not to show too much emotion, he put his hand on my swollen abdomen and began to pray for me and our unborn child.

"Our fears lifted somewhat as we trusted in God. Where else could we go? Only He could help our baby now.

"The day my husband took me to the hospital, we were calm, and purposed together to love and protect this little one, no matter what the cost! Hearing the cry of our newborn child, somehow, by faith we knew he would be fine. And he was! A beautiful, healthy baby boy, our son, still thrives today. If we had a thousand lives, we could never thank our heavenly Father enough!" she smiled.

Contented and playing on the floor, the beautiful child was completely absorbed in his toys. Bright, alert, and healthy, he and his brothers were the joy of Grezena and Daniel's lives.

Inasmuch

The seminars were almost over. Soon it would be time to leave this family they had learned to appreciate.

Sitting at the large table, eating bowls of steaming soup, they were fully engaged in conversation, when the doorbell rang. Rarely had they found time to sit and talk for long, because the pastor's home was so busy.

Ruth, the young woman who had interpreted for Esther during the seminars, stood at the door. Beside her, an old woman held tightly to her arm.

"Come in!" said Grezena. "Now, who is this little Baba?" she asked, while leading the feeble woman to a comfortable sofa in the living room.

"I found her on the train," said Ruth. "Alone, frightened, and vulnerable, she seemed lost. I said to myself, *If that were my mother, wouldn't I want someone to see that she was OK?* Leaving my seat, I went to ask her if she needed help.

"'God bless you,' she murmured. Tears stood in her eyes as she whispered, 'I am running away from my own daughter! I have lived with her in the same house, locked up in an attic. I am neglected, forgotten, and ignored by my family.'

"I couldn't believe her story," said Ruth, "but the woman went on. 'My daughter took away all of my clothes except this thin sweater and old summer dress. She was afraid I would go if an opportunity presented itself. She was right. One day when she forgot to lock the attic door, I climbed down the stairs and ran outside. Entering a cruel, unfriendly world, I shivered with cold and didn't know where to go. Somehow, I reached the train station, took all the money I had sewn in my slip, and bought a train ticket for Prague. Not even knowing where I would go when I arrived, my only thought was to get away from the awful situation I had been living in for so long!"

Looking at the old woman sitting on Grezena's sofa, they saw that, indeed, she wore only a light sweater and summer dress. Outside, the wind rattled the shutters on Grezena's apartment windows. Most of the leaves had already blown off the trees, their limbs reaching out stark and naked toward the empty, dark sky. Soon winter would be on them, and the snow and sleet would cover the vast land of Czechoslovakia.

"What could I do?" asked Ruth. "What would you have done? I couldn't leave her on the train with no one to

care for her, so I took her with me. I knew somehow you cold help!"

Grezena left her seat to sit close to the little grandmother. Already, she held a cup of hot soup in her work-worn hands. Hungry and shaken, she eagerly devoured it all.

Her faded, gray eyes looked trustingly into Grezena's as if to say, "Yes, these kind people will help me."

The next day, although filled with previously arranged obligations, plans had to be changed. Grezena and Daniel deciding to put first things first, knew this Baba must have a new home.

Calling one rest home after another, Daniel found out nobody wanted her! There were too many older people like herself out there. Already the homes were filled to capacity. They couldn't be bothered with one more.

The pastor and his wife went to the police. Surely, they would help.

"No, we can't do anything for her," they shrugged. "This problem is between her family and her. Take this woman home where she belongs."

"Yes," thought Daniel, "that just might be the answer to this dilemma."

The grandmother wept when Daniel presented this idea to her.

"No! No!" she cried, holding onto him. "I cannot go there! My daughter leaves me alone—all alone. I don't have clothes. I don't have enough to eat. I am always hungry and so cold! I am so lonely! Please don't take me there pastor… oh, please don't!"

That night, she slept on the living room sofa again.

Before shutting off the lights, Grezena took the wrinkled hand into her own, and prayed that God would make a way. The Baba smiled trustingly, closed her faded gray eyes, and went into a deep, warm sleep. These people, she knew, would not put her out into the street.

The next day, with Baba sitting in the back seat of the car, they took her to an old people's home. Finally, somebody wanted her. Toothless and exuberant, the old woman smiled. Yes, God really did answer prayer. Maybe she wanted to be His child after all.

That night they talked.

"Leaving older people is a common occurrence in our cities. Unfortunately, it happens too often," the pastor's wife said sadly. "No one wants them when they grow old, so they leave them somewhere to die."

I thought of the seniors in America. Though many are in rest homes, usually they are cared for, and their children and friends come to visit. But this...?

"We always have an open home and open heart to help. We don't have much, but are happy to share what we do have. Christ did the same. Should we not follow in His steps?" said the pastor.

The woman was hungry. They gave her meat. She was thirsty, they gave her drink. She was a total stranger, they took her in and gave her the best accommodations they had. Some day,

> *...the King shall answer and say unto them, Verily I say unto you, Inasmuch as ye have done it unto one of the least of these my brethren, ye have done it unto me.... Come, ye blessed of my father, inherit the kingdom prepared for you from the foundation of the world* (Matthew 25:40, 34).

FAREWELL

As Gordon went to start the car and drive the trailer out of the churchyard where it had resided for almost two weeks,

Esther, Grezena, and Daniel watched beside the big church. Putting her arms around the woman she had learned to appreciate, Esther expressed her thanks for her kind hospitality. In this young woman, she had seen a life totally dedicated and surrendered to the Master she served wholeheartedly.

Climbing out of the car, Gordon came to say good-bye. Two big men embraced, as tears ran down their cheeks. When would they meet again? A friendship had been formed, and blessed was the tie that bound them together in Christian love.

As they drove out of the churchyard, with crisp, dead leaves crunching under their car tires, they drove into another world.

Now what new ventures for Christ were in store for them, and those to whom they would minister? Only their Father knew. Assured, anew, they put their trust in Him.

Anticipation and excitement filling their hearts, they drove to the next place of ministry.

Warsaw to Minsk—1989

In Poland again, the seminars had gone well in Warsaw. Though they were weary, their next destination was Minsk. With a population of 955,000 souls, it was the capital of Beloruss in the Soviet Republic.

Usually the journey from Warsaw to Minsk could take up to eight hours, but how long would they be at the Russian border? Would the guards take everything apart again? The answer, they knew, was always unknown until they were there. This made it difficult to even calculate what time they would arrive at their next destination.

Esther's alarm clock peeled shrilly, awakening her at 6:30 A.M. What an unearthly hour to get up when they were so tired! But, as arranged the night before, they planned to leave Warsaw early in the morning. Quickly, but reluctantly, Esther crawled out of her cozy, hard bed.

Washing her hair in cold water in a small, discolored sink, was often a time-consuming ordeal in itself. Today was no exception. She winced as the freezing water covered her head. *Will I ever get used to this?* She doubted it.

They had planned to meet their hostess for breakfast at 7:00. She was ready—but what about her husband?

Deciding to sleep in two separate bedrooms while there was room available in the Bible school building, they knew, in light of what lay ahead, this would be a wise idea. After heavy schedules, like they had just encountered, rest was essential. Gordon was a heavy snorer and they both knew it. This way, they would be rested for their next time of ministry—at least they hoped so.

Going to Gordon's door, Esther knocked. Why wasn't he answering?

Then she heard it. Loud, rhythmic snoring came from the other side of the closed door. He was still sleeping!

A combination of frustration and relief came over her. Yes, he would be the one who would be driving, and needed the extra rest. And yet, he was also the one who had suggested they leave early!

Knocking louder now, finally, she heard a shuffle. Unlocking the rusty door, he stood there. Pale and disheveled and pulling his fingers through his hair, he asked, "Hey what time is it? Did I oversleep?" He knew he had.

Hurrying, he slipped into his clothes and together they walked toward the Piaseski apartment for breakfast.

The cold meal went down! Of necessity they must eat before driving into Russia. Restaurant locations were always unpredictable, and if they found a place to eat, the food would probably be unpalatable anyway.

At 8:30 A.M., they bid their hostess good-bye and drove toward the Russian border.

They were beginning to feel accustomed to this, but knew the ordeal ahead was always uncertain. What would happen today? Only God knew.

At the border, there was a long line of cars. Everyone was waiting to go across the border. How long would it take? When they parked, quickly other cars drove in behind them. At least seventy were ahead.

Esther, always keeping track in her journal wrote:

> At the moment, we are at the Russian border. A cold wind is rustling through the golden leaves. It is fall, and a chill is in the air. Where did the summer months go?
>
> The sun is making a feeble attempt at warming us—but I can barely see it because of clouds covering the sky. The cars ahead of us are about a mile or more long. Will we ever get through? We are waiting to reach the front of the line to have our passports and visa's checked.

A little later, she wrote;

> We are still waiting. We left Warsaw at 8:30—it took 7 hours to get this far—hopefully we don't have to wait much longer.
>
> I have a problem. I need a bathroom! But where to go?" Gordon is still not in the car. No doubt the officials are asking him questions—they always do!
>
> I have to go! But where?

Finally, leaving the car, she walked in search of a bathroom. She never realized how happy she would be to find dirty, outdoor facilities—but standing not too far away, there were actually two! What luck! She couldn't wait to get there!

Walking inside, she tried to close the rusty door. There was no way she could do this. The floor, seats, and holes were completely covered with human feces! A mixture of wet, and dried human excrement covered everything—everywhere! What should she do? Gagging, she groped toward the door. Once outside, she wiped her odorous feet on the grass and frantically looked for a place to relieve herself.

Running down the dusty road toward a few small trees, she saw a barbed wire fence dividing the Polish and Russian borders. Border guards stood everywhere.

Knowing she couldn't go there, either, Esther continued her hapless search. Passing cars, she choked on the smell of exhaust and dust. Others, she saw, were looking for facilities, too.

Beyond caring if someone saw her, she finally found a scant grove of small trees. What a relief, and release!

Running back to the parked car, she saw Gordon was already there. As he drove up a few more feet, the KGB border guard told him to park over the big trench in the pavement so they could look under the car. Carefully checking, it took a long time before they emerged.

Esther felt the stern eyes of the austere official as they bored into hers. "Now, take everything out of your car and trunk," he ordered.

Wearily, they began to remove dirty clothing, food, books, seminar material, cooking pots, gifts purchased in Poland for the Russian people—everything had to come out. After such a long time in travel, their clothes were soiled, rumpled—and smelly. Their shoes were piled on the pavement to be checked. All their merchandise was piled single file. Nothing was omitted. As Esther watched them going through her personal items, she began to feel resentful and

angry. But there was nothing she could do but comply to their requests.

Spiritually speaking, they were in God's hands, but physically, they were in the clutches of the *regierung*. They had to obey!

Later, in her diary, Esther continued her entries:

> Observations:
> Tall, electric and barbed wire fences at the border are everywhere. Long deep trenches in the pavement make access to check under vehicles…
>
> Every shape and model of car stands waiting in line to get to the border…
>
> I see dozens of border guards—their khaki green suits with bright, green hats, and accessories flaunted in arrogance…
>
> One official holds a stick and is waving it around like a baton. Uncertainty—questions—troubled hearts surround us…
>
> People talking Polish, Russian, and German are everywhere! Cars, spewing out diesel, oil, gasoline—makes the air polluted and dark!
>
> I feel like a prisoner of war for no crime at all!

After eight hours of this treatment, they asked for Gordon's car registration. Pulling the visor down, he reached for it. But it wasn't there! Pulling the visor toward him—it still wasn't there. But it had to be! It had always been there! Where, oh where was it now, when they needed it so desperately?

"Dear God," he prayed as sweat dropped into his eyes,

"please help me find the registration. I have to have it!"

Rummaging around in the back seat, Esther wept. If they couldn't find it, what would happen? She could guess!

Miraculously the corner of a piece of paper showed from under the seat. Could it be? It was the registration papers! "Thank you, God!" they exclaimed through their tears. He had intervened once again!

They soon realized they were getting hungry. Putting their small camp stove together, they opened a can of soup from Germany. Cutting a few slivers of cheese, they sat down on the ground and had the nourishment their bodies so desperately needed.

Driving over the border into the USSR brought a sense of relief on one hand, and foreboding on the other. What was in store for them this time? How could they know? Their lives were in the hands of Almighty God. They put their trust in Him alone.

They breathed a sigh of relief. A huge moon, hanging in the darkened sky, shone ahead on the dusty, unpaved road as they drove toward Minsk. Many more hours of driving loomed before them...and they were so weary. A busy time of ministry had just concluded in Poland, and now another would begin tomorrow, in the USSR.

With anticipation, they drove toward the city. By faith, trusting in His help, they would assist a hurting people there. He knew what was ahead. They would be fine—because their Father planned it all!

32 BACK TO SEATTLE

Time was moving on and the girls were choosing their careers.

Charlene's Vocation

Esther could still hear Charlene ask, "Mom, what should I be when I grow up?"

Answering her own question years later, with no doubt in her mind, she decided to become a nurse.

Esther held her breath when she came home one day carrying Freida, the cat cadaver. An assignment given to her at the University of Washington, she was expected to dissect the hapless creature, while studying the parts of its body.

Working for days in the garage, the odor of formaldehyde permeated the house, but Charlene didn't seem to mind. Totally absorbed in her work, she carefully studied

each body part of the cat, preparing for the vocation that lay ahead.

"Mom," she called, "come in here and see the small heart and liver! Look at the kidneys and stomach! Mom, this is really exciting!"

Patiently she worked long hours on this scientific project until finally it was completed.

Esther never did see Freida. She would rather hold her own living, healthy cat in her arms, and let the other body parts stay where they were.

Yes, Charlene would make a wonderful nurse. Her parents knew the empathy she displayed toward others who were ill. God had known long before she was even born that she would choose this important profession. Esther and Gordon were pleased as they faithfully prayed for her.

GRADUATION—DECEMBER 13, 1989

The auditorium was packed. Many parents, grandparents, and other loved ones and friends had come early so they could sit at the front of the large auditorium. Gordon, Esther, and Corinne, along with Steve and his family, were part of the fortunate ones. A long row of about twenty filled the crowded pew. The big day had finally arrived!

They were all there to witness a procession of new nurses walk down the long aisle to the front of the auditorium to receive their diplomas. But they had eyes for only one. Charlene, they knew, had put her soul, mind, and body into long hours of concentrated study and practical work to come to this important day in her life.

As soft music filled the auditorium, Esther was reminded that they had given both girls to God when only newborn infants. Then, years later, in Switzerland, Charlene informed them that she wanted to stay in Europe and continue her education. She had little money, but a lot of courage and trust in an awesome God. Their hearts were moved as they drove away leaving her standing on a windswept hillside, surrounded by the majestic Swiss Alps. Leaving her in the care of her heavenly Father, they knew He had promised to look after her. Yes, it was their obligation to let go and let God take over.

"Mom," whispered Corinne, "are you with us?"

Esther smiled and wondered when the procession would begin. Gently she squeezed her daughter's warm hand. How quickly the years had flown by!

The lights dimmed. Except for the music, the auditorium became still and dark as people stopped talking. Then, thirty-five nurses dressed in white, each carrying a lit candle in her hand, began their procession to the front.

Eagerly they watched for their daughter. There she was! Tall and regal, her long hair cascading down her shoulders, she walked straight and confident. They were all so proud!

When Charlene reached the platform, she, along with the others, put her candle in a designated place. There they softly flickered in the semi-darkness of the room.

To hear the International Council of Nurses pledge, recited by the graduating nurses, was moving as they pledged to care for their patients, "with all the skills and understanding we possess, without regard to race or creed, politics or social status… in order to conserve life and alleviate suffering and promote health."

"I will do my utmost to honor the International Code of Ethics as applied to nursing and to uphold the integrity of the nurse," they concluded.

When her name was called to receive her diploma, she walked confidently toward her instructor, shook his hand, smiled, and walked back to her place in line.

They cheered and clapped—laughed and cried. She had done it! She had beat the odds and obstacles that had been in her path and was now a Registered Nurse.

A few weeks later, she received her grades from the state board examination. Though these tests had been long and challenging, she had passed with high honors.

A job in a nearby hospital was opened to her almost immediately. She was one of four classmates chosen.

Charlene had found her calling in life and she was happy!

Corinne's Graduation—1990

Pomp and circumstance dissolved into smiles and shouts of joy as 8,125 baccalaureate and graduate degrees were awarded at the University of Washington in commencement ceremonies on June 9, 1990.

The auditorium was packed as the grads waited in the side rooms of the Edmondson Pavilion. Soon they would enter and make that long walk down the aisles to receive their earned diplomas. For both the morning and evening exercises, 14,000 spectators sat in the bleachers, looking for their special graduate.

Grandpa, Grandma, Charlene, Steve, Gordon, and Esther carefully climbed high into the bleachers to find a place to sit. By the time they arrived, almost every available seat was taken. Though they had to climb many steps, they would have the advantage of seeing Corinne without having to look around hundreds of heads.

Grandma stopped for breath about half-way up. They could hear Grandpa breathing heavily, but finally they found a place to sit.

Everyone had looked with anticipation to this special afternoon. Corinne had worked hard at her university studies, and would reap the reward of all her efforts this night.

The music began. Thousands of young men and women, two abreast, wearing gowns and mortarboards, walked slowly to the front of the vast pavilion.

They strained their eyes to catch a glimpse of Corinne, but couldn't see her. Esther pulled out her binoculars to make it easier to see the graduates. But where was Corinne?

Suddenly, she spotted Corinne and her best friend, Kim, ceremoniously walking down the long aisle. Corinne's long hair cascading down the back of her dark robe, looked almost luminous in the subdued light. Her radiant face peered from under the mortarboard. They were all so proud!

She looked up to the bleachers, straining her eyes to find her family. Finally she spotted them. Gordon, standing tall, waved his arms, to let her know she had located them in that vast audience. Others did the same. She smiled and waved back, acknowledging that she had seen them.

Amazingly, it didn't take long for the many graduates to receive their diplomas. With meticulous planning so far in advance, everything went like clockwork as, one by one, their names were called and diplomas put into eager hands. Eventually the time came when Corinne shook hands with the president. Receiving the long-anticipated diploma, she knew this paper was her passage into a new life.

Smiling, with the precious document in her hand, she went back to her seat and stood with her classmates.

In his address, Dan Evans had some practical advice for the graduating class of 1990.

"Shed those black robes of conformity and begin making your unique and distinctive contribution to our world," he said. "Test your limits, endure the discomfort in challenging the common order. Fight for your beliefs with vigor!"

In response to this challenge, hundreds of mortarboards flew through the air. And then it was over.

The graduates walked out the exit, to a glorious day of sunshine and bright hopes for the morrow.

It took longer for the guests to file out of the crowded building, but soon they, too, were out in the warm sunshine.

Finding Corinne, they all took turns congratulating her. Hugging her tightly, Esther knew her daughter would go a long way. Were those tears in Gordon's eyes as he kissed her on the cheek? She knew they were. Hastily he wiped them away with the back of his rough coat sleeve. Grandpa and Grandma were proud as they, too, expressed God's blessings for her future. Charlene and Steve stood nearby with camera in hand.

THE PARTY

The house shone from top to bottom. Fresh rolls, sliced turkey, red meats, and salads, along with an assortment of other food, stood in readiness on the long dining-room table. Corinne was expectantly awaiting the arrival of her guests. She and her Mom scurried around in the kitchen, attending to last-minute details.

Suddenly the door bell rang and Corinne jumped up to greet guests as they arrived.

Over and over the chimes vibrated into every corner of the big house. Soon all her friends were there, congratulating the guest of honor who had just earned a degree in radio and broadcasting.

Having lived abroad for years, it was plain to see Corinne's guests included a wide variety of cultures. She was comfortable with them all.

They had a grand time! All the rooms in the big house were put to use. The air was pregnant with festivity. Colorful balloons, streamers, and scented flowers, together with the strains of Chopin's classical music, made them want to grab a partner and dance around the room.

The food went fast as most of the guests came back for more. Charlene's decorated cake gracing the middle of the table, was inscribed with a special message of congratulations and best wishes to the guest of honor. Moist and delicious, it, too, was consumed rapidly.

One by one, the guests went home, leaving paper cups, streamers, and empty dishes, but in Corinne's heart there was a glow that would not go away so soon.

The girls went into the library after the guests were gone and had their own quiet party. Talking till late, the sisters expressed their desire of good will for their future lives. They knew God was aware of the pathway ahead.

After the dishes were stacked in the dishwasher, and the decorations stashed away, the house was quiet again. Esther tiptoed into Corinne's bedroom.

"Mom, can you rub my back?"

Esther stepped up to the bed like she had done when her daughter was small, sat down, and began to massage her tight muscles.

"Thanks, Mom, for a terrific party!" she said.

Esther bent down to kiss her cheek, mixed emotions flooding her heart. One day soon, though she lived nearby, she, too, would be gone and her bed empty. But tonight she was still here—and Esther was grateful.

As she slipped out and closed the door, she whispered, "Good night, Sweetheart!"

"'Night, Mom, I love you!"

Empty Nest

The house was so big!

Esther walked into the empty rooms, remembering when childhood voices rang throughout the halls.

"Run, Charlene, I'm going to catch you!"

"Bet you can't, Corinne!"

"Here I go!"

Almost knocking the plants over in their haste to play hide and seek, they ran to find a place to hide. Then, giggling and tired after being found, they fell to the floor.

These same halls were now so still. Would she ever become used to this?

It seemed only yesterday she sat beside their bed at night. Sometimes they talked—about boys, friends, school, church. Feeling free to share dreams with their mother, they knew she would give advice when necessary, but mostly just listen. They liked that the most. In this busy world, it is hard to find someone who will just be quiet and hear what a child has to say. In her heart, Esther gathered and hid their precious secrets, keeping them to herself and God.

CORINNE

Corinne's room was the most recently vacated. Esther went in and picked up her old, comfortable nightgown. It was one in which she loved to sit and lounge. It gave off a distinct aroma of Corinne's favorite shampoo. So often when she was home, Esther sat beside her bed, massaging her back. She said this was the most wonderful way to relax that she knew of. Those were times they talked and shared. Esther sensed the aroma of her dusty perfume.

But this time was different. Corinne wasn't there. Esther squeezed her eyes together to control the hot tears… but they came anyway.

Fritz, Corinne's big gray cat, came into the room. Searching for her, he sniffed the old aromatic sneakers lying beside her crumpled bed, and jumped up to crawl between her covers. Fritz and Corinne always had a special rapport. When he almost died last summer, she sat with him in the hospital for hours. They think he "willed" to live because of her love for him. The vet said Fritz was the first cat to live with such a serious disease. Now the little animal restlessly paced around her room.

Where is Corinne? He couldn't figure it out, but continued to search for his beloved master.

"I am planning to move to Los Angeles, Mom and Dad," she had announced.

"Los Angeles?" answered her astonished father.

Both Gordon and Esther were reluctant for this change. They realized, after counsel, that she had made up her mind to try her wings. She needed a job in her field which constituted video and TV promotions. They all knew it was difficult to find this kind of work in Seattle, so they had to let her go, committing her to God.

It was Friday morning when she drove out of the yard bound for the big city of Los Angeles. The old van was packed with her earthly possessions. Both Gordon and Esther wept as they embraced her. Bravely she held back the tears, while swallowing a lump in her throat. But she was determined to go. Esther and Gordon were proud, though their hearts hurt.

Esther watched the van disappear down Fremont Avenue North. So often Corinne had driven there, but this time was different. She wasn't coming home! Once again hot tears stung her eyes. Esther's mother, Katy, must have had the same emotions when Esther left for Winnipeg. Now she understood. Her youngest was gone!

They would miss Corinne. For seven years, she had been the capable office manager for their Marshall Foundation. Efficient and intelligent, she operated the mission like a well-run business. When they were audited by the IRS on several occasions, they always were impressed with her work. Never again would they find capable office personnel such as this.

Young people in Poland had loved Corinne. Always patient and kind, drawn to her, they listened carefully while she taught.

With an exuberant, magnetic personality, not only the Poles were drawn to her. Everywhere she went, Corinne left sunshine in her path. Los Angeles would be a difficult city to conquer, but they knew God would go before and lead her in paths she should go.

CHARLENE

Maternal instinct compelled her to walk into Charlene's empty room, as well. It, too, was hollow and still. A picture of her smiled from the dresser beside the one of her mom and her taken in the Swiss Alps.

Some of her old, stuffed toys still sat in the chair by Max's window. Her old cat loved to climb the big tree beside the window. There he cried till she let him in. Snuggling down beside Charlene, he settled down in sweet peace, his body vibrating with contented purrs. No one else really cared much for that old cat, but he was satisfied because Charlene loved him. That's what really mattered. After Max died, the big tree was cut down, too. How everything had changed since the few precious years when the girls were home.

Charlene's wedding gown still hung in the closet, together with the veil and hoop. The silk bouquet she carried to the altar on her wedding day was still on her dresser. It seemed like yesterday when they watched their first-born walk down the aisle in her flowing, white wedding gown to become the wife of her intended.

Both Gordon and Esther asked them to wait until Charlene had graduated from college, but the couple were convinced this was the right time.

"Are you sure you want to get married now?" queried Gordon.

"Yes, Dad, I love Steve!" she answered simply.

Love continued to radiate between them.

How fast time flies! The years melt into one!

"We spend our years as a tale that is told," said the Psalmist so long ago (Psalm 90:9). Did time fly rapidly in those days, too?

What was this nostalgia and loneliness that swept over Esther in waves? Yes, it must be the empty nest syndrome. Now she had no babies to hold, no childish hurts to kiss and make better. Suddenly she felt older and useless. This phase in her life was over.

CHALLENGES

Wait! Perhaps a new and different phase in her life had begun? Esther held her head high as this realization swept over her. She would continue to pray and support her children. She would always be there when they needed her. Mother love is stubborn. She vowed to love and cherish them through all the difficult times as well as the good times. Her work was not over! There was still so much to do!

"Mom!"

Tuning her ear for sounds that really were not there, she answered loudly, "Yes, my dears, I am here. I will always be here!"

Softly closing the door to Charlene's room, she walked over to Corinne's to do the same.

Now she could look ahead with joy. There would be new and different challenges to face. Perhaps one day grandchildren would sleep in their mother's old room, dreaming dreams of their future.

She planned to be there for them, too. Always.

Balisky Family Photos

Gordon and Esther in Adelboden, Switzerland.

Gordon in his ukrainian costume.

Gordon, Esther, Charlene and Corinne taken in Abbotsford, BC.

Mary and Bill Balisky, Gordon's parents.

Henry and Kathryn Peters, Esther's parents.

Corinne, Charlene and Esther at Tunner See in Bern County.

Gordon, Esther, Charlene and Corinne in Seattle.

Corinne in front of her apartment in Los Angeles.

Murray and Nancy Marshall with us in our living room. Murray wrote the foreword for this book.

Harold and Hazel, (Esther's brother and sister-in-law) and Paul and Martin.

Alexis and Nicholas – Grandpa and Grandma's pride and joy.

The Balisky – Dittoe Family (Photographed in 2001)
Front to back: Nicholas, Charlene, Gordon, Corinne, Alexis, Steve and Esther.

TO MY LITTLE GIRLS
From Mama

It seems only yesterday you were a baby
I held close within my arms,
Today—you are a little girl,
filled with sweetest charms.
Yesterday, I gently rocked you
and sang a lullaby,
Nestling close to me in confidence,
you closed your big, blue eyes.

Yesterday I well remember how you,
my toddler, cried with glee.
As you held out your wee hands
and unsteadily came to me.
Yesterday—your first step—today
you run with joy to play,
Blonde curls flying—quick feet running,
along your merry way.

'Twas today you lost your first tooth
and excitedly came to me
You held it proudly in you hand,
for Dad and Mom to see.
Yesterday it seems to me—you grew
your first tooth small,
What an event—what celebration—
what a little doll!

Today I took your little hand
and went with you to school…
Your first long day—you bravely went
to learn the golden rule,

My eyes grew misty as I left you—
then blinded me with tears,
My little babe of yesterday
had changed throughout the years.

The time rolls on—before I know it
you will be a teen—
That blue-eyed, lisping, little girl
no longer will be seen,
Replacing her—a sweet young lady,
with plans and joys ahead,
School—then college—a vocation,
as by God's hand you're led.

Today I'm thankful to be a mother—
what a privilege rare.
I look ahead, and when you need me,
I always will be there.
Yesterday has gone so quickly—
memories linger near,
Yesterday, today, tomorrow—
I will always love you, Dear!

New Developments

Though the children were gone, Esther's life went on.

Slavic immigrants from the Ukraine and Russia began arriving on the West Coast. She would never forget the strategic day in the spring of 1990, when she and Gordon sat in the front pew of their own home church in Seattle. This was the place where, over twenty years ago, they knelt at the front of the sanctuary, while the elders, deacons, and pastors commissioned them in prayer to go to Eastern Europe and Russia as missionaries.

Incredible, but true, now looking around her, Esther saw the sanctuary filled with people from these countries. Carving out a new future for themselves in the United States of America, the people continued to come. Due to religious persecution during previous times, in vain they had made petitions to the government to leave the country. Now that the face of Russia was changing, they were given freedom.

Families who arrived first, sacrificially sponsored their loved ones to come to the United States, as they, too, fled the country where they had suffered for their faith.

Now here they were—fathers, mothers, young people, and children—sitting in rapt attention as their pastor shared from God's Word. Women with colorful *Babushkas* tied around their heads, wearing drab, colorless clothing, wiped tears from their eyes as truths from the Bible were revealed to them. Young people, already looking too mature for their years, silently and respectfully listened. The children sat in front benches where their parents could keep an eye on them. Little girls, with big ribbons tied in long, silky tresses, folded their hands neatly while praying to the heavenly Father who cared for them. Little boys, scrubbed clean behind the ears, sat quietly—stiff and uncomfortable in their Sunday attire.

Esther glanced sideways at her husband as the music began. Tears running down his cheeks, he, too, could never have imagined what they were seeing that day.

The singing began. Each verse in the minor key was sung slowly, thoughtfully, prayerfully. And easily, expectantly, the entire congregation of Slavic people slipped to their knees to pray. Some raised their arms in praise to the heavenly Father who brought them out of bondage into a land flowing with milk and honey. Many prayed audibly, some quietly, but together, Esther was certain they were making the courts of heaven ring.

As in Russia in former days, poems were recited at length, Scriptures read, and many musical selections rendered.

Gordon and Esther, deeply moved, looked around them. They saw people who had suffered severely in Russia to keep the faith of their fathers. They observed women who had waited patiently while a pastor-husband was in prison, their children growing up without the tutelage of a father in the home. They saw work-worn hands holding tightly to a treasured Bible, a gift they received since coming to America. In Russia, they often had copied the sacred words on paper because there were no Bibles. Now they owned the precious Book! How could they be so blessed?

Gordon and Esther observed men and women with whom they had worked in the former Soviet Union in past years. Coming from Odessa, Rovno, Black Sea, Lvov, Moscow, and Kiev, now amazingly—500 strong—they were worshiping in their own North Seattle Alliance church. Tears filled Esther and Gordon's eyes as the choir sang about "The Deep, Deep Love of Jesus." Unashamedly they allowed the tears to course down their cheeks. They had given over twenty years of their lives to tell these people about the great love of God. Their hearts were overflowing now!

Bowing her head, Esther remembered clearly how, on her wedding day, she had quoted the famous words of Ruth to her mother-in-law, Naomi, as she said,

> *...whither thou goest, I will go; and where thou lodgest, I will lodge: thy people shall be my people, and thy God, my God* (Ruth 1:16).

Little did she realize, as a young, perhaps naïve and inexperienced woman, how prophetic these words would be. Since that day, while working in Communist countries, Esther and Gordon had traveled thousands of miles. She had gone where he went. They had stayed in countless Slavic homes, sleeping in a variety of beds—some lumpy and uncomfortable, where the springs rose up to meet them. Sometimes they slept on the floor, other times in trailers or tents, but she lodged where he lodged. Most strategic of all was the prophecy that Gordon's people would become her own. This statement had become a reality!

Seeing hundreds of Slavic people worshiping in their church was almost too overwhelming for them to believe. These were their people. Esther had made this promise to Gordon over thirty years before—and she meant it more on this day than ever before.

The elderly pastor then asked Gordon and Esther to sing. Going to the beautiful grand piano, she felt her fingers slide over the familiar ivories. The twenty-third Psalm, which they had sung many times in the former Soviet Union, and a favorite with the people, echoed across the big sanctuary. Remembering well, women softly wiped tears away. Men sniffed and children listened quietly. They were standing on holy ground. The Lord, their Shepherd, was among them.

Shaking hands, one by one, they greeted them after the lengthy service was over. Men, crushing Gordon in their big arms, kissed him on one cheek and then the other. Women held Esther close to their hearts.

Surely, their Father had planned this, too!

HELP FOR A NEEDY PEOPLE

Since that day in 1990, the Balisky home became a public place for hurting refugees to come for help. Their strength was offered, day and night, to assist in any area of need. Their kitchen became a place to feed people who needed a meal. Their privacy was relinquished to help the hurting. They took in refugees for the night. Sometimes that

one night turned into months. What else could they do?

Once again Gordon answered the doorbell as it peeled into the late hours of the night. Two young men stood at the door. With no place to call home and no food in their bellies, the hopeful immigrants asked for assistance. They had recently arrived from Russia and their English vocabulary was limited. With no jobs or money, to whom could they turn? Where could they go? A place to sleep, something to eat—was that too much to ask?

Sometimes in recent nights they had gone to fellow Russian homes to sleep, but they were already filled to capacity. Often families with many children lived under one roof. How could they ask others to join them when there were no beds and little food available? Gordon invited the homeless lads to stay with them for a few nights. Taking turns sleeping on a couch or in a car because of lack of space, the boys were weary and hungry. Could Wasyl help? They would go over and see.

Esther watched from the window. What had these boys eaten for breakfast, lunch, or dinner? Her heart reaching out, she went to the door. "Gordon, bring the boys in. I have soup on the stove. We can make a bed downstairs."

Never having seen this auntie before, the boys were amazed to be invited into an American home. Timidly walking into the kitchen, soon their empty stomachs were filled with warm, nourishing food.

Then a big fire was built in the fireplace downstairs. A sofa was converted into a bed, sleeping bags taken out of storage, pillows fluffed up, fragrant, clean sheets spread carefully over the mattress, and the boys were ready to move into their new home. Fed, warm, secure, and comfortable, they drifted off to sleep.

This was only the beginning. Many Slavic young men who needed food and shelter, now came to live at the Baliskys.

God had brought the mission field to their front door! Almost daily, they were immersed with a flood of Russian immigrants. It would be difficult for these people to break old habits and customs and blend into American culture. They had to help!

Most of the immigrants were coping with language problems, so Gordon, trying to get them into colleges in the Puget Sound area to learn English, was overwhelmed with calls. Green cards and visas must be obtained from the immigration offices in downtown Seattle. This took many hours of travel and telephone calls. To find low-cost housing was another area of responsibility. Most had large families, so consequently, homes or apartments with ample room must be found.

To have twenty people come to the house in one day was not unusual. Esther sometimes longed for privacy and time for herself, but those days were filled with a myriad of duties. She made sure a large pot of homemade soup was always simmering on the back burner.

Sometimes, at the end of a long day, both Esther and Gordon were exhausted. But to know some now had a home in which to live, clothing on their backs, and food on their table, was a blessing they could not put into words.

The Scriptures in Matthew 25 became her solace:

> *And he shall set the sheep on his right hand, but the goats on the left. Then shall the King say unto them on his right hand, Come, ye blessed of my Father, inherit the kingdom prepared for you from the foundation of the world: For I was an hungered, and ye gave me meat: I was thirsty, and ye gave me drink: I was a stranger, and ye took me in: Naked, and ye clothed me: I was sick, and ye visited me: I was in prison, and ye came unto me.*

> *Then shall the righteous answer him, saying, Lord, when saw we thee an hungered, and fed thee? or thirsty, and gave thee drink? When saw we thee a stranger, and took thee in? or naked and clothed thee? Or when saw we thee sick, or in prison, and came unto thee?*
>
> *And the King shall answer and say unto them, Verily I say unto you, Inasmuch as ye have done it unto one of the least of these my brethren, ye have done it unto me.* (Matthew 25:33-40).

Would He also say to Esther and Gordon, "Well done, thou good and faithful servants—enter into the joy of thy Lord?" The Master looked tenderly upon His weary children and assured them that indeed He would say, "Well done."

Gratefully, Esther put her head on the pillow and went to sleep. Knowing God would give strength for each day, peace filled her heart.

* * *

The number of immigrants coming to the United States continued to grow.

Early in the morning the phone rang again. Gordon excused himself, leaving a group of needy refugees on the doorstep.

"There is a family of fourteen arriving from the Ukraine," said the voice on the other end. "We need a place for them to live. Can you help, Wasyl?"

Already, they had found homes for many, but here was another opportunity to assist. "Yes, I think I can help. When do they arrive?"

"This week, Wasyl. Please do what you can so this family can have a home when they come. In our house we have absolutely no room. We can't help!"

In a few days the large family stepped off the airplane.

Dazed and in shock, they viewed the affluence around them. Everyone seemed to be rich and in need of nothing here. How could it be? How would they fit into this new culture? They had nothing. "Can we survive here?" worried the Slavic mother. "How about the children? Soon they will need to go to school. Can they learn the language so fast?"

Several children hid behind the mother's ample skirt, as she, carrying a newborn, stepped into the house Gordon had prepared for them. Wiping her eyes, and putting down her heavy burden, in wonder, she looked around her. So, this would be their new home. Never in Ukraine had she seen such a house! Excited, the children ran from room to room, calling their parents to come and look.

"Daddy! Mama! Here is a place to make a fire and a machine to wash our clothes like we saw on TV! Hey, there is a rug on the floor!" Oh joy! This was almost too much! Yes, they would like living in this wonderful place.

Though simple by American standards, little furniture graced the rooms, and no curtains hung on the bare windows, but the family were more than grateful. This place far exceeded their dreams and hopes for the future.

"*Sposeebo*! *Sposeebo*!" (thank you) exclaimed the big Ukrainian. Extending his hand, he shook Gordon's, his lower lip quivering with emotion.

But this family must have food, beds, warm blankets, and cooking utensils to survive. Esther knew what she had to do!

Phoning a Ukrainian pastor's wife, together they went to a second-hand store and gathered cart loads full of clothing and necessary items with which to set up a household. These provisions were plain, but necessary. They would be adequate.

The immigrants in the United States were concerned about their relatives. Could they, too, by some miracle, come to live in this land flowing with milk and honey?

Dedicated to the Russian Woman

There she stands—the little Russian woman
Holding firm, but gently to her baby's hand.
Stepping onto foreign soil in culture shock
In America—a strange, but bounteous land.

The sounds are new and vastly unfamiliar;
So this is English—she will have to learn.
With mixed emotions—visualizing Russia
For motherland and home her sad heart yearns.

The young child cuddles closer to her mother
Sensing, too, that she is far away from home.
Where's Grandpa? Where's Grandma? Where are all her small friends?
She feels frustrated—abandoned—alone.

Where are the cattle grazing so peacefully
On hillsides and meadows where she often played?
And where is the thatched-roofed home of her childhood
The place her father fashioned and laboriously made?

America—a great land of bounteous harvest
Where nectar from her mighty rivers flow.
Spacious wheat fields—food in abundance
Is where the immigrant must learn to grow.

I'll take your hand, dear Russian sister,
As you become accustomed to our ways.
A wondrous miracle—God brought you here
Lift up your voice in thankfulness and praise.

33 THE MENNONITE BRETHREN

The Mennonite Brethren, many of whom had their roots in the Ukraine, watched closely as they observed miracles taking place. Should they become involved in assisting these immigrants who had lived in the place where their own forefathers had suffered to keep the faith?

Many of the older Mennonites who were born in the Ukraine still vividly remembered the difficulties they had encountered while living there. Now, were there not thousands of Slavic believers, some of whom were tortured for their faith, in the Ukraine and Russia, asking for asylum? Would God have them assist immigrants who so recently came to America? Would He not want them to help those who were already here, trying to assist their own loved ones in the Ukraine?

The Russian origin of the MB denomination and the Slavs' exposure to Mennonite Brethren believers during the years of shared persecution, helped establish a natural link between the Conference and the new immigrants when they settled in the United States.

After much prayer and careful consideration, the Mennonite Brethren Conference decided to contact Gordon and Esther.

Asking them to be the liaisons between the Slavic people and themselves, they felt this could be a joint effort in reaching out to the immigrants in the United States.

Several of the MB leaders came to Seattle to talk this matter over with the Baliskys.

Seated in the living room on Fremont Avenue North, Esther was amazed how God was bringing them together with her own people to reach the Slavic populace (Gordon's people), right in their own country.

How mysteriously God works! Tears filled her eyes as they talked and made preparations to make Esther and Gordon a part of the conference for a period of time, to help plant and establish churches for the newly-arriving immigrants.

"Church buildings are very important," emphasized Gordon, "because their main worship service runs two to four hours. Dual worship services just do not work, because of the duration of the services."

They discussed this challenge, as well. Slavic congregations, they knew, were among the few congregations in the Conference where growth was being hindered by the size of the facilities. The Slavs needed buildings large enough to accommodate all their people. One reason they grew so rapidly, was because new arrivals of additional families from the Ukraine and Russia continued to come. "This influx is going on all the time," added Esther. "Every person who has a permanent residence in the United States can continue to sponsor family members who want to come. Consequently, these churches continue to grow."

Having worked in the Ukraine and Russia for years, Gordon and Esther knew that Slavic churches have a heart for reaching their own people. This, too, would be another reason for growth. Church plays an important part in the life of Slavic people.

Putting their hands on Gordon and Esther, the Mennonite Brethren leaders prayed for the couple who had so unselfishly given their lives to help these people overseas, and were now willing to help establish and plant churches in the United States, also.

The room was hushed as they rose from their knees. Awed, because God had put them together with the Germanic people who had lived in the former Soviet Union, and now had a burden to reach the Slavic people who had immigrated from there, Gordon and Esther clearly saw the hand of God in this transaction. Shaking hands as the brethren left, they knew Someone much greater had this transaction in His omniscient plans years ago. Their place was to be obedient in that plan. With God's help, they would be, because their Father planned it all!

They had hoped to establish ten new churches in five years, however in just over a year, eleven were born. The first congregations were in Washington and Oregon. That area remains the center of Slavic activity. But since that time, as immigrant families dispersed to other parts of the country, Slavic congregations from Sacramento, California, Salt Lake City, Utah, and Minneapolis, Minnesota, were interested.

New contacts kept emerging. Could they keep up with these demands? Gordon and Esther were heavily involved with work in Eastern Europe and Russia and now with immigrants in the United States. "How thin can we spread ourselves?" they wondered. Their days did not seem to be long enough. But they rejoiced in knowing God was performing a

modern-day miracle and He was using them to be a part of the action.

The First Slavic Church

Finding the first church building for a group of about 400 Ukrainians was a challenge. Growth could be hindered if the size of the building wasn't adequate. New families were continuing to filter in from the Ukraine, so the future must be reckoned with. The Slavs also wanted to reach out to their own people who did not attend church regularly. But where could they meet?

Gordon felt he should speak with the pastor of the Fifteenth Avenue Bible Church where he had pastored before moving to Europe. The large congregation there had

Gordon and Esther with a few of the Slavic and American pastors from the Pacific Northwest.

The first Slavic MB Church in Seattle, WA. Terry Robson and Gordon on left.

decreased to where they were not using the sanctuary for worship services, but instead met in a smaller room in the church. Would it be possible for the Ukrainians to meet in the large sanctuary? Earnestly praying, he sought God's will. The Mennonite leadership, too, prayed for God's will to be done.

When Esther heard there was a possibility this arrangement could be made, she was ecstatic. To think God would allow them to be back in the church she had dearly loved so many years ago, would be an awesome miracle. But was this possible?

One day Zoya, a Russian pastor's wife, and Esther, standing at the back of the spacious sanctuary, decided to pray together about this possible development.

Esther was reminded of the wonderful times of blessing she and her family had spent in this place. Was He now bring-

ing the Slavic people, with whom she and Gordon had worked in the Ukraine, to this place?

Zoya put her hand on Esther's arm. Then, in her mother tongue, she prayed for God to make it possible for them to use this building for their worship services. Esther followed, praying in English, that God would cement this important decision.

Tears springing between closed eyelids, she talked to God. "Lord, You remember the precious times of fellowship we had in this church together with Your people. You allowed us to minister here and bring unity to a hurting body. May You open the doors to allow the Slavic people for whom You died, to come into these doors with thanksgiving in their hearts. Make this sanctuary available for a grateful people. Thank You, God!"

After negotiating with the Pastor and board of the church, the decision to rent the building to the Slavs became a reality. The Fifteenth Avenue church people still planned to meet in the blue room and use an adjacent Sunday School facility. Otherwise, the building was available to the Slavic people.

Glory be! God had performed a miracle! The Mennonites cooperated to make this house of God a unique place of worship and praise.

Repairing God's House

There was a hustle of activity at the Fifteenth Avenue Bible Church during that week in June. Diligent Mennonite Brethren "U Serve" members were working to repair the building.

Men, high on scaffolding, prepared to paint the complete interior of the large church. Others industriously worked with hammer and nails, creating a new look in the building. The fence around the property was in dire need of repair. Work on the grounds and in the interior of the church was going forward.

June 1 marked the beginning of the agreement to lease this valuable property to the Slavic congregation. At that time there were 28,999 new immigrants in the Puget Sound area and many would need a church home. This sanctuary would accommodate about 400 of them.

Gordon was quoted in a nation-wide periodical as saying, "This development of the Mennonite Brethren Center for Slavic ministries, marks a milestone of missionary outreach in North America."

During the week of repairing the building and grounds, excited Slavs joined the industrious workers. *Borscht*, *holopsie*, and *verenike*, graced the crowded tables, as busy Slavic women stood ready to serve at a moment's notice. The Mennonite Brethren had sent their own people from various states to help bring about the neccessary tasks that must be completed before the waiting congregation could move in.

Esther watched the proceedings with joy. The sun shone through stained glass windows on a freshly painted sanctuary, while the entire, re-created building had an aura of cleanliness and warmth.

Now the Slavic congregation had a new church home! Gordon and Esther could see clearly that God had opened the doors to let these grateful people in. Here, they would worship, unmolested, and their children would be taught the Word of God!

To God be the Glory

Songs of praise rang out from the Fifteenth Avenue Bible Church as the Slavic/Mennonite Brethren Center was dedicated to God on Sunday, June 14, 1990.

About 450 people crowded into the brightly re-decorated sanctuary. Spilling over into the large foyer, people continued to arrive. Chairs, filling the aisles, accommodated many who otherwise would have no place to sit.

For several weeks, men and women had worked together as they gave the thirty-foot-high ceiling two coats of paint. Many had lent willing hands and dedicated hearts to make this house of God a place that would honor and glorify His name. Long hours were spent in physical labor as well as in concentrated prayer to bring them to this anticipated day.

The service began at 1:00 P.M. People sat quietly as several Russian pastors shared from the Word of God.

Gordon and Esther, newly appointed catalysts to spearhead this new venture, shared in the meeting. Gordon capably spoke in the language of the people. Of course this endeared him to them. Expressing appreciation, they chorused a unanimous “Amen!”

Rev. Scott Golike, the present pastor of the Fifteenth Avenue Bible Church, informed the people he and his congregation were happy to share the building with the Slavic group.

Terry and Kristin Robson, sponsored by the Zoar Mennonite Brethren church from Inman, Kansas, where, long ago, Esther’s parents attended, were in the Seattle area to teach English to the immigrants. They, too, took part in the lengthy service.

Afternoon hours went by rapidly as the people sat quietly. Even children were silent, realizing God had brought them to this special hour.

Prayer time is vital in a Russian service. Slipping to their knees, on several occasions, the large body of believers prayed earnestly. With tears in their eyes, they thanked Him for bringing them to this house of God.

Music plays an important role in the church, too. Several special numbers, including a large choir, brought blessing and encouragement to the congregation. Many wept as the young people sang about their glorious hope when they will all be with the Lord in heaven. Some, especially the elderly, longed for that time.

Esther played the big church organ as she had done so many years ago. Victorious praises of "To God be the Glory" filled the auditorium as people filed out, making their way to the dining room upstairs.

Long tables were filled with copious amounts of Russian cuisine. The women made certain there would be enough to feed everyone. Later, there were enough leftovers for several needy families to take home.

The atmosphere was filled with joy and laughter as different cultures sat around the laden tables. This was an occasion to celebrate! Now the Russians had a place to worship. God had caused this dream to become a reality!

THE FIRST THANKSGIVING

The Slavic/MB Church on Fifteenth Avenue was filled to capacity as two Slavic immigrant congregations met to celebrate Thanksgiving on November 27. Chairs were placed in the aisles to accommodate the overflow. Still the people came.

As Esther looked across the sea of faces, she was reminded of a similar scene in history when, in 1620, a group of English pilgrims came across to America as immigrants, and gave thanks to God in a similar fashion. They celebrated their first Thanksgiving in a new country, after founding a colony in Plymouth, Massachusetts.

As Gordon and Esther entered the beautiful sanctuary, vegetables, fruit, and grains decked the front. Tastefully arranged, they added to the aura of festivity.

The Slavic congregation sat quietly as a group of young people, accompanied by guitars and keyboards, sang

Part of the dedication of the First Slavic MB Church were tables laden with ethnic foods.

for about an hour, their voices ringing throughout the crowded church.

Poems were recited at length. It is always the custom to have not only one sermon, but several, and this Thanksgiving celebration was no exception. Tears filled the eyes of many, as their pastor expressed thanksgiving to God for allowing them to come to the United States of America. As he stressed gratefulness for health, peace, and joy, the people echoed affirmatively. He challenged his congregation and the Slavic visitors present, to continue to grow in the Lord as they settled in their new country.

One by one, bright-eyed children filed to the front of the church. This was their opportunity to share in the service. Smiling, little girls with large ribbons in their hair, sang songs they had been rehearsing for some time. Their clear, young voices blending as one, young boys clothed in Sunday attire, joined them.

Pungent aromas from the kitchen began to fill the sanctuary. After the closing prayer when the kneeling congregations prayed aloud in unison, the service was over.

Aware that a feast was imminent, the people made their way to the dining room. Quickly walking through the crowds, Esther took pictures of the feast before the large body of believers filled the room. Foods of every description were there. Watching kitchen helpers carve six beautifully roasted turkeys made everyone feel hungry.

Food enough to accommodate 500 people disappeared rapidly as they indulged in the sumptuous fare.

Everyone expressed thanksgiving as they had fellowship around the tables. But the children were getting weary. They had been in church for about six hours. The women efficiently cleared cluttered tables and chaos in the kitchen. Gathering their families together, they left for their homes.

It had been a wonderful Thanksgiving! The people were satisfied. They had been spiritually and physically fed. Everyone rejoiced.

Humanitarian Aid

By 1994, there were 350,000 to 400,000 Slavic immigrants on the west coast. Besides that, many were scattered throughout various parts of the United States.

Slavic churches began springing up across the country. Eventually having contact with about eighty new churches, the demand for buildings was increasing rapidly.

Gordon, keeping contact with rapidly growing conditions in Russia and the Ukraine, also worked with churches he and Esther had helped to plant there. Through daily contact with the people overseas, the work was supervised from America. From letters, fax, telephone, plus immigrants who kept in touch with loved ones in Europe, he had a broad picture of what was happening.

Though the Baliskys worked hard to help the immigrants become established in their new country, it was difficult for the people to settle in an unfamiliar environment. Needing a great deal of encouragement, often they looked to Gordon. Living on the edge of poverty in churches numbering 300 to 600, the people were not able to support their pastors, but eventually, with financial aid, the shepherds of their flock could continue to teach their people.

Meanwhile, the political and economic situation in the Ukraine and Russia was getting worse. With independence, economic instability increased. The average wage of a worker was not comparable to how much was needed to support his family. The economy in Russia and the Ukraine had collapsed. The international monetary fund saw no hope for the economy of that country, unless momentous changes took place. Realizing the terrible plight which their people faced in their former homeland, scores of Slavs in both America and Russia appealed to the Baliskys for financial assistance.

Gordon sought the face of God. How could he help the immigrants in his own country, as well as scores in the Ukraine and Russia? He prayed all night. In the morning, coming down to the aroma of freshly perked coffee, he greeted his wife.

"Good morning, Honey. I have made a decision. I know God wants me to help Slavs who need food, not only here, but also in the former USSR."

Looking at the weary lines etched in her husband's face, Esther was concerned. "What kind of a plan do you have?"

"We will set up a plan in the United States as well as the Ukraine and Russia, to develop a humanitarian aid mission manned by Slavic nationals there, and Slavic immigrants here."

How can he spread his time and energy any farther? Esther wondered. But encouraging him in this new venture, she smiled and encouraged him to go about his business.

The Slavic people were euphoric! It brought great satisfaction to be able to help their families who were suffering in their homeland. Many nights had been spent in worrying about how their loved ones would survive in the midst of an economic crisis.

Various companies donated food, others reduced their prices, and soon the large warehouse on Fifteenth Avenue was filled to capacity. Made possible through special grants to cover shipping and the cost of containers from the U.S. to the countries from which these immigrants came, expenses were cut down.

Gordon, spending countless hours organizing, calling, and planning, was pleased that details were coming together so efficiently.

"The average wage of a worker in the Ukraine varies," said Wolodya, the assistant pastor of one of the churches. "But sometimes he will make about 7 dollars per month. This is not enough to provide for a large family."

People in Lvov, they heard, complained because they could not survive on this low income. "Money," they said, "quickly loses its value. We must spend it as fast as we get it."

On a sunny day in summer, scores of Slavs carried boxes out of the storehouse into the container outside.

Carefully addressing each box to a family overseas, and including a return address, the people were assured their relatives would soon have food to put on the table. Laughing and talking, the immigrants filled the container. When it was finished, they started on another. In the beginning stages, from the Seattle region, over thirty containers (56,000 pounds each) were shipped to the Ukraine. Shipped to Georgia, southern Russia, and other places, the number of shipments continued to increase as needs grew greater.

Newly-formed congregations from Portland, Oregon, Sacramento, California, and Cleveland, Ohio joined in this ministry to help loved ones in their former homeland.

Eagerly, Ukrainians in Rovno, Ukraine, unpacked the boxes that had arrived from the U.S.A. When the warehouse was filled, they used their own vehicles to deliver humanitarian aid to the addresses on the boxes. At least some of Ukraine's hungry people could sit down to some food on the table and enjoy God's bountiful goodness because someone cared!

GRATEFULNESS EXPRESSED

The recipients' gratefulness was expressed in some letters from Dushanbe, Tajikistan, very recently:

> God gave us comfort from these verses in Habakkuk 3:17-18 (NIV): *Though the fig does not bud and there are no grapes on the vines, though the olive crop fails and the fields produce no food, though there are no sheep in the pen and no cattle in the stalls, yet I will rejoice in the Lord, I will be joyful in God my Savior.* (From an evangelist in Dushanbe.)

> We treasure every slice of bread and drop of milk… every time I pour (your donated) milk into my baby's bottle, my heart melts in tears because of your love. (From a mother of six in Dushanbe.)

> With the sounds of heavy artillery and guns outside our home, our children shake with fear and plead with God. It's okay if they don't receive presents at Christmas, they just pray that the war will end." (From a mother in Dushanbe.)

> Every day our life is tears. We're often on our knees in prayer. We fear that my daughter might not come home from school safely. Many times bandits take young girls. (From a mother of a sixteen-year-old in Dushanbe, October, 1993.)

It is encouraging to see Slavs in the U.S.A., who have left their country and homes with nothing but a suitcase and a few personal belongings, willing to do so much for their friends and families in the Ukraine and Russia.

ABUNDANCE

> They sit around their laden tables and eat to heart's content
> God in loving mercy has His abundant blessing sent,
> They eat until they're satisfied, and can devour no more,
> While bountiful provisions are in their coffers stored.

A visit to the grocery store will replenish all their needs
Then on numerous varieties their affluent families feed
So few know the pain of hunger in their abundant land
For God in love supplies their needs by His almighty hand.

Do they ever stop and thank Him for blessings rich and free?
Do they take this love for granted, or can they thankful be?
Golden grain waves in the fields to become their daily bread
"I will supply your needs, My child," so graciously God said.

But across the world children cry for a taste of milk and bread
While at nightfall an anxious mother gently tucks them into bed.
Will there be food enough tomorrow? desperately she cries
Or will her children starve until one by one they die?

Let us bow the knee and worship God who supplies our needs
Who gives us food and drink abundant and generously our family feeds.
Would it be too much to share His gifts with others who will die
From lack of food and sustenance? It is up to you and I.

Bethel Church Finds a Home

Gordon and Esther were not only instrumental in helping to find a church home for the large, Slavic congregation in the former Fifteenth Avenue Bible Church in Seattle, but they assisted an Ethiopian congregation to work out a plan to have their services in the same building.

Berhanu, the pastor of the Ethiopian church, came to Gordon one day. "Please help us, Brother Gordon, we need a place to meet. Our congregation is growing and we don't know where to go!"

Soon it was arranged for them to come to Fifteenth. Joyfully, they thanked God for this miracle and moved in. On Sunday, April 7, the church rang with a different kind of music. This time not only Slavic, but Ethiopian. Their first Sunday in this church marked an important milestone in their lives.

Berhanu, the senior pastor, and his wife, Mulu, came from Ethiopia to the United States some years before. Berhanu completed his training and received a degree in theology, while Mulu earned hers as a pharmacist, and worked in a local pharmacy. In order for Berhanu to spend time with their people and all that is associated with planting a church, she worked many hours in order to help support herself, him, her aged mother, and a small child. Besides that, she was active in their local church.

After moving into the big church, the congregation chose to call their church, Bethel.

So while the Slavs occupied the main sanctuary, the Ethiopians met upstairs. A Korean congregation used a large room in another part of the building, while the English congregation which had moved out of the sanctuary, still met in the blue room on the main floor. Was it possible for four cultures and languages to meet under one roof? They proved it was! Who but God knew that in the future, this building would be filled like this? Surely the Father planned it all!

Special Meetings

"Please," said a grateful Pastor Berhanu, "Come to our services. Pastor Selishe Eshete will be our speaker and is flying in from Nigeria where he pastors a growing congregation of over 7,000."

"Thank you for the invitation, Berhanu," said Gordon. "We will plan to be there."

For two and a half weeks in May, he led four sessions

encouraging believers in the church to a closer walk with God.

Gordon and Esther attended part of the conference. Walking into the familiar building the first night, they were greeted by Pastor Berhanu, Mulu, and Sisay, who is helping in a teaching ministry in the church.

The service had been scheduled for 6:30, but typically, Ethiopian style, it didn't begin until 7:30. Eventually, the church filled as people walked into the sanctuary.

"We are here to be a blessing," opened Pastor Berhanu.

After leading in prayer, he introduced Daniel Agonafer, a gifted worship leader. Singing in Amharic, while Mathius played keyboard, the congregation worshiped God. Clapping enthusiastically, and raising their hands high, the people stood for an hour.

Women, singing in a high obligato, complimented the bass voices of the men. One great choir, in four-part harmony, echoed throughout the building. Gordon's eyes were moist when he realized how God had made this possible. Yes, he, himself had a part in it, but he knew God had done it!

Dark, curly-haired children, with big, black eyes, joined their parents in worship. They, like the Slavic children, were accustomed to long services.

Once a pop singer in Ethiopia, Herut Bekele accepted the Lord seven years ago and now used her fabulous voice to glorify God. "I love you all!" she smiled as she introduced her music. While she sang, the congregation clapped their hands. When she sang the third verse about the coming of Jesus, the worship grew even more animated.

As Pastor Berhanu introduced the speaker, the congregation waited in expectancy. Reading from Proverbs 19:21, Pastor Eshete stressed the fact that, in Christ, they are somebody and Jesus can make somebody out of nobody. "We have true identity through Christ," he emphasized. When he posed the question, "Who am I?" in the same breath he answered, "I am God's masterpiece and His workmanship created in Christ Jesus!"

As the congregation voiced their praise, he continued, "Use your life for Him. The greatest tragedy on earth is not death, but a life lived without purpose. Don't waste time. Purpose is more important than plan. You, God's masterpiece, are important to Him," the pastor emphasized.

Praise filled the room again. He continued, "Satan will start throwing stones, but walk on the stones he throws at you. You are somebody in Christ!"

When the congregation rose to their feet to pray, they had been encouraged and challenged to realize their position in Christ.

Thoughtfully, they left the sanctuary after the three-hour service. All were encouraged. They had met with God!

As Gordon and Esther walked out of the sanctuary where he had been pastor so many years ago, they, too, were challenged to realize their position in Christ.

"Come again!" invited Pastor Berhanu as he shook Gordon's hand, "and you, too, dear Sister Esther," he added. "Thank you both, for helping us find a church home!"

With mixed emotions, they stepped into their car and drove home. Who could have realized this church would be home to several ethnic cultures? Only their heavenly Father knew—after all, He had planned it all many years ago!

34 A JOURNEY TO EUROPE

Though Gordon and Esther were busy planting and establishing Slavic churches in the U.S.A., there were leaders in the Ukraine who invited them to come and teach there. It was difficult to pull away from present responsibilities, but after prayerful consideration, they decided this would be the time to go.

The telephone rang in Corinne's apartment in Los Angeles one fall day. "Corinne, how would you like to come to the Ukraine with Dad and I? We could spend New Year's and Christmas there. Could you get away from your job for awhile?" asked Esther.

Corinne sounded excited and decided to check into her job situation. Would they allow her a leave of absence for a few months? She wasn't certain.

The phone rang in Esther's kitchen a few days later. "Mom! Good news! I have made arrangements to go with you! When do you want to leave?"

Preparations were soon underway. Someone, they knew, must stay in their house while they were away. The office would be run by a capable young woman who had recently started her job there. Other numerous details attended to, soon it was time to leave.

Corinne had arranged a flight to Seattle from Los Angeles, so they could fly together.

Arriving on a crisp, fall day, her parents greeted her at the airport. This would be a good change for them all, and they eagerly looked forward to ministry in Europe again.

Hours later, arriving in Frankfurt, Germany, Cori exclaimed, "This feels like home! It's like we've never been away!"

Recalling the days when she had gone to school at Black Forest Academy and made many friends there, brought moments of nostalgia. Where had the years gone?

It was wintertime in Europe as torrents of rain beat on the windows of their rented vehicle. A cold wind made them all shiver, but it didn't matter. This truly was their second home!

Christmas Eve in Adelboden, Switzerland

Before leaving for the Ukraine, they found themselves walking down snowy streets in the little *dorf* of Adelboden, situated high in the Swiss Alps. Esther pulled her warm hat around her ears. Snow, falling gently, covered the frozen earth, while a cold breeze blew in from the mountains.

The villagers were in an unusually jubilant mood. Everywhere, clad in colorful snowsuits and scarves, they hurried along the snowy streets, making last-minute preparations. Shops, still open, displayed suggestions for a variety of gifts. Though it was cold, tables filled with merchandise stood on the sidewalks to make it easier to choose those final selections.

Perched on ladders, leaning against store fronts, warmly-clad men prepared to stretch Christmas lights from one building to another. Soon the town would be alive with color. Wide-eyed children pulled their mittened hands away from their parents to go and see—explore.

Casting shining rays on the street below, already the trees were decked in brilliance. Covered with a layer of snow, and glistening lights, their branches reached high into the darkened sky. What a wonder! What a sight to behold!

Esther still felt the cold penetrate her ears, though she wore a warm hat. Fingers tingling in her gloves, she moved them from side to side to keep the blood flowing. Stamping on her feet, slowly she felt warmth return. Invigorated, she breathed in deep draughts of fresh, cold air.

The German and Swiss people purchase their Christmas trees on December 24. With awe and anticipation, children wait for that important night.

Tonight, parents along with their warmly-clad offspring, looked over the assortment of trees. Children, screaming with delight, carefully chose the largest they could find.

"This tree will look beautiful in our home!" cried the eldest. "*Vatie*, let's buy this one!" Pulling and tugging her father's arm, she led him to the chosen tree.

Tying it to their car, the happy family drove through the sparkling *dorf* to take their treasure home.

In short order, candles would be placed on the tree while the excited children watched. Spellbound, they knew they would not be lit until evening. This was a tradition they had respected all their lives.

Nestled beneath the base of the towering Swiss Alps, chalets were soon brilliant with light. Their reflections, dancing on the snow outdoors, depicted the most incredible picture post card!

Suddenly, horses pulling sleighs filled with joyful young people crowded the narrow Haupt Strasse. Scarves flying in the wind, they called, "*Fröhliche Weihnachten*!"

Smiling, the Baliskys waved back, "Merry Christmas to you, too!"

The laughter died away as they drove toward the mountains were a Christmas party would take place momentarily.

Feeling a surge of excitement, Esther followed the sound of their laughter with her eyes as she looked toward the towering, snow-capped mountains surrounding Adelboden. Rising high above the town, their majestic beauty was beyond description.

Then, walking toward Boden, another *dorf* where they had often skied together as a family, they saw cross-country *loipers*, skiing in the freshly fallen snow. Carefully staying in the *spuren*, effortlessly they glided past. Their brightly colored scarves blowing in the wind, and faces ruddy with cold, they greeted them.

Everyone was happy! It was Christmas Eve!

Darkness had fallen quickly. As lights twinkled across the snow, they walked toward Pension Hari.

Sometimes, after ministry in Eastern Europe, they came here to relax. Esther claimed there was no better place to forget about the outside world. Here, they were sheltered. Here they could rest.

They were greeted enthusiastically by their hosts, the Hari family. Happy to extend hospitality to them, they enjoyed the atmosphere in this friendly, quiet place.

The new *staamhaus* recently carved out of new, white lumber, was aglow with lights when they arrived.

After stomping the snow from their boots on the rug outside, and loosening the scarves around their necks, they entered the house. Their glasses, foggy with steam when they entered, reminded them they had been out in the cold. Blowing her nose, Esther knew she must look like Rudolph, the red-nosed reindeer. But who cared? Everyone looked the same!

An aura of Christmas permeated the warm, cozy *Saal.* Fragrant aromas from the big kitchen, filling every corner, reminded them they were hungry. Something festive, they were certain, would soon be served.

After showering and changing their damp clothes, they were soon in the dining room for dinner. About 160 guests sat at prepared tables. Candles glowing everywhere bathed the room in soft light. Outside the big windows, they could see snowflakes floating to the frozen earth.

Dinner was served with elegance. Turkey and all the trimmings reminded them of home. Were their loved ones taking part in a feast such as this? They knew they were.

Someone came to their table. "*Guten Abend*, *Frau* Balisky," said the smiling *Saal* chaplain. "Would you play the piano for this *Heiligabend*? We will be having a service soon."

Esther was aware that many of the traditional carols sung in the States were different than in Europe, however she accepted his offer. "Yes, I would be happy to!" she smiled.

When they entered the *pension* sanctuary, it was filled with an expectant people, sitting in the candlelight, quietly waiting for the service to begin.

Beside the glowing Christmas tree, Esther was seated at the piano. "Silent Night," and "*O du Fröeliger*" along with other carols she did not know, soon filled every corner of this sacred place.

Understanding the service in the language of the people, they, along with others, savored these *Heiligabend* memories. Tomorrow was their Savior's birthday.

All during the service, the children couldn't wait until it was time to open the gifts under the big Christmas tree.

Finally wriggling free, exclaiming with delight, they tore into the colorful wrapping paper. Eyes shining like stars, they thanked their parents. While holding their treasures tightly, soon mothers and fathers took them to their rooms. It was late and far past their bedtime. No one really cared. It had been an evening to treasure!

"Good night, *Gott segne ihnen*!" they called after them.

The children were too excited to respond.

Going to the spacious outdoor balcony off the meeting place, Gordon, Esther, and Corinne viewed the starry, Christmas night. Towering mountains in the distance were edged against the inky sky. Covered with a blanket of newly fallen snow, their peaks reached upwards. The air was so still—one could almost hear it. What a holy evening! Sensing the presence of their God, they stood there a long time. Not wanting to break this hallowed moment, they drank in breathtaking, awesome beauty. Finally, hearts filled with peace, arm in arm, they walked quietly to their room in the *pension*.

Gratefully, Esther sank into the luxury and warmth of the big, Swiss feather comforter, and savored the events of this day. Tomorrow, December 25, they planned to celebrate the events of the day—traditional Christmas Day in the Western world—together with the Swiss people.

Christmas in Rovno, Ukraine—January 7, 1994

Arriving in Kiev, Ukraine, they entered the shabby airport terminal. To think President Clinton had been there only days before, made them wonder how he had adapted to the poor surroundings.

But even though rain continued to pelt on the Ukrainian countryside, here, too, in spite of primitive living conditions, they felt at home. This was the place where they had often ministered in the past. Now they planned to do so again.

• • •

As the Christmas tree lights blinked in the crowded living room in Rovno, they were reminded it was time to celebrate their Savior's birth.

"I hope you are comfortable here," smiled their hostess, Valentina Mularchuk, as she put sheets on the small couch were Corinne and Esther would sleep. It was like a board box. A small mattress in the living room was flanked by the back of the couch and two small arms. *How can two of us sleep in such a small bed?* they seriously wondered.

And where would Gordon stay? Was there room in this small house for one more? Valentina made sure there would be room for all her guests.

With a curtain stretched between their couch and his, he at least had room to stretch out. *Are we going to hear him snore through the flimsy material? Will we sleep at all?*

Trying to think positive thoughts, Corinne graciously thanked their hostess for the sleeping quarters. Crawling into bed, as the Christmas tree lights blinked off and on, they smiled into the darkness. Lying close together, they pulled the small quilt around them.

Amazingly, they didn't hear as much snoring as they had anticipated. They actually slept that night!

CHRISTMAS DAY (JANUARY 7)

"Good morning!" called Gordon from behind the curtain. "Merry Christmas!" So this was Christmas in the Ukraine! Thoughts of home nagged at them, but here they were. How different would it be to celebrate here than in the U.S.? They would soon find out.

After quickly dressing, they went to the kitchen and slipped onto the bench behind the small table. Hot tea, cold meat, and salad were quickly consumed. Excusing themselves, they put on warm coats, boots, and headscarves, and left for church with Pastor Mularchuk.

Entering the large sanctuary, they sucked in their breath. No one had told them that the place they would worship that morning was so beautiful! Huge glass chandeliers hung from the high, domed, vaulted ceiling. Six round pillars, gilded with gold and made of pure marble, ran from floor to ceiling. Stained glass windows, with brightly painted pictures, adorned the front and sides of the massive building.

A beautiful pipe organ, which was not played that morning, stood at the front. Esther could imagine the majestic music filling the room.

As one, the large congregation stood to their feet and began to sing about the birth of Christ.

A preschool had been started by Nadya Filuk, a young woman they met that morning. In earlier years, this, of course, would have been impossible, but now to hear the little ones perform on Christmas day was a wonder. To celebrate Christmas openly was a miracle. This had to be done in secret during the Communist era.

As Nadya capably led, the children's uninhibited voices echoed throughout the majestic building. In their own language, "Joy to the World" and "Silent Night," were sung with gusto!

Making the motions to "His Banner Over Me is Love," eagerly the children performed for their proud parents.

Gordon, in the language of the people, gave one of the morning messages. Challenging the people, he told them, on this Christmas day, to cleanse their hearts before Almighty God. Eagerly they listened. Yes, this would be a wonderful gift to give the Lord on this special day.

After a small lunch at Nicholai and Valentina's house, they went for a two-hour walk in the quaint Ukrainian village. There was no sunshine. The sky was dark, as a blanket of fog hung over the town, but they saw glimpses of weather-beaten cottages and foliage through the haze.

How quickly the afternoon went by. It was time for evening church already!

The service was long. A group of about 2,000 Slavs worshiping as one, was only one phase of the varied program. Music filled the large church as different musical groups took part.

Esther and Gordon made their way through the crowd as they walked to the big platform. As Esther ran her fingers over the keyboard, Gordon introduced the song they had chosen.

"*Slava Bogu*!" smiled the audience when they were finished.

"God bless you!" "*Zbogom*!" They knew He had.

MONDAY, JANUARY 10

Corinne awakened with swollen glands and a sore throat. One thing they vowed never to do, if possible, was to become sick in Eastern block countries. But when it happens, what does one do? With few medications available, and doctors they would rather not see, where could they turn?

Perhaps she needed rest. After getting to sleep at 5A.M., they slept for a few hours in the afternoon while Gordon and Pastor Nicholai went to Rovno to unpack the humanitarian aid containers.

Later Nadya, the young woman they met in church yesterday, came by to visit. Over a cup of hot *chi*, they talked.

"Yes, I have family in Canada. Sometimes they send us medication. Just recently we received antibiotics and I would like to share them with Corinne."

They were delighted. Hopefully, they would solve the problem without having to seeing a doctor.

They had another problem, too. They had run out of water. There was no mineral water left in the stores in the village. What should they do? They had to have water.

As their hostess boiled water tainted by Chernobyl on the stove, they knew they had to drink. Tasting bitter and warm, Corinne wrinkled her nose as she had a sip. Without water, her fever would not come down.

Nadya did bring the antibiotics and as Corinne swallowed her first one, Esther prayed this would be the remedy she needed.

RAIN—JANUARY 11

Another overcast, foggy day. They had anticipated snow at Christmastime, but instead, there was lots of rain, mud, and cold wind. So much for picturing romantic, showy Christmas scenes from the heart of the Ukraine.

While Gordon assisted the Ukrainians with the humanitarian aid project, Corinne and Esther stayed with Valentina. Always ready with a bite to eat or a cup of hot *chi*, she did her best with what she had. *Borscht*, tea, and day-old bread became daily breakfast fare, while they longed for a traditional American meal. What about coffee and toast? It was amazing how, together, they communicated in a mixture of Polish, Ukrainian, English, and Russian. But they understood each other as they sat around the table in the kitchen.

Esther was proud of her daughter. This girl was a trooper!

Corinne's fever continued to rise, while her glands, swollen and inflamed, did not get better. But eventually, as the antibiotics took effect, she began to feel like herself again. They breathed a sigh of relief.

Evening arrived. Nadya's brother, Walter Filuk, drove

into the Mularchuk yard blowing the car horn.

After putting their coats on, they all crowded into his old Lada car—Nadya's nephew, Corinne, Esther, Gordon, Walter, and Nadya.

Where were they going? It sounded like an adventure!

They were still in need of water, so Walter informed them they were on their way to St. Nicholai's where the water was clean to drink. This well, considered sacred, and cared for by the Orthodox Church, was used by some of the village people as well as others from the surrounding areas of about a thirty-kilometer radius.

Thirsting for clean water, Corinne bent down and filled her cup. Satisfied after drinking deep draughts, she handed the cup to her mother. Quickly, tastefully, the cool liquid went down her throat. What a different taste than the boiled, Chernobyl water!

Filling some plastic jars, Walter put the water into the trunk of the old Lada. Who can realize the value of water until you don't have any!

NADYA'S PARENTS

As they bumped along the muddy, corrugated road, suddenly, without warning, the front tire went flat. Quickly repairing it, they were soon on their way again.

Where were they going this time? Walter seemed to be full of surprises.

Looking down into a green valley, a small house with lights shining in the windows appeared. "We will visit here," he smiled.

Heartily welcomed by an older woman and her husband, they were asked inside.

"These are my parents," smiled Nadya. "This is where I grew up!"

Sitting beside the hot brick stove in the wall, they warmed their backs. A small, pregnant, cat shyly crawled into Corinne's lap, snuggled close, and went to sleep. Thinking of Fritz and Pumpkin Rose at home, she gently stroked the fur on the little animal.

It wasn't long before Nadya's mother had lunch on the table. Yes, they were hungry. It had been a long afternoon.

In small, glass cups, she served tea, grown in the valley from outdoor herbs. Refreshing and nourishing, they slowly sipped until it was gone. Eggs fried with bacon and potatoes was amazingly tasty.

Watching Corinne eat as she conversed with Nadya, made Esther happy. Her daughter was feeling better again.

But where was the bathroom? Quite certain it was not in the house, Esther decided to ask Nadya.

"It is very dark outside," she answered, "and the toilet is far away." Here, she demonstrated squatting down behind the barn, "you can just go in the barnyard."

Grateful for a place to go, they followed suit.

After praying and reading God's Word with the older couple, they said good-bye. Nadya, gently putting her arm around her mother, fondly smiled at her toothless father at the same time.

"Thank you, thank you!" they said as they walked out the door. Going up the hill toward the Lada in total darkness was a challenge, but together, they made it.

Later, snuggling under the small quilt, they were grateful for their "board bed."

But what was that noise? Loud, incessant scratching coming from under their board bed, they jumped up to check. Was it a mouse? What could they do?

They found nothing. Deciding to ignore the sound, they pulled the small quilt over their heads again and tried to go to sleep. It had been a good day!

"'Nite, Mom!"

"'Nite, Cori!"

"'Nite Gordon!"—but he was already snoring.

The alarm rang. Was it morning already? Hearing Nadya's voice from the kitchen, they knew she had arrived to pick them up. They had arranged yesterday to go shopping in Rovno. It would be interesting to see what kind of merchandise these stores carried.

But what was this? The shelves in the first store were almost empty. There was so little to buy and what there was cost a great deal of money.

Suddenly, while they were browsing, a worried-looking woman came and asked what they were doing.

"We are trying to shop," explained Nadya.

"Well, what do you think of my store?" she asked.

Expressing ourselves as positively as we could, she seemed relieved.

"People live in fear around here," Nadya told us later. "Living within themselves, they are constantly afraid of losing their jobs." So this is why the woman was so worried.

After buying a few trinkets, Corinne and Esther went to Nadya's apartment for lunch. Sitting around the small table, eating cheese, bread, and coffee, they talked freely about her family (whom they knew) in Canada. "Yes, I want to go there soon," she said. They hoped this would be possible.

Later, expecting Walter to come for them, they prepared to go.

A Visit with Walter's Family

Hearing the familiar *putt-putt* of the little Lada car, they ran out to meet him.

They had been told everyone was going swimming. Though it was getting late, they donned their swimsuits, and drove to the swimming pool. Esther knew she was not a good swimmer, but the cool, clear water refreshed and invigorated her.

Still later, piling into Walter's Lada again, they drove to his home. There, Katya, his wife, had a big dinner waiting—and yes, they were hungry after all that exercise!

Nine children shyly stood on the staircase and stared as the strangers walked into their house. This house held memories for Esther.

Years ago, they had come here for a large meal around this same table. Charlene was sick then. While holding her stomach in pain, they drove to their hotel room. Esther prayed, earnestly, sincerely for the health of her daughter. An answer came when, running toward the bathroom, she lost the heavy dinner. Pale and shaken, she crawled back into her bed and slept like a baby. Gratefully, with tears in her eyes, the mother thanked God for a quick healing.

Gradually now, sitting around the same table, Esther noticed the children beginning to open up to these strangers from the West. Soon everyone was laughing and talking.

Hugging Katya, and saying thank you, they filed out to the little Lada car.

Sleep didn't come easy that night. Corinne and Esther, hearing the "thing" in their room again, crawled under the bed to see what it was. Laughing hard, they held their sides, but couldn't see it. What or who could make noises so loud? It must be strong! Talking themselves into believing this was the heat radiators making the terrible noise (which secretly they knew it wasn't), they went to sleep about 5 A.M., quite exhausted. They were thankful for another interesting day.

GIFTS FOR AUNT MARTHA

Date: New Year's Eve 1994
Place: Ternopyl, Ukraine

Standing together in a small living room in the heart of the Ukraine, gratefully Aunt Martha clasped their hands. Tears filling her eyes, she thanked them on behalf of herself and her family, Nusha and Bogda, for coming to see them.

For over twenty years Gordon and Esther had traveled and worked with the people in Eastern Europe and Russia. Often they had wanted to visit with these family members, but due to stringent Communist control, were not allowed to be in their home. Before they entered the country, their trip was always scheduled in advance. Knowing the time of their arrival, everyday activities, as well as their departure, they were watched at all times. They were often followed. Esther would never forget the time they veered off their course, and became lost in the country. Very soon the KGB caught up and ordered them to go back to the city. They carefully followed the KGB car until they were on track once more. It was wise not to allow this to happen again!

Martha, who had never accepted Christ, was afraid if they tried to visit, she, too would be questioned by police and what would happen to her and her family?

Out of deference to Aunt Martha and the regulations they were expected to follow while in that country, they never went to see her until now.

Because the structure of government in the country had changed in recent years, with new freedom to go wherever they wanted without being followed by the police, or endangering the lives of others, Gordon, Corinne, and Esther made plans to meet these members of the family.

Gordon's Aunt Martha grew up in Ternopyl, Ukraine,

with her father, mother, and siblings. When her parents decided, many years ago, to migrate to Canada, all were allowed to go except one sister, Martha, who supposedly had an eye problem. Leaving her with friends, they assumed she could come later. Though letters were exchanged and efforts made to release her, it had never happened. Eventually, she married. A daughter and son were born to this union. Now she called this her home.

The day they left for Ternopyl dawned overcast and rainy. As the rain splashed onto the windows in the pastor's home in Rovno where they stayed, they knew this would be a wet day.

The soil, quickly turning to thick, red mud could make the journey difficult, but they didn't want to change their plans now!

They left the house in an old U.S. army truck. Their chauffeur, a Slav, drove them to a huge warehouse in the area first. Would they like to see the humanitarian aid sent to their country from America? He knew they would.

Here, supplies arriving from their warehouse in Seattle were put into storage, ready to be distributed to the people of that country.

Having sent several forty-ton containers to the Ukraine before leaving Seattle, they, along with the Slavs, were concerned that the latest shipment had not arrived. Victor, an immigrant from Seattle, visiting his parents, checked numerous times a day to see if the goods had come. Everyone was anxious. Had they gone astray? Did the Mafia steal them? There must be a reason why they had not arrived. They planned to find out.

But God's timing was perfect! The air was filled with excitement, when hundreds of apple crates with return addresses from Seattle and surrounding areas, arrived while they were there. To see packages, here in Rovna, from Everett, Kent, Lynnwood, and Renton was exciting.

Each box was designated to a different area in which loved ones were located. Now the relief would be distributed. Hungry families would benefit from sacks of flour, sugar, cereal, rice, vitamins, medication, and clothing.

Placing her hand on the nearest box, Esther whispered a prayer of thanksgiving to God. At least a few needy people would be fed and clothed.

At that time, the Slavic churches on the West Coast, together with the help of the East Europe Evangelism and Marshall Foundation, were responsible for shipping fourteen 40-foot, 40-ton containers to the Ukraine. It was a miracle to see their own warehouse in Seattle filled to capacity just before shipment each month—sometimes twice a month. They planned to send several more containers in January. They were committed to continue to assist in this worthwhile project.

Working in the Ukraine for several weeks, they saw extreme poverty everywhere. They could not help everyone, but here relatives of the West Coast immigrants would benefit—and they were grateful!

Packing the army truck with several boxes filled with necessary items not available in the Ukraine, they resumed their journey to Aunt Martha's in the mud and rain.

On the entire trip which took about two and a half hours, they saw very few vehicles on the road. Wondering why, when in the past there had been more traffic in the country, they asked their chauffeur.

"There is no gasoline," he answered. "And if there were, it would be too costly for the average person to fill his tank. So people take public transportation or just walk."

The pouring rain, mixing with heavy, wet soil, turned

into gumbo. The farther they drove into the countryside, the more their tires clogged up with mud.

They drove into a small village and stopped. Rolling down the splattered window, they asked for instructions to Aunt Martha's house. They figured people in remote areas usually knew everyone.

A toothless Baba, wearing a *Babushka* on her head, informed them excitedly. "Go to the right at the next intersection." Curious as a cat, she watched them. *Who were these strangers? Could it be possible that long-lost kin had arrived to see Martha?* She planned to find out later.

Following the instructions, they drove to where the muddy road ended, and pulled up beside a cottage. With the courtyard swept clean and colorful geraniums gracing weather-beaten window boxes, the cottage was like most others they had encountered. A bench sitting in the front yard, they knew, was often occupied by those who wanted to chat or gossip about the latest news.

Behind a weathered fence, stood a little Ukrainian woman. Smiling broadly, she knew where Martha lived. "Go about a kilometer down the road. She lives there!"

"But what road?" they wondered. There was no road. Later Aunt Martha told them that, though they had worked for the Government all their lives, there never was a road built to her place.

Impossible to drive even their powerful army truck through the deep mud, they wondered what route to take. They couldn't walk. They would lose their boots.

Did God bring us this far, only to have to turn back? They didn't think so.

An Angel?

Suddenly an unexpected answer came. Along came a

wagon pulled by two strong horses. The driver, commanding his animals to stop, smiled broadly. Gesturing for them to climb aboard, he offered to take them to Aunt Martha's house.

How did he know their dilemma? Where had this man come from? They hadn't seen him earlier. He seemed to have emerged out of thin air. Did God send an angel in the form of an old man?

"Watch your step," Gordon called, trying to help Corinne out of the truck. Holding her coat shut in the wind, and stepping into the gumbo, carefully she climbed into the primitive conveyance.

Esther's boots were caked with mud as she, too, stepped into this convenient, but crude, mode of travel.

The wind blew manure and big chunks of mud into their faces as they sat, single file in a wooden, V-shaped wagon that had been used to haul manure earlier in the day. The driver had scooped some of the matter out, and put straw into the trough, so it wouldn't smell too badly. At this point they really didn't care. Blankets, covering the weather-beaten seats, kept their clothing from mixing with the remains of the manure that still clung there. Their sides heaving, the horses strained to pull the wooden-wheeled wagon through the gumbo. Could they pull seven people even a few kilometers farther?

Sitting and shivering, they watched the wooden wheels, now coated with gumbo, straining without turning through the debris. Would they make it? They had to!

Rain continued to pelt the countryside. It was gray everywhere. The road, sky, fences, their faces, and even their clothing and boots were stained with mud. Cottages along the road were drab and colorless. Stained, gray geese, their heads held high, paraded in single file through the puddles—their feathers streaked with mud.

Esther's hair hung in kinky ringlets. Corinne's fur hat was so drenched, water was dripping into her eyes.

Suddenly everything became lighter. Two women stopped abruptly as they drove up beside a little Ukrainian house. The younger one, dropping two buckets, and promptly tripping over one with a muddy boot, raised her arms high and ran toward them.

"Gordon! Gordon!" she screamed. "It is you! You have come!"

Recognizing him from pictures sent by Gordon's mother at an earlier date, and expecting them to arrive in Ternopyl any time, she expressed her excitement unreservedly when she saw her cousin for the first time. They had sent word a few days before informing them they were coming. But due to poor phone connections, were never certain if they received the message. Obviously they had.

Carefully climbing out of the muddy wagon, they embraced. A lump caught in Esther's throat when she saw Martha. There, peering at them from beneath a Russian *Babushka*, was a face with the likeness of Gordon's mother. Shyly she smiled and took them in her arms. So this was Gordon, her sister Mary's eldest son! Tears filled her faded blue eyes, as she gently kissed him on one cheek and then the other.

Walking into the crowded front porch, they quickly removed their muddy boots and coats.

Rows of shoes and boots stood neatly in a row. Someone had carefully washed off the mud. They were clean for the next trip outdoors.

Immediately Nusha, her face flushed with excitement, hurried into the small kitchen to prepare a New Year's feast. There wasn't much money and food in Slavic homes, they had visited, however, they always brought out the best because they saved it for guests who may come to visit.

It didn't take long for the triangular table in the tiny living room, with a colorful cloth, to be filled with traditional foods such as *holidettes*, cabbage, salads, and *verenike*. More fortunate than city dwellers, they had fresh or canned produce on hand.

Standing beside the crowded table, they held hands and asked God's blessing on this bountiful array of food. Not accustomed to praying before a meal, Nusha stared. Did God really hear?

Eating didn't stop them from talking at the same time. There were so many things to share!

Then the conversation turned toward spiritual matters. "Aunt Martha," said Gordon in Ukrainian, "God has fashioned us according to His own image. He loved you enough to give His life for you and your family."

Interested now, she answered, "Gordon, I have been reading literature sent to us from Billy Kaju. For years, in these books, I have read the same story you are telling me now!" Tears filled her eyes again.

Billy Kaju, a Ukrainian evangelist, had led Gordon to the Lord in Canada when he was a child! Now, in the heart of Communist Ukraine, was Gordon hearing that his Aunt Martha was interested in the Gospel as a result of this man's faithful witness? Incredible!

As the chickens scratched in the courtyard around the little house, the cows waiting to be milked lowed in the barn, and pigs squealed in their pens, the family listened as Gordon shared the message of salvation. Carefully, simply, he outlined the message of the cross.

Suddenly the mood was changed. Hearing singing at the front of the house, Nusha ran to open the door. Greeted by a group of young people singing traditional New Year's songs, she invited them in.

"Happy New Year!" they chorused.

"Happy New Year!" answered their listeners, "and thank you!"

Their singing died away into the night, as slowly, they made their way to other houses in the area.

"I have to go to the bathroom," Esther whispered, nudging her husband. Cori, too, was sensing the urge of nature.

Informing Nusha of their plight, they walked into the small porch. Putting on their jackets and muddy boots, they walked out into the rain. Yes, the privy was outside! Walking between pigs, chickens, and cows in the barnyard, while dodging animal feces, they came nearer to their destination. The familiar odor of an outdoor toilet was not drowned out by the rain. The smell, fresh and rank, Esther went in first, while Corinne waited in the rain with Nusha.

Piled high in a frozen heap, the feces were heaped on the cold, wooden seat.

How could she handle this? Long ago she learned, that where there is a will, there is a way. She had to find it!

Coming out into the rain, now it was her daughter's turn to commit to the challenge.

It was soon time to leave. Corinne put her arms around Aunt Martha, tears filling her eyes. So this was her flesh and blood!

The older woman, placing a work-worn hand on Corinne's sweater, lovingly caressed the soft, pure wool. The young woman, touched, took the sweater off and handed it to her aunt.

"*Nyte*, *nyte*!" said Auntie.

"Please, *pozyalosta*," said Corinne.

Putting the beautiful sweater over her simple housedress and big apron, Aunt Martha finally had something pretty! She would wear it often.

Slipping into her once shiny Nordstrom boots, which were now shapeless and caked with mud, Esther noticed Aunt Martha looking at her feet.

"You're feet look just like ours!" laughed the woman.

Bogdon started his jeep. Here was a vehicle able to drive in muddy conditions such as they had that night. Steadily they crawled to their U.S. Army truck some kilometers away.

Waving until Aunt Martha and Nusha disappeared, they drove on into the distance.

The wind whipped around them, tore open their coats, and flung their hair around as they transferred the apple crates of humanitarian aid into Bogdan's waiting vehicle.

Suddenly Nusha appeared. There was no room for her in the crowded vehicle, so she ran down a higher side road where there was more grass, in order to be with them again. Helping transfer the goods, she worked alongside them. "I just wanted to see you one more time," she laughed. "Now that I found cousins, I don't want to lose them so soon!"

Ransacking their own suitcases, they added more to the growing pile of clothing in Bogdon's car. Perhaps there were needy neighbors? Usually there were.

Lost in thought, they slowly drove back to Rovno.

Was it coincidence that three large containers of humanitarian aid arrived while they were in the area? Was it mere chance that a man with a wagon and horses arrived to transport them to Aunt Martha's house just when they didn't know what their next step would be? Was it luck that they brought humanitarian aid, not realizing, though Nusha and Bogadan were employed, they had received no remuneration for several months? Living off Aunt Martha's meager widows' pension, they wept when Gordon gave them a gift of money and other aid.

God's timing is perfect. They had been obedient and

He used them to bless their extended family and others who were hungry.

As the old U.S. Army truck slithered through the mud on this dark, New Year's Eve, Corinne and Esther rested their heads on the cold back seat. It had been a big day and, though they were tired, their hearts were full of gratefulness to God. It had been a New Year's Eve to remember!

Hours later, the old Army truck continued to bounce along the muddy corrugated road toward the Mularchuk home. With the heater running on high, they dozed off.

"We are here!" announced Gordon from the front seat.

With muddy boots, soiled clothing, and dirty hair, Esther walked to the house. In the porch, she carefully pulled the boots off her swollen feet.

Running water into the small bathtub a little later, she felt the dirt leave her body. What a relief! Putting on her nightgown, she climbed into the board bed.

Corinne followed soon afterward. Even the small bed felt comfortable after slithering around in the army truck.

Just about to doze off into a peaceful sleep, the "creature" started to scratch and crunch the plastic in Esther's suitcase. Was he trying to eat the chocolates they had bought in Germany?

Putting her earplugs into her ears, she tried to shut out the noise. Finally about 2 A.M., they both went to sleep.

What a day it had been! They had traveled six hours on a terribly muddy road. After miraculously getting to Aunt Martha's house, they bonded with family they had never met before. Sensing a kinship, they were satisfied and happy to have made the effort to meet their extended family.

In the morning, Esther checked her suitcase. The plastic on the box of chocolates was torn to shreds. Yes, the "creature thing" was serious! He was hungry!

UKRAINIAN COUNTRYSIDE

While Gordon continued to help the Ukrainians with the humanitarian aid, Corinne and Esther faced a long day in the house with Valentina and the "creature thing."

Putting their boots on, they went for a long walk in the village. Here was the real Ukraine! Small houses, with blue windowpanes and lacy curtains, lined the streets. Boxes of geraniums standing in the windows reminded them acutely of Mary Balisky, who had once lived in this area, too.

Most of the houses, flanked by muddy, dirty streets, looked similar. Sometimes a small courtyard divided one house from the other. Usually these were neatly swept clean, but now heavy mud covered everything, everywhere.

Invariably a family dog was tied up with a rope beside the house, and barked furiously when they walked past. Warning his owner there were intruders nearby, he had done his duty.

Often the family cat, resting on the windowsill, meowed as they walked by. Some, arching their backs, came toward them for a gentle stroke.

Because the families are usually large, children were everywhere. This was the holiday season, and they were not in school.

That night the "creature thing" was busy again. Corinne and Esther put food under the bed for him and Esther closed her suitcase so he couldn't eat the treasured chocolate bar. In the morning, the food under the bed was all gone.

Realizing they would soon be leaving this village, they knew he must be christened. So they dubbed him Leonard Bihate. Now the "creature" (who turned out to be a large mouse) had a name!

SUNDAY

After taking part in the Sunday service the next day, they went to another home for lunch. Mara and Yuri and their family were moving to Seattle soon. Boxes and piles of things stood everywhere.

Around a long table filled with food, they asked questions about their new home. "How big is Seattle? Are the houses like the ones in Ukraine? We heard the United States is like heaven. Is it true?"

Corinne and Esther exchanged glances. Not speaking out loud, they both knew that, indeed, their country was like heaven in comparison. They could hardly wait to get there again.

This family knew that life would be challenging when they moved to the States. Living on welfare and becoming adjusted to a new country is never uncomplicated. They would have to find out for themselves. But these people looked with anticipation to living in the land flowing with milk and honey. Was not everyone rich there? They hoped someday, they, too, would have a lot of money.

To the Baliskys, it seemed a little sad this family was willing to leave a good church home, a comfortable house, uproot their many children, and leave their furnishings (including a piano) behind. Just before their departure, the hostess took Corinne to a cupboard filled with dishes and crystal. Reaching in, she presented her with a lovely crystal bowl. "I can't take all these things with me," she sighed. "I want you to have this!"

Corinne knew the value of a dish such as this and thanked her friend with sincerity.

"Esther, I want you to have these dishes," she said, as her guest followed her to another cupboard. Taking a beautiful gold and maroon tea set from where it had stood for years, she gave it to Esther.

"Thank you! I will treasure it always. It will have a special place in my home!" replied Esther.

GOOD-BYE

Later, saying good-bye to Valentina and Nicholai, they thanked them sincerely for the love they had shown to them.

"How can we repay you for all you have done for us?" choked the big man. "God bless you!" Kissing Gordon on one cheek and then the other, the men embraced.

"God bless you, Nicholai and Valentina!"

The humanitarian aid from the United States was greatly appreciated by the people. What would they have done without it?

A letter and Certificate of Appreciation were sent to their offices in Seattle from the U.S. Department of State, recognizing the work in which East Europe Evangelism and Marshall Foundation were involved.

Containers are still being sent to Ukraine and Russia today.

OPERATION SUPPORT FREEDOM

May 5, 1995

Mr. Gordon Balisky
The Marshall Foundation
19506 Fremont Ave. N
Seattle, WA 98133

Dear Mr. Balisky:

In our recent edition of our newsletter, "The Humanitarian," we announced an award program acknowledging the work of select organizations participating in Operation Support Freedom.

Based on our information, The Marshall Foundation has shipped 31 containers to various locations in the former Soviet Union. In recognition of this contribution to Operation Support Freedom and the people of the New Independent States, MPRI-NIS is presenting you with this "Certificate of Appreciation." Your efforts have improved the lives of the citizens of the NIS and helped make OSF one of the United States' most successful programs. This award is simply our way of letting you know your contribution has not gone unnoticed.

Congratulations and best wishes for continued success.

Sincerely,
James W. Bayer
Project Director

CERTIFICATE OF APPRECIATION

In recognition of continued participation in "Operation Support Freedom" and tireless dedication to improving the lives of the citizens of the New Independent States, The Marshall Foundation is presented with this certificate on May 1, 1995

James W. Bayer Charles R. Hardest
Project Director Dir., Humanitarian Assistance
MPRI-NIS U.S. Department of State

35 ALENA'S NEW LOOK

"Let's leave!" called the chauffeur. "It's time to go!" After packing their bags and bidding Nicholai and Valentina farewell, they boarded the old army truck again.

Ralph Balisky, Gordon's cousin, had been in Kiev recently. Phoning him before leaving Seattle, he told them about Ryesa and Anatoly.

Their first and only child, Alena, a victim of the Chernobyl disaster in Kiev, was born with a deformed lip. Determined to find help, the couple looked all over the city for a doctor who could operate. Could this problem be corrected with surgery? The emphatic answer was "*Nyet*! There is nothing we can do!" When realizing their little girl would have to live with an impediment for the rest of her life because there was no help, miraculously, Ralph had come along. Yes, he decided, he would take the family to Canada. Perhaps they could operate there. Anatoly said good-bye to

Anatoly and Ryesa with daughter Alena.

his wife and daughter, and went with the uncle from Canada first, expecting to send for them later.

Now, Gordon's part in the saga was to take Ryesa and Alena with them to Canada. Putting herself and her child into God's hands, though she had never seen the Baliskys before, she would trust them. Yes, she would go with these people. Her family agreed. What else could they do?

Walking up a flight of stairs, they met Ryesa and her family face to face. Greeting them at the door was a beautiful young woman. Gesturing, she invited them in to meet the others. Baby Alena, shyly peering at them from behind her mother's skirts, smiled crookedly, displaying a new, white baby tooth. Grandma, Grandpa (Ryesa's parents), Vera, her sister, and others shook their hands.

The aroma of beet *borscht* wafted in from the kitchen. "Please be seated," smiled Vera, "I have made soup!"

The table was so small, only some of them could sit. The rest, helping themselves, ate cafeteria style. Quickly the hot soup went down.

Grandma, many times during the evening, tried to hide the fact she was wiping tears from red-rimmed eyes. Her daughter and grandchild were leaving! When would she see them again? Perhaps never?

Taking the tiny hands of the toddler's in her own, she carefully guided her around the crowded room. Proud of her first steps, the child laughed out loud. Could the doctors in the West repair a lip that disfigured the child's face so? They sincerely hoped so.

But where would everyone sleep? The one-bedroom apartment was tiny. How would they all manage? After the five-hour trip from Rovno in the rickety old truck, they felt the need to rest. Tomorrow, they knew, would be another big day. Then, the day after that, packing, driving to the airport, and leaving for Vancouver, there were many details to be looked after.

Baby Alena's crib was in the living room. Grandma and Grandpa chose to sit in chairs nearby. Ryesa and Vera, too, would sleep on the floor. What about Esther, Gordon, and Corinne? Where would they sleep?

"Here, Corinne and Esther," smiled Ryesa, "you can sleep in our bedroom." The room was packed with boxes and clothing, but they were grateful—and embarrassed to take the only bed.

"Gordon, you can pull this chair into the kitchen. That is all we can offer you."

Taking his chair with him, he wondered where to park. Everything was full!

Corinne and Esther, feeling rather selfish, couldn't hide the giggles coming on. Turning their faces to the wall and trying to stifle the sound, they laughed until their faces were red. Gordon didn't think it was funny! And really, it wasn't. It was easy to laugh when one was not supposed to. But, secretly, they couldn't help it.

January 17—Exploring the City

Breakfast was waiting when they woke up from a fitful sleep. *Holopsie*, salads, bread, and porridge soon filled their stomachs. They realized Vera must have risen early to prepare such a feast. Of course, Gordon had to move his chair out of the kitchen at that hour, too.

They noticed Grandma stayed with Alena every moment she could. While holding her small hands in her own, it was evident that the child, too, loved her grandma. It was not easy for the aging grandparents to be willing to let their children go, but they knew that if Alena was going to have a normal life, they would have to.

The old truck appeared at the apartment. Were they ready to go downtown? This would be exciting!

They were told the population of Kiev, one of the largest cities in Russia, was three and a half million. Though many of the historic buildings were in need of repair, the city was full of historical adventure.

Lying on the Dnieper River, in a region rich with farms and industries, it was an important railroad center and had many factories. Esther noticed thick, gray smoke curling steadily from many industrial buildings.

Kiev was known as one of the most beautiful Soviet cities, as well. The old section, once strongly fortified, stood high on a cliff overlooking the Dnieper.

They thought it was exciting when Ryesa told them the city was the sight of Russia's first Christian church, built before AD 944.

Rebuilt after the German forces caused severe damage in World War II, the city completed a new subway and sports arena seating 15,000 persons.

After giving them this information, the driver deposited them on Main Street.

The day went by rapidly as Ryesa took them from shop to shop. How did she find time to do this when she was leaving the day after tomorrow? Perhaps she had done most of her packing already?

Corinne's eyes lit up when valuable, Russian icons caught her trained eye. With her American dollars, she purchased them for only 15 dollars each. She knew just the spot where she would place them in her apartment in Los Angeles.

Hailing a taxi some time later, they were soon at the crowded apartment again—and again dinner was ready. Grandma still walked around with her precious grandchild. When Ryesa entered, her eyes filled with tears. How could she bear to part with her loved ones?

Everyone talked at once as they sat down to eat their *borscht*. The apartment was cold, but with many bodies, gradually it warmed up. Drinking hot *chi* helped, too.

Morning dawned. Only one more day in the Ukraine.

That night, before they all retired, Ryesa burst into the apartment and announced, "Hey, everyone! It's snowing!" Looking outside, they saw big, white flakes fly past the window, and settle on the soil below. Covering mud and debris, the streets appeared like a picture post card. Finally, after all

the mud and rain, it was snowing! And tomorrow they had to leave!

Ryesa had errands to run so, along with Corinne, they combed the streets of the city again. Corinne, enjoying the action, willingly went with the young woman who had things to do.

Calling the apartment some time later, they informed Esther that there was an opera in the big theater that night. Would they like to go? It was *Don Quixote*. Yes, they would love to go! At home, a performance such as this could cost up to 200 dollars per person. Here, in Kiev, when the girls purchased the tickets, they found the cost was 2.50 dollars a piece. The price was right!

Entering the huge Belshoi opera house, they were soon seated near the front. The three-hour presentation left them breathless! With elegant costuming, famed operatic singers, and wonderful acting, they listened spellbound and intrigued. When the huge curtains came down, the applause was almost deafening! Of course, they clapped louder than anyone else! Going to an opera in the middle of a snowy winter in the heart of this great city, was an experience none of them would forget.

At the apartment again, hot soup simmering on the stove, soon disappeared. The cold weather, increasing their appetites, had made them as hungry as small cubs.

The hour was late. Still no one wanted to go to bed. Carefully, thoughtfully packing the last of the necessary items she would take to Canada, Ryesa wiped tears away. But soon she would see Anatoly—that was something special. Would arrangements for Alena's surgery be made soon? She would find out shortly! The small apartment was feverish with activity. Vera, attempting to tidy the small kitchen, tipped over boxes and suitcases.

Grandma put the last of Alena's baby clothes into her crowded bags. Some of Ryesa's suitcases stood in readiness by the door, while other boxes and bags cluttered the small apartment. When could they go to bed? Corinne nudged Esther. She was very tired, but Ryesa was packing in the bedroom. So they sat… and waited.

The phone peeling into the lateness of the night, never seemed to stop. In between calls, Corinne called her friend, David, in Los Angeles. Was the news they were receiving about a 6.6 earthquake in California correct? She had to find out.

Amazingly, she made connections. "Hello!" came David's voice. "Yes, Corinne, we have had an earthquake, and it's been devastating."

"How is my apartment?" she asked, fear edging her voice.

"Your pictures and some other things smashed to the floor and are broken. Your dishes are fragments and the house is cracked," he answered. "The lights in the city are out, and thirty-one have been declared dead already. Thousands of homes have been leveled and destroyed, and freeways and bridges are out."

Dazed, Corinne put down the receiver. Had she been there, perhaps she, too, would have been hurt—or worse—killed? Thanking God she was not present when the earthquake hit, Corinne knew she was blessed. Temporary values could be replaced but God had spared her from possible injury and emotional trauma. Also, thankfully, common sense told her to pack her prettiest things away in a box before making the trip to the Ukraine. How could she be so fortunate?

No one went to sleep until morning. Corinne and Esther, finally pulling the covers over their heads, tried to catch a few hours of rest. Gordon, in his chair in the

kitchen, was wide awake. How could he sleep when chaos reigned? He didn't. Perhaps he could get a few "winks" in the airplane later.

January 18—Departure

In the morning, the water pipes were frozen, the heat rads closed off, and the apartment icy cold. How could Vera prepare breakfast for her departing guests? Somehow she managed. She had to.

Excitement and tears ran hand in hand as Ryesa's departure drew closer. The house was still a medley of phone calls, suitcases scattered everywhere, and people coming in to say good-bye. Hugs, prayers, and blessings surrounded the young woman who had always made Kiev her home. How could she leave everything—and everyone?

The doorbell rang again.

"Ryesa, your chauffeur is here! Time to go now!" called her father from the other room. Letting go of Alena's small hand, Grandma, along with seven others, stepped into the waiting vehicle.

Someone had to stay at the apartment because there wasn't room for everyone in the crowded bus.

Grandpa, holding daughter and granddaughter in a fierce bear hug, had to let go. They were leaving. Waving as long as he could see them, slowly, tearfully, he shuffled into the empty apartment. But maybe the little family would come back soon? Alena's surgery would be over then. Encouraged, he looked out the window and watched the white snow fall gently to the ground.

The suitcases outnumbered the amount allotted to take on the plane, so capably, Gordon shipped several on ahead to Canada. Still there was a lot of luggage because Ryesa had to pack for herself, as well as her child and husband. There seemed to be no end of baggage, but she claimed it was all necessary. Ours added to the enormous pile.

Going through passport control and baggage claim took a very long time. Finally, heaving a sigh of relief, they stepped onto the small aircraft. They were on their way!

Alena began to cry. Then her cries turned to screams after they were airborne. Ryesa, at the end of her self, slumped wearily onto the back of the seat. Alena, throwing herself from side to side, wouldn't stop crying. Finally, after a long time, exhausted, she and her weary mother dropped off to sleep.

The Baliskys were happy when the wheels of the plane had left the runway of Ukraine soil. Now it was good to feel them touch ground in Frankfurt. Corinne breathed a sigh of relief. "I feel like kissing the ground," she smiled. "Now we are really home!" Esther agreed.

Driving to the Ramada Inn after collecting all their baggage, Ryesa, in awe and wonder, looked around her. Kiev, with it's teaming millions, was nothing like this. Clean, wide streets, and huge, efficient buildings stood everywhere. Well-dressed men and women, hurrying to and fro, were intent on business at hand. Wherever she looked, everything seemed to be in order.

There were no poisonous fumes belching from chimneys, no old cars and trucks. Here, she could breathe freely. *Could heaven be a little like this*? she pondered.

After checking into rooms 1012 and 1014, they went to the dining room for dinner.

Oh, the aroma of *rahm schnitzel* (beef cutlet) and fresh, strong coffee! Corinne couldn't wait to see a menu. Ryesa, in shock, just stared. Trying to keep Alena quiet was a problem. Once again, the child, wriggling in her arms, and eventually breaking out in screams, seemed to be uncontrollable. How could they have dinner under these circumstances? Ryesa tried in vain to quiet the little girl. Tears welling up in her eyes, she wished Anatoly was there to help.

Placing her order, Esther gently took the young mother and child up to their room as Gordon arranged for a dinner to be delivered there.

Corinne, Esther, and Gordon enjoyed the elegance, efficiency, and good food while they dined in peace. Ryesa, on the other hand, quieted Alena as she bathed her in the sink. When the child finally went to sleep, she enjoyed her dinner quietly. So this was German cuisine? Admitting she liked it a lot, the young mother ate every crumb.

Morning arrived too soon. They had a plane to catch. There was no time to relax in their comfortable quarters.

Taking all the luggage out of the hotel rooms and into the airporter bus was a big job. Gratefully, Gordon was still with them, although he'd had to make arrangements to take a different flight due to previous commitments.

Going through baggage control, after checking everything in, they were told to go and identify each piece of their luggage. What a pain! But carefully looking through dozens of suitcases and packages, they finally found their own. Then, thankfully, it was time to board.

Esther carried Alena while Ryesa and Corinne's arms were loaded with carry-on bags.

Alena screamed as if she was being tortured. While wriggling in her arms, Esther held the child tight. What was wrong with her? Did she sense the seriousness of this upheaval?

Finally, they were all settled in their seats, quietly resting. Alena ceased her tantrums, and dozed in the arms of her overwhelmed mother.

The trip went by quickly. "Ladies and gentlemen, we

are now nearing the Vancouver airport. Please fasten your seat belts."

What? Already? Ryesa silently wondered what came next. Would her Anatoly be there to meet them?

Looking out the window on her side, Esther saw the mountains appear far below. The sun, casting light onto the massive range, caused the mountains to glow with an ethereal brightness.

They felt and heard the familiar thump. They were on Canadian soil! The Ukraine seemed a world away.

The wheel on Esther's crowded cart broke after much straining and puffing, to pack all the luggage inside. Then every piece had to be unloaded! Sweat stood out on Corinne's forehead as she lifted it into another cart. Ryesa carried Alena, so getting all the luggage through passport control was the responsibility of Esther and Corinne.

What a relief to push the crowded carts into the terminal! But where was their ride? Would Gordon's cousin, Larry Balisky, be there, or perhaps Anatoly?

While calling their names, two young men searching through the crowd, came toward them.

"Here we are!" shouted Corinne waving her arms.

Larry had sent them. Bless his heart. It was a relief to let them push the carts out to the waiting vehicle.

Driving through the city toward Abbotsford, Alena and Ryesa were strangely quiet. Would this be their new home? No matter, Anatoly would look after that. Ryesa resting in this fact, could now relax.

Driving into Grandpa and Grandma Balisky's familiar yard in Abbotsford, it was wonderful to disembark and great their loved ones.

"Did you see my sister, Martha?" asked Gordon's mother, with a look of anticipation in her eyes.

"Yes, we have so much to tell you!" laughed Corinne. "Come on, Grandma, let's go inside."

Of course she had dinner on the stove.

By the time the little family from the Ukraine were reunited, Ryesa clung to the man who had promised to be her protector. He held baby Alena close and vowed to help his family to adjust to this strange, new country. Alena, he was certain, would have a changed countenance once the anticipated surgery was over.

Larry, true to his word, had sent the boys to pick them up at the airport. Now smiling, he greeted them all in Ukrainian. When Esther and Corinne replied in that language, he laughed. "You and Corinne speak well! You have learned a lot!"

Paul Milken, an immigrant from the Ukraine, had come all the way from Seattle to take Esther and Corinne home. Gratefully, they thanked him. Gordon's flight would not be arriving for some time. He would have to arrange for his own ride when he reached Abbotsford.

When they arrived in the familiar yard on Fremont Avenue North, Fritz and Pumpkin Rose came to meet them. Purring and kneading affectionately, they greeted their favorite people. Corinne would have to leave for her home in Los Angeles soon, but tonight, contented, they were home.

Surgery

Surgery for baby Alena was imminent. But how could this be accomplished? Thousands of dollars were necessary to do such extensive facial surgery. Gordon, knowing he had a big God, started to make calls to various hospitals.

Meanwhile, the Ukrainian family living at Larry's felt a little apprehension. Did they come all this way just to be turned down? Life everywhere for their Alena would be difficult without surgery. Surely God cared enough to accomplish a miracle for a little Ukrainian girl who had been adversely affected by the Chernobyl disaster? Yes, He did!

"Doctor Balisky, tell us about the Chernobyl disaster," said the specialist, phoning from Shriners Hospital in Portland.

"When the nuclear reactor exploded in April of 1983, it sent radiation in steam that mingled with the air to a high level of 20,000 feet. The lower radiation traveled in lower areas. One cloud went southwest, another traveled over the city of Gomal in Russia. It has a population of 450,000 people and was severely affected. The clouds continued up past Minsk, over Latvia and Finland and across Norway and Sweden—then through England and Scotland. Some radiation was even detected in the Pacific Northwest. There, too, they were taking milk off the grocery shelves," replied Gordon.

"Yes, I remember that," said the doctor. "What were the long-range effects and how did they affect the people?"

"Deformed children are still being born today," answered Gordon. "Physical and psychological agony of mothers and children were beyond description during those terrible days, and many are still suffering."

"Being more specific, what are the long-range effects?" asked the doctor.

"X-rays have shown functional organs such as liver, lung, and kidneys to be deformed," answered Gordon. Kidneys sometimes resemble long string beans rather than their normal shape. Lungs take up an entire chest cavity, hearts are greatly enlarged, bone structure has often been deformed. Blindness and stomach problems are common."

"Is the soil still contaminated?"

"Yes. People dig vegetables from that same soil because they have to eat. Potatoes, beets, and carrots, too, are poisoned. Grain used for bread is still contaminated."

"You say, Doctor Balisky, the child Alena has been affected?"

"Yes, Sir," he answered. "Do you have a solution?"

"Bring the child into Children's Hospital. We will take a look to see what can be done."

"Thank you!" Gordon exclaimed as he hung up the phone. God was at work!

The phone rang in Larry and Loraine's house in Chilliwack. "Please bring Alena to Seattle as soon as possible," said Gordon. "The doctor wants to look at her."

Larry was excited when he called Anatoly and Ryesa to his side. Soon they were speeding toward Gordon and Esther's house in Seattle. The next destination would be Portland, Oregon.

"Please, God, make it all right!" prayed Ryesa. "Please heal our little girl!" She knew nothing was too hard for Jesus. No man could work like Him!

The doctors at Shriners Hospital knew there was hope for the little Ukrainian girl. They promised to do the surgery on Alena's lip at no cost to the parents.

Gordon was elated. After many hours on the phone, he knew this was a direct answer to everyone's prayers, including his own.

Surgery was scheduled. Ryesa, Anatoly, Esther, and Gordon stayed nearby. The hours ticked by, while capable doctors worked to restore the face of the child. Ryesa, pacing back and forth, wrung her hands. Surely these doctors would make her child beautiful? But to the mother, she was the most beautiful child in the world with or without surgery.

Watching the clock, Anatoly shuffled his big feet. It was difficult to sit still when he knew their only child was under the surgeon's knife. Gordon and Esther prayed. Surely she would be okay?

Awakening, bandaged and dazed, the little girl stared at unfamiliar surroundings. Hearing her mother's voice, immediately she was alert. Her fears calmed, she held onto her daddy's big hand.

Alena was in the hospital under observation for days, while the parents, staying nearby, were with her most of the time.

"You can take the child home now," said her surgeon one day.

But where was home? Would they go back to Canada or stay in Seattle with Gordon and Esther?

They stayed with Gordon and Esther for three months. Slowly Alena's lip healed, giving her a brand new appearance. Red, raw skin replaced by new, tender skin, gave the parents joy and hope.

Many times Ryesa, longing for her family, unburdened her heart to Esther during those days. Yes, she was lonely. Not understanding the language, and unfamiliar with the culture and ways of the American people, often she was frustrated. How does one turn on a microwave oven? How does the countertop stove work? How could she wash her baby's clothes when she didn't know how to use the washing machine? These were a few of the simple but complicated questions for which she needed answers.

Patiently, tenderly, Gordon and Esther helped the couple meet their needs. Larry and Lorraine Balisky did the same when the family went to live with them in Canada.

Life was different in America and Canada, but they vowed, as their daughter grew stronger, to live there and become adjusted to the new culture. And after time, they did.

Gratefully clinging to Esther when they left Seattle, Ryesa thanked her for solace and guidance during the most difficult time in her life. Alena, too, putting her small arms around Esther's neck, wouldn't let go. Though they came

from different cultures, they were one in the bond of love.

God had given the Baliskys wisdom to assist a family in need and that family would never forget.

Ralph Balisky, who planned it all in the first place, died soon after this, but his legacy lives on.

36 MARY BALISKY GOES TO SLEEP

It was April 7, 1994, and Esther and Gordon were visiting his parents in Abbotsford, B.C. in Canada. After returning from the Ukraine, they continued to share their experiences.

Esther turned to her mother-in-law and said, "Mother, would you like to come and stay with us in Seattle next weekend?"

"Yes, I would like that," she answered.

It had been a difficult time for Mary. Struggling to keep back the tears, the promise that they would come back to Abbotsford for her, put a light in her tired eyes.

Yes, she would be waiting.

Hugging her, they said good-bye.

Watching them till they were almost over the hill, they heard her call, "See you next week-end!"

Their visit never did transpire. Mary went to be with the Lord the following Sunday, the day they had planned to bring her to Seattle.

SHOCKING NEWS

The phone rang shrilly. Esther rose to answer it.

"Hello? Yes, this is Esther... No, Gordon is not here right now, Sheila. A few days ago, he was called away to help plant another Slavic church in Portland. Can I have him call you when he gets home?"

"Yes, please do," she answered. Her voice was strained and hushed. "I just wanted to tell you that Mom went home to be with the Lord this afternoon."

"What?" Esther was stunned. "What happened?"

"She went to church this morning with Aunt Pearl. Together, they took communion and sensed the presence of the Lord. After making lunch for Daddy, she said, 'I am tired, Bill,' and went to rest. Covering herself with a light blanket, she was soon asleep. He went to check on her later, because she had slept so long, and found that she was not breathing! Mother was gone!"

"I will call Gordon in Portland right away. God bless you, Sheila!"

Sheila said good-bye, her voice filled with tears.

Planning to go to Abbotsford as soon as Gordon arrived, they were too late. Now she was in her heavenly home. They knew there was no better place to be, but how they would miss her!

This was all so sudden! Gordon was shocked when Esther told him his mother had gone to her eternal home. Everyone was.

"I planned to be home today, so we could go to Abbotsford and get Mother," he said, his voice choking.

How could it be? Yesterday, though tired, she seemed to be fine... today she was with her Father in heaven.

On April 13, 1994, somber and shocked, the family viewed the body of the one who had been a vibrant, loving mother.

Esther put her arm around her father-in-law, as together, they stood looking at the woman who had been his faithful helpmeet and companion for so many years.

"Rest in peace, Mother, rest in peace," she murmured.

Funeral Service

The Abbotsford Baptist church was hushed as the family walked silently to the front of the crowded sanctuary. All were there to pay tribute to a woman who had walked with God.

While Joyce Warkentin played the organ prelude, everyone sat in the presence of death, yet they knew death was swallowed up in victory. Would they wish her back?

"How Great Thou Art," "What a Day That Will Be," "Safe in the Arms of Jesus," and "Trust and Obey" were songs she would have chosen. Reverently, softly, the congregation joined in, meditating on each verse as they sang.

Esther, at the request of the family, went to the front and shared the Tribute To Mother with the silent congregation.

At the cemetery, Corinne, Charlene, and Steve stayed beside their grandmother's grave after the others had gone. Quietly grieving, they distinctly heard and felt a breath of wind flow gently over the closed casket. Was this God's benediction?

Mary Machuk's Family

The Moses Machuk family—Mary's parents—migrated from Domuninka, Ukraine, to Alberta, in the spring of 1929. Mary, born into a loving family of seven children, was the second child.

Settling on a homestead, Moses built a small log cabin for his family, consisting of one room. Here, the family lived, loved, and integrated into the community.

Later, moving to Highland Park, Alberta, Mary worked

for a man whose wife had passed away leaving four children.

Bill Balisky, a young man in the community, heard about the hard-working young woman. "She must be a responsible person to look after all those children," he mused. "I want to meet her."

And meet her he did.

God brought Bill and Mary together. To this union, six children were born.

Their simple and sincere faith was not only communicated in word but in deed in every part of their lives. Their home was always open to neighbors and visitors.

Her culinary talents extended to many. Freshly baked goods, especially her apple pie, according to her sister, Pearl, appealed to many guests. Ukrainian *holopsie*, perogies, *verenike* and home-cooked soup were more of her specialties.

The Joy of Serving

Esther had known Gordon's mother was a good cook before they were married, but afterwards she had more time to sample her delicious culinary delights.

As a new bride, Gordon took her to his home one weekend for the first time as his wife. Entering the house, intoxicating aromas greeted them. She still remembered the flavor of the sweet and sour meatballs. Delicately browned to perfection, they swam in a rich brown sauce that was unforgettable. Crusty brown rolls, fresh from the oven, were moist and soft on the inside. Fluffy mashed potatoes smothered in dairy butter, melted in her mouth. Succulent deep apple pie was served for dessert along with freshly perked coffee.

Gordon's old bedroom had been carefully prepared for them. Esther would find that his mother always took pride in freshly laundered sheets and pillowcases. Giving off a sweet outdoor scent, they reminded her of blooming lilacs on a summer day.

Waking from sleep in the morning, another aroma made Esther realize she was as hungry as a young cub.

Freshly perked coffee, the sweet smell of bacon and eggs, and toast browning in the toaster over, caused her to nudge her sleeping husband. Upon awakening, he, too, inhaled the tantalizing aromas that wafted throughout the house. It didn't take long to dress. Laughing, they raced down the stairs. And breakfast was as delicious as it smelled. In this house, Esther knew her girlish figure would disappear quickly.

Since that week so long ago, Esther's mother-in-law served them royally whenever they came home. There was always ample food on hand. Dad saw to that. He loved to shop. The deep freeze downstairs was filled with food, from homemade rolls and desserts to fresh meat and frozen *borscht.*

Charlene and Corinne enjoyed going to Grandma's house, knowing that she would always have something good to eat. They were never disappointed.

Several of Mother and Dad Balisky's children lived in the vicinity of their parents' home. Everyone always felt free to come home. Joyfully, she took time for them and her many grandchildren—everyone feeling welcome and special to Grandma.

And others coming from far and near sensed a warm atmosphere as she welcomed them into her home.

Birthdays were never forgotten as carefully she selected a special card for each one.

Then she became critically ill. Languishing, she spent many weeks in the hospital.

Her busy hands lay idle—her feet usually active, were still. After numerous tests, vigilant doctors and nurses carefully watched her in the intensive care unit. Calling the hospital often, they waited prayerfully, hoping their mother would be well again.

Finally, arriving home, weak and exhausted, she had no energy to entertain guests or do her work around the home. A nurse was called in to help with tasks mother could not accomplish in her weakened state.

It was difficult for her to sit by and watch others do what she had enjoyed doing for so many years. The light in her eyes was gone, her smile faded. The joy of living had disappeared.

Slowly time went by, and gradually some of her energy returned.

The phone rang one day. She was having guests from out of town. Excited, she began to prepare a meal for them, working slowly and carefully. Color came into her wan cheeks and light came back into her listless eyes as she set the table with her beautiful china. Once more the house was filled with tantalizing aromas as apple pies baked in her oven, and colorful *borscht* simmered on the burner.

Going to answer the ringing doorbell, happily she welcomed her guests into the house.

The joy of living had returned! Mother could serve others again!

Mary Balisky had very little formal education, however, the school of experience and God's wisdom was much more valuable than any education could have given her.

The Lord was preparing to take her home as her health deteriorated. He snatched her away from suffering and pain to be with Him forever.

IN MEMORIAM

God looked around His garden
And found an empty space.
He then looked upon His earth
And saw your tired face.

He put His arms around you
And lifted you to rest.
God's garden must be beautiful—
He only takes the best.

He knew that you were suffering,
He knew you were in pain.
He knew you would never get well
Upon this earth again.

He saw the road was getting rough
And the hills were hard to climb,
So He closed your weary eyelids
And whispered, "Peace be thine."

It broke our hearts to lose you
But you never went alone.
For part of us went with you
The day God called you home.

-author unknown

Disappointment

While Esther and Gordon were away on another trip, Ryesa and Anatoly lived in the house and looked after Esther's cats. Upon arriving home again, Fritzy did not come to meet them. What was wrong? A concerned Anatoly came to the car and told them their little companion was in the hospital.

"What happened?" Esther asked, while Pumpkin, happy to see her, purred in her arms.

"I found him outside on the road. Apparently a car had driven over his head and left him to die. I was scared," he said. "What should I do? I ran to the neighbor, and Cheryl, across the street, took him to the vet. He is in the hospital now."

Anatoly looked worried and sad. Could he have prevented this terrible thing from happening? "Meanwhile," he said, "Pumpkin has cried for his brother, and refuses to be comforted."

Esther didn't take time to go into the house. Racing in her car to where her little friend lay mortally wounded, she ran inside. "I would like to see Fritzy Rose. How badly is he hurt?"

"We are doing everything we can," answered the vet.

When Esther entered the room, her cat was moaning in pain. Laboriously turning his head when he heard her voice, the wounded animal cried piteously. Yes, his dearest friend had come.

She couldn't hold him, or stroke his fur, but her presence seemed to comfort him momentarily.

Painfully his eyes followed her when she moved. Esther couldn't stand it! Weeping softly, she talked to him, trying to console her frightened, little friend.

In frustration, he tried to get up but it was not possible. Would he die?

CORINNE'S VISIT

Grandma Balisky passed away just a week before the cat did. When Corinne heard that her beloved Grandma was gone, and Fritzy had been mortally wounded, she wept. Tears fell into her suitcase as she prepared to go home to face two deaths.

Quietly she talked to God. He would help her through.

She arrived home just before Fritzy died. Knowing her voice, he revived for a moment, but soon closed his eyes for the last time.

Corinne, Esther, and Gordon planted three apple trees in honor of Corinne's surrogate Grandpa Art, Grandma Balisky, and Fritzy Rose.

Can Mother see the tree planted in loving memory of a mother who had done her work well? they wonder. They believe that because she loved green things and gardens, she would smile and say, "Well done, my child! Help yourself to an apple."

A Ukrainian New Year's Celebration

The New Year's celebration lasted for nine hours. On December 31, Esther and Gordon, along with 400 other Slavs, attended the Watch Night service in the Slavic Mennonite Brethren church in Seattle.

In Russia, in former years, believers were not allowed to have Watch Night services in their churches, due to stringent Communist control. Usually they would gather in homes to sing and pray. Even this was not safe.

Since coming to America, they were now free to worship as long as they desired. Oblivious to the hours, time seemed to stand still as they worshiped God. No one would stop them here!

Upon arriving at the church at 9:00 in the evening, in spite of snow and icy conditions in the city, the Slavic congregation already filled the large meeting house.

Tastefully decorated, the sanctuary shone with Christmas lights. A seven-foot tree aglow with twinkling lights, accentuated the holiday spirit. Near the pulpit, the front wall was ornamented with shining stars encircling a wreath aglow with lights. Accented by large red ribbons, a heavy garland of tinsel was draped across the entire stage.

As was the custom, there was a great deal of music during that eventful evening. All portraying thanksgiving to God, joyfully they sang numerous times during the long service. A group of young musicians blessed the congregation as their music echoed from corner to corner.

Before Gordon and Esther went to the piano to sing an arrangement of Psalm 103 by O.E. Ford, the entire congregation stood to their feet as a pastor read the timeless Psalm.

A visiting pastor from the city of Lvov in the Ukraine, updated the people on conditions in their former homeland. Emphasizing trials and testing in uncertain conditions in their former country, where breakdown of law and order in every level of society prevail—he challenged the congregation to pray for their brothers and sisters there.

He went on to say that conditions leave the people with little hope in the midst of instability, uncertainty, and tremendous changes. Food shortages, lack of medical supplies, black market racketeering, and multiple murders, put fear into the hearts of the people.

After a series of lengthy messages by various pastors, Esther watched the hands of the clock as they neared the midnight hour. The year was almost over!

As the service neared completion, Pastor Stephen Gorkovchuk emphasized the importance of wisdom for the coming New Year. Taking his passage from Matthew 25, he referred to the parable of the Ten Virgins. Five were wise and five were foolish. "A wise man," he said, "realizes he must give an account of his life before God and others so he must learn to walk wisely and carefully at all times."

Quoting an ancient Russian proverb, he continued, "The person who realizes he needs wisdom and help from God has already become wise."

From the passage in Matthew, he emphasized the importance of realizing the economics of *time*. "There never seems to be enough," he said. Concluding his message, he said, "It is too late on our dying beds to evaluate how much time we have wasted!"

Christmas lights accented the rugged faces of the people as they listened in rapt attention.

At 12:30 A.M., the entire congregation slipped to their knees. Praying aloud simultaneously, each one thanked God for the miracles He had done for them that year.. Gratefully they gave thanks.

Rising from their knees, friendly embraces and smiles were exchanged as they wished one another a "Happy New Year!"

But the evening was far from over. The day before this celebration, the Slavic brethren had borrowed Balisky's old Ford pickup truck and transported tables, borrowed from another church in the city, to the Slavic center.

Placing them in rows in the large dining room, everyone realized that this would be the first time they could all be seated around tables while having a feast. On previous occasions, people stood or sat in chairs while they ate.

The Slavic women had come early to set the tables, gracing them with long, white tablecloths and table centers.

Upon entering the crowded dining room, Esther could

see dozens of varieties of ethnic foods, including *holopsie*, *verenike*, sauerkraut, and Ukrainian *kielbasa*.

She had never indulged in a New Year's feast at 1:30 A.M., but it was novel and the food outstanding!

As the hours passed by, no one seemed to be tired. Women scurried around, refilling empty serving plates, as children laughed and played, and adults conversed freely.

Esther, growing weary, realized her eyes would not stay open. About 3 A.M. she drove home on the icy streets of their wintry city. But fellowship around the tables lasted for several more hours. When Gordon arrived home at 6 o'clock, there were still people at the church.

This had been a New Year's celebration to remember!

How faithful and good is the God who cared for the Slavic immigrants in their migration to the United States! They knew He would see them through another year as they became adjusted to their new culture.

He who has helped thee hitherto,
Will help thee all thy journey through!

(see 1 Samuel 7:12)

After countless hours of time, prayer, and effort, Slavic churches were being formed. An appreciative people wept as they said "Thank you."

A Community Celebration

On Sunday, May 30, at 4:00 P.M., in Portland, Oregon, eight Ukrainian and Russian churches met together for a community celebration of worship. Four Slavic/Mennonite Brethren churches were represented at the rally.

The New Hope Community church, seating about 3,000, was almost full. A spacious balcony, encircling the entire back of the sanctuary, accommodated hundreds.

Pastors, wearing dark suits and white shirts, representing various Slavic churches in the area, took their places at the front of the beautiful church. Bowing together in prayer, the service was committed to God.

Everyone settled into padded pews and joined the thirty-voice choir from the Slavic MB church in Portland, as they sang about the ministry of the blessed Holy Spirit in the lives of God's children.

A large, stained glass window overhead cast brilliant colors of violet, blue, and gold across the front of the sanctuary.

Husbands and wives, grandparents, young people, and children sat side by side, anticipating to hear from God during the long service ahead.

Pastor Vakulsky stood and greeted the large assembly in Russian, then in fluent English. "The Russian and Ukrainian churches have gathered together today," he said, "in one big service. They have rented this church to accommodate everyone at the same time. In celebration of the Day of Pentecost, we are here to exalt the name of Jesus Christ our Savior. We welcome you," he concluded. "Let us praise God together on this special day."

Cameras flashed and video recorders hummed as this memorable service was recorded for future blessing.

Hundreds of children were present. Little girls, groomed neatly, wore frilly dresses and bright ribbons in their hair. Young boys, with white shirts and carefully pressed trousers, sat quietly beside proud parents. Nursery accommodations had been provided for small children and babies, however, the parents often preferred to have their children sit with them during the service.

Baby carriages stood in a row at the back of the crowded church. Attentive mothers and fathers endeavored to keep their babies still, but as time wore on, many little ones became restless, crying for attention.

Some went to sleep in their mother's arms, still others sat on the floor in the aisles, trying to amuse themselves.

There was a rustle as about 3,000 people knelt to pray. Their prayers were not silent or whispered, but unanimously they cried to God who heard and answered prayer. An elderly man beside Esther wept as he talked to his heavenly Father. Pastors, with arms outstretched, knelt together with their joint congregations.

Time fled by as daylight hours turned into night. Still the service continued.

Each participating church had a part in the community worship. Special musical numbers, including solos, duets, trios, male chorus, instrumentals, and choirs, filled the passing hours. Five talented musicians, sitting in a semi-circle, played several selections from the works of Bach.

Eight children, along with their parents, were accustomed to performing for large audiences, as from the eldest to the youngest, they sang joyfully from hearts full of love for God. Christian Slavic children, taught to sing, recite poetry, and even preach in the church during their tender years, continue to do so for the rest of their lives. Performing in front of an audience is a natural occurrence.

The musical selections during the community celebration were all outstanding. Dedicated talent displayed itself in various ways as each group took part. Eleven sermons were preached with gusto!

Wondering if they would ever stop, Esther stretched in her seat and tried to stifle a yawn.

It was a relief, before the last sermon, to stand and greet others nearby. Words such as "*Slava Bogu*" and "*Zbogom*" ("Praise the Lord" and "May He bless you") were exchanged as thousands heartily embraced or shook hands.

After the next sermon, the people stood to their feet

and recited the Lord's prayer. The service was finally over at 9:30 P.M. Leaving the auditorium, the crowd dispersed to their homes.

They would remember how the messages in song and word had stirred their hearts. The first cooperative service was the beginning step in developing community, and a positive identity for the newly-arrived immigrants from the Ukraine and Russia.

During the course of the evening's ministry, attention had been focused by the speakers, on problems and challenges facing them in their new country. Each time they pointed out that solutions were found only in a strong dependence upon God and His Word.

Future community services were planned on a quarterly basis. The people looked with anticipation to be together again. A community of Slavic believers had been formed and they planned to cooperate.

37 A CHANGED LIFE

The phone rang one more time in Esther's office. "Mom, Dad," came the frightened voice of their daughter.

"Corinne, where are you?" asked her dad on the other phone.

"I have been in an accident," she wept.

"What happened?" asked her mother, bracing herself.

"I am calling from a pay phone here in Los Angeles. My car is wrecked—totaled! Someone called a tow truck to come and take it."

"And how are you? Are you all right?" they asked in unison.

"No, I am hurt badly!" she cried. Panic filled her shaking voice.

If only they were closer. What could they do?

"Hold on, Corinne," encouraged her father. "Get some medical help immediately."

"I will," she sobbed.

The helplessness of parents 1,000 miles away, while their child is in peril, is unspeakable! What could they do? Bowing in prayer, they cried to God to give their daughter peace… to send medical aid… to calm her fears… to give wisdom to those who assisted her….

"Oh God," prayed Esther, with her head in her hands. "How badly is she hurt?" In agony, she wept before God.

After medical attention, someone took Corinne home, and she called again.

Sitting near to the phone for hours, they grabbed it on the first ring.

"Mom, Dad," she whispered in a small voice.

"Corinne, how are you?" they cried.

They could barely hear her, as she answered, "The pain in my back is terrible. I can't hardly walk and it is hard to talk. I am so weak and shaky. Can you help?"

"I will be on the next plane to Los Angeles," promised her dad, before they hung up.

Reluctant to let go of the phone, Esther continued to hold it to her ear after the voice of her daughter was gone. With miles separating them, how could she be of assistance to her youngest? How could she soothe and comfort? Or would it even help?

It seemed the flight could not reach Los Angeles quickly enough. Gordon, sitting in his seat, wrung his hands and prayed for his youngest. There were details to look after. He would be there to assist in every way possible.

Because she was happy in the city of the angels, had a good job, and a myriad of friends, why did this tragedy strike now? God was in control, he knew, but why this?

Finally, after it seemed hours of flight time, he disembarked. Taking a taxi, he was transported to Corinne's house.

Then he saw her! Lying on her side, she looked up at him and burst into tears, her eyes revealing great pools of suffering. He held her close. What was next? Only God knew.

He learned that an eighty-year-old man had driven through a red light with his big car without stopping. Driving fast, he crashed hard into Corinne's small Toyota in the intersection. Had he hit her only a fraction closer to the front door, Corinne knew she would have been in heaven at that moment.

After checking on the car sometime later, he looked after other details as well. Knowing it would be difficult to meet her financial obligations there, he suggested she move back to Seattle. Perhaps she could stay at home until she was able to work again.

This was not Corinne's plan. Living in Los Angeles made her happy. The beautiful beaches with huge waves crashing onto the shore, the warm sunshine with little rain, a good job, friends… how could she leave?

But how could she pay her rent? If she was not able to walk steady, how could she work?

"I will have to make a decision, Dad," she wept. She decided to move.

Renting a large truck, Gordon and some of her male friends packed her belongings. Lovingly she looked at her attractive apartment. A spacious living room with shiny hardwood floors, a beautiful area with amenities close by—it was hard to leave.

But her dad thought it was best. Did she agree? What else could she do?

The journey to Seattle was painful, slow, and careful. Each jar caused her to cry out in pain as she sat in the front seat of the big truck with her dad and Paul, the driver.

Piling her beautiful belongings into the place where

she grew up, and putting some in storage, reluctantly she moved into the "David" room at home. With a bathroom and walk-in closet, she would be comfortable. Settling down into the big bed, her body hurting, emotionally wrought, she prayed to God.

"Why? Why? Why? Do I have to start all over again?" Her job as a movie producer and specialties in video and communications would be difficult to pursue in this city. Would there be a job for her when she recuperated? Or would she recuperate? A thousand questions filled her heart.

During the months of healing, God was with her. Holding Pumpkin's furry body close to her, he, in his own way, tried to comfort and bless. And he did. Corinne bonded deeply with the little animal.

Slowly, ever so slowly, her muscles mended to the point where she could walk more freely. But would she ever heal completely? That remained to be seen.

Moving into an apartment, months later, Corinne was encouraged. Slowly recovering, she integrated friends, church, a job, and her family into a new phase of life in the Pacific Northwest. Courageously she started again. Purchasing a lovely home gave encouragement and incentive. Corinne found a new purpose. Her life had been radically changed. In her adjustment, more than ever, she bonded with her heavenly Father. He was her source of strength and wisdom. He would look after her future, too.

> *And he said unto me, My grace is sufficient for thee: for my strength is made perfect in weakness...* (2 Corinthians 12:9).

CORINNE

You were born in beautiful B.C.
A precious gift for your dad and me.
We loved you fiercely from the start
As you wound yourself around our hearts.
With big blue eyes and curly hair,
You and your sister were quite a pair!
Playing together, you generously shared,
You knew in your heart how much we cared.

Accepting Jesus when you were small,
He kept you safe so you wouldn't fall.
Singing His praises, you raised your voice,
Knowing for Him you had made your choice.

You had many friends and you loved to play
Especially at twilight—your best time of day.
Running outdoors while the sun bid good-bye,
You didn't want to come in—your spirits were high.

Barbies were some of your favorite toys,
Later, that fun turned into playing with boys!
In school your grades were higher than the rest.
You were never pleased till you'd done your best.

Now specializing in production and TV
Your work is excellent—that's plain to see.
Your music has become a worthwhile choice.
When you sing, dear, I feel my heart rejoice!

Thank you for your life—a precious gift from God.
Though sometimes you're chastened by His mighty rod,
Yet always you thank Him—His ways are best.
You gave Him your life—He'll look after the rest!

—Mom

The First Grandchild

A short while later, Esther and Gordon were delighted to be told that Charlene was pregnant. Their first grandchild! What could compare to this joy?

But what would she do with her cats? The prospect of having a baby and two felines, seemed too much for her to handle.

Corinne's tender heart was stirred. "No! They can not be put to sleep! I will take them to my new home."

Dusty Rose and Bunny Rose were taken to Corinne's house. The cats, exploring their new home, were apprehensive at first, but as time went by, they found peace and security in this place. Two warm bodies cuddling in Corinne's lap were contented and happy.

The Rose family were all settled.

THE BIRTH

Grandparents, aunts, and uncles waited with baited breath outside the delivery room in the Providence Hospital. They listened for the newborn cry of an infant. There was no cry. Esther held her breath.

"The baby's here!" cried Corinne from inside closed doors.

"Isn't she beautiful?" shouted the new father.

Her color was not good. There was still no cry. Charlene waited, anxious and tense. "Please, Little One, make a sound… even a small one. Are you alive?"

Capable medical staff fighting to save the baby's life, were silent as they utilized all the expertise known to them. Suddenly there was a small whimper. At least she was alive!

Carrying this precious little bundle of humanity to the Emergency Child Care Center, the new father, though concerned, had a smile on his face.

Esther saw her then. So small! So vulnerable! "My first

grandchild!" she breathed, as a choking sensation filled her throat. "O God, please let her live!"

Love filled Esther's heart like a strong current, as she remembered when she held her own newborn infants so long ago. Where had the years gone? How she loved this helpless little girl!

Silently, at the Emergency Child Care Center, Esther stood looking through the glass that separated her from her granddaughter. Why was she so gray? Tears filled the new grandmother's eyes and slid down her cheeks as she prayed for this vulnerable little one so valiantly fighting for her life. But she was strong. She would make it.

How quickly she became a toddler, coddled and loved by doting parents, aunts, uncles, and grandparents.

They named her Alexis, meaning Protector. The suggested character quality is defined as a victorious heart. And what a heart! Needless to say, Gordon and Esther were proud. It is so good to be a grandparent!

A FAVORITE RECIPE

You will need:
1 honest face
1 head of silver hair
2 eyes that twinkle
1 pair of lips for affectionate kisses
2 arms to hold children of all sizes.
Add to this:
1 smile
2 ears that listen with undivided attention
1 clean and starched dress
1 homemade apron
1 lap to sit on

Mix with:
A grandchild's love and kisses
and a place in a rocking chair on the front porch.

Yield:
1 old-fashioned Grandma

Note:
This recipe will come out very sweet,
especially if the temperature is warm.

BONDING

The Christmas tree lights glowed softly, filling the room with light. A little girl gently placed her tiny hand into her grandma's, and looked up at her with an expression of love. Leading Grandma to the Christmas tree, her eyes were big with awe and wonder. What a sight to behold! Carefully she scrutinized each ornament placed there by the hands of a loving mother.

It was her second Christmas. Last year she had eagerly torn off the colorful wrappings from gifts placed under the tree. What a time of joy and celebration that turned out to be! This year she understood the true meaning of the season. It was Jesus' birthday and she planned to enjoy it.

In the past, Esther had told her the wonderful story of how angels welcomed the Savior's birth, singing, "Glory to God in the highest, and on earth peace, good will toward men (Luke 2:14)." She loved that part. How exciting those angelic beings were to her.

Earlier in the day, she had been thinking about the angels. Suddenly she looked at Esther with her big blue eyes and exclaimed, "Glory to God in the Highest!" Her mother looked at Esther and smiled.

"Where did she get that from?" Charlene asked in surprise.

Alexis had remembered. "Read me a story, Grandma," she said.

As they sat in the soft glow of the tree, Esther opened the large Bible Storybook and automatically turned to the old, yet ever new account of their Savior's birth. Sitting under the tree, she and her grandma were alone, except for the presence of the Christ who was once a baby. Now no longer a child, He was probably smiling His approval from His home in heaven, as He observed the scene below.

They read the story once. Totally comprehending as Esther read, Alexis turned the pages to the beginning again. Once more they went through the wonderful story, but that was not enough. They read it again. Now the truth was firmly implanted into the heart of an eager two-year-old. She knew the meaning of Christmas afresh, and her heart was touched.

Joy filled Esther's being as she held the child fiercely to her heart. Then soft, wee arms entwined her neck. Yes, Alexis and her grandmother had bonded. They were real friends. They had shared God's love together.

"I WUV YOU GRANDMA!"

"I love you, Alexis!"
Silky arms enfold me.
Soft red mouth kisses my cheek,
She sits upon my knee.

"I wuv you, Grandma!"
Blue eyes search my face.
They play with toys—she takes my hand,
"Come, Grandma. Quick, let's race!"

"I wuv you, Grandma!"
Laughing, she looks back at me
To see if I am right behind her.
Satisfied, she cries with glee.

"I love you, Alexis!"
We sit on the floor.
Soon toys are scattered everywhere,
And she runs back for more.

"I wuv you, Grandma!"
We play for several hours
"You be Mrs. Tan," she says,
"Who lives in a tall tower."

"I love you, Alexis!"
Our imaginations flowing,
Mrs. Tan and friend have tea,
Bonding strong is growing.

"I wuv you, Grandma!"
"Now yet's go to the park!"
Jumping, climbing, sliding,
We play till after dark.

Walking hand in hand toward home,
We view the evening stars,
"That's where Jesus lives," she says,
"Beyond the sky so far."

"I love you, Alexis!"

Now it's finally time for bed.
I read a favorite story,
To my precious sleepyhead.

Soon big blue eyes close,
And she is fast asleep.
Bending down, I kiss her cheek,
And ask the Lord her soul to keep.

38 WELCOME HOME NICHOLAS

Esther startled when the phone rang. "Hello," answered Gordon.

"Hi, it's me—Steve." Their son-in-law sounded elated and exhausted.

Esther held her breath.

"Our little boy just arrived!"

Esther grabbed the cordless phone. "Is Charlene all right?" she cried.

"Yes, she's fine."

"And the baby, how is he?"

They could almost see Steve smiling across the miles. "Everyone's fine. Nicholas Steven is so big!"

"What does he weigh?" asked the excited grandpa.

"You wouldn't guess!"

"Well he must be big!" said Gordon."

"He's 10 pounds, 2 ounces… I think we have a heavyweight here," laughed the proud father. "Come to the hospital and see for yourself.... Yes, Alexis is here too. She'd love to see you."

It wasn't far to the hospital, but it seemed they just couldn't make it there fast enough! Finally, they ran up the stairs of the hospital, and made their way to the maternity ward.

Corinne and Alexis, standing in the hallway, came to them. Alexis looked so small in her little white sweater and pants. Running to her grandma, her small arms were soon wrapped around Esther's neck.

"I have a new baby," she smiled.

"Yes, I know," Esther whispered, her face almost hidden in the child's silky hair.

"Are you happy, Dear?" asked Gordon.

"Yes. I want to take him home with me soon," she smiled.

"Here, I have a present for you," said Esther.

Not wanting her to feel left out now that her new brother was getting so much attention, Esther had wrapped a toy bunny in brightly colored paper.

Her eyes wide with anticipation, quickly she tore open the colorful wrappings. Then, holding the fuzzy toy close, she took her grandma's hand as together they walked to Charlene's room.

"Congratulations!" smiled the proud grandpa. "What have we here?"

Charlene smiled one of her "Rolls Royce" smiles and uncovered the face of her newborn son.

Steve, bursting with pride, watched as they looked at the face of their first grandson. Red, wrinkled, and beautiful, he wiggled and made baby noises.

"What a big baby!" cried Esther.

"Yes, Mom, I know, I just delivered him!" laughed Charlene. "Here, you can hold him," she offered.

Taking the bundle of energetic life from her weary arms, Gordon and Esther were awed at the miracle that had just taken place. Another grandchild! Praise be to the Creator of life!

It was time for Alexis to go to bed. Corinne excused herself to take the little girl home, and quickly left the hospital room. Alexis waved as long as she could see them.

"Good night, Sweetheart!" cried Esther. "Sweet dreams!"

"Bye Grandma and Grandpa! Bye Mommy! Bye Nicky!" she called over her shoulder.

It wasn't easy for her to leave Mommy in the hospital, but she knew Auntie Baah was planning to stay the night at her house. That softened the blow. She could wait until tomorrow. Maybe Mommy would be home then.

A big sign across the door of his new home greeted the new baby the next day. "Welcome Home Nicholas," it read. They all knew this baby would be pampered and well-loved like his big sister. They would see to that!

Alexis' First Church school Nicholas's Enthusiasm

Softly, Esther knocked at the door. Immediately she could hear little feet running down the stairs.

"Grandma! Grandma!" shouted Alexis as she flew into Esther's arms, with Nicky close behind. This was an important night for both of them. "I will be on the stage tonight," Alexis boasted.

"Are you going to sing?" asked Grandma.

"It's a secret," she grinned.

"Come on, Grandma! Mommy's ready to leave!"

Climbing into the Ford Explorer, Charlene did up the seat belts. Then they drove out of the yard. They were on their way! "Yes, Grandma," Alexis teased, "I will be with the other kids in my school program, but what I am going to do is a secret!"

"I can hardly wait!" replied Grandma.

The four-year-old wiggled and moved around in her car seat. Too excited to sit still, Esther saw her eyes glow. Soft, blonde hair, cascading down her back, shone in the Christmas lights. A frilly, long dress made the excited youngster look like a little angel.

Soon they arrived at the church. Charlene, who'd had surgery recently on her foot, hoisted her crutches out of the car and let the children out of the back seat.

Esther carefully held their hands, because their mother could not. Both children pulled and tugged to enter the Lutheran Church School before the other kids.

They were blessed because they arrived early enough to sit in the front seat. This would make it so much easier to see Alexis perform. Nicky would love that!

Like a big girl, she took her teacher's hand and went to the back of the church to line up for the procession toward the big stage.

The church was packed. Proud parents, aunts, uncles, sisters, and brothers came to hear their preschoolers. What an event!

Cameras clicked and video cameras hummed as two by two, the children came down the aisle.

Where was Alexis? Nicholas, sitting on Esther's knee, craned his head to find his sister.

"Sausey, oh where is Sausey?" he cried.

Then he saw her. Confident, unafraid, her head held high, and her eyes shining like drops of water on a petal, she walked forward.

Standing in front of them, she smiled. Yes, she was going to do her best for those she loved.

They were proud as she joyfully launched into song.

Totally uninhibited, forgetting others around her and remembering only to do her best, she thoroughly enjoyed herself.

Nicholas, sitting in Esther's lap, was mesmerized.

Waving his little hands, he called, "Sausey, Sausey!"

Then doing the actions to songs the group sang, he tried to sing along. It was hard to keep him still, because had she let him go, he would have nudged in beside his sister on stage and sung along with the bigger kids. He loved every minute of the enchanting program.

Alexis not only sang and did the actions, but she told the whole story of the songs with her facial expressions. Her hands, also, keeping in time with the music and words, caused others to notice the little performer.

Suddenly, her cousins and aunty walked in and came to sit with the rest of her family in the front pew.

Alexis saw them. Diverted and waving her hands delightedly in the air, she cried, "Emily, Carman! Hello, it's me, Alexis!" They smiled as, undaunted, she went back into her role in the program.

Cookies, cookies, cookies. They went into the auditorium after the little singers had completed their program to have a snack. Alexis, proudly hugging her cousins, introduced them to her teacher.

What was the secret she had mentioned earlier? Singing, only for them, and doing her best, was the four-year-old's goal. Now her secret was out!

A Fun-filled World

"Come Gramma, let's play choo-choo train," the little boy cries
As Thomas, the caboose, climbs the hill. Nick's a regular guy!
"Beep-beep," blows the whistle, "puff-puff" pants the train,

Laughing, enjoying, he cries, "Engine, do it again!"

"Come Gramma, let's play baby." We're done with playing train,
Now I'm a baby with an "owie"—my tummy's feeling pain!
Please take me to the doctor, he can see what's wrong,
In our new car we have to hurry, the ride will not be long.

"Gramma, let's play dress-up!" He quickly runs to get a gown,
High-heeled shoes, a hat and gloves, he dances round and round.
Tossing off his finery, he has a perfect plan—
Running away he cries, "Gramma, catch me—catch me if you can!"

"Come, Gramma, let's play Sunday School. I'll be the teacher now."
When we pray to God our Father, quietly our heads we bow.
"Let's sing about David and the sling that went round,
And the five little stones in the brook that he found!"

"Come, Gramma, let's play in the park. I know there's a swing,"
The child is delighted, as he runs, jumps, and sings,
He loves the teeter-totter, merry-go-round, and slides
And the colored, wooden horses that go round when he rides.

He's ambitious—mischievous—a fun, loving boy,
So many things to do—so much to enjoy!
Nicholas Stephen, have as much fun as you can
Because tomorrow you'll be a regular man!

–From Grandma, July 11, 2001

Peters Reunion

"Hello, Esther, this is your cousin Phil calling from Kansas."

"Hi, Phil, what's on your mind?"

"We are planning a Peters reunion here. Would you be interested in coming?"

She certainly was interested.

Checking with other family members, all of them replied in the affirmative. Excitement was in the air! They would finally see cousins with whom they had not been in contact for a long time. Coming from a closely-knit family, they looked with anticipation to this time of celebration.

Esther would never forget when her father, Henry, had taken most of his family to Kansas by car when she was a child. Because their parents' roots were buried deep in this state, they wanted to show them, not only tell them, about the place where they were born.

She would never forget that trip. Bonding with cousins, she made friends for a lifetime. Visiting Henry and Katy's respective homes where they had lived even before they were married, gave her such joy. Many times they had told her stories about happenings in their lives when they were young. Now she saw firsthand, where they had taken place.

Then in later years, after Gordon and Esther were married, they were often invited to come and share the Slavic ministry at the Zoar Mennonite Brethren Church where her grandparents and parents had made their church home.

Making wonderful friends with cousins, other relatives, and new acquaintances, during their visits, Gordon and Esther looked with anticipation to seeing them all again.

Since Kansas is a long way from Washington state, they flew to the reunion. As they landed and heard the familiar thump of the airplane's wheels on Kansas soil, they knew they

were not strangers there. Their ties to this state were bonded closely to her forefathers.

About 100 family members of the ten children of Jacob and Anna Peters met for their first reunion on August 7-10, 1998, at Bethel College.

Hosting the reunion were Jim, Phil, and Peggy—Esther's first cousins. It seemed appropriate that these grandchildren would invite the rest of the family to the state of their original family home for a reunion.

Hugging members of her own Peters clan, Esther was delighted to see them again—especially in this place where their parents were born.

The reunion included a tour through the then ultra-modern home that Jacob and Anna (Esther's grandparents) had built in 1907. The house is still standing today in the middle of the section. Proudly it stands as a witness to those who lived there so long ago.

Driving their car a little farther, Esther swallowed a lump in her throat as she viewed the place where her mother had lived and loved from childhood to teenaged years.

Storytelling will forever be a part of family history. At the reunion, recordings were made and were available for future generations. About twenty grandchildren were present.

A highlight of the three days together was a "parlor talk" where these twenty cousins sat around a table and swapped a variety of interesting stories with each other. It was a bonding force as around the theme, "Celebrating the Blessings of Our Family," everyone took part. God's faithfulness to a family who risked everything to re-establish themselves on another continent and culture, was clearly the focus of the time together. Thankfulness to God was expressed in singing together and telling stories of God's blessings on individuals and families.

Some copies of Esther's new book, *In Grandpa's Shoes*, hot off the press, were sent directly to Kansas for this family reunion. She had not yet seen the completed work. Excited, she tore open the carton containing books on which she had worked so long.

She was given an opportunity to tell others about the family book at the first meeting. From then on, interest was generated and the books sold quickly. Signing as fast as she could, Esther's family stood in line to purchase her first book.

Because *In Grandpa's Shoes* is a book relating to their family, many at the reunion wanted to read it. Some bought copies to pass on to their own children and grandchildren, and other relatives who were not able to attend the reunion.

The families enjoyed being together to such an extent, that another reunion was immediately scheduled in Manitoba for the year 2000. Bill Peters and his brother planned to host this one.

After that, the Peters family invited their cousins to another which would be hosted by Bob—Esther's brother, in Grande Prairie, Alberta, Canada, in 2002, where many of their parents and grandparents once lived.

What a great idea! Warmed by fun and fellowship, they had bonded with family. They would do so again!

Pumpkin Rose

Esther's cat looked at her with large, suffering eyes. Nestled limply in the arms of his favorite person, she thought he knew it was almost time to go.

How will I know when we should put him to sleep? Esther often wondered during those difficult days.

Pumpkin Rose was diagnosed with cancer of the liver just weeks before. Every day his appetite dwindled, until lately, he wouldn't eat anything offered to him. Even delicacies from the pet store didn't tempt him.

"Please eat," pleaded Esther, but he wouldn't. Pumpkin had been with them for sixteen years and was an intricate part of their family.

When they drove into the yard, he was always there to meet them. Rubbing his glorious fur against Esther's leg, he begged to be picked up. Soon, in the crook of her arm, he purred until his entire body vibrated with contentment.

When going on a trip, he would jump into the suitcase. Pleading with her not to go and leave him again, his big, round eyes searched her face.

His face filled with expression, was full of love for those dearest to him. Even if he could have, there was no need to express his thoughts verbally, because they always knew what he wanted. Gratefully saying thanks, he cuddled close.

Pumpkin was in ecstasy when he could lie on Corinne or Esther's lap, or cuddle closely under the left arm. What could be better? Drooling with contentment, he closed his eyes and went to sleep.

One Monday morning, Esther called her cat, but there was no answering cry. There was no greeting as a little fury body rubbed against her leg.

Lying in his little bed, Pumpkin was motionless. Talking softly and stroking his downy fur, Esther heard no response.

Picking up his bed, she ran to find Gordon. "Pumpkin is not moving," she cried. But together, they noticed there was still a little life.

"It's time," said Gordon.

Calling the Veterinary Clinic, they explained what had happened.

"Bring him in," said the sympathetic doctor. "Yes, it's time."

Lying peacefully in his bed, together, they took him to the clinic. Totally unaware of their presence, he seemed to be asleep, but they knew it was a prelude to the sleep of death.

Quietly, Esther put her hand on the little animal as Doctor Phillips injected the final lethal solution. "He's gone," he whispered.

Corinne, Gordon, and Esther lined the inside of the grave with flowers, fall leaves, and juniper, and carefully placed his stiff body into this prepared place under the apple trees in the backyard. Reminded again, that these trees were planted in honor of their Grandma Balisky, Grandpa Art, and Fritz Rose, now their little friend had joined the others.

Buried just outside Esther's bedroom, clearly she could see the grave. No, he couldn't cuddle in the crook of her arm anymore, but he was resting quietly close to her in a special place.

"Good-bye my little friend," whispered Esther. The only reply she received was the wind gently rustling the flowers on his grave. Pumpkin was at rest.

Dusty Rose

Corinne was preparing to go to Europe for a vacation. Sitting in her pet carrier, Dusty looked alert—inquisitive.

Corinne had just come back from taking her cat to the Veterinary Clinic.

"We will give her antibiotics—perhaps that will clear up her problems," said Dr. Phillips.

But it didn't. Gradually Dusty wasn't interested in food. Corinne brought delicacies from the pet store, but nothing tempted her. Even water stood untouched in her bowl. Usually drinking from the sink in the bathroom, now she couldn't jump that high. Her body, too heavy for her weakened legs, could not carry her anymore. Was she going to die, too? It couldn't be. On Monday, they had put Pumpkin to sleep. Now would his mother be gone as well?

Corinne doted on her cats. Dusty, and her daughter, Bunny Rose, had lived with her for four years. Corinne called them "her girls."

What fun it was to come home at night, knowing they were there to meet her.

Now is Dusty going to leave me, too? she wondered.

Giving her water from a dropper, Corinne and Esther watched the nourishment reluctantly go down the suffering cat's throat. Then putting her gently in her bed, she became motionless. Was she already gone?

That night, Charlene came to say good bye to her faithful friend. Together the girls watched the suffering animal.

When morning came, Corinne put her friend into the pet carrier, and took her to the place where Dusty, too, would receive the final lethal injection. Yes, it was time. Three days after Pumpkin's demise, Dusty, too, was gone.

Gordon and Esther came to her house soon afterward. Dusty's body lay quietly under a clean, colored towel.

They buried her in Corinne's back yard. Lining her grave with red roses, carnations, and juniper leaves, carefully Corinne placed her friend in the soft earth, facing the kitchen and study windows.

"Has she seen her babies?" thoughtfully, they wondered. "Where do these little creatures go when they breathe their last?"

But they wouldn't worry about this. God had every thing planned long ago. If He sees the sparrow fall, surely He has a place for Dusty, Fritz, Pumpkin, Molly, and Stripy Rose.

"Good-bye, Dusty Rose," whispered Corinne as she walked toward the house.

Bunny Rose came to meet her, rubbing her furry body against her. She seemed to know something was different. Now she would be an "only cat." Would she like that?

As Corinne carried her into the house, the little animal nestled in her arms. Did she need comfort, too?

Together, Corinne was assured, they would both be fine.

Warm Glow of Christmas

"Mom, would you like to go to the Lights of Christmas with us on Friday?" asked Charlene. "We have been there several times. The kids love it!"

Pulling her warm, British wool sweater over her head, Esther was soon ready to go.

"Are you ready?" she called to Gordon.

"Coming!" he answered, while zipping up his warm leather jacket.

It was December and the weather was crisp. With no rain, the frosty earth crackled as they walked to the car.

Soon, ringing the knocker on Charlene's door, they heard the pitter-patter of little feet.

"They're here!" cried Nicholas.

"Looking out the side window to make sure it was them, Nicholas and Alexis ran to open the door.

"Grandma! Grandpa!" they cried, hugging them.

"We're going to the Lights of Christmas. Can you ride with us?"

Soon they were all driving toward Warm Beach Christian Camp where almost a million lights would welcome them.

Now, in its fifth year, the Lights of Christmas was established to give something back to the community, while also making better year-round use of the camp. During its four years, the Lights of Christmas drew more than 150,000 people to the five-acre facility.

While the Lights of Christmas may make the boldest statement, the lineup also includes a heavy dose of music, drama, food, and crafts.

"Come see the baby Jesus!" said Alexis, while together they pulled their grandma to the site where He was featured.

But before they even saw it, they heard carols coming from that direction. "Look at the baby Jesus!" exclaimed Nicholas. There they saw a lighted Nativity with 8-foot-high figurines and five entertainment stages.

Other features they visited that day were Tinhorn Town, and The Children's Theater, home to the Soda Shop Christmas Hop. New to the offerings was the Doo-wop Diner. The animal petting farm is always a favorite to youngsters. Touching the soft creatures, Alexis sighed with delight.

Steve had just come from work, so he was hungry. While dining, music filled the room again. Unreservedly, Nicholas walked toward the stage. Dancing in time to the music, his little face was flushed with excitement. Alexis, a little shy, joined him near the end. Wearing red, both resembled Santa's helpers.

When they went to 10-foot Bruce the Spruce, billed as Washington's only talking Christmas tree, the children finally reached the front of the line. Shyly, Alexis hung her head, while in a whisper Nicholas talked to Bruce.

Ride options included ponies, a draft horse wagon, and the Polar Express Train. Both were delighted to mount the ponies and go around the track.

Then carolers dressed in Victorian costumes sang about the birth of Jesus Christ.

Finally, it was time to go home. Walking toward the car, Esther's heart was filled with joy as the children held her hands.

Almost a million lights twinkling overhead made this a

wonderful festive occasion and they planned to come again.

"Good-night Grandpa and Grandma!" they called. "Merry Christmas!"

Conquering the River

Putting her hands over her eyes, Alexis cried, "No! I don't want to walk over those stones to cross the river!"

"Neither do I," answered Charlene. Esther silently agreed.

The river ahead blocked the path on which they were hiking. In order to reach the other side, they had to cross the raging torrent. White foam dashed against the sharp, slippery rocks as the water wildly made its way to the big river below.

Steve and Gordon were already on the other side. Calling to the women, they tried to hear, but the sound of the river was too loud.

"What?" they shouted back.

Cupping his hands over his mouth, Steve yelled. But what was he saying?

A few minutes earlier, Gordon had made his way cautiously across. As he did so, Alexis and Esther had prayed. What if he fell? The stones were sharp. He could hurt himself. When his foot touched the bank on the other side, they all shouted and cheered. Now who would be next?

Cautiously, carefully, Steve shuffled back toward them. "Come on Nicholas!" he shouted.

The four-year-old stepped onto the nearest rock.

"I can't look!" cried his sister.

But when Nicholas grabbed his father's hand, his confidence grew. Gordon cut and trimmed a tree branch and, grasping it firmly, held it out to the boy. He made it!

When Alexis reluctantly decided she would make her way across the dangerous rocks, they all held their breath.

But when her daddy held her hand, and with the other, she reached out to Grandpa's stick, she was soon on the far shore. Once more, everyone clapped.

"Yes, Alexis, you made it!" cried Nicholas. Hugging his sister, everyone laughed.

Now it was Esther's turn. Could she make it?

The water churned and foamed against the slippery rocks. The sound reverberated like thunder into the chilly atmosphere.

"Here I go!" she determined.

Walking toward the water, she lifted her foot to step onto the nearest rock. It was too slippery. She tried another. Her foot held.Was the next one going to be too slippery too? She had to take that chance. The children were cheering her on from the other side.

"You can do it, Grandma!" they shouted. The roar of the water was too loud to hear, but she knew they were watching. She didn't want to disappoint them.

Finally, reaching Steve's outstretched hand, she hung on. While clasping his shirt with the other hand, slowly they made their way toward the other bank. Once more Gordon's stick was a refuge as she reached for it—and made it across! The shore felt safe and solid as she stepped onto the firm ground.

Now what about Charlene? She'd had two foot surgeries recently and today her feet were throbbing with pain. What if she fell?

Everyone else was on the other side, so she had no choice but to try. The roar of the water seemed even louder as she put her foot out onto the rock.

"Steady now," cautioned her husband who stood with bated breath as he watched his wife slowly come toward his outstretched hand.

Charlene held her breath. Could she reach the big rock where Steve's feet were firmly planted? She had to! Everyone else had taken the challenge—and won.

When her cold hand touched Steve's, she knew she would be OK. Smiling now, clasping his hand, she made her way to her father's stick. Holding onto it, she, too, stepped onto the shore.

The children ran to their mother. "Good job, Mom!" they shouted. "Now we're all here!"

Charlene and Esther breathed a sigh of relief, as once again they continued their ascent to the top of the mountain. They hiked up the narrow path. Laughing, teasing, panting, they looked with anticipation to the view from the top of the mountain.

Now what was this?

"Nicholas," called Steve, "come and see what I found!"

The boy pulled his hand away from his grandma's and excitedly followed his dad. His eyes grew big with wonder and awe. He had never seen a cave before!

"Follow me inside, Son," said Steve, as he took the small hand in his.

The others watched from the mouth of the big cave as the two disappeared into the damp, cold, dark interior. They could hear the voices echo inside as father and son explored the depths in this new adventure. Weary from their walk, they sat quietly on the big rocks and viewed the majesty of God's creation. The river, the mountains, the expansive blue sky—everything spoke of His work.

It wasn't long until they were making their way down the path again. "Look at the flowers!" smiled Nicholas. "These are Indian Paintbrush, you know," he informed them. Yellow, pink, red, and white flowers were scattered everywhere, clinging to the mountainside.

"Can we pick some?" asked Alexis.

"No," said her mother. "In a park like this, we are not allowed to pick flowers."

All too soon they heard the roar of the river. Of course they had to cross it again! Silently dreading this encounter, no one spoke of it until they arrived there.

"I trust Grandpa," said Alexis, "because he has that big stick. He and Daddy will help us across."

As Esther viewed the situation, a challenge raced through her mind. Could she do it by herself this time?

Holding onto a big tree trunk jutting out into the water, she stepped onto the first rock. Why not try? As she went a little farther, she realized how dangerous this was. Why did she venture out alone? Could she make it?

Getting down on her knees this time, she groped for the next rock with her hands. Crawling along the slippery rocks while the water foamed and lashed beneath, carefully she made her way to the middle of the river. She held her breath. Determined to make it, she crawled onto the next rock. It held. Then the next, until she was actually on the other side. No one could believe it! Everyone cheered, wishing they, too, were there.

Gordon was getting his stick ready, when suddenly, to his horror, he lost his balance! He felt the cold water envelope him as his feet hit the bottom of the river. Quickly he regained his balance, and, soaking wet and cold, he made his way to the nearest rock.

Relieved he wasn't hurt, Esther joined her family as they doubled over with laughter. Gordon didn't think it was so funny at first, but eventually he also began to see the humor as he surveyed the situation.

Thankful everyone had made it across the river again, they walked through the delightful Bavarian town of Leavenworth, WA, with its German architecture and quaint stores. Going into the candy shop, the children were soon sampling the delicacies.

"Give me a bite of your chocolate, Grandma!" said Alexis when she saw the delicious morsel her grandma was eating.

Steve, sitting on a bench nearby, smiled. "I saw you take a bite of Grandma's chocolate," he teased.

"Mmm, this is s-o-o good!" she said, licking her own piece of candy.

They were growing tired. Charlene and Steve's vacation apartment had been fragrant with the aroma of roast beef when they had left earlier, so they knew dinner would be ready.

Later they all sat down at the table and enjoyed Charlene's good cooking. Looking out the window, they could see the massive mountains, the luscious green pastures, and the river beyond.

"Mom, I'm hungry!" said Nicholas, his mouth filled with food.

Everyone was too busy eating to comment.

That night, as they closed their eyes to sleep, visions of mountain flowers, steep hills and valleys, and roaring rivers filled their heads. It had been a memorable day. They had found a big challenge and won! Maybe they would cross that river again some day!

39 An Iron Curtain Falls on Fremont

"Statue of Lenin arises—and sets off
a furor of revolutionary style."

This article, appearing in the Seattle Post Intelligencer in 1999, evoked a great deal of interest. Vladimir Ilyich Lenin, the founder of the Communist party, ruled Russia until his death in 1924. Now, a hulking 18-foot bronze statue of him, the stern architect of Russia's Revolution, stared across a parking lot in Seattle's Fremont neighborhood, which, on Sundays, is transformed into a throbbing mecca of flea marketers.

In 1993, Lew Carpenter of Issaquah, Washington, was teaching English in Poprad, Slovakia, when his students took him on a field trip. There in a public dump, he saw Lenin lying on his metal face.

Carpenter was taken with it and persuaded the town to sell it to him for 13,000 dollars. This would be better, he

Gordon at the statue of Lenin In Russia.

thought, than to have history melted down for park benches like dozens of other Lenin statues across Eastern Europe.

Carpenter, who died in a car wreck soon afterwards, mortgaged his home in Issaquah to pay the nearly 28,000 dollars in transportation fees to Seattle. He tried in vain to sell it.

Instead, the big, bronze statue languished in a pasture behind his house. After his death, the family found themselves with a giant statue of Lenin which no one wanted to buy. For a time, the city of Issaquah thought about displaying it, but eventually, declined.

In April, Peter Bevis, a Fremont sculptor, heard about the statue and came out for a visit. He marveled at what he saw and had it carted to his foundry, where he spent several months restoring it.

The Chamber of Commerce then voted to hold the statue in trust until a buyer was found. The asking price was 150,000 dollars, of which the chamber would take 35 percent to spend on maintaining existing public art exhibits. The rest was to be divided between Bevis and Carpenter's family.

Some say they don't want the hulk in their city, though it is an icon of Russian history, it is also a defunct military symbol.

Lenin's goals were the destruction of free enterprise (privately owned and controlled businesses) and the creation of a classless society (a society without groups of rich and/or poor people). His ideas were based largely on the theories of Karl Marx, a German philosopher. According to Marx, free enterprise would some day destroy itself.

Lenin set a pattern for Communist revolutions, using force and terror to work toward his goal.

Later, more than a billion people lived in countries ruled by Communist party dictatorships. The Communist world considered Lenin and Marx its greatest heroes.

Lenin suffered a third stroke on March 9, 1923, and on January 21, 1924, he died of a brain hemorrhage. The government preserved his body by a special process. Lenin's tomb, in Red Square in Moscow, is one of the country's most honored monuments.

In 1978, Gordon, Esther, Charlene, and Corinne stood at his tomb in Red Square, which attracted thousands of visitors each day. A glass-covered casket containing Lenin's entombed body lies inside the huge memorial.

His fist raised and clenched, it is as if the dictator is still speaking in death. "Religion," he seems to repeat, "is the opiate of the people! There is no God. Communism reigns supreme!"

During his reign of terror, thousands of Christians were imprisoned and persecuted for their faith in Russia.

In their years of travel and ministry in Russia, Gordon and Esther comforted, consoled, and prayed with many who had been in prison, or had relatives there. Grieving and brokenhearted, they still clung to the faith of their fathers. Never would they recant or give up!

"This statue has no place here or anywhere in our country! It has no place in our free society!" stated many citizens of Seattle.

Now as Gordon or Esther drive past the statue, they are vividly reminded of the many who suffered for their faith during his reign of terror.

A Decade of Blessing

About 3,000 Slavs crowded into plush seats at the Conference Center Auditorium in Des Moines, Washington, on Friday, September 3, 1999.

Coming from across the United States for this great tenth-year celebration and reunion, all of them had immigrated from the Ukraine and Russia. Some came as Christian Pentecostals, who were among the most persecuted of all religious groups in the former USSR.

Several had arrived years earlier, but most since 1989, and some only recently. With the Soviet Union loosening its immigration restraints under Gorbachev's policy of *glasnost*, and the West opening its doors to those seeking political and religious asylum, they fled by the tens of thousands.

Familiar-looking people, to whom Gordon and Esther had ministered in their motherland, extended hands of greeting and welcome when they arrived at the center. Members from several Slavic churches expressed joy that God had brought them there.

The celebration service was scheduled to begin at 7:00 P.M., but as is customary, most were still streaming into the building after the designated time. Eventually all the seats were filled and chairs placed in the aisles to accommodate the overflow crowd.

Almost an hour later, a fifty-voice choir took their places on the massive platform. Rich, clear voices flowed reverently across the auditorium when they began to sing about salvation and redemption through the blood of Jesus. The women were dressed in long, black skirts, white blouses, and wearing traditional *Babushkas* on their heads, (showing deference to God and their husbands). Finally the service began.

The main floor and balcony were filled with a mixture of faces. Older women wore scarves and floral dresses. Most of the younger ones were more contemporary in their attire, yet many still wore the traditional headpiece. Dozens of babies, with baby carriages alongside, were coddled and held to keep them quiet throughout the lengthy service.

Although the service was long, hundreds of children throughout the congregation sat remarkably still. Most

belonged to large family groups. All school children spoke the English language fluently, and had integrated into the American culture very well.

The services featured many Bible messages, poems, and musical numbers. Often, the congregation was called to prayer. Standing or kneeling, everyone prayed out loud at the same time, as they expressed their supplication and thanksgiving to God. The emotion quickly swelled as the crescendo rose, then gradually decreased, until the room was hushed.

Among the many pastors who shared the Word, one came from Woodburn, Oregon. Speaking directly to his fellow immigrants, he emphasized that their people, for generations, had prayed that God would break the doors of Communism wide open. Then the Iron Curtain fell, and the doors opened!

"The first family," he continued, "came from Siberia. A church was built, and as more immigrants arrived, it was soon filled. Many of our people have moved to different areas of the United States. Now they are scattered everywhere, and the mighty hand of God is at work among them. He has always gone before them."

Anatoly Desatnyk, from Odessa on the Black Sea, pastoring a church in Seattle, challenged the people to praise God for His goodness to them. "Our heavenly Father who is rich in grace and mercy looked on us with favor in bringing us to this land of America. We have labored little, and received so much. He gives us health and strength from His great hand. Out of His abundance, He has blessed us, so we in turn must bless others. It was the presence of a loving heavenly Father, and not an organization, that has brought us this far," he concluded.

In 1977, Gordon and Esther ministered to his suffering congregation in Odessa. What a miracle that now they are free to worship with them in their great nation, the United States of America.

Other pastors shared during the celebration. Peter Sayenko, President of the Slavic Community on the West Coast, addressed the congregation many times, challenging them to have a grateful spirit. Stephen Gorkavchuk from the former First Ukrainian Church in Seattle was present, as well.

Saturday morning, over 5,000 Slavs filled the spacious Overlake Christian Church sanctuary, in Redmond, Washington. Peter Tishenko, a Slavic pastor from Vancouver, Washington, spoke in the morning service. Enthusiastically, the people praised and worshiped God, knitting every heart together in joy and thanksgiving.

It is not Slavic tradition to leave a celebration without food, so despite the large crowd, everyone was fed. Esther was reminded afresh of the ancient Biblical account where Christ fed 5,000 men, women, and children. No one went away hungry!

Behind the scenes, thousands of chickens were barbecued. Dozens of salads in king-sized bowls stood in readiness. Tables were laden with varieties of Russian foods. Diligent planning and organization made the feast a culinary event to remember.

In the last service, which lasted from 6:00 until after 10:00 P.M., Pastor Vasily Vakulsky, from Portland, Oregon, opened by calling the vast group of Slavic immigrants once again to prayer. Corporately, they praised God who had brought them from persecution to a land where they have freedom to worship. It was emphasized continually that they must not forget to be grateful and remember how God has blessed them.

"This is a land where food and other commodities are plentiful, and we have a great deal of abundance all around us. In our country, people are starving for lack of bread. Thank God every day for your blessings!"

While babies slept in their carriages, and toddlers clung to their parents, the last song was sung.

With joyful hearts the vast audience dispersed. It had been a wonderful day! They would not forget God's blessing in graciously opening a new door of freedom for them. They had come through that door, and a new life had begun.

Worshiping with Our Slavic Family

(as printed in *The Christian Leader*, August 24, 1999 by Don Ratzlaff, editor)

The language is foreign, the length of service more than two hours. Fortunately, much about Slavic worship transcends translation and mere endurance.

We pull into the parking lot of the Slavic Christian Church in Portland, Oregon, about twenty minutes before the Sunday morning service is to begin. The spaces are filling fast, the parking strategy here is already discernible: squeeze in one more car. By the time the service begins, the lot and the side streets will be bumper to bumper with cars. Likewise, worshippers will fill the pews inside in much the same style. Maybe 500 in all. The main floor and balcony are filled with a mix of faces, young and old, thin and round, handsome and homely. The children, many of them sitting together in rows, smile and giggle. Once the service begins, though, these youngsters are remarkably attentive, considering the length of the wait expected of them.

The adults are more sober, focused. The dress code for young men ranges from the modern double-breasted suit to open collar and shirtsleeves. The older men prefer the simple, plain-cut gray or black suit—a carry-over from a not too distant time past when clothes were bought for function, not fashion.

The older women have that stereotypical *Babushka* look —round figures adorned in neat but simple dresses. Most of the younger women, though, are more brightly attired. Married women, young and old, heed the literal words of Scripture by covering their heads with a scarf when they worship.

A Testimony of Faces

But the real story of these people is written in their faces. The older adults, their stark and rugged features chiseled by years of hardship, now radiate renewed hope and gratitude. Who could have envisioned the sudden and dramatic plot change penned in these chapters of their lives?

I recall the dinner conversation the night before with Yuri Savinskiy, 66, a former civil engineer in the Republic of Georgia. With the help of an interpreter, he described the challenge of being Christian in a totalitarian Communist state. Secret house-church gatherings late into the night. KGB agents tearing apart family pillows and mattresses in a desperate search for Bibles and other damning evidence of Christian allegiance. The twenty years of hard labor in a Soviet prison. Now, though, there is a joy in Yuri's face that belies his years. God has liberated him and his family.

As I survey the faces of these older saints, I wonder how many could tell me similar tales. I will never know for sure. English is still a barrier for them, even though some have been on U.S. soil for almost four years. As in most immigrant situations, fluency in English correlates conversely with the age of the person. Here, most of the children speak English without a trace of accent. The youth and young adults are becoming fluent as they enter school and the job market. But

for many older adults, who have few outside contacts, managing a new language seems an almost unattainable goal.

For the young to middle-age adults, language is the key to employment, which in turn is the key to economic stability. In their eyes I see a mix of optimism and apprehension in this new environment. On their backs rests the burden of transition. They carry the responsibility to support not only their children but, in many cases, their parents and sometimes members of their extended family.

Those working closely with the Slavic churches say the employment rate among attendees varies from area to area. In some churches, as many as 90 percent have found jobs; in others, the rate is closer to 50 to 60 percent. Construction and manual labor are the primary sources. Language limitations and years of living in a state-regulated employment environment have resulted in few Slavic-owned business ventures to this point.

BEYOND TRANSLATION

For me, the challenge of language suddenly takes on new meaning when the worship services begins—in Russian. Now I am the one grasping for understanding in a foreign environment. Gordon Balisky, who has served as a liaison and translator for us among the Slavs in the Pacific Northwest, offers an occasional explanation, but the content of the songs and messages is lost on me.

Fortunately, there is much about Slavic worship that transcends translation. Most North American Mennonite Brethren would fixate on the sheer length of the services. Two and a half to three hours is not uncommon—five hours is not unheard of. But the time moves quickly. Interspersed between the three or more Bible messages featured in each service are periods of corporate prayer, reading and recitations by children and women, and rich music—some congregational singing, but many numbers from the choir and smaller ensembles.

What fuels a Slavic service along more than anything is the intensity of the experience. The preaching is impassioned, whether the speaker is an elder of long standing, or a young man given the opportunity to test his gifts. During this service, pastor Vasily Vakulsky, quiet and reserved before the service, now punctuates his message with vigorous gestures and intonation. As the head pastor, his is the final and climactic message of the service. He leaves no doubt the Word of the Lord is being spoken.

And it seems to take hold in the pews. At the conclusion of each Bible message, the congregation is invited to respond in corporate prayer. Unlike the traditional Mennonite Brethren service, where corporate prayer usually means the pastor or leader prays audibly on behalf of the congregation, the Slavs express corporate prayer quite literally: everyone prays—audibly and simultaneously.

For such a sacred moment, no one sits passively in the pew. Some stand, the rest kneel on the floor facing the front—no small feat amid these crowded pews. Immediately, a low rumbling of righteousness rises from the congregation. The emotion quickly swells. Within moments, the sanctuary is filled with a cacophony of confession and petition. Tears flow. Some believers raise their arms heavenward, others bury their face in their hands.

After several minutes, as if on unspoken cue, the tide of prayers subsides. Pastor Vakulsky, the last one praying, concludes the time with an "Amen." Whether these expressions of piety and devotion, as sincere as they appear to the visitor, become routing and mechanical for those who follow them service after service, I don't know. For this "foreigner,"

though, the visible evidence of their deep and potent faith is certainly one gift they offer the rest of us in their newly adopted denominational family.

CELEBRATION OF FAMILY

Two other components of the morning service make it special, if not uncommon. The first is a child dedication. Children are celebrated and cherished in Slavic households. In contrast to their new American culture, where families average the proverbial 2.5 kids and a dog, Slavic families bring with them high regard for larger broods. Four to six children per household is more the norm than the exception. Some families have more.

On this morning, three young families come forward to receive a bouquet of flowers, words of affirmation, and a prayer of dedication from Pastor Vakulsky. Working his way down the line, he holds each infant warmly. Judging by their smiles, the parents are obviously pleased—with themselves, the pastor's blessing, and a faith family that welcomes and nurtures a new generation in a new land. The cycle of life continues unabated.

Later in the service, another family is called forward. Balisky tells me the couple and their three young children have just arrived in Portland from the former Soviet Union. They have been invited to the podium for a word of public welcome and prayer.

As they step onto the stage and stand self-consciously before the congregation, I see in the faces of the husband and wife both gratitude and fear. This must be a traumatic time in their lives. I try to put myself in their place. What would prompt me to uproot my family from a familiar environment to a foreign one? Yes, the future of the Commonwealth of Independent States is uncertain, but what kind of future awaits them here in this strange new land?

I recall the conversation I had the previous day with Peter and Nelly Tishchenko. Peter is the pastor of the Slavic Christian Church of Vancouver, Washington. Through the translation of a family member, I asked him about the fears he and his family had about being in this country. He seemed hesitant to respond. I wasn't sure whether he didn't understand the question, or was merely reticent to admit to fears. Given the language barrier, I was helpless to clarify my intent.

Nelly, who is further along in English, broke the silence first. "We wonder if our kids well keep our culture," she said. Peter nodded his agreement.

It wasn't the answer I expected, to be honest. I thought they would express concern about the threat of North American materialism and secularism to their faith. Or the hazards posed by crime, gangs, and substance abuse, especially for their youth. But to be concerned primarily about their language and foods?

I wanted to probe their response with more questions, but decided not to. They had been honest with me. And, the more I thought about it, the more appropriate their response seemed for an immigrant people. In truth, I had to admit it mirrored a primary concern of the first Mennonite Brethren immigrants who came to the United States from Russia 120 years ago. I could only hope their Slavic brothers and sisters would gain a healthy perspective on the connection of faith and ethnic traditions more graciously and quickly than the rest of their adopted denomination had through the years.

These broader issues, I'm sure, are far from the minds of this young family which now stand before us on the stage. A place to live, a job to support the family, a language to learn—these are concerns I see in their eyes. And I breath a prayer of thanks that they have a local church family committed to helping them make the transition.

Time for Connections

Then, almost abruptly, the worship service ends. The meetinghouse empties slowly. Because my opportunities for conversation are limited, I grab my camera and head out a side door to survey the scene there. Across the crowded parking lot, pockets of people coagulate to catch up on the latest news and events of their lives. A few cars inch their way toward the exits, but no one seems in a great hurry to leave. These people value each other and take the time to make the connections.

"What lies ahead for the Slavic Mennonite Brethren connection?" I wonder as we finally drive away from the church. God has opened doors for them that no one had even imagined three years earlier. The potential for denominational numerical growth is significant, but so are the challenges of assimilation.

Some wonder whether the Slavs are committed to stay with us for the long haul, or are merely interested in a short-term step up to something else. Others wonder whether the denomination is truly committed to incorporating these new people, or interested only in a short-term step up in growth statistics.

Questions like these can't be answered after one whirlwind reporting tour in one isolated region. But having listened to our denominational leaders who work most closely with these churches and to the few Slavic leaders I have had the opportunity to encounter, I sense the key to the long-term outcome may lie more with the denomination than with the Slavs.

I leave wondering: Are we interested only in hosting a

few thousand out-of-town guests for a brief visit, or will we invest the resources necessary to enlarge the house and invite our adopted brothers and sisters to take their rightful place at the family table?

Update

After eleven Slavic churches had been established in the United States in just over a year, Gordon and Esther completed the fruitful time of ministry as liasons and translator for the Mennonite Brethren.

The ministry went ahead, however, as the Baliskys prayerfully continued the work their heavenly Father had planned for them—both in the United States and abroad.

A Visit from Poland—2000

"Hey, Esther! Guess what?"

Whenever Gordon came in saying that, Esther knew there was a surprise at hand.

"What?" she smiled.

"Martin and Powell from Poland are coming to see us! Can you believe it?"

"When?"

"They will be here in a few days. Let's put them in the apartment in the basement. That way they will have privacy and rest," he added, his voice filled with excitement.

It seemed all too soon that Gordon was speeding toward Sea Tac airport to pick them up.

Esther had a pot of *borscht* simmering on the stove when they arrived at the house.

Looking very similar to the young boys they taught on several occasions at Camp Konev, near Lubartow, two grown young men stood at the threshold.

"*Ciotka*!" offered Powell, extending his big hand.

"Is this really you?" asked Esther.

"It is really me and this is Martin!"

"My goodness! You have grown so tall! You are both men now!" she smiled.

Times goes by rapidly. It seemed such a short time ago when they were children.

Gordon didn't notice the change so much because he had been in Poland in December and January of that year. Powell, with a sensitive heart, transported Gordon from one place of ministry to the next while he was there. Spending time with the boys then, this was only an extension of their time together.

Terry and Kristin Robson, from Kansas, who helped with camp work at Konev, years ago, dubbed the older one, "*Duji* Powell," which simply means "Big Powell." Even as a child he showed signs of becoming a big man. Now he was.

Martin, the youngest in his family, still had the same loving smile on his face.

Taking him in her arms, gratefully he returned Esther's embrace.

"Here *Ciotka*! We have something for you."

Powell was holding a large basket of dried Polish flowers—all the way from his country.

"We carried this bouquet everywhere, and had a stewardess look after it on the plane. Both of us wanted to give you something fresh and nice," said Powell, handing the basket to Esther.

"Thank you so much!" she answered, truly grateful for the wonderful remembrance of fresh flowers in the spring—and from Poland yet!

"Here, let me take your coat," said Gordon.

"And I made *borscht* especially for you," said Esther. "Please be seated."

After washing their hands in the sink, gratefully they sat down at the big kitchen table.

Sighing, Martin remarked that the *borscht* tasted just like his mother made at home. She had hoped it would.

Both boys were weary after the long flight across the water. Taking them to their sleeping quarters, they were glad to be able to go to bed.

The house was quiet again while they slept. Gordon had a faraway look in his eyes.

"Remember the fun we used to have at children's camp when Martin and Powell were there?" he reminisced. "*Duji* Powell loved to eat! Especially the spaghetti went down fast," he laughed.

Martin and Powell were born in Lubartow, very near to Lake Konev. None of them realized then that someday there would be a camp for children and youth in the area and that God would help them purchase a piece of property by the lake. Only their great and wise heavenly Father planned it all. He was aware, long before, that many young people and children would come to know Jesus as Savior and go on into Christian service as a result of being there. In turn, they would lead others to know Him, too.

Powell and Martin were two of these choice ones!

They were brought up in a devout Catholic home where the name of Jesus was honored, but not known on a personal basis. Making up a large part of Poland's Catholics, they, too, adhered to the letter of the law as they worshiped not the Creator, but His earthly mother.

When Powell and Martin came to children's camp one year, they were pleased when everyone accepted them. Feeling as if they had been there every year, the boys' inhibitions disappeared. Joyfully they joined in sports, classes, and food.

Who could eat more than *Duji* Powell? No one knew.

As each year went by, their parents gave the boys permission to attend camp. Soon their sister came, too.

As time went by, the boys became more interested in the God their leaders and some of the campers always talked about. He must be wonderful! Gradually the Bible stories became alive as they learned about Jesus. Silently, wistfully, the desire to know Him personally filled their hearts.

One day while *Ciotka* Esther was telling a story in chapel about how God sent His Son to earth to die for them, they realized it was time to make a commitment to follow Him.

Why is my heart pounding so? wondered Powell. Looking across the room at his brother, he saw his head was bowed. Were those tears running down his cheeks, too?

> *Behold, I stand at the door, and knock: if any man hear my voice, and open the door, I will come in to him, and will sup with him, and he with me* (Revelation 3:20).

Was this not the verse his leader had shared earlier?

Breathing heavily, Powell bit his lower lip with his teeth. Was this restlessness, Jesus speaking to Him? It had to be!

He wasn't certain then that the Savior was wanting his attention.

"Whoever wants to let Jesus come into your heart," said *Ciotka*, "please raise your hand."

Without hesitation, the older boy's hand shot up. Martin followed suit.

Later, after another leader prayed with them, two boys, their faces beaming, told them what had happened in their lives. Praying the sinner's prayer, their desire now was to follow the Lord.

Soon afterward, their sister, too, made the same decision. One after another, several members in their family also came to know Him in a personal way. Now He was not only a name, but a personal, living entity in their lives.

Gordon and Esther became good friends with the family. Encouraging them where to go to church and grow in the Lord, several followed their advice. Mentoring them, especially the boys, from year to year, they watched them grow in the faith.

Eventually, both boys graduated from seminary. They found there was a burning desire in their hearts to let others know about the God they served now. Uninhibited, they shared their faith.

Looking across the table at the two young men who were now in Seattle, caused a tug in Gordon's heart.

These, like many others like them, were their adopted children in the faith. Now spiritual leaders in Poland, they worked alongside others they had led to Christ and mentored in the faith. In turn, they challenged still others to the saving knowledge of truth.

"Thank you, God," breathed Gordon, roughly wiping the tears from his face.

Taking them to the Bible College from which Esther and Gordon graduated in Alberta, Canada, Powell and Martin encouraged the young people there to go all the way with God.

Young men and women listened carefully as *Wujek* and the boys shared for hours. The challenge had been given. Would they follow it? Powell and Martin had made the decision to do so and had never been sorry. How would the students respond?

Later they heard that hearts had been challenged. God was speaking to them, too.

After mentoring the boys in their home in Seattle for months, soon the time came for them to go back to Poland

and minister to their own people. Now, fortified in the Word, they planned to share what they had learned.

Powell was so tall, Esther stretched to meet his embrace.

"Good-bye, and remember, God will never let you down," she said.

Martin stayed in Seattle a little longer. When the time came for him to leave, he promised to come back.

"You have been a blessing to us—in Poland and now in your home," he said, while swallowing a lump in his throat.

"And you to us," gulped Gordon, while taking the young man in his arms.

"God bless you, my boy! God bless you!"

Watching him as he disappeared into the aircraft, they knew within Martin's heat there burned a desire to follow in Jesus' steps. Together the boys would be faithful to their trust and tell others the wonderful story of love, because someone had told them first.

Surely the Father had planned it all!

Slavic Christian Center Dedication —January 20, 2002

When Gordon and Esther drove to the new Slavic church in Tacoma, Washington, they saw cars everywhere. Barricades stood at entrances where parking lots were already filled.

Gordon drove their compact Toyota toward an area that was congested with cars. Smiling, the parking attendant beckoned them to come through. But where could they park? A space just large enough for their small vehicle seemed to be reserved for them. Others were still driving around looking for a spot. Many parked outside on the streets around the massive church.

The next question remained, where could they sit? The foyer was already filled to capacity. Looking inside, the big church was crowded from the back to the front.

Suddenly an usher walked toward them.

"Please follow me," he greeted.

Leading them around the back hallway of the church, to the front, he showed them where to sit.

Crowding in, they saw two empty seats beside the pulpit. Gratefully, they sat down. Had they known then that the service would last for four hours, they would have been even more thankful for a place to be seated.

Flowers flanked the front of the choir loft where a seventy-five-voice choir raised their voices in praise to God. When with one voice and heart, they sang the "Hallelujah Chorus" in the Russian language. The great building filled with praise.

Esther, finding herself singing the beautiful anthem along with the choir, felt her heart swell.

Though the crowd of Slavic believers gathered there on that lovely Sunday was large in number, everything paled in comparison to the greatness of the God who made the occasion possible.

Pastor Peter Seyenko stood behind the pulpit of this place where God had given him leadership, and with a broad smile on his face, he greeted the vast audience.

"When we get to heaven, we'll have a great deal to talk about and remember!" he said.

The praise was so loud, it resounded to the four corners of the big church and, no doubt, into heaven's portals as well.

Another pastor said, "We will remember this service for a long time." And they certainly will, as pastors and their wives came from all across the United States to attend this memorable event. People from Florida, California, Kansas,

Washington, Moldavia, USSR, Beloruss, and Ukraine were present. Everyone stood in awe to see how God had opened the doors of this house of God for a needy people.

With tears running down his cheeks, another pastor said, "Nicholai Kruschev made a statement in the 1960s that by the 1980s there would be no Christians left in the USSR! Not only are there thousands of believers there," he said, "but here in the United States, there are over a million Slavic people who regularly worship God!"

Still more tears flowed, as another continued, "I remember when we lived in constant fear when we went to church in Russia. Would they take one of us to jail because of our faith in God? Sometimes it happened. But we never knew when it might take place. Young people hid in the closets and under the beds, because they thought the police were coming. We were always apprehensive! But thanks be to God, that is over now!"

Thanksgiving and praise filled the large building as with one voice they thanked Him for releasing them from bondage and fear.

"Thank you," said Pastor Peter, "for those of you who made this event possible," then named Gordon as one of them.

The service went on and on, as nineteen speakers graced the pulpit and dozens of musical renditions were offered.

Gordon's thoughts turned to the events preceding this day. Ten years ago, he remembered, a small group of immigrant believers from the Ukraine and Russia met for worship in a small Salvation Army hall in Tacoma. From this group, they chose Peter, a young man from Kiev, to be their pastor and leader.

As they met, they prayed together like they had in their homeland. Here there were different issues and challenges, but the same enemy, the prince of darkness—but God was the same.

Their number steadily grew, so they moved into another building. Again they outgrew this larger one. Never did they endeavor to purchase land until this time.

Driving by a large, vacant bus barn, in the heart of this sprawling metropolis, they talked about enquiring how much the city wanted for it.

"It must be very costly," said Peter. The elders agreed. Because there was a large acreage and several other buildings included, they knew this land was valuable.

"We will trust God together," said Peter, as he presented the need for a larger sanctuary to his people.

"Amen!" they chorused.

Then, as a group, they went to the city officials. "How much money are you asking for the vacant bus barn?" asked the elders from the church.

Emphatically, they were told it would be 960,000 dollars. "Even this price," they said, "would be a bargain for this choice piece of property."

"How could we raise money like that?" they wondered. But God had the answer. He always does!

Gordon shifted in his chair. The service was still going on as the hours of the big clock ticked away. He remembered how the congregation in Peter's church continued to pray.

The old bus barn was almost a city block in size. With such huge, high ceilings in this domed building, so much could be done to make it an attractive house of prayer. And it was large enough to accommodate their growing congregation. They continued to fast and pray.

Finally Peter and the elders decided to go to the city officials again and offer to give them 250,000 dollars. Would this be enough?

The city did not respond for some time, because they would lose money on this absurd offer When they did, an

incredible miracle had taken place. They offered the building to the immigrants for 250,000 dollars! Incredible, but true! How they rejoiced and thanked God for this miracle! Their God, Jehovah, had manifested Himself. He cared about them! Their faith had been strengthened.

Applications for permits to change the former use of the building to the status of a church, code changes, renovations, and years of work were challenging issues ahead. But God helped them with each one.

Slowly, daily, the house of prayer took shape.

Today several thousand were celebrating the dedication of their house of God. Everyone was awed by this evident answer to prayer. God had done this! After the service, making their way to the large dining room area in another part of the building, they found that it, too, was filled with people.

Plates of food soon graced the many tables. Fellowshipping as they ate, everyone praised God, who had made this wonderful miracle possible.

Now Gordon and Esther could see the fruit of their labors clearly. Already, over 600 Slavic churches had been born across the United States as the immigrant population swelled to over a million. Surely their Father had planned it all years ago and they were grateful!

Because we shared His love with others
and obeyed the Master's call,
From grateful hearts of joy we know—
our Father planned it all!

Reminiscing

The Balisky's attended this remarkable service in Tacoma, as they had many other similar meetings in the recent past.

Esther, sitting in their pew with her husband, vividly recalled times of fellowship with persecuted believers in Russia as well.

There, the Scriptures were not available to them. If one had such a priceless treasure, however, others would laboriously copy pages from God's Word by hand. Infinitely valuable to them, they often memorized large portions and hid them in their hearts. Here, no one could take them away!

Now in the United States of America, believers were blest to have their own Bibles. How their faces glowed with gratitude to God who brought them to a country where they could worship freely. What more could they ask?

Looking into the blue eyes of a smiling child sitting in front of them, Esther knew she would have opportunities here that would never have been available to her in Russia.

Observing teenagers, sitting together across from them, she knew they too, were becoming acclimated to this new land of opportunity. With God on their side, He would help them face challenges ahead, and in faith they would trust Him.

Fathers and mothers reverently bowing their heads, quietly breathed their thanks to God who had made it possible to be free from fear. Anytime in Russia, in the former regime, their children could be taken away from them. The government frowned on religious activities in the home and church. Now they were free at last!

Esther's heart was full, as she thought of their own precious family.

Her husband, who had sacrificed so much to help these hurting people – sometimes working day and night to assist in what ever way he could.

Their girls, who had faithfully travelled to many countries, helping them share God's Word – their lives a living testimony to God's glory.

Their son-in-law, who purposes in his heart to serve God with all his heart.

Their grandchildren, who are following in the steps of their parents and grandparents.

Looking at Esther, Gordon clasped her hand and smiled.Was she thinking along the same lines as he? He was certain she was! His heart too, was overflowing with gratitude and praise because their Father had planned it all!

As humble servants, their earnest desire was that one day the Saviour would look on them with favor and say, "Well done thou good and faithfull servants. Enter into the joy of the Lord."

APPENDIX ONE

Preparation for Service

Before we were born, God had a divine master plan in mind for us. He scheduled each day of our lives before they ever existed. Psalm 139 clearly states He knows everything about us.

We were not aware that God was preparing us for ministry in Eastern Europe and Russia. However, as children, both of us were keenly aware of God's call on our lives. Gladly, willingly, we surrendered to His leading.

We met during several years of training for the great task of launching out into the work He had for us. Our goals were similar. To serve the Lord was a priority.

Gordon was brought up in a Slavic community in Canada. His father, a businessman, owned a store in the country. Many, coming from far and near, did their weekly shopping there. Slavic immigrants from various countries set-

tling in the area made this their place of business, too. Bringing their families with them while they shopped, the children were told to go out and play till they were finished.

Eyeing each other, shyly the children bonded. Soon, on a first name basis, they played until their parents were done.

Speaking in their mother tongues, everyone tried to understand each other. Children have a way of having fun together—no mater what culture they come from. These times were no exception.

Quickly Gordon learned several languages. Coupled with the Ukrainian language they spoke at home, he became fluent in others.

One day, at the age of six, his mother, tying the boy's shoes, informed him he was old enough to go to school now. "But, Son," she smiled, "you will have to learn English!"

"What was English like?" he wondered.

It wasn't long before the extroverted child learned that unfamiliar language, as well.

What a preparation for service! When traveling into the East, he conversed freely in several languages in various countries.

Esther was brought up in a home where both High German and a Low German dialect was spoken.

"Esther," her mother said in later years, "when you were two years old, you spoke German fluently. *'Wo sol Ich meine Hut lassen?'* was one of your favorite phrases," she laughed.

God knew we would live in Germany for years. Neither Gordon nor the girls spoke German at that time. Esther would be the spokesman until they learned.

We came across many in various countries who spoke Low German freely. Even in parts of Eastern Europe and Russia, she could communicate in either language.

God knew all these languages would be important in order to communicate. He planned it all. What a preparation!

When Esther was a child, God gave Henry and Katy, her parents, a rare ministry. Today, she sees this as another preparation for ministry in Eastern Europe and Russia.

Slavic immigrants settling in Alberta, Canada, needed someone to minister to them. Services in the Ukrainian language were organized in the Novelesky home. Katy and Henry felt a burden to help, but how could they? The language was foreign, but somehow, they felt the need to assist.

They offered their musical talents. Henry playing his electric Hawaiian guitar, joined in with Katy as they sang in English or German.

Silently, the immigrants wiped tears from their eyes, as the dedicated couple sang about a Savior who loved them enough to die for them.

Though they did not understand English, they sensed the presence of the Lord through their music.

Esther, squirming and wiggling through the long three-hour services, didn't know that in future years, she would sit in long services as both she and her husband would take part in ministry like this.

God knew. He planned it all eons before.

Pastoring in several churches in the United States, Gordon received an education. Through times of pressure and blessing, we learned to work with people. Some lessons would be invaluable for the rest of our lives.

Higher education, we found later, would be essential as we worked with heads of state and country. Going through Eastern block borders, too, Gordon would be respected as Doctor Balisky. God knew this, as well.

Was not the journey of Esther's ancestors as they fled persecution from Holland to Prussia, to Russia, and finally to the

U.S. and Canada, a well-paved road for them to follow? Suffering to preserve the faith of their fathers, many were murdered. No one gave up. All were willing to die for this cause.

Later, their great-granddaughter married a Canadian of Ukrainian-Polish decent, and together they returned to minister in lands where their forefathers bled and died.

Not realizing they would go through hard times of testing in these countries as well, later they knew their Father planned it all in advance.

Was it a coincidence that Esther dreamed about being imprisoned in Russia on several occasions, long before the call to Eastern Europe and Russia ever came? Often in her dreams, she found herself in a Russian cell, wondering when she would be released. How could she have known that one day, she and her husband would be kept under surveillance in Russia? Not given permission to leave, they wondered when and if they would ever be home again.

God had a plan for our lives. Faithfully He prepared us for service in His great vineyard.

Purchasing our home in Seattle, many years ago, we sometimes wondered, "should we buy this big house with six bedrooms and 6,000 square feet of floor space?" But God supplied and gave peace when we made the final decision.

How could we know then, that many Slavic immigrants would make this spacious house their home until they were settled on foreign soil?

God knew before we were even born.

Was it a coincidence that on her wedding day, Esther quoted the words of Ruth as a pledge and vow made before her new husband?

> *...for whither thou goest, I will go; and where thou lodgest, I will lodge: thy people shall be my people, and thy God my God* (Ruth 1:16).

Little did she realize the implications of the pledge she had made, but God did. Was this another preparation? They now know it was.

God paved the way from before our birth. While making preparations all along the way, we know now, our Father planned it all!

Appendix Two

Donald M. Best

Donald M. Best, Senior Vice president of Best Lock Corporation, died September 17, 1980, in Methodist Hospital, Indianapolis. Don worked for the Company all his adult life; most of that time he was involved in sales work. Whether in a sales territory, working as the sales manager, or promoting international sales, he always brought vision and great enthusiasm to his job.

His vision also resulted in his involvement in many Christian activities. Upon returning to the Indianapolis area from the west coast, he found there was a lack of Christian schools there. Characteristically, his thought turned to the establishment of a Christian school near the Company. Working with Walter Best, the vision became a reality and has had immeasurable impact on the lives of hundreds of young people over the ensuing years.

An interest in churches behind the Iron Curtain led him to establish East Europe Evangelism as a vehicle for supporting Christian ministries in those countries. On one of his trips behind the Iron Curtain, Don was disturbed by the Russian media giving tremendous play to the Russian Cosmonauts' claim that they had proven God did not exist because they didn't see Him when they were in space. Don's thoughts turned to their own astronauts, particularly to Colonel James Irwin who, after his trip to the moon, announced to the public how God had touched his life in a very deep and meaningful way during his three-day stay on the moon in 1971.

Through many contacts and much planning, Don arranged for Colonel Irwin to visit Russia in 1978, and accompanied him as the sponsor of that trip. Needless to say, the Russian Christians were greatly encouraged by the first-hand testimony of an astronaut who had walked on the surface of the moon and who had a personal talk with God. The

ministry of East Europe Evangelism will be carried on by Mr. Gordon Balisky, a friend and associate of Don's in the ministry to Christians in Communist lands.

Don also participated in several organizations active in the local scene. As a member of the Broad Ripple Christian Fellowship, Christian Business Men's Committee, and the Gideons, his influence was widely felt. His participation was not limited to organizational memberships. For several years he traveled weekly to the Boys' School in Plainfield to work with the inmates of that institution. Also, many churches have enjoyed Don's singing voice as he used that talent in many varied ways.

East Europe Evangelism

Since accepting responsibility for the ministry and leadership for East Europe Evangelism and Marshall Foundation in 1980, Gordon and Esther Balisky have seen much blessing and fruit. Children reached by the Gospel of Jesus Christ from the '70s to '90s are now becoming leaders in their own countries. They are leaders with a sure foundation and faith in Jesus Christ.

East Europe Evangelism and Marshall Foundation is an international ministry, chartered in Canada, U.S.A., and Europe.

East Europe Evangelism has no source of endowment, but is funded by the voluntary contribution of individuals, businesses, and organizations around the world. Donors may designate the projects for which their contributions are to be applied. All contributions are carefully used as designated by the donor. All gifts to the East Europe Evangelism and Marshall Foundation are acknowledged with tax-deductible receipts.

All projects of East Europe Evangelism are administrated under the direction of its Board of Directors. Over more than fifty years of operation, some of its projects have been:

1. Development of vocational schools, colleges, and seminaries in third world countries.
2. Shipment of medical equipment and medicines and the provision of professional medical assistance to countries suffering serious hardship.
3. Development of children's orphanages, youth camps, and other facilities beneficial to caring for their physical needs and the development of their moral character.
4. Development of programs that assist the nationals in broadening their cultural and ethnic understanding through Christian training, literature, multi-media, and other avenues.

In essence, their overall goal is to motivate nationals to become productive and self-sufficient, so they can, in turn, be of help to others.

The Marshall foundation seeks to work closely with governments and agencies within North America, Europe, and needy third world countries.

Glossary

Due to the fact that other languages use alphabets other than our own, the Russian and Slavic words may be spelled phonetically.

Baah	Corinne's nick name
Baba	grandmother (Russian)
Babushka	head scarf (Russian)
Bahnhof	train station (German)
Begosh	cabbage dish with meat, onions, and pork fat (Polish)
Berioska	tourist stores in Russia (souvenirs and gifts)
Bozimi	Oh, my God! (Slavic: Ukraine, Poland, Russia)
Borscht	cabbage and beet soup (Slavic)
Brat	brother (Slavic)
Cashtan	store for tourists in Russia
Chi	tea (Russian)
Chleb	bread (Slavic)
Ciotka (Chocha)	aunt (Polish)
Dasveedanya	good-bye (Russian)
Djien dobri	good day (Russian)
Dobry dzien	good day (Polish)
Dobra niez (Dobranoch)	good night (Polish)
Dorf	small town, village (German)
Dovejenya	hello (Polish)
Duji	big (Slavic)
Dzie kuja (Djenkuye)	Thank you
Faspa	a light afternoon lunch (German)
Forecelt	awning (German)
Frau	woman or Mrs. (German)
Frauen	women (German, Swiss)
Frauen Spital	women's hospital (German, Swiss)

Fröhliche Weihnachten Merry Christmas (German)
Gasthaus guest house, a bed and breakfast
Glasnost acknowledgement of a rest time in a nation, peaceful reform
Holidna hungry (Ukraine)
Gott segne Ihnen God bless you (German)
Guten Abend Good evening (German)
Guten Tag Good day (German)
Haupt Strasse main street (German)
Heiligabend Christmas Eve (holy evening) (German)
Holidettes head cheese (Slavic)
Holopsie cabbage rolls (Slavic)
Ich will meine Tauchter sehn I want to see my daughter (German)
Kielbasa (Cubasa) sausage (Slavic)
Kinapke open-faced cold meat and cucumber sand wiches (Polish)
Kommen Sie mit mir Come with me (German)
Koogle scoop (German)
Loipers cross country skiers (German, Swiss)
Lupsha noodles (Slavic)
Mamushka name of endearment for mama (Slavic)
Maslo butter (Slavic)
Mockowiz poppy seed (Slavic)
Nyte no (Russian)
O Du Fröeliger O Happy One (German)
Pann Mr. (Polish, Ukrainian)
Pension hotel or boardinghouse (German, Swiss)
Pommes frites (German) French fries
Pozyalosta please (Russian)
Pirenna quilt or duvet (Polish, Ukrainian)
Rahm schnitzel beef cutlet (German)
Regierung government or to govern

Saal	hall, auditorium (German)
Schrank	storage unit (German)
Sehr	cheese (Slavic)
Slava Bogu!	Praise the Lord! (Slavic)
S'niadanic (Sneydanik)	breakfast (Polish)
Soltice	government appointed policing agents (Slavic)
Spuren	ski tracks (German, Swiss)
Sposeebo	thank you (Russian)
Staamhaus	main house (German)
Touflee	shoes (Ukrainian)
Vati	name of endearment for father (German)
Vehrmacht	army (German)
Verenike	thin pancake (Polish, Ukrainian)
Verruyuschiye	believer (Russian, Ukrainian)
Wasyl	William
Wasyl Was Ylovitch William,	son of William
Wie Heist deine Tauchter?	What is your daughter's name (German)
Wo sol Ich meine Hut lassen?	Where should I leave my hat? (German)
Wujek (Vooyuk)	uncle (Polish)
Ya	yes (German)
Zbogom	God bless you (Polish)
Zloty	Polish currency